T0244185

TOLKIEN
in the
TWENTY-FIRST
CENTURY

ALSO BY NICK GROOM

The Vampire

The Gothic

The Seasons

The Union Jack

The Forger's Shadow

Introducing Shakespeare

The Making of Percy's Reliques

TOLKIEN
in the
TWENTY-FIRST CENTURY

THE MEANING OF
MIDDLE-EARTH TODAY

NICK GROOM

PEGASUS BOOKS

NEW YORK LONDON

TOLKIEN IN THE TWENTY-FIRST CENTURY

Pegasus Books, Ltd.
148 West 37th Street, 13th Floor
New York, NY 10018

Copyright © 2023 by Nick Groom

First Pegasus Books cloth edition September 2023

All rights reserved. No part of this book may be reproduced in whole or in part without written permission from the publisher, except by reviewers who may quote brief excerpts in connection with a review in a newspaper, magazine, or electronic publication; nor may any part of this book be reproduced, stored in a retrieval system, or transmitted in any form or by any means electronic, mechanical, photocopying, recording, or other, without written permission from the publisher.

ISBN: 978-1-63936-503-6

10 9 8 7 6 5 4 3 2 1

Printed in the United States of America
Distributed by Simon & Schuster
www.pegasusbooks.com

To Joanne, Matilda, and Dorothy:
thank you for looking after me.

Every song a new song, each song newly sung;
Every song a true song, only just begun:
Every note ran true and sweet,
Every word with every beat,
Every tale a world complete –
When every song was new, when every song
   was new.
    Mick Ryan, 'When Every Song Was New' (2013)

We sail within a vast sphere, ever drifting in uncertainty, driven from end to end. When we think to attach our-selves to any point and to fasten to it, it wavers and leaves us; and if we follow it, it eludes our grasp, slips past us, and vanishes for ever. Nothing stays for us. This is our natural condition and yet most contrary to our inclination; we burn with desire to find solid ground and an ultimate sure foundation whereon to build a tower reaching to the Infinite. But our whole groundwork cracks, and the earth opens to abysses.

    Let us, therefore, not look for certainty and stability. Our reason is always deceived by fickle shadows; nothing can fix the finite between the two Infinites, which both enclose and fly from it.

                    Blaise Pascal, *Pensées* (1670)

Whither is fled the visionary gleam?
Where is it now, the glory and the dream?
        William Wordsworth, 'Ode: Intimations of
                Immortality from Recollections
                of Early Childhood' (1807)

Contents

Acknowledgements

I would first like to thank my undergraduate, postgraduate, and international summer school students at the universities of Exeter and Macau for the opportunity to discuss these ideas for several years with intelligent and knowledgeable readers and fans: it has been a pleasure and a privilege. Among Tolkien scholars, I owe significant debts to Mark Atherton, Andoni Cossio, Dimitra Fimi, Lynn Forest-Hill, Peter Gilliver, Andrew Higgins, Stuart Lee, Tom Shippey, Martin Simonson, and especially Will Sherwood. At Exeter, where I taught for several years, I would like to thank my colleagues Henry Bartholomew, Jo Esra, Karrie Anne Grobben, Eddie Jones, Tim Kendall, Joanne Parker, Esther Raamsdonk, Debra Ramsay, Mike Rose, and Andrew Rudd. A few words, phrases, and ideas are taken from my earlier publications on Tolkien, but I have endeavoured to present significantly new readings here, if not unharmonious with my previous work from which the occasional idea has been adapted.[1]

My present colleagues, including Man Yin Chiu, Josh Ehrlich, Rhett Gayle, Matthew Gibson, Victoria Harrison, Damian Shaw, and Sun Yifeng, have assisted in many ways that have meant a great deal to me, though their natural generosity of spirit means that they may not realize what a help they have been; likewise the Dean of the Faculty of Arts and Humanities

Professor Jie Xu and the Vice-Rector Professor Michael Hui have provided much-appreciated support. One dear friend and colleague has always gone the extra country mile during the difficult time in which this book was written: William Hughes – thank you, Bill, I hope that I can do the same for you one day. John Goodridge has greatly encouraged me in my work for some thirty years, and it was a pleasure to find that our interests dovetailed in this project; typically, John kindly read several chapters in draft, which I very much appreciated. I also received help, in different ways, from Nicholas Allen, Iago Elkin-Jones, Jonathon Green and Susie Ford, Ronald Hutton, Alan Lee, Siobhán McElduff, Andrew McNeillie, Mick Ryan, Reverend Paul Seaton-Burn, Lubna Speitan, Fiona Stafford, and Michael Suarez, SJ.

I am particularly grateful to Shaun Gunner and The Tolkien Society (which I first joined many years ago, and have since rejoined to find it equally welcoming, enthusiastic, and informed); it was a privilege to be the Guest of Honour at the Society's 2022 AGM, after which I received welcome comments and communications following my talk – several of which were perceptive and refreshingly insightful and have belatedly informed this book. In particular, I had the pleasure of corresponding with Tolkien Society members Jennifer Brooker, Chris Walsh, and Jessica Yates – all of whom had written on similar areas. Brooker made a simply brilliant point about Great War passwords that I should have considered – 'friend' being the conventional response in the Allied Forces' challenge 'Friend or Foe?'; Walsh offered an incisive counterpoint (often in harmony) to many of my own suggestions; and Yates, typically perceptive and informed about everything in Middle-Earth, was very helpful about the Spiders.[2] All three exemplify the support one can expect from members of The Tolkien Society.

The existence of this book, however, is primarily down to two people who have had an enduring impact on my life as a writer: James Nightingale, my editor at Atlantic, and David Godwin, my agent. Without them, there would be no *Twenty-First-Century Tolkien*. Furthermore, in production Atlantic favoured me with the most meticulous and learned of copy-editors – Tamsin Shelton; I am extremely grateful that she has applied her extraordinary editorial rigour to this book; any errors that remain are, of course, my own. My abiding debt to my family is, I trust, clear in my dedication.

Finally, I would like to remember those with whom I shared my early experience of reading Tolkien. My parents, Elisabeth and Michael, were very understanding when their young teenage son suddenly became captivated by Tolkien's work, and they spent countless hours taking me to gaming events and what are now called LARPs, which must, at the time, have been mystifying to them; they also bought me many books by and about Tolkien, which I still treasure. But there were also a handful of people with me on the 'frontline' of Middle-Earth, some of whom, I am pleased to say, I remain in touch with: David Bennett, Mike Cattell, Martin Deacon, and Andy Morgan, as well as Jules Cowley, Michael Goodwin, and Neil Roberts. Thank you for those memories, which forty-plus years on have been stirred by writing this book.

Lastly, I should stress that in spite of comments in my conclusion, this is not a 'lockdown book' – it is a book about Tolkien, first conceived many years ago, if written under more recent, and more trying, circumstances. However, the impact of the Covid-19 pandemic is inescapable and has, I hope – at the end of things – provided an opportunity to show how Tolkien's Middle-Earth writings are strikingly relevant today.

Nick Groom
Séipéal Iosóid

Notes on the Text

Terminology

In this book, the names of the prominent peoples of Middle-Earth are capitalized in the same way in which national or ethnic identities are capitalized, such as Danish, Roma, or Gothic: this distinction reflects individual languages and applies to Dwarves (evidently Tolkien's preferred plural has been adopted), Elves, Ents, Hobbits, Humans, and also to Orcs (and, in *The Hobbit*, to Goblins too). However, this distinction does not imply that these peoples of Middle-Earth constitute different races: rather, they are different species.[1] The 'Race of Men' is usually referred to as 'Human' in this study, as umbrella-terms such as 'Mankind' are now rightly considered patriarchal – even if these words were not consciously gendered when Tolkien was writing.

Moreover, intelligent species within Middle-Earth such as Dragons, Eagles, Spiders, and Trolls are generally capitalized – Tolkien himself tended to capitalize these, although inconsistently. I have chosen to capitalize Horses as well because they clearly have knowing sentience and a bearing on the plot, but not deer or dogs or smaller creatures, which barely feature in the texts under discussion. Wizards perhaps deserve to be capitalized as a distinct species, but the general use of this term outside Middle-Earth alongside Tolkien's specific use within it would risk confusion.

'Middle-Earth' itself is Anglicized and therefore capitalized. Tolkien's own preference for not capitalizing the second word of a name following a hyphen appears to derive from Nordic usage; however, this runs counter to his claim in Appendix F of *The Lord of the Rings* to have 'Englished' the language, and one cannot, for example, imagine Sackville-Baggins being rendered 'Sackville-baggins'.[2] In any case, to use the form 'Middle-earth' would have created an inelegant inconsistency in my own title. Nevertheless, there is complete fidelity to other authors' preferred capitalization in quotations and titles cited. The Shire is always given with the definite article, as this is how it appears on the map of Middle-Earth, and, again for consistency, 'Bag End' is unhyphenated throughout, which is Tolkien's preferred style in *The Lord of the Rings* (but not *The Hobbit*). The term 'Anglo-Saxon' (first used in Latin in the eighth century AD, and in English by 1602) is generally used in preference to 'Old English' as it reflects the hybrid nature of English identities in the pre-Conquest period, and to resist the appropriation of the term by far-right groups.[3]

The First World War is usually referred to as the 'Great War', as would have been familiar to Tolkien. The Second World War, which went under a number of different names while Tolkien was writing *The Lord of the Rings*, maintains its common appellation – although I was tempted to call it the 'Six Years' War' after one of Tolkien's counter-factual narratives.[4] *The Silmarillion* (italicized) refers to the published work of 1977, 'The Silmarillion' (sometimes 'Quenta Silmarillion') refers to unpublished drafts of the text as Tolkien was writing it.

References

Although there are several different editions of *The Hobbit* and *The Lord of the Rings* in circulation, it is not difficult to access a digital copy to find a particular quotation. For this reason although references for all direct quotations are given, they are, for frankly sentimental reasons, keyed to the page numbers of my beloved and battered copy of the third edition Unwin paperback of *The Lord of the Rings* (1979), unless I am referring to material unique to the first, second, or subsequent editions; likewise *The Silmarillion*. The preferred text of *The Hobbit* is *The Annotated Hobbit* with an introduction and notes by Douglas A. Anderson (2002) as it includes important additional material – again, unless a point is being made about an earlier edition. To help distinguish between the books and the major films, the Peter Jackson movies of *The Lord of the Rings* are collectively called *Rings*, and his films of *The Hobbit* are collectively *Hobbits*.

Foreword

The love that dare not speak its name.
Lord Alfred Douglas, 'Two Loves' (1894)

This is a book unlike other books on Tolkien and his visionary creation of Middle-Earth. To begin: I first read *The Lord of the Rings* aged thirteen, and was totally enraptured by Middle-Earth. The finest analogy I have found to my experience is in the words of the much-loved and greatly lamented writer Terry Pratchett, who described his first encounter with *The Lord of the Rings* in the most reverential terms: he read it as a teenager, babysitting on New Year's Eve – 'I have never since then so truly had the experience of being inside the story.'[1]

This book is about being inside the story, a wild story. It is not an (apparently) straightforward introduction to Tolkien's world – not only are there plenty of such primers, guides, and encyclopedias, but they tend to get rapidly bogged down in the minutiae of Tolkien's 'legendarium' or 'mythos' (his complex architecture of gods and goddesses, the intricate lore of the many peoples of Middle-Earth, and their entangled histories and tales across thousands of years). Within a few pages, these books are preaching to the converted and are lost in the arcana of the 'Ainur' and 'Maiar', and purveying imaginary deities to perplexed readers rather than doing what they should be doing, which is, simply, explaining the value of the writing. Neither is this book an academic study of the challenges that Tolkien's work poses to his readers in such areas as the twists and turns of invented languages and alphabets, or the workings of Catholic theology. Such extreme erudition stifles the appreciation of the works as literature, and as a wider culture – indeed, this work could be deemed worthy but worthless; of undoubted scholarly significance, but of interest only to the cognoscenti.

In contrast, *Twenty-First-Century Tolkien* takes as its starting point the Tolkien phenomenon today: a multi-media mix and fix of literature, art, music, radio, cinema, gaming, fandom, and popular culture – a never-ending Middle-Earth. We cannot return to a purely literary Middle-Earth independent of, primarily, Sir Peter Jackson's extraordinary films. We should therefore accept that any assessment of newly published works drawn from the Tolkien archives – as well as new adaptations of his tales and imagined histories – are inevitably going to be deeply coloured by the multifaceted twenty-first-century Tolkien 'industry', for want of a better term.

In that respect at least, Tolkien can be compared with Shakespeare: he is not simply an author and a body of work, but a vast and growing field of cultural activity and products. This 'discourse' – and I will try not to use that word again – combines Tolkien's earliest influences and sources (from *Beowulf* to *Peter Pan*), biographical details (two world wars and half a century of university politics – mainly at Oxford), and an astonishingly rich variety of texts (poetry, drama, fiction, literary criticism, philological scholarship, and so forth) with the dazzling efflorescence of adaptations that began in his lifetime and have since expanded to Himalayan proportions. Even before the publication of the final volume of *The Lord of the Rings* (itself one of the bestselling books of all time), Tolkien had received a proposal for a BBC radio adaptation. The rage for adaptation is, however, seen most markedly, of course, in six films that in the past two decades have each grossed close on $1 billion.[2] This stratospheric ascent has also happened remarkably quickly. In the case of Shakespeare it took at least a century for the reputation of th'immortal Swan of Avon to take flight and another century for the Bard to become an international icon and the foundation of a global market; in the case of Tolkien it was already happening in his lifetime and was cemented within thirty years of his death. Since then, things have accelerated even more rapidly: the unparalleled worldwide success of *Harry Potter*, in tandem with the Tolkien film franchise, was achieved within a dizzying five years. We will never see such a phenomenon again. Never again.

This book is published to coincide with another major intercession in this passionately debated and zealously defended – and protected – artistic world. The Amazon Prime Video TV series of *The Rings of Power* is, at a rumoured $1 billion, the most expensive television series yet made; it premièred on 2 September 2022. *The Rings of Power* is set in the 'Second Age', thus pre-dating the events of *The Lord of the Rings* by several thousand years, yet including some of the same immortal characters – principally the rebel Elf warrior-queen Galadriel. This material is gleaned from the appendices of *The Lord of the Rings* (which run to 150 pages) and from passing evidence in the text (and, less so, in *The Hobbit*) such as that provided by songs and in fragments of historical detail. It is also worth pointing out that some episodes from the novel have in any case never been filmed (or been developed as games), so there may well be an opportunity to incorporate these incidents as well.

The viewers of this new series – and indeed the vast majority of those who enjoy Tolkien's books, and the radio series, films, games, and artwork inspired by his work – have at best only a passing interest in Tolkien's Anglo-Saxon and mediaeval learning, the composition of his works, his obsessively detailed invented languages, or his Roman Catholicism. Any popular book on Tolkien needs to grasp this nettle: Tolkien is not only for the academics, the fans, and the self-styled experts, but has a far broader appeal. A straightforward example: among the 'castaways' on BBC Radio 4's *Desert Island Discs* who selected *The Lord of the Rings* to accompany the Bible and the works of Shakespeare are figures as diverse as primatologist Dr Jane Goodall, mountaineer Sir Edmund Hillary, botanist David Bellamy, and folksinger Mary O'Hara – none of whom are philologists specializing in Old English.[3]

The appeal of Middle-Earth can best be addressed and enhanced, then, by moving Tolkien away from the dusty antiquarian and highly specialized commentaries and towards more contemporary ways of understanding the extraordinary creative achievement of his work. His writing is enthrallingly intricate, tentative and absorbing. This speaks to us today. Tolkien's open and experimental approaches can demonstrate his striking relevance for the most pressing issues confronting the Human condition in the twenty-first century. Writing predominantly in the 1930s and 1940s, Tolkien clearly could not anticipate the crises of the present, but through often surprisingly prescient episodes and especially in the retelling and reinvention of his characters and narratives in different formats, his work is becoming a touchstone of current concerns. More and more, we are beginning to think through Tolkien.

So while there is always room for Tolkien purists – not least because through the volumes of Middle-Earth writings and specialist websites, Tolkien has become a culture that requires keen-eyed custodians, curators, and critics – mention of Tolkien or Middle-Earth or *The Lord of the Rings* is no longer rooted in the books. Rather, the books are the source of a radical typology of characters and places and plots that can be reinvented across film, television, and computer gaming, as well as art and music, LARP (live-action role-play) and tourism, and many other activities.[4] There are, for instance, some 100,000 hits on the online art gallery DeviantArt simply for the word 'Hobbit'.[5]

Consequently, the huge anticipated global audience for the Amazon Prime Video TV series may well benefit from a book on Tolkien that cuts across the past eighty-five years since the inaugural publication of *The Hobbit* to identify why the books and media adaptations have been so popular. The answer to this is definitely *not* that Tolkien invented, say, a highly complex language system for Elves (although this does have some curious implications), but rather, I suggest, because his writing is creatively open-ended, humane (and yet intensely aware of non-Human perspectives), and environmentally sensitive. In a word, Tolkien, in his many guises, offers a richly rewarding re-enchantment of the world – something we desperately need after a global pandemic, repeated national and international lockdowns, and growing social isolation, as well as in the wider, apocalyptic contexts of political extremism and instability, climate change, and ecological disasters such as snowballing species extinction. Tolkien's vision increasingly has value today: more than ever, this is the Tolkien moment.

Twenty-First-Century Tolkien will accordingly consider areas such as uncertainty and the indeterminate, failure, friendship, the contradictions of his environmental imagination, the significance of things and objects (both inanimate and animate), and the weird and eerie in the books and films and games (and, more broadly, in Tolkien's other work) – as well as Tolkien in a post-Covid age. I begin with the multiple Tolkiens that existed, then survey his often frantic professional life and attempts to write for the press, and outline his love of Anglo-Saxon and mediaeval sources, before turning to the thorny problems of the composition of his major works.

After that, more treacherous waters: radio and film adaptations, and some spin-off computer games. Yet it cannot be stressed too strongly that this book does not privilege the published canonical texts over later reworkings. Most readers (if they read the books at all) now come to them through the Jackson films and/or computer games, and soon they will be coming to those Jackson experiences (and perhaps eventually the books) via the Amazon Prime Video series *The Rings of Power*. But *Twenty-First-Century Tolkien* respects this 'multi-platform' Tolkien in a non-hierarchical and, I hope, non-judgemental way. But although I say 'non-hierarchical', one cannot escape the books, and they have an immensely powerful and irresistible gravitational pull. The commentaries presented in the following pages are meant to open up the interpretation and appreciation of Tolkien's work rather than closing it down, introducing unexpected contexts and readings derived from his unruly and wayward working methods, and the abundance of subsequent adaptations. So although my primary aim is to answer the question 'Why Tolkien now?', I certainly hope that those who have enjoyed the films but are yet to read the books might be moved to do so after reading my own book, this book. As the seventeenth-century printers John Heminges and Henry Condell said of an earlier writer (pretty well known today), 'Read him, therefore, and again, and again, and if then you do not like him, surely you are in some manifest danger not to understand him.'[6]

The huge amount of material inspired by Middle-Earth since the late sixties, when its sudden popularity on university campuses yoked it to rock music and the counterculture, and since then in everything from the genesis of the role-playing game *Dungeons & Dragons* to Peter Jackson's era-defining films means that I have had to be increasingly selective in my examples. This has been particularly the case in popular (and, admittedly, relatively unpopular) music. There are several volumes to be written in this area – I have only a few paragraphs. However, I hope that I have been fair, representative, and ultimately persuasive in my overall points, and that my examples are recognizable rather than recondite, and I am sorry if I have missed particular favourites here, or elsewhere – this book is, sadly, finite. But more to the point, perhaps – just listen to the music, any of the music.

Finally, in writing this book I have repeatedly been brought up against the extraordinary problem that many people unfortunately read *The Lord of the Rings* with their eyes shut, misreading it as a simple fairyland conflict between good and evil in which good inevitably triumphs. This reading is not only prevalent at the lowest level of ignorant commentators who make the most basic mistakes in the plot, but also among some of Middle-Earth's most ardent fans. All I ask you, as readers or potential readers, is that you read the words on the page, and then attend – assiduously – to the films. Only at that point should you judge them and make of them what you will. But frankly, if Middle-Earth was a facile good/bad dichotomy, you would not be reading this book, and I would not have bothered to write it – in fact, it would not have been possible to write this book at all about a twenty-first-century Tolkien . . .

ONE

Myriad Middle-Earths

I smell a man of middle earth.
William Shakespeare,
The Merry Wives of Windsor (1597)

We begin:

HWÆT!
WĒ GĀR-DEna   in geārdagum
þēodcyninga   þrym gefrūnon,
hū ðā æþelingas   ellen fremedon.[1]

These are the opening lines of *Beowulf* (*c.*AD650–800), with which Tolkien would habitually begin his lectures. The poem was well over a thousand years old when Tolkien strode into the room, throwing out the lines. But today they may be oddly familiar too, having a Tolkienian timbre: those mysterious letters 'þ' and 'ð', those words 'þēodcyninga' and 'æþelingas': their meaning is present, if just out of reach.[2]

The lines can be translated as

Lo! [or 'Behold!', or 'Hark!', or 'What!', or even 'Oi!'] We have heard of the glory of the kings of the Spear-Danes in days of yore – how those princes did valorous deeds . . .[3]

Listen . . .

How Many Tolkiens?

John Ronald Reuel Tolkien, John Ronald, Ronald, Philip, J.R.R.T. (and occasionally 'JRsquared'), Gabriel, the 'Home Secretary', Lieutenant Tolkien, Professor Tolkien, Tollers, Fisiologus, N.N., Kingston Bagpuize, Oxymore, John Jethro Rashbold ('J.J.R.'), Spurius Vectigalius Acer (or T. Portorius Acer Germanicus), Eisphorides Acribus Polyglotteus, Ruginwaldus Dwalakōnis, Rægnold Hrædmoding, Arcastar Mondósaresse.[4] He was baptized Anglican, familiarly known as Ronald (a name he delightfully recognized as derived from Norse), and took the name Philip at his Roman Catholic confirmation. He was Gabriel or the 'Home Secretary' to close school friends (the T.C.B.S., see below), Tollers to close colleagues (the Inklings), and Rashbold in a semi-fictionalized account of himself. He rendered his name Vectigalius Acer in Latin and Eisphorides Acribus in ancient Greek ('vectigal acer' and 'eisphorides acribus' punning on the words 'toll' and 'keen'), and, more literally, Dwalakōnis in Gothic and Hrædmoding in Old English – the latter for an Anglo-Saxon poem he wrote for the poet W.H. Auden's sixtieth birthday in 1967 (by which time Auden had joined the Tolkien Society of America and renamed himself 'Gimli').[5] He had earlier (1910–37) published poetry under the pseudonyms Fisiologus, N.N., Kingston Bagpuize, and Oxymore. Tolkien himself provided a derivation of his surname, stating in a letter that it was originally German, from Saxony – *Tollkühn* – and meant 'foolhardy' (hence, 'Rashbold'); he then straightaway declared that he was more of a Suffield (his mother's maiden name), and that it was to the Suffield side he owed his love of philology and mediaeval romance.[6] Indeed, he identified as an Anglo-Saxon West Midlander with an affinity for the Welsh Marches and Wales.[7] So there are many Tolkiens (or Suffields), not to mention his self-appointed artistic heirs; Tolkiens, Tolkienians, and Tolkienists may even perhaps merit their own collective noun: a *gramarye*.[8]

But what is interesting here is the very profusion of Tolkien's names. We all have various nicknames, but Tolkien's seem more manifold, deliberately proliferating, and in tension with Suffield. And this is also true in his writings.[9] The character Aragorn is variously Estel, Thorongil, Strider, Aragorn, Isildur's Heir, the Renewer, Longshanks, Elfstone, Wing-Foot, and Elessar Telcontar – names that, at least initially, often mean little to other characters or to us as readers, except to impart a sense of growing presence and inscrutable meaning. Gandalf, meanwhile, has so many names he even forgets the very name of Gandalf at one point: he is Olórin, Mithrandir, the Grey Wanderer, the Grey Pilgrim (and the Grey Fool to the sardonic Denethor), Tharkûn, Incánus, Greyhame, Stormcrow, Láthspell, and eventually the White Rider.[10] Other names are less stable: Treebeard's name is growing, or unfolding.[11] These names are in part the consequence of the number of languages spoken in Middle-Earth, but also a feature of the fluctuating identities and changing status of the characters. Characters are defined and named by others, by circumstances, by context. They do not assert an individual identity, but are pluralistic, persistently fashioning and refashioning themselves, or being reinvented by other forces. This is most notable when Gandalf the Grey becomes Gandalf the White, but even characters such as Frodo bear different names, such as Mr Underhill, Elf-Friend, and Ringbearer – and this is something all-too-familiar in the current age of social media avatars: selfhood is no longer fixed, but fundamentally fluid. The many Tolkiens are also evident in his range of creative activities: lecturer and tutor, scholar and literary critic, philologist, editor, translator, poet, artist, children's author, novelist, dramatist, cartographer, occasional (and memorable) performer, speculative linguist, and – it has to be said – experimental writer.[12] Even Tolkien's academic work hums with competing voices: his acclaimed lecture on *Beowulf*, 'The Monsters and the Critics', includes phrases in Anglo-Saxon, Icelandic, and Middle English, as well as coinages from Lewis Carroll's 'Jabberwocky'. And despite his professed dislike of allegory, this piece contains not one but two allegories on the poem's treatment by critics and commentators.

Tolkien's own constellation of shifting characters is borne out by his biography, so it is worth summarizing the chief events of his life to show how his changing names and revisions in his identity are reflected in his various roles and experiences.[13] He was born on 3 January 1892 at Bloemfontein in the Orange Free State, a province of South Africa. The family was from Birmingham, but his father was a representative of the Bank of Africa, so from the beginning the young Ronald was a person in exile.[14] While in Bloemfontein, Ronald was bitten by a 'sun-spider' or 'camel spider', and he later claimed, rather improbably, to remember racing through the grass away from the creature, as well as later paddling in the Indian Ocean.[15] But he was not more than three years old at the time, so these memories are likely to be examples of Tolkien's later ongoing reimagining of himself: a flight through an Edenic garden, a moment of childhood innocence bathed in a sunlit sea. As it was, both he and his mother were suffering so severely from the intense heat that in 1895 she returned to Birmingham with Ronald and his younger brother Hilary. He also claimed to remember parts of the three-week voyage to England: looking down at the sea, arriving at a harbour beyond which was a great city (Lisbon) – a vision highly suggestive of his later depictions of Elfland or Faërie as a magical isle reached only by enchanted craft.

In Birmingham he was brought up by his mother and her Suffield grandparents. His father was due to join them as soon as he could leave the bank, and in February 1896 Ronald dictated a letter describing himself to his father as 'a big man' because he now had a man's coat.[16] The letter was never sent. His father died the following day of a haemorrhage brought on either by rheumatic fever or typhoid.

In 1896, the single-parent family moved to the hamlet of Sarehole on the outskirts of Birmingham in 1896; this proved to be an idyllic and formative experience of the English countryside for Ronald. He learnt Latin and German at his mother's knee, as well as admiring her beautifully calligraphic handwriting, and she read him Lewis Carroll's *Alice* books and Andrew Lang's *Fairy Books* – which included the tale of the Viking hero Sigurd and the Dragon Fafnir.[17] She also unexpectedly converted to Roman Catholicism, precipitating a family rift.

The tale of Sigurd and Fafnir, which appears in *The Red Fairy Book* as 'The Story of Sigurd', is worth pausing over. It is a key episode in the thirteenth-century Old Norse *Völsunga Saga*, which Tolkien later translated into taut, terse poetry, and in recalling his mother reading the tale aloud to him, he presents it as effectively the primal scene of his first encounter with Dragons. Lang's version begins with a king dying on a battlefield because his sword breaks; nevertheless, the shards are kept by his pregnant wife to forge anew for their young son. She straightaway disguises herself as a maid to escape her husband's foes, is captured by Danes, and questioned before the king because she looks too regal for a maidservant; consequently, she is treated well in the royal household and gives birth to Sigurd, who grows up in the palace. In time, Sigurd's tutor, Regin, tells him of the Dragon Fafnir: Regin and Fafnir were originally brothers, but Fafnir killed their father and seized a hoard of cursed gold (other versions have Fafnir's greed, or Dragon sickness, causing him to become a Dragon). Regin consequently seeks revenge, and persuades Sigurd to slay Fafnir, forging a razor-sharp sword from the shards of his father's broken weapon. Sigurd hides in a pit and stabs the Dragon as it passes over him, and Fafnir curses the gold again as he dies. Regin then asks Sigurd to cut out Fafnir's heart and roast it for him. As Sigurd does so, he licks his fingers and so tastes the heart, which gives him the power to understand the speech of birds – who are all chattering about Fafnir's gold and Regin's plans to betray Sigurd. Sigurd accordingly decapitates Regin, whereupon the birds sing a chorus that the warrior-maiden Brynhild lies in an enchanted sleep nearby. Sigurd equips himself with 'the Helm of Dread' from the hoard of Fafnir – a helmet that confers invisibility upon the wearer – and rides to Brynhild, imprisoned in a castle ringed by fire, and frees her. They of course fall in love, and Sigurd gives her a ring from the cursed hoard; he then rides off to another kingdom and meets the princess Gudrun, whose mother mixes a potion causing Sigurd to forget Brynhild and marry Gudrun. Gudrun's brother, Gunnar, then determines to marry Brynhild, but cannot reach her through the circle of fire, so he magically disguises Sigurd as himself to rescue Brynhild a second time. They exchange rings, and Sigurd then gives the cursed ring to Gudrun. At the wedding feast, Sigurd comes to his senses, remembers everything, but keeps his peace. Brynhild and Gudrun then quarrel, and Brynhild recognizes on Gudrun's finger the ring she had received from Sigurd and thought she had given to Gunnar – 'and she knew it and knew all, and she turned as pale as a dead woman'.[18] She accuses Gunnar of deceiving her, and drugs his younger brother with serpent's venom and wolf's flesh; he becomes maddened and slays the sleeping Sigurd – whereupon Brynhild's heart breaks. Brynhild and Sigurd (and his mighty steed) are placed in a longship that is set alight and carried away on the tide, thus fulfilling the curse of the gold.

I have described Lang's version of the tale in some detail to suggest the captivating hold it must have had over the young Tolkien's imagination, and to draw out parallels with his later writing and with the work of his followers. A Tolkien buff will immediately recognize some of the contours of the tragic tale of Túrin Turambar here. Túrin attacks the fearsome Dragon Glaurung as it passes over him, and his assault is alluded to in *The Lord of the Rings* when Sam stands beneath Shelob, raising the sword Sting above his head as she impetuously impales herself upon the blade. Likewise, the complicated love interest is reflected in Túrin's own relationships, although these are, catastrophically, incestuous, and also influenced by the tale of Kullervo in the Finnish national epic the *Kalevala*. The roasting of the heart, the slaying of Regin, the love triangle Sigurd–Brynhild–Gudrun, and Gunnar's disguising of Sigurd are dark materials for a children's tale, but they are part of an overall theme of masking, shifting appearances and multiple identities, concealment, and deceit. The story thus hinges on revelation and recognition – not least through the strange, unearthly language of birds – and on the fallout from slaying a Dragon. The cursed ring from the Dragon's hoard is the key actor in this legend: it is both a prized treasure and a wedding band that brings misfortune to those who possess it; it is as if the ring has an inimical sentience. The long shadow of 'The Story of Sigurd' thus reaches not only into the comfort of Bag End, but as far as the self-destructive Dragon sickness of Thorin Oakenshield in the film *The Battle of the Five Armies* (2014). For Tolkien, such memories of reading were sifted and nurtured: they are a conscious and deliberately constructed personal history of language, land-scape, letters, and legends – a shorthand for the formation of his character. This is not to say that they are false memories, but rather that his recollection is selective – if forgivable – self-mythologization.

In 1900, Tolkien passed the entrance exam to King Edward's School, then housed in an imposing mediaevalist Gothic Revival building designed by Charles Barry, the architect responsible for the Palace of Westminster, which had been rebuilt in the three decades following 1840.[19] As it was a four-mile journey to school, the Tolkiens regrettably left Sarehole for Moseley, a district of Birmingham near the railway. It was a ghastly move after four years in the countryside. There followed an unsettled period moving house and moving school, a period of home-schooling from his mother, and eventually a return to King Edward's on a scholarship. Tolkien remembered that he was stimulated by the unfamiliar languages that now entered his life: he had his First Communion in Latin, he pondered the Welsh names painted on coal trucks that passed on the train tracks, and at King Edward's he was introduced to Greek: 'The fluidity of Greek, punctuated by hardness, and with its surface glitter captivated me. But part of the attraction was antiquity and alien remoteness (from me): it did not touch home.'[20] Again, displacement and dislocation, and the lure of enigmatic meaning.

Then, in 1904, his mother became diabetic and died in November of the same year. It was a devastating blow; Ronald was just twelve years old. He and Hilary were taken under the care of Father Francis Xavier Morgan – an ebullient half-Welsh, half Anglo-Spanish pastor of the Birmingham Oratory – and lodged with a Suffield aunt.[21] The two brothers spent most of their home time at the Oratory, where nearly every morning they served Mass before Fr Francis provided breakfast as they played with the Oratory cat.

At school, Tolkien immersed himself in language and literature. He read Chaucer's *Canterbury Tales* and the Arthurian poem *Sir Gawain and the Green Knight*, and his English teacher introduced him to Anglo-Saxon and the epic poem *Beowulf*; he also taught himself Old Norse so he could now read of Sigurd and Fafnir, Brynhild and Gudrun in the original languages. Perhaps fancifully, Tolkien felt that Anglo-Saxon (and the later poems *Sir Gawain and the Green Knight* and *Pearl* in particular) was part of his West Midlands Suffield literary inheritance – but of course he was a young orphan seeking identity (or identities), and he seems to have found considerable solace in words and language. Words held a magic for him – they were the rich remains of previous epochs, carrying the history of the region, imbued with the cultures and values of the past, and at the same time the most sophisticatedly modern medium of thought and communication. And his memories of his mother were rooted in learning language.

While his best friend Christopher Wiseman was teaching himself Egyptian hieroglyphics, Tolkien had discovered the Gothic language in 1908 or 1909 via Joseph Wright's *Primer of the Gothic Language*. Little of Gothic survives – there is, for instance, no poetry – but it nevertheless stirred in him 'a sensation at least as full of delight as first looking into Chapman's *Homer*'.[22] Tolkien also found the Gothic script beautiful, and enjoyed writing Gothicized inscriptions; and, undaunted by the lost vocabulary and literary culture, he simply invented missing Gothic words and ultimately wrote his own Gothic poetry. King Edward's held an annual debate conducted in Latin, but Tolkien also addressed the assembly in Greek, Anglo-Saxon, and Gothic, displaying an extraordinary linguistic fluency, and, not content with languages ancient and modern, he began to invent his own. The first of these invented languages was perhaps a three-page letter in pictorial code to Fr Francis, but he also worked with his cousin Mary on Nevbosh, a 'New Nonsense' language, and then on a language based on Latin and Spanish he named Naffarin. In his last months at King Edward's he discovered Finnish and the Finnish national epic the *Kalevala*, which would provide the foundations of another new language he would call Qenya, which he worked to perfect throughout his life.

At school, Tolkien enjoyed the male camaraderie of small clubs, forming the Tea Club and Barrovian Society, or T.C.B.S., named after a favoured tearoom at Barrow's Stores where he would meet with his three closest friends. They debated and gave readings – Tolkien typically introducing his companions to *Beowulf*, *Sir Gawain and the Green Knight*, and the *Völsunga Saga*. He was also a corporal in the school's Officers' Training Corps (the cadets), and sufficiently highly thought of to be one of eight King Edward's cadets selected to attend the coronation of George V. By his final year at King Edward's Tolkien was a Prefect, a Librarian, the House [Rugby] Football Captain, [Rugby] Football Secretary, Secretary of the Debating Society, an editor of the *King Edward's School Chronicle*, and an actor in various school plays (including Mrs Malaprop in Sheridan's *The Rivals*, performed after his first term at university); he also received several school prizes. He was remarkably involved in the school and exceptionally industrious in his work. Any spare time not devoted to invented languages was spent painting or writing poetry. His earliest dated poem was written in March 1910, inspired by reading the poems of the Roman Catholic opium addict and one-time outcast Francis Thompson, of whom he was an ardent admirer, and also by seeing a stage production of *Peter Pan* in April 1910, which 'I shall never forget . . . as long as I live'.[23] Some of his poems were published in the school magazine, along with his reports on school activities and sports. But another form of solace had come with his friendship of Edith Bratt; she too was an orphan and, for a time, had a room in the same house in which Tolkien and his brother lodged. Their friendship rapidly blossomed into romance, necessarily conducted in secret, but news of their clandestine relationship soon reached Fr Francis. At the time, Tolkien was being tutored for a scholarship to study 'Greats' (classical Greek and Latin) at Oxford – a scholarship to cover expenses and fees being a necessity for one in Tolkien's position. Fr Francis was severely disappointed in Tolkien's behaviour, which he saw as a distraction from his academic studies, and moved the Tolkien brothers to new lodgings. Tolkien and Edith nevertheless continued to meet, leading Fr Francis to forbid contact until Tolkien's twenty-first birthday, although the two did occasionally contrive to chance upon each other 'accidentally'.

In 1910 (at his second attempt) Tolkien was awarded an Open Classical Exhibition to Exeter College, Oxford – an Exhibition providing less financial support, but, with an additional bursary from his school and the help of Fr Francis, it was sufficient to enable Tolkien to attend. He duly took up his place in 1911, reading Greats (or Literae Humaniores, as Classics at Oxford is known). There, in addition to his lectures and tutorials in ancient Greek and Latin languages, literature, history, and philosophy, he was tutored by Joseph Wright in Comparative Philology – Wright being the author of the *Gothic Primer* that had so enthralled Tolkien. He also attended Mass regularly, continued writing poetry (some of which was published in magazines), learnt to ride with a territorial cavalry regiment, and began teaching himself Finnish and Welsh. Clubbable as ever, Tolkien formed a literary society – the Apolausticks – and served as its first President, before this group transformed into the Chequers Clubbe.[24] In the meantime he was elected to the Exeter College Essay Club (becoming President in his third year) and the Stapledon Society (the JCR, or undergraduate student body, of which he became President in his second year, and Secretary in his third year). He sometimes got involved in high-spirited student escapades, including taking and driving a bus full of excitable students around the centre of Oxford, and entertaining the Stapledon Society one evening who 'listened with breathless interest to the respectively frolicsome, frivolous and fearful adventures which had befallen Messrs. Tolkien, Robinson and Wheway'.[25] Notwithstanding this, he also won the college Skeat Prize for English in 1914, with which he bought William Morris's *The House of the Wolfings* (Morris, coincidentally, having been an undergraduate at Exeter sixty years previously). During the vacations he painted, and at Christmas wrote and performed in little seasonal plays. He also travelled: in the summer of 1913 Tolkien was employed to take two Mexican boys being schooled in England to Paris to join family members, and to act as their tutor. Sadly, though, the trip proved to be highly traumatic as one of the boys' aunts was killed in a traffic accident and Tolkien, not especially fluent in French or Spanish, had to make the arrangements to have her body repatriated to Mexico. The experience did little to warm him to the French or French bureaucracy.

Halfway through the second year of his four-year degree Tolkien was faced with university exams (Honour Moderations), which he not only needed to pass in order to remain at Oxford, but pass sufficiently well to retain the award of his Exhibition. His performance was frankly poor, only just placing him in the Second Class cohort, but he produced an exceptional paper in Comparative Philology – his saving grace. This led the college to recommend Tolkien switch courses to English Language and Literature, which would enable him to focus on language, philology, and Old and Middle English; he was also allowed to keep his Exhibition. He now had papers in Anglo-Saxon literature, Middle English literature, Chaucer, Shakespeare, English literary history, the history of the English language, Gothic and

Germanic philology, and an optional paper in Scandinavian philology (which included his beloved *Völsunga Saga*).

In the midst of this in 1913 he came of age at twenty-one years, became independent of Fr Francis, and duly proposed to the staunch Anglican Edith. She would have to convert if they were to marry, and accordingly began taking instruction while Tolkien continued his studies throughout the year, visiting her when he was able to do so. Then came the signal experience of his generation. It was 1914; on 28 June Archduke Franz Ferdinand of Austria was assassinated, and by 5 August Britain was at war.[26]

Tolkien was permitted to finish his degree before joining up, although the delay was extremely uncomfortable and incurred family – and public – disapproval. There was an overwhelming expectation that all eligible men would enlist: Tolkien's brother Hilary as well as many of his undergraduate peers joined up in the weeks immediately following the outbreak of war, many doubtless in response to hectoring propaganda demands to serve one's country. In the event, Tolkien was able to drill with the Officers' Training Corps and take classes in signalling in anticipation of enlisting when he completed his studies, even if university life – particularly the meetings of clubs and societies on which he relied for expressing his multifaceted mind – was severely curtailed. Undaunted, by October 1914 Tolkien had begun a translation of the Kullervo episode from the *Kalevala*, and read a paper on the Finnish epic to the Sundial Society at Corpus Christi College (at the invitation of his T.C.B.S. compadre Geoffrey Bache Smith), and in 1915 also read to the Exeter College Essay Club. The translation of Kullervo was never finished, but later, with the Sigurd story, formed the core of his Middle-Earth 'Great Tale' of Túrin Turambar.[27] The four members of the Tea Club and Barrovian Society had endeavoured to keep the club active throughout university, and Tolkien spent a weekend before Christmas back together with the group, discussing their hopes and ambitions as writers and artists. Faced with war and the likelihood of one or all of them being killed, the group's integrity and its role as a catalyst for the creative imagination began to verge on the sacred, especially for Geoffrey Bache Smith. For Tolkien too, this penultimate meeting seems to have drawn his emerging literary world into sharp relief.

By the second half of 1914, Tolkien was writing recognizable Middle-Earth poetry such as 'Sea Chant of an Elder Day', and he had read 'The Voyage of Éarendel the Evening Star' to the Exeter College Essay Club on 27 November 1914 (see below). Indeed, by 1915 in addition to his undergraduate essays he appears to have been writing or revising poetry or painting regularly – sometimes on a daily basis. It is also worth bearing in mind that Oxford in the early years of the Great War was one of the crucibles of early Modernism and so buzzed with artistic innovation. Tolkien's immediate undergraduate contemporaries included the immensely tall and near-blind writer Aldous Huxley, whose first collection of poetry was published in 1916. Tolkien also encountered Thomas Wade Earp – a charming, foppish aesthete and promiscuous gay socialite who was already moving in rarefied circles and on his way to becoming a notable art critic. Earp was some sort of cultural force of nature at the time, and it was inevitable that Tolkien would be drawn into his orbit: he was President of the Exeter College Essay Club when Tolkien read 'The Voyage of Éarendel the Evening Star' in November 1914, and dined with him that evening; they had also debated together.[28] Earp was also President of the Psittakoi (the 'parrots', founded by the radically minded Classicist E.R. Dodds in 1912), at which Tolkien read a piece of literary criticism in May 1915. T.S. Eliot was also in Oxford in 1914 and 1915, and apparently read 'The Love Song of J. Alfred Prufrock' at a meeting of the Psittakoi – although it is not known whether

Tolkien was present on this occasion.[29] But Tolkien clearly had a dalliance with the iconoclastic early avant-gardists at a personal level. Moreover, Earp was one of Tolkien's first publishers: he included the poem 'Goblin Feet' in his edited anthology *Oxford Poetry 1915*, which appeared when Tolkien had already left Oxford and was on basic military training.

Despite being, unfortunately, a sickly piece of fairy verse that Tolkien would later disown, 'Goblin Feet' clearly caught the mood of the time and quickly gathered admirers. Fairy verse was a refuge from the war. In May 1916, the charity 'Good Fairies for Unfortunate Fighters' sent food parcels to prisoners of war, explaining that 'soldiers who have fought and suffered for their country, turn to us, like children, for the one small pleasure they are allowed. Beneath the unromantic string and brown paper covering Parcels for Prisoners lies a whole world of dreams and memories.'[30] Reproductions of Estella Canziani's painting *Piper of Dreams, or Where the Little Things of the Woodland Live Unseen*, which pictured a seated Bombadil-like figure with his back against a tree and playing a pipe while fairies circle around him, sold some quarter of a million copies in 1916, the year in which military conscription was introduced.[31]

The fashion continued in the aftermath of the conflict. Ruth Fyleman's *Fairies and Chimneys* had an edition published for schools each year from 1920 to 1925, and the collections of fairy stories edited by Andrew Lang, the Brothers Grimm, and Hans Christian Andersen were republished.[32] Cicely Mary Barker's first book, *Flower Fairies of the Spring*, was published in 1923; Enid Blyton's *Real Fairies*, a book of poems, was published in 1923, and *The Enid Blyton Book of Fairies* followed in 1924. 'Goblin Feet', meanwhile, was later included in the Longmans *Book of Fairy Poetry* (1920) in the impressively canonical company of Shakespeare, Milton, Keats, Tennyson, and Yeats, and in the popular *Fifty New Poems for Children*, first published by Basil

Blackwell in 1922. As for T.W. Earp, Tolkien later recalled, perhaps with grudging affection, that Earp's name and behaviour had inspired the mildly disparaging term 'twerp' – conceivably in exasperation among contemporaries that Earp was somehow ineligible for military service.[33]

Tolkien's last months of undergraduate study culminated in his final 'Schools' examinations, which finished on 15 June. He immediately began acquiring his personal military equipment, and on 28 June applied to join the Lancashire Fusiliers on a commission for the duration of the war – his aim being to serve alongside his T.C.B.S. friend Geoffrey Bache Smith. His degree results were published on 2 July: he achieved First Class honours. Tolkien then returned to his poetry and painting, before being commissioned as a second lieutenant and undertaking his basic training at Bedford – meaning that he was forced to delay his graduation until March 1916. He specialized in signalling, which involved a number of devices and skills, from flying flags and launching rockets to learning Morse code and handling carrier pigeons – and he continued to write poetry while in training, planning to publish a volume of fairy poems. He moved to a billet at Lichfield, Staffordshire, and became part-owner of a motorbike so he could visit Edith in Warwickshire, and the T.C.B.S. met for the last time. During his training at Brocton Camp, near Lichfield, Tolkien and Edith were hurriedly married on 22 March 1916, and honeymooned for a week in Somerset. Warwickshire and Oxford were by now woven into the rich, ever-evolving tapestry of his imaginative creation, and after the newly-weds visited Cheddar Gorge that too joined those other, quintessentially English locations in his mind.

Tolkien left for France on 6 June 1916. There was little time or opportunity for writing, although he did take notebooks with him. He later commented: 'You might scribble something on the back of an envelope and shove it in your back pocket, but that's all. You couldn't write. You'd be crouching down among fleas and filth.'[34] It wasn't actually quite all – he did write some poems, and he could still muse over and map out his legendary histories so that when he came to write them down they already had the mnemonic contours of oft-told tales.

Within the month, Tolkien's unit were marching to the front-line, and on 1 July the Battle of the Somme commenced; nearly 20,000 Allied servicemen were killed on that first day. Tolkien himself was in the thick of the offensive, often living in dug-outs and trenches. News then came that Robert Quilter Gilson, one of the T.C.B.S., had been killed. Although Tolkien himself escaped injury, by 27 October he was sick with Trench Fever (a debilitating louse-borne disease caused by the bacterium *Bartonella quintana*) and was sent behind the lines to a Red Cross hospital, before being shipped back to Britain in November and admitted to a makeshift ward at the University of Birmingham (nominated 1st Southern General Hospital). Within a month Geoffrey Bache Smith had died of shrapnel wounds; the T.C.B.S. had been reduced to two surviving members: Christopher Wiseman, who was serving in the Royal Navy, and Tolkien.

Tolkien's recovery was slow, and perhaps while still in the 1st Southern General Hospital, he began *The Book of Lost Tales*, his first legendary cycle, and reworked the language Qenya by placing its origins in another invented language, Primitive Eldarin. Primitive Eldarin also gave rise to a third language, Goldogrin (later called Sindarin), which was elaborated with a grammar and a lexicon, and Tolkien began writing copious notes to add depth to his imagined territories, histories, and lore. Edith helped by transcribing the texts of *Lost Tales* from Tolkien's drafts into 'fair copy' as his productivity increased and his legendarium became deeper and more complex.[35] Tolkien was frequently transferred around the country, but they were often able to stay together. At one point in June 1917 the young couple visited a wood together and Edith danced among the hemlock. The scene made a profound impact on Tolkien: he was to recreate it in the key 'Great Tale' of Beren and Lúthien, the otherworldly love story that was the tale closest to his heart. It is usually overlooked that Edith was expecting their first child when she danced and was nearing the end of her first trimester, so was perhaps beginning to be visibly pregnant. Against the backdrop of the Great War and Tolkien's persistent illness, this brings an extraordinary poignancy and sense of hope and the future to the scene.

Their first son, John, was born in November; a week later Tolkien received promotion to full lieutenant. The next year was much the same: light duties, frequent repostings, but also recurrent relapses with a sometimes shocking deterioration in his condition (in August 1918, for instance, he lost nearly two stone in weight). Tolkien nevertheless continued to write and paint, wrote an introduction to the poems of Geoffrey Bache Smith (published as *A Spring Harvest* in June or July of 1918), and began learning Russian and practising his Italian and Spanish. Apart from a period of some two months when he was assessed as fit for general duties and sent to the Humber Garrison, Tolkien stayed in Britain for the remainder of the war, convalescing or on light duties and training, eventually being deemed fit only for sedentary employment. He returned to Oxford with Edith and John, and began working for the *Oxford English Dictionary* as a lexicographer. Within a few days, on 11 November 1918, the war ended.

Tolkien's work for the *OED* (which lasted until May 1920) included entries for *wake* and *walrus*, but more significantly his immersion back in academic philology stimulated him to refine further his invented language Qenya alongside further work on *The Book of Lost Tales*.[36] Yet within six months he had abandoned the book, his first sustained attempt at a legendarium.

This may have been partly in consequence of reading William Blake's prophetic books for the first time, as in their calligraphy, illustrations, and mythic narrative scope he must have seen the remarkable congruence of Blake's work with his own ambitions, as well as the heights to which he might – must – aspire. In addition to working on the *Dictionary* he was now tutoring for the university, often teaching female undergraduates who were placed under his supervision on account of his status as a married man with military service (interestingly, he had also in 1909 defended the militant suffragette movement in a school debate). Indeed, until he was demobbed in July 1919 Tolkien habitually wore his officer uniform around the city, but also had a dapper taste in clothes and furnishings, perhaps in response to the fashionable Modernism of the post-war period – certainly his watercolours at the time display a luminous abstract quality strongly reminiscent of the work of Wassily Kandinsky. He also gradually returned to some of his old pursuits, such as attending meetings of the Exeter College Essay Club.

His neglect of *The Book of Lost Tales* was also probably due to a major academic opportunity he received around mid-1919: the chance to write a Middle English vocabulary for Kenneth Sisam's anthology *Fourteenth Century Verse & Prose*. Sisam had been one of Tolkien's undergraduate tutors, so this was not only a prestigious commission, but also a clear endorsement of a potential university career for Tolkien. However, towards the end of 1919 he was drawn back to writing poetry again, and also returned to 'The Voyage of Éarendel the Evening Star'. A key moment came on 10 March 1920, when he read 'The Fall of Gondolin' to the Exeter College Essay Club. This was an account of the siege of an Elvish city that had first been drafted in *The Book of Lost Tales* and was subsequently repeatedly reworked in different versions of 'The Silmarillion'; early drafts were also heavily influenced by his experiences at the front. Reading 'The Fall' to an audience shows a marked increase in confidence in divulging his fairy legends, despite the rather lengthy apology with which he began.[37] The reading was warmly received, the Secretary recording this 'new mythological background' to be 'exceedingly illuminating' and in the tradition of William Morris, George Macdonald, and Friedrich de la Motte Fouqué; 'very graphically and astonishingly told, combined with a wealth of attendance to detail interesting in extreme'.[38] Perhaps encouraged by this response, he began to rewrite *The Book of Lost Tales* based around the Anglo-Saxon mariner 'Ælfwine of England'.[39]

Tolkien's academic career then suddenly took off with his appointment as Reader in English Language at the University of Leeds in July 1920. Tolkien moved to the city while Edith initially stayed in Oxford to give birth to their second son, Michael (born 22 October); he also almost immediately applied for Chairs at the universities of Liverpool and Cape Town (he was offered the De Beers Chair at Cape Town, but declined). Tolkien then cultivated the prodigious work rate that would characterize the following decades, tirelessly combining the demands of university teaching and administration with his own, highly charged, creative ambitions. He designed the English Language parts of the Leeds course, rewrote most of *Lost Tales* and improved Qenya, and, when he returned to Oxford in December, composed the first of his 'Father Christmas letters' for his children – which immediately became an annual commitment.[40]

The family decamped and settled in Leeds in April 1921; it was one of the most polluted industrial cities in the country: the tons of soot and tar in the atmosphere cut sunlight by 17 per cent, stunted the growth of trees, and acid rain and arsenic particles poisoned grass and plant growth.[41] This may have been a contributing factor in the severe case of pneumonia Tolkien contracted in 1923. Nevertheless, for the next four years Tolkien

worked in the university – and in another Gothic Revival building. He recommended E.V. Gordon, a postgraduate student, to
be appointed Assistant Lecturer, and the two worked closely
together until Gordon's untimely death in 1938. To popular-
ize their Old Icelandic courses, Tolkien and Gordon formed
the 'Viking Club' for students, which involved drinking beer,
readings from the sagas, and singing songs jokily translated into
early Northern languages – such as 'Éadig Béo Þu!' to the tune
of 'Twinkle, Twinkle, Little Star'.[42] They also joined forces to
co-edit a student edition of *Sir Gawain and the Green Knight* for
Oxford University Press. At the same time, Tolkien had returned
to the overdue *Middle English Vocabulary*, finally submitted early
in 1922, thankfully published in May as a single volume and
then as part of *Fourteenth Century Verse & Prose*. He continued
his legendarium, and wrote both serious and comic verse for
Leeds magazines *The Gryphon* and *The Microcosm*, departmen-
tal and university anthologies, and a volume of *Yorkshire Poetry*.
To make some much-needed money, he also started marking
School Certificate examination papers, to which he would
patiently attend every summer for the next few years.

By 1923, Tolkien had agreed to edit a selection of Chaucer's poetry and prose, known as the 'Clarendon Chaucer' – the
Clarendon Press being the academic imprint of Oxford University Press.[43] The first proof sheets arrived at the end of the
year, and continued into 1924 alongside proofs for the yet-to-
be completed *Gawain*. Tolkien worked on the Chaucer edition
throughout the year and was rewarded by promotion in October
to the new Professorship of English Language at Leeds. His
third son, Christopher, was born on 21 November, and he finally
completed the Chaucer glossary in December – just before
penning a pair of Father Christmas letters. Part of most evenings were in any case now taken up in concocting outlandish
stories for his children ('The Orgog', see p. 25, dates from this

period). At the same time, he embarked on his translations of *Beowulf*, finishing a prose version by the spring of 1926 (the version in alliterative poetry was never completed), and became External Examiner to the Oxford English degree (i.e. a guest examiner appointed from a different institution to oversee marking standards). He was also assiduously working on his legendarium and invented languages – now, principally Noldorin. Sadly, in the midst of all this, the Tolkiens' house was burgled at the end of 1923.

Come 1925, Tolkien's prolificacy had become habitual and he was sedulously applying himself to an extensive spectrum of assorted activities, from oral storytelling for children to the cerebral annotation of Old English texts to creative mythography. He was now translating the Middle English allegorical poem *Pearl*, part of the same manuscript book – so presumably by the same poet – as *Sir Gawain and the Green Knight*, and had become an accomplished composer of alliterative verse himself. He continued work on *Gawain* and the Clarendon Chaucer, became a contributor to the survey of scholarship *The Year's Work in English Studies*, and published a short academic article on the Devil's coach Horses. *Sir Gawain and the Green Knight*, edited by Tolkien and Gordon, appeared on St George's Day (23 April) 1925. The proofs to the text of Chaucer were finally completed in the middle of the year, although Tolkien still had to write the notes – but he was now occupied in applying for the Rawlinson and Bosworth Chair (Professorship) of Anglo-Saxon at Oxford, which had become vacant, as well as versifying the tales of his legendarium. He was swiftly appointed at Oxford in July, narrowly beating Kenneth Sisam – his old tutor and now colleague and editorial advisor at Oxford University Press; Sisam evidently took the defeat at the hands of his former student in his stride. Before taking up his new appointment the family holidayed at Filey in Yorkshire, where a series of events – his son

Michael's lost toy dog, a violent coastal storm – led to Tolkien making up a story about the plaything, which in time became the illustrated children's story *Roverandom* (see pp. 25–6). He was required to teach at both Oxford and Leeds in the autumn of 1925 to fulfil his contracts, but still found time to continue annotating the Clarendon Chaucer, and, satisfyingly, E.V. Gordon succeeded him as Professor of English Language at Leeds. The family moved to Oxford at the beginning of January 1926, and, apart from the odd trip to Leeds to help with lecturing, Tolkien settled down to professorial life in Oxford.

How Many Tales?

As Tolkien's biographer Humphrey Carpenter drily notes, after his return to Oxford, 'you might say, nothing really happened'.[44] He worked in Oxford exclusively until his retirement and lived in the city with Edith for the next forty-two years. He gave lectures and tutorials, attended Faculty meetings, was an active reformer of the English syllabus and elector of new staff, and chaired various examination boards. He was a popular (if often inaudible) lecturer; a conscientious undergraduate tutor and thesis supervisor and examiner of research students; a diligent researcher and writer – and although he published little academic work under his own name, he remained incredibly busy and committed to an ever-broadening range of subjects and projects.[45] He soon found time to plan a full outline of what was developing into 'The Silmarillion' (known as the 'Quenta Silmarillion'), revised the key episodes (some, again, in verse), and in due course produced an annotated map of his imagined world. His poetic career continued with poems published in *Realities*, the *Inter-University Magazine*, the *Stapledon Magazine*, the *Oxford Magazine*, and even the *Chronicle of the Convents of the Sacred Heart*, and he resumed his painting and drawing – notably during a prolific summer holiday to Lyme Regis in 1928 in which he produced a series of paintings of the still-evolving legendarium. He also started a new cycle of poems, 'Tales and Songs of Bimble Bay' (1928), and translated Breton verses (which became *The Lay of Aotrou and Itroun and The Corrigan Poems*, published in 2016). He returned to his accustomed ways by reading at the Exeter College Essay Club and forming the Kolbítar ('coalbiters') – a social club translating passages from the Icelandic sagas and taking its name from those who would sit so close to the fire that they could bite the coal. He also joined more sober groups such as the Philological Society and the Society for the Study of Mediæval Languages and Literature, and was an honorary board member of the British Esperanto Association. Tolkien continued contributing to *The Year's Work in English Studies*, and by April 1926 had completed his translations of *Beowulf* and *Pearl*, which he sent to Oxford University Press – but the Clarendon Chaucer had faltered. In May of the same year he met C.S. Lewis (1898–1963) for the first time, and, while marking School Certificate papers that summer, he possibly wrote the first words of *The Hobbit* on a blank sheet of exam paper.

More of his work for children followed: *Roverandom* illustrations in 1927, the picture book *Mr Bliss* in 1928, and the Father Christmas letters every year – and another child, Priscilla, was born on 18 June 1929. Meanwhile, *The Hobbit* was being relayed to the Tolkien children as a bedtime story by 1930, perhaps earlier.[46] It is, then, worth reflecting on Tolkien's reputation and ambitions as a children's author (of which more in Chapter Two). Tolkien started writing what became *The Father Christmas Letters* for his children in 1920, and they continued until 1942. They recount, of course, the annual adventures of Father Christmas, the accident-prone North Polar Bear (named Karhu: Finnish for 'bear'), and his two cubs as they prepare for Christmas. The letters rapidly became episodes in an ongoing saga involving Goblin attacks aimed at thwarting Christmas. The manuscript letters themselves are beautifully presented in coloured calligraphy with added illustrations, and Tolkien's eye for detail went so far as designing North Pole stamps for the envelopes. Neither could he resist migrating elements of his extensive legendarium into these seasonal dispatches. While the Goblins have their own alphabet (based on Finno-Uggric Lapp pictographs, often used on shamanic drums), the language of the North Pole was actually Tolkien's Qenya Elvish, and Father Christmas's secretary was called Ilbereth – a name that would later reverberate through Middle-Earth as 'Elbereth', the divine Queen of the Stars.

But there were other tales too. Tolkien punned with street signs such as 'Bill Stickers Will Be Prosecuted' and 'Major Road Ahead' by turning Bill Stickers into a villainous mountain of a man and Major Road into his nemesis in a long-running series of farcical episodes told to his children between about 1926 and 1930.[47] Another character in these comic oral tales was Timothy Titus, a name Tolkien briefly recruited for the landlord of The Prancing Pony at Bree in *The Lord of the Rings*.[48] A further early personality was Tom Bombadil, based on a Dutch doll belonging to Tolkien's son Michael: Bombadil not only became fully the most eccentric character in *The Lord of the Rings* (see the Conclusion), but Tolkien also eventually published poems and a whole book of poetry in his name. There was also 'The Orgog', which survives as an inscrutable fragment and an accompanying illustration of 'A Shop on the Edge of the Hills of Fairy Land'. *Roverandom*, in contrast, was a story Tolkien was telling to his children in 1925, which was then written down in 1927 as a coherent, illustrated narrative. As mentioned, the family had been on holiday to Filey and Michael had lost his toy dog on the beach. In Tolkien's version, Roverandom is a real dog that has been turned into a toy dog by the wizard Artaxerxes. The toy Roverandom is bought by a boy who then loses him, and is turned back into the real Roverandom by the sand sorcerer Psamathos Psamathides. Roverandom is taken to the moon by a seagull, where he meets the Man-in-the-Moon (who also has his own dog). On the moon they encounter giant lunar Spiders, as well as a Great White Dragon. Roverandom has further adventures at the bottom of the sea, having been taken there by a whale, before eventually being reunited with the little boy who had bought him as a toy.

Roverandom is essentially an 'Immram': it is based on mediaeval Irish tales of saints' travels to the Otherworld, and in fact Tolkien would later work on his own Immrama such as 'The Death of Saint Brendan'.[49] The story also contains references to Arthurian legends, fairy tales of the sea, and Norse myth (the Midgard serpent), as well as Lewis Carroll's *Through the Looking-Glass* (1872) – Tolkien was, in a very real and self-conscious sense, in the tradition of Carroll. Carroll (1832–98), whose real name was Charles Dodgson (he too played with names), had been Mathematics Lecturer and Fellow of Christ Church, Oxford, and was renowned for his scholarly nonsense writing for children.[50] There are, moreover, some obvious links with *The Hobbit* in *Roverandom*, such as giant Spiders and a Dragon, and Tolkien's illustrations for *The Hobbit* are noticeably similar to those he prepared for *Roverandom*.[51] The geography over which Roverandom travels also connects at some points with the emerging landscapes of Middle-Earth (especially the Cottage of Lost Play and the Path of Dreams, and Elvenhome in the far West). But *Roverandom* is also an utterly whimsical romance that presents fairies as creatures tiny and frivolous: the moon-gnomes ride on rabbits and the sea-fairies travel in sea-shells pulled by fish.[52]

Although details are sparse, at about the same time he wrote the first draft of *Farmer Giles of Ham* (published in 1949). This too began as a children's story, and according to Tolkien's eldest son was first made up after the family were forced to shelter from the rain following a picnic. The story is a wry fairy story, a mix of Dragons, derring-do, and droll humour. Farmer Giles achieves fame when he shoots a marauding Giant and is rewarded with an old sword from the king's armoury. This turns out to be a magic Dragon-slaying weapon, which comes in useful when a real Dragon, Chrysophylax, appears. While the king's knights are routed by Chrysophylax, Farmer Giles manages to subdue and capture the Dragon with his sword Caudimordax, takes the Dragon's hoard, and establishes a little kingdom of his own. Tolkien gradually reworked the tale into a more adult satire laced with philological jokes and references to Oxford and its environs. Despite the elements of fantasy Tolkien resisted adding elements of his legendarium, and steadfastly maintained the story's setting as Oxfordshire between the third and sixth centuries – a conceit that went so far as to present the finished text as a translation of an earlier manuscript. By this time the tale had become a hybrid: something for bookish children versed in mediaeval scholarship, or adults fascinated by recondite word games and tickled by academic frivolities.

Tolkien also wrote and illustrated the absurdist caper *Mr Bliss*. Despite grumbling about the Morris Cowley factory in East Oxford – and indeed about cars in general – when he returned to the city in 1925, Tolkien had nevertheless bought a Morris Cowley in 1932. 'Jo', as the vehicle was known (after its number-plate), seems to have become a much-loved family member: it not only inspired the antics of *Mr Bliss* (Tolkien had various prangs the first time he took Jo out), but also enabled Priscilla to take all of her cuddly toys on holiday to Sidmouth in 1934. Edith, Christopher, and Priscilla travelled by train; John and Michael bicycled; and Tolkien and the teddy bears drove there.[53] Mr Bliss too buys himself a car: a yellow car with red wheels. He crashes into friends transporting cabbages and bananas, which he is then obliged to give to three bears. He takes the bears and a donkey to visit his friends and crashes into their wall. They all fly out of the car and land in a picnic. The bears gorge themselves and are chased away by dogs; everybody gets back into the car and is towed along by Horses ... and so it goes on. There is plenty of eating and conviviality and slapstick in this ridiculous yarn – which is what children like.[54]

Tolkien's academic publications were, however, at this stage often nugatory and hardly groundbreaking – such as the foreword to *A New Glossary of the Dialect of the Huddersfield District* (1928), or a note on the name *Nodens* for an archaeological report (1929, published 1932). An academic article on 'Ancrene Wisse and *Hali Meiðhad*' (1929) was, however, rather more substantial, and initiated an invitation to edit the text. The thirteenth-century *Ancrene Wisse* was a 'guide for anchoresses' in Tolkien's cherished West Midlands dialect. The invitation to edit the *Ancrene Wisse* (also known as the *Ancrene Riwle*) came from Kenneth Sisam, and prompted some further discussion about the Clarendon Chaucer – Tolkien not having had any reply from one of his collaborators for some two years. Sisam agreed to allow Tolkien to edit the *Ancrene Riwle* and complete his Chaucer; the *Ancrene Riwle* would be part of the Early English Text Society series, an imprint published by Oxford University Press.

As Tolkien's scholarly publishing commitments mounted, his friendship with C.S. Lewis really blossomed in 1929, their passionate talk ranging from Northern sagas to university politics to theology. In November, for example, they stayed up for three hours discussing the Norse gods. A year later they talked together about the Christian faith with Hugo Dyson, an English academic at the University of Reading, until after three o'clock in the morning; such discussions brought Lewis, an agnostic, back into the Protestant Church.[55] This closeness in turn inspired Tolkien to start showing Lewis his fiction, poetry, and the sprawling legendarium. Lewis was among the very few confidants of Tolkien's early work-in-progress – and when Tolkien first approached him, Lewis responded with over a dozen pages of commentary. Moreover, the friendship with Lewis seems to have spurred Tolkien to rewrite the tales of the legendarium again in 1930 – this time a prose 'Silmarillion' – and return to the grammar of Qenya. He also wrote poems variously based on episodes in the Anglo-Saxon *Beowulf* and the Icelandic *Völuspá*. But from such sublime moments Tolkien also occasionally strayed into the ridiculous: in 1930, he was also the unlikely performer in two dialogues for a Linguaphone course on how to speak correct English: 'At the Tobacconist's' and 'Wireless'; today, they have an almost Beckettian quality to them.

It is worth remembering that, despite being in the most cloistered of ivory towers, Tolkien was working in an atmosphere of extreme political turbulence and instability with the rise of Nazism and the eventual outbreak of the Second World War: Adolf Hitler became Chancellor of Germany in 1933, and Britain declared war on 3 September 1939. Tolkien, however, continued to work with his characteristic energy at a hectic pace of unceasing application – even if he was anything but single-minded and also (as discussed further in Chapter Five) often displayed an extreme diffidence in completing things. He continued to teach and examine (including external examining at the universities of Manchester, Reading, and London), and met the administrative demands of a senior academic as an active participant at meetings and on committees. He committed himself (again and again) to completing the Clarendon Chaucer. Although by October 1932 the Press were forced to issue an ultimatum, they were still discussing Tolkien's contribution in 1936 – indeed, from October 1936 to October 1938 Tolkien was freed from some of his university duties by the award of a

Leverhulme Research Fellowship, so it looked as though the Clarendon Chaucer would finally be realized. He also worked with E.V. Gordon on translations of the Anglo-Saxon poems 'The Wanderer' and 'The Seafarer' for Methuen Old English Library, and translated the mediaeval poem 'The Owl and the Nightingale'. It was also perhaps in this decade that he translated the Old English 'Exodus' (eventually published in 1981) and the Finn and Hengest sections of *Beowulf* (published in 1982). Most significantly, he worked with Simonne d'Ardenne on an edition of 'Seinte Katerine', and wrote some (very few) academic articles: a two-part essay on the Anglo-Saxon word *Sigelhearwan* ('Sigelwara Land', 1932 and 1934 – an unusual translation of the Latin word for Ethiopians) and an analysis of Chaucer's use of dialect (1934). In fairness, he was also effectively co-editor of d'Ardenne's research thesis *An Edition of the Liflade ant te Passiun of Seinte Iuliene*, published by the University of Liège in Belgium as a requirement for her professorship. She privately acknowledged that it was a collaborative work, and E.V. Gordon wrote to Tolkien to complain that he was 'grieved that your name is not attached to it, because . . . practically all that is especially valuable in it is recognisably yours. There is really no other piece of Middle English editing to touch it. And the financial interest in it is not sufficient reward or return for the wealth of new material you have given.'[56] Consequently, the work stands as a testament to Tolkien's generosity of spirit, his commitment to his discipline rather than the acquisition of personal accolades, and his support of junior – especially female – colleagues in the patriarchal hierarchy of academia. But Gordon was also right in his assessment of the work: the account of mediaeval literature in the edition is outstanding – and recognizably by Tolkien.[57]

His creativity too was overflowing. He continued to write poetry, including two poems in Old Icelandic on the Völsungs;

Mythopoeia, a meditation on myth, fairy tales, and Christianity, which he wrote while invigilating exams; nearly a thousand lines of *The Fall of Arthur*; and the short Anglo-Saxon radio drama *The Homecoming of Beorhtnoth Beorhthelm's Son.*[58] He resumed, then abandoned, the versified legendarium, and from about 1933 to 1937 was writing, revising, and rewriting the prose 'Silmarillion'. In addition to the myths and legends themselves, he added chronicles, essays on languages, phonology, alphabets, etymologies, and orthography – as well as maps – and he developed his invented languages with invented alphabets, and even gave a paper on invented languages ('A Secret Vice', which was later published).[59] By 15 November 1937 he had completed a version of the 'Quenta Silmarillion', which was sent to the publisher George Allen & Unwin, and although his translation of *Pearl* was rejected by the publisher J.M. Dent, it nonetheless captured the interest of BBC radio and part of the translation was broadcast on 7 August 1936.

Typically mixing business with pleasure, Tolkien and Lewis formed the Cave, a pressure group to reform the Oxford English School, and also joined the Inklings – effectively a creative writing workshop for members to read and comment on each other's unpublished fiction and poetry.[60] The Inklings was founded by Edward Tangye Lean – brother to David Lean, who later directed some of the seminal films of the twentieth century. Lean was a precocious undergraduate, and so dons were welcome to attend the meetings held in his college rooms. Tolkien and Lewis joined in the early 1930s; Tolkien read his poem 'Errantry' (a piece of fairy verse, later adapted for *The Lord of the Rings*) and acted as secretary. When Lean graduated in 1933, Lewis maintained the Inklings for a small circle of his friends. They met before lunch on Tuesdays in the landlord's sitting room at the Eagle and Child pub, lubricated by beer from the barrel, and on Thursday evenings in Lewis's rooms at Magdalen College eased by his drink allowance.[61] Tolkien also occasionally joined Lewis and his students for 'beer and *Beowulf*' evenings.[62] Tolkien seems to have been inspired by these peacetime, one might almost say secular, versions of wartime comradeship. The set they formed around themselves, in its way more influential than the Bloomsbury Group, was deliberately anti-Modernist – even fogeyish – in their tweeds and waistcoats and pipe-smoking, certainly English (sentimentally so, not tub-thumpingly nationalistic), but provincial (Oxonian), and generally Christian (ranging from Tolkien's Roman Catholicism to Lewis's Ulster Protestantism). In 1931, in addition to Lewis and Tolkien, the Inklings comprised Lewis's brother Warren, R.E. Havard (a doctor), Owen Barfield (a solicitor), Hugo Dyson (a fellow academic), and Charles Williams (of Oxford University Press).

By the end of 1932, Tolkien had finished a draft of *The Hobbit* and immediately entrusted it to Lewis, who had both read and enjoyed it by the beginning of February 1933.[63] This early draft ended with the death of Smaug, although Tolkien had narrated the concluding chapters verbally to his children.[64] Three years later, in the first months of 1936, the publishers George Allen & Unwin contacted Tolkien, inviting him to revise the translation of *Beowulf* prepared by John Clark Hall; it had first been published in 1911 but remained the standard undergraduate translation of the poem. Tolkien was too busy to revise the edition and graciously recommended that Elaine Griffiths, his research assistant on his edition of the *Ancrene Riwle*, be commissioned, but he nevertheless discussed the project with Susan Dagnall, an editor at Allen & Unwin who visited him in Oxford. While there, she heard about *The Hobbit*, borrowed a typescript of the novel, and read it. Tolkien was encouraged to finish the story that he had continued working on in infrequent spare moments, and by August 1936 it was virtually complete; he sent it to the publishers in October.[65]

Things then moved very rapidly. Within three days, Tolkien's life – or at least his subsequent reputation – was transformed. His professional standing peaked on 25 November 1936, when he gave his acclaimed and immensely influential lecture '*Beowulf*: The Monsters and the Critics' to the British Academy. It remains to this day the most significant piece of criticism ever published on the poem, and, unusually for Tolkien, is a passionate demand for literary criticism rather than philological analysis. 'The Monsters and the Critics' is, in fact, one of the most idiosyncratic and heartfelt pieces of literary criticism ever published, and its allegories and digressions, erudition and playfulness, acute insight and perception rank the paper alongside the literary criticism of Samuel Johnson, Samuel Taylor Coleridge, and Oscar Wilde. Almost straightaway his fiction also made the giant step from receiving the appreciation of close friends to the endorsement of a major publishing house. On 28 November, he was again visited by Dagnall to discuss *The Hobbit* and, presumably, its illustrations – Tolkien, with his usual obsessive attention to detail, having prepared no fewer than five maps for the book (it was eventually published with just two maps, but several more of his illustrations). The publishers were also interested in his other children's stories, and so Tolkien gave Dagnall copies of *Farmer Giles of Ham*, *Roverandom*, and *Mr Bliss*, as well as the translation of *Pearl*. Middle-Earth was about to become a global property.

But what – or where – is 'Middle-Earth'?

How Many Middle-Earths?

Middle-Earth is, simply, the world. The *Oxford English Dictionary* defines *middle earth* as:

> The world, the earth, regarded as a middle region between heaven and hell ... Sometimes also: the inhabitants or

things of the world, esp. as opposed to those of heaven; worldly things as opposed to divine or spiritual things.[66]

The word is used in *Beowulf* (l. 75), 'The Wanderer' (ll. 62, 75), *Sir Gawain and the Green Knight* (l. 2,100), and Laȝamon's thirteenth-century poem *Roman de Brut*.[67] The *Brut* is the earliest history of Britain written in the country's native language, which at the time was Anglo-Norman heavily influenced by Anglo-Saxon poetic conventions of alliteration, concision, and compound words. It tells the nation's story in a chronicle that mixes myth and legend into a fabulous history, describing the founding of Britain by the Roman Brutus; the arrival of the Angles, Saxons, and Jutes; and King Arthur.

Laȝamon's various spellings of 'middle earth' include *middilherpe*, *middel ærde*, *middelerpe*, and *middel-eærde*. The *OED* provides over forty variant spellings, before tracing the history of the word back to the Anglo-Saxon *middenerd* (thirty-plus variant spellings) and the Middle English *middle-erd* (in over forty different versions), derived from Old Saxon (*middilgard*), Old German (*mittigart*, *mittilgart*), and Gothic (*midjungards*). At a conservative estimate, then, there are well over a hundred different versions of 'middle earth', and the word survived long into the nineteenth century. In Thomas Ruddiman's 1710 edition of Gawin Douglas's glossary to Virgil's *Æneis*, he defines *Myddill erd* as 'a phrase yet in use in the N[orth] of S[cotland] among old people, by which they understand *this earth in which we live, in opposition to the grave*: Thus they say, *There's no man in middle erd is able to do it*'.[68]

A century later, the *Edinburgh Magazine* carried some fairy lore, describing a woman who, 'Having narrowly escaped thrice being confirmed in her fairy state, she visited her friends on this "middle eard", with whom she dwelt for seven years, disclosing the manners and explaining the customs of the Fairy Land.'[69]

The word also appears in E.R. Eddison's 1922 fantasy novel *The Worm Ouroboros*, which Tolkien knew well.[70] Tolkien had met Eddison with Lewis, and thought very highly of his work: 'I still think of him as the greatest and most convincing writer of "invented worlds" that I have read'.[71] A few years later in 1951 (before the publication of *The Lord of the Rings*), Tolkien's friend and admirer W.H. Auden (1907–73) likewise used the word in his 'Phi Beta Kappa' poem 'Under Which Lyre', delivered at Harvard in June 1946: 'What high immortals do in mirth/Is life and death on Middle Earth'.[72]

As for Tolkien himself, he positioned middle earth (*middan-geard*) at the very inception of his subsequent legendarium. Holidaying in Cornwall (the uttermost West, one might say) in 1914, he was especially moved by two lines from Cynewulf's poem *Crist*. Very few Anglo-Saxon poets are named or have poems attributed to them – although this did not stop Tolkien imagining that the poet of *Beowulf* was one Heorrenda, to whom he alludes in his legendarium. But Cynewulf's name has survived, and in his poem on Christ, two particular lines captivated Tolkien:

> Eala earendel engla beorhtast
> Ofer middan-geard monnum sended.[73]

The lines have been rendered 'Hail, heavenly beam, brightest of angels thou,/sent unto men upon this middle-earth!' – but the word *earendel* is mysterious; it has been translated as a proper noun meaning 'Rising Sun' or 'Dayspring', and for Tolkien it clearly held a linguistic power.[74]

Tolkien was spellbound by these cryptic lines during the long, hot summer months of 1914. From Cornwall he visited Warwick, and then his aunt in Nottingham, and it was while here that on 24 September 1914 he wrote the poem 'The Voyage of

Éarendel the Evening Star', his first witness to Middle-Earth. In effervescent lines he tells the story of the celestial mariner Éarendel and his transit of the night skies, before disappearing into the dawn:

> Éarendel sprang up from the Ocean's cup
>   In the gloom of the mid-world's rim;
> From the door of Night as a ray of light
>   Leapt over the twilight brim,
> And launching his bark like a silver spark
>   From the golden-fading sand
> Down the sunlit breath of Day's fiery death
>   He sped from Westerland.[75]

Tolkien later commented, 'I felt a curious thrill, as if something had stirred in me, half wakened from sleep. There was something very remote and strange and beautiful behind those words, if I could grasp it, far beyond ancient English.'[76] He was perplexed by Cynewulf's lines: he told his T.C.B.S. friend Geoffrey Bache Smith that he could not understand why. Smith asked what the verse meant; 'I don't know,' replied Tolkien, 'I'll try to find out.'[77] So there is a sense of discovery here rather than of invention.

By the end of 1914 he had expanded the tale of Eärendel (now spelt thus) into a long narrative poem that linked the celestial mariner with Faërie and the Elvish city of Kôr, and he was simultaneously developing his latest invented language, Qenya. So the two great components of his vast legendarium – the literature and the language – arose within weeks of each other, and within a few short months of the outbreak of world war. His watercolours also aligned with his vision of a new cycle of invented legendary tales. Tolkien's limitless legendarium therefore began as a threefold synthesis of linguistic invention, the literary composition, and visual artistry that complemented, contributed to, and indeed sometimes contradicted each other.

He rewrote 'The Voyage of Éarendel the Evening Star' (or 'Éala Éarendel Engla Beorhtast') some five times, and Eärendel also appeared in 'The Bidding of the Minstrel' (written in the winter of 1914), which in turn became 'The Lay of Eärendel'. 'The Voyage of Éarendel the Evening Star' was read to the Exeter College Essay Club on 27 November of the same year. In other words, it was written at the end of the innocent summer that was the prelude to the Great War, and shortly afterwards shared at Oxford as Tolkien's inaugural piece of Middle-Earth writing. At the same time memories of the sea off the Cornish coast were evoked in 'The Tides', dated 4 December 1914 but possibly written *in situ* on The Lizard as it is a deeply impressionistic poem of the booming ocean with a sense of the immense gulf of time. This was revised the following March as 'Sea Chant of an Elder Day', and again in 1917 as 'The Horns of Ylmir', by which time it was thoroughly knitted into *The Book of Lost Tales*. An explanatory sentence introducing this version of the poem states that Eärendel is the son of Tuor, making the lines part of Tolkien's 'Great Tale' of 'The Fall of Gondolin'.

Critics have focused on the name 'Eärendel', but the phrase 'Ofer middan-geard monnum sended' is equally important. The reason why 'Middle-Earth' (as I will style it) is so crucial to Tolkien is because it is the place of incarnation. It is only in the real world that the miraculous can occur. The miraculous is, obviously, an unremarkable event in Heaven; but on earth, on *Middle-Earth*, the miraculous is a once-in-a-lifetime experience (if that). And what Tolkien always has in his mind are the Gospels: four witnesses to God's manifestation on earth. Tolkien's faith is robustly ordinary – he is not a mystic, he has no pretensions to saintliness, but he does understand that the relationship of the everyday to the divine is simply (and necessarily) a daily engagement. The divine does not occupy a separate, sacred space in Tolkien's thinking or in this theology: its value is that it is part of the everyday world, every day. And that, in a word, is why there are no churches in Middle-Earth: the divine is not separated from the commonplace.

But it seems to have taken some years before Tolkien identified part of his imagined world as Middle-Earth. More than a dozen years after the publication of Eddison's *The Worm Ouroboros*, Tolkien drew a series of maps ('Ambarkanta', c.1937) and noted that, 'in the North and South . . . Middle-earth extends nigh to the Walls of the World'.[78] In a letter written some years later he explicitly identified his lands with the Old and Middle English Middle-Earths and therefore with the prehistory of our world.[79] At the same time he was completing and publishing *The Hobbit*, and although there is no mention of 'middle earth' in the book itself, it would of course retrospectively be recognized as the foundational Middle-Earth narrative (at least in print). But the Middle-Earth of the first edition of *The Hobbit* is an odd place, mixing references to our own world (the Gobi Desert, Shetland ponies, the Hindu Kush) with the Middle-Earth that had begun to develop in Tolkien's imagination since before the Great War through references to Gondolin and the enmity between Elves and Dwarves. Mentions of our own world as well as other fictional worlds (notably Lilliput) were removed from the second edition – as were such things as tomatoes – when the work began to be aligned with *The Lord of the Rings*, and in the third edition Tolkien added allusions to Bree, Weathertop, and the Fords of Bruinen (although he did not mention them by name), and made the dates more precise. Middle-Earth thus became more remote from our own world, but also more tangible.

But in fact, all of the settings of Tolkien's creative writing are effectively Middle-Earths because they all overlap. Both Tolkien and Lewis entertained literary ambitions, so in 1936 or early 1937 they each decided to write a novel: Lewis's on space travel, Tolkien's on time travel. From this agreement (possibly even a bet) came Lewis's book *Out of the Silent Planet* (published in 1938 and the first of his 'space trilogy'), while Tolkien drafted a narrative on 'The Fall of Númenor' – a version of the Atlantis myth that eventually became the 'Akallabêth' section of *The Silmarillion*. 'The Fall of Númenor' was to be at the heart of his novel *The Lost Road*, an unfinished philological treatise about time travel.[80] The central character, Alboin Errol, is an academic and expert in the old Northern languages. Since childhood, he has been haunted by dreams of a drowned isle called Númenor and through words that come to him like the echoes of primal languages, languages he calls variously Elf-Latin or Eressëan, Beleriandic, and Germanic. These words seem to have arisen thousands of years ago: they have travelled through time. The island of Númenor appears to lie beneath the waves of the Atlantic a few miles west of the coast of Cornwall, and is glossed as Lyonesse, a lost stretch of land from Land's End to the Isles of Scilly that is connected to Arthurian legends. But Númenor was also another invented myth developing in tandem with the legendarium. So although *The Lost Road* is set in contemporary Cornwall, it is very much a Middle-Earth work. Alboin (the name is a version of Ælfwine, and the character is based in part on Tolkien himself) subsequently dreams of Númenor and his meeting with the Númenórean freedom fighter Elendil, who is resisting the government of Sauron. Sauron has introduced machines, iron ships, and even flying boats to the island, a technological revolution that has carried with it totalitarian rule, mass surveillance, and the extinction of Human rights. Tolkien quarried his legendarium to add depth to the Númenórean struggle – at one point introducing a Genesis myth that is recognizably a draft of the prose 'Silmarillion'.[81] Alboin is then invited to travel back in time and experience the epoch of Númenor. Tolkien may have hoped, then, to write a novel along the lines of Rudyard Kipling's *Puck of Pook's Hill* (1906): a series of time-travelling episodes that exemplified key moments of English history and national cultural identity. Indeed, Christopher Tolkien suggests that *The Lost Road* could have included overlapping stories of the Lombards, Norse ship burial, the Straight Road to Faërie, the Tuatha Dé Danaan of Celtic myth, cave paintings, the Ice Age, Elendil, Gil-Galad, and (of course) Númenor. It was to be a profound synthesis of myth.[82] Tolkien seems to have been struck by the layering or stratification of history that comprised the sheer magnitude of the past and the varieties of historical evidence that could give it expression: not only archival, archaeological, folkloric, and oral, but also memorial, psychic, spiritual, and sacred.[83]

It is not only Númenor that haunts this unfinished story: there are also connections with *Beowulf* via references to the god of harvest known as 'King Sheave', to Tolkien's own translation of *Beowulf*, and to the historical Goths and their legendary island home of Scandza.[84] The narrative of *The Lost Road* is further entangled with the figure of Ælfwine, a time-travelling Anglo-Saxon poet and 'Elf-Friend' who moves through both British and Irish mythology as well as through Middle-Earth and the realm of Faërie, and who at one point sings of Mirkwood.[85] Moreover, Anglo-Saxon verse recited by Ælfwine was later adapted by Tolkien in a draft of *The Silmarillion;* his worlds were amalgamating.[86] This perpetual ebb and flow of textual exchange is also shown by Tolkien's habit not only of writing Anglo-Saxon poetry (such as *Sellic Spell*) but also of translating his chronicles of the events of Middle-Earth into Anglo-Saxon.[87] Ælfwine himself was then developed in *The Notion Club Papers*, another strange and unfinished novel that Tolkien began writing in about 1944 when he found it impossible to continue work on *The Lord of the Rings* (see Chapter Three).[88] It is worth pointing out at this stage that Númenor also haunts the digressive discussions of the Notion Club: the language of Númenor is analyzed and appears in Anglo-Saxon, and the submerged forces of Númenor seem able to summon a devastating storm.[89] There is also a ship named *The Éarendel*, and Zigūr, a Sauron figure.[90]

If *The Lost Road* was soon abandoned in order to write up *The Hobbit* and so did not progress beyond a handful of chapters and notes, it nevertheless reveals a set of preoccupations that Tolkien was to explore in very different ways in *The Lord of the Rings*. The centrality of Númenor and the character Elendil (later to be recast as the Númenórean ancestor of Aragorn) certainly mark the book as Middle-Earth writing, as does Tolkien's mystic philology. Strange words have strange powers in *The Lord of the Rings* (see the Conclusion); words seem to have a will of their own; they are the custodians of ancient cultures and thus infuse the present with the past. Furthermore, Alboin articulates one of Tolkien's key beliefs: that different literatures are emanations of particular languages – the language is 'in some way related to the atmosphere of the legends and myths told in the languages'.[91] The 'lost road', the road to enchantment, the road to Faërie, is, then, language itself. The fear of totalitarianism also hangs over *The Lord of the Rings* like a nightmare, from Mordor to The Shire – again dictated by Sauron and his methods of surveillance, from spies to the probing searchlight of his fiery Eye, as well as by his broken minion Saruman. In other words, while *The Lost Road* is explicitly about the burning political issues of the 1930s, these matters are only implicit in the later Middle-Earth writings – but *The Lost Road* can help to unlock them.

Tolkien's unfinished poem *The Fall of Arthur* is another Middle-Earth, with more references to Eärendel, Tol Eressëa, and Númenor.[92] Reciprocally, certain elements of the Arthurian legends were also incorporated into Middle-Earth, such as the similarities between Lancelot's travels and Eärendel's voyage, and the departure of Lancelot compared with that of Tuor.[93] But I will not dwell on these. Instead, I have tried to give a sense of the astonishing networks of connections, correlations, and correspondences between the different tales and poems Tolkien was writing, writings that were both intimately interwoven and entangled, deeply complex and confused.

•   •   •

Out of this confusion came *The Hobbit*, and eventually *The Lord of the Rings* – books that, conceived against the inchoate character of the developing legendarium and alongside Tolkien's overwhelming professional obligations, nevertheless began to cleave to a narrative logic and decisive conclusions. Within the chaos that surrounded him, Tolkien's stories found a voice, rooted in the turmoil of the restless mythology itself. But, almost inevitably, his tales – especially his longest tale – would be anchored in the ground of Middle-Earth. And yet despite the apparently firm footing, this was a mooring in shifting sands. Not only did the legendarium continue to ebb and flow like an ocean of story, but both *The Hobbit* and *The Lord of the Rings* wrote back to Middle-Earth in reshaping the Dwarves and recreating Galadriel. The proliferating tales became reciprocal, symbiotic, siblings: *The Hobbit* rewrote 'The Silmarillion', *The Lord of the Rings* more so – and the legendarium was never published in Tolkien's own lifetime.

What I find extraordinary – and inspiring – is that rather than change the plot of a tiny tale such as *The Hobbit*, Tolkien preferred to revise the twenty-year project of his invented mythology. He knew when stories worked. And the whole saga of the Rings of Power itself emerges from *The Hobbit* rather than from the legendarium. Tolkien – characteristically – did not allow the Elven wars of the legendarium to govern the history of the Rings of Power, but instead extrapolated a whole new chronological span to explain both the Second and Third Ages of Middle-Earth in the context of this one accidental feature: a ring – even (and rightly) subordinating the whole history of his beloved Númenor to the One Ring. Among hours of story-telling and reams of writing, then, Tolkien knew when he had hit on the right story. When he did, he went with the tale itself; his whole elaborate constructed background became marginal: the truth was in the telling.

TWO

Uncertainty

If a man will begin with certainties, he shall end in doubts;
but if he will be content to begin with doubts, he shall end
in certainties.

Francis Bacon,
The Advancement of Learning (1605)

Tolkien's works are full of uncertainty both in their unsteady
textual states and in their unstable morality. With regards to
the former, the episode of the Ring in *The Hobbit* was variously rewritten, retold, and republished in different forms,
while poems canonized in *The Lord of the Rings* were unexpectedly rewritten and sentimentalized in the later collection *The
Adventures of Tom Bombadil* (1961). Literature for Tolkien was
embodied in processes of transmission and change, so few of his
texts exist in a single definitive version: they are defined by flux
– and this recurrent flux also undermines the moral certainties
of his books.

Moral instability is profound in *The Hobbit*, and all-too

evident elsewhere in Tolkien's work. It is worth remembering that Tolkien was a traditional (Tridentine) Roman Catholic, and yet there is barely any institutionalized religion in Middle-Earth save for the heathen rituals of Númenor in its decadence.[1] Likewise, there are no churches or services, few funeral rites, possibly just a single prayer (Faramir's 'Númenórean Grace'), and no identifiable God or Christ-figure, intercessionary saints, or holy writ.[2] Possibly there are angels, and indubitably there are demons of Morgoth – but there are no clerics. Is this a godless place, driven by the enigmatic forces of 'providence' or 'fate'? Or are these same forces evidence of a divine plan? Nevertheless, it does appear to be an insistently secular world, in which morality is vague and, at best, contingent: characters repeatedly mislead, deceive, lie, cheat, and steal. Hobbits are famously gluttonous, Elves and Dwarves are materialistic, Hobbits and Dwarves are lazy, Humans are wrathful and proud – most of the deadly sins are evident.[3] Yet these moral shortcomings are not identified or punished: Bilbo, for example (employed as a 'burglar', lest we forget), lies and steals with impunity and retires with a healthy profit.

The previous chapter went into some detail about the range of writing on which Tolkien had been engaged in the quarter of a century before the appearance of *The Hobbit*. Much of this found its way into the novel to create a work that not only occupied our world and Middle-Earth, but several other realms besides. *The Hobbit* was in part compiled from materials Tolkien already had to hand: his surfeit of fiction and poetry (much of it unfinished or abandoned), lecture notes and scholarly research, as well as memories of his mother reading to him and stories he was himself telling his own children. For *The Hobbit*, Tolkien drew on everything from the Anglo-Saxon epic *Beowulf* to his own cursory Bimble Town poems.

Tales of the Unexpected

The first sentence of the story – one of the most famous in British children's literature – was, according to Tolkien's own myth of origin, jotted down on a blank page of a school exam paper he was marking to make extra money for his family. So the genesis of *The Hobbit* was immediately part of the domestic economy of the Tolkien household and the professional chores Tolkien was obliged to fulfil every year. The line is a bald yet baffling statement of apparent fact: 'In a hole in the ground there lived a hobbit . . .'[4]

The year was perhaps 1926, perhaps later – there is uncertainty over the origins of the tale, much as there is uncertainty in the profound moral ambiguity and shifting geographical ground of *The Hobbit*. Tolkien gave various different accounts of the genesis of his book, some decades later, and he was both a raconteur who knew the value of a good anecdote and the most impishly unreliable reporter when it came to discussing his own fiction and his role in writing it, often presenting himself as, at most, a translator or editor. Having written that sentence, he then sought to *discover* what Hobbits were – alluding to the central method of mediaeval rhetorical reasoning: *inventio* – which actually meant discovering (rather than simply inventing) arguments. And this process entailed telling the story of the Hobbit – or, it transpires, many Hobbits. In a brilliant blog post, the writer and critic Adam Roberts comments on Tolkien's later mock-etymology for the word *Hobbit*, emphasizing that (in spite of much web-based misinformation) it means 'hole-dweller, hole-liver'.[5] Roberts then argues that 'there are at least five peoples in The Hobbit who can be described . . . as Hobbits: Bilbo's people; the Dwarves; the Goblins – and Gollum (both of whom live in the caves under the Misty Mountains) and Smaug himself'; indeed, Tolkien noted that the name Smaug derived from the Germanic *Smugan*, meaning 'to squeeze through a hole' (as does Sméagol).[6] Roberts actually overlooks the Elvenking's palace in underground caves, but his overall point is strikingly valid: 'The titular "*The* Hobbit" starts to look like ironic understatement.'[7] Nearly everyone in *The Hobbit* is a Hobbit of sorts – living in a hole.[8]

Tolkien's children certainly remembered the story being read to them at bedtime, although these early drafts were quite different from the version that was finally published – most obviously in the characters' names. Gandalf, for example, was originally called Bladorthin, whereas the Dwarf Thorin was named Gandalf; Beorn was originally named Medwed, and Smaug was Pryftan. The tone was different too: as Roberts puts it, the plot of the first *Hobbit* is of a group of incompetents encountering various monsters while on a preposterously dangerous quest, but later versions become weightier, more sinister, and, of course, effectively a prequel to *The Lord of the Rings*. It became part of a bigger plan in which everything required a rationale, and so was 'retconned': retrospectively revised.[9] The process is analogous to the drafting and redrafting of scholarly research notes as understanding deepens and more connections are made: but as we saw in the last chapter, Tolkien's academic publication was often painfully slow. Much of his voluminous work on *Beowulf*, for example, was not published until over forty years after his death – nearly a century after he had begun it.

The Hobbit, however, was in print within possibly a decade of that first sentence being jotted down. Tolkien signed the contract with the publishers George Allen & Unwin on or around 2 December 1936, and within days was being sent sample pages, in discussion over the maps, redrawing illustrations, and designing the book's dust jacket. The company was also enthusiastic about the other three stories he had sent, as well as the updated translation of Clark Hall's *Beowulf*. In the event, of these only *Farmer Giles of Ham* reached the press in his lifetime, but within a couple more months there was an American publisher for *The Hobbit* as well, and very soon there was interest in translations too. By February 1937 he was correcting proofs, but unfortunately due to a number of rewrites the text had to be reset and consequently reproofed; at exactly the same time he was proofing the text of his British Academy lecture, *Beowulf: The Monsters and the Critics* – hardly an easy task. But in early August 1937, Tolkien received an advance copy of *The Hobbit*, and the book was duly published the next month, on 21 September. In less than three months the first printing of 1,500 copies had sold out and it immediately went into a second impression (2,300 copies).[10] Meanwhile, Tolkien had used part of his £25 advance to replace his car, and Edith had very much taken to motoring trips. Yet the version of *The Hobbit* read by nearly everyone today is the third edition of 1966, and, with a few exceptions concerning revisions (notably of Gollum, see below), that is the familiar text to which I will refer.

From the outset, the tone is jovial, instructive (on what Hobbits are), and slightly conspiratorial, with all the direct address and verbal inflections of a tale best read aloud in the evening. The authorial voice of *The Hobbit* is strong and deliberate, directed at an implied reader (or listener) who is young and attentive.[11] The narrator (who is certainly not consistently omniscient) speaks to the reader in different tones and anticipates questions; this, together with a profusion of textual allusions, means that the story revels in its status *as* a story.[12] Within the first two pages it is playful, quirky, curious, and engaging, restlessly shifting perspective. Then Gandalf arrives on page three, and starts playing language games. He quizzes Bilbo Baggins on what he means by 'good morning', offering four and then five possible readings of those two words – 'Do you wish me a good morning, or mean that it is a good morning whether I want it or not; or that you feel good this morning; or that it is a morning to be good on? . . . Now you mean that you want to get rid of me, and that it won't be good till I move off.'[13] He then turns his rigmarolatory to the phrase 'I beg your pardon'.

All of this is strikingly redolent of Humpty Dumpty in Lewis Carroll's *Through the Looking-Glass*, who variously declares that 'glory' means 'there's a nice knock-down argument for you', and that 'impenetrability' means 'we've had enough of that subject, and it would be just as well if you'd mention what you mean to do next, as I suppose you don't mean to stop here for the rest of your life.' Alice reasonably observes, 'That's a great deal to make one word mean', to which Humpty Dumpty replies, 'When I make a word do a lot of work like that . . . I always pay it extra.'

For Humpty Dumpty, using words is a constant power-struggle in which he intends to gain complete mastery – 'When *I* use a word . . . it means just what I choose it to mean'.[14] This is quite the opposite of Tolkien's scrupulous philological pursuit of words and their meanings through different eras, different languages in order to track their meanings and associations, but it is nevertheless an aspect of Middle-Earth. Words have power of life and death in Bilbo's riddle-game with Gollum, as well as being able to open doors (Moria), summon aid (from the puzzling character Tom Bombadil), and curse the dead to a half-existence as the undead (the Oathbreakers: see Chapter Four and the Conclusion). There are, it becomes apparent, many connections between the *Alice* books and *The Hobbit*. Humpty Dumpty deciphers the strange poem 'Jabberwocky', which contains a profusion of invented words and is a parody of how old English ballads were presented in eighteenth-century literary antiquarian editions (which Tolkien himself mimicked in, for instance, *Farmer Giles*); likewise, Elrond decrypts Thrór's map.[15] Humpty Dumpty's explanation of portmanteau words – 'there are two meanings packed up into one word' – a Victorian version of the Anglo-Saxon poetic *kenning* or compound word – could effectively be applied to many of Tolkien's own coinages such as 'skin-changer', *mithril* (meaning 'grey brilliance' in Elvish), 'staggerment', and 'Wilderland'.[16]

These last two, 'staggerment' and 'Wilderland', are among the many instances in *The Hobbit* of what could be called Tolkien's technique of confustication and bebotherment.[17] He enjoyed reviving obsolete and archaic words – *confusticate*, *bebother*, and *bewuthered* – words that would be absent from the standard family dictionary but could just about be deduced by a philological child.[18] Another, oft-repeated example is *gledes* (meaning burning embers), which also significantly appears in *The Fellowship of the Ring* in Isildur's account of his taking of the Ring: again it is absent from the *OED*, which instead offers *gleed*.[19] Tolkien is playing with words and their histories to touch the imagination at a point beyond scholarship – as he does in the case of 'Wilderland', coined by Tolkien from *wilder*, meaning 'wander', 'astray', 'bewilder'. It is a word that immediately appeals and has developed a life of its own, being beautifully taken up by the incomparable singer-songwriter Joni Mitchell in 'I Think I Understand' (1969).[20] It had previously been adopted as the name for a pioneering environmental community in New Zealand (1964), and has since been used by a touring wildlife film festival in the UK (2019), and, in the plural, as the name for a rewilding project (2021). It is a testament to Tolkien's influence that such exploratory wordplay has become a staple of fantasy writing, most notably in the Latinate incantations taught at Hogwarts: *Expecto Patronum*.[21]

To return to Humpty Dumpty. The Dumpty ditty, 'In winter, when the fields are white', is part of the nonsense song tradition enthusiastically taken up in *The Hobbit*. In addition to riddles and more serious, prophetic songs, the book includes several pieces of pure nonsense: the washing-up song at Bag End, the singing at Rivendell and even at Goblin Town, as well as Bilbo's goading of the Spiders with his daft doggerel. Even Humpty Dumpty's 'un-birthday present' ('A present given when it isn't your birthday') has a direct analogy in Hobbit celebrations, where the custom was to give rather than receive presents on one's birthday.[22] More generally, Alice's abiding sense of being lost in a strange and overpopulated adventure – somebody else's story – looks towards the dislocation that Bilbo feels as he travels through an outlandish landscape meeting crowds of exotic creatures. Indeed, following Gandalf's visit, thirteen Dwarves are about to start piling through Bilbo's front door. And Tolkien was also wondering about the nature of wizards: were they Humpty Dumpties – wragglers in wordplay – or were they something more: weavers of wonder? The young Ronald had read the *Alice* books at his mother's knee, and it is no surprise that Tolkien later clearly enjoyed alluding to Carroll.[23] Indeed, when his publishers added a blurb to *The Hobbit* describing it as reminiscent of *Alice's Adventures in Wonderland*, Tolkien matter-of-factly remarked that it was much closer to *Through the Looking-Glass*.[24]

Within the first pages, then, Tolkien introduces several disparate elements. Hobbits (hitherto unheard of), their life-style and habits: they are Edwardian English in their visiting and entertaining, reminiscent of characters from a classic P.G. Wodehouse novel – except that Hobbits are half the height of Humans and live in well-furnished burrows (or holes in the ground).[25] Appropriately enough for a Wodehouse caper, we are then told of Bilbo's heritage and inherited wealth – albeit with the eccentric rumour of a remote ancestor taking a wife from among the fairies. Dwarves, magic, and a wizard follow in short order, with Dragons and Goblins and Giants – but so does pipe-smoking and fireworks and then even Bilbo's grandfather's enchanted collar-studs that obeyed commands to fasten and unfasten themselves. This last, most incongruous of wonders bizarrely unites the fashions of Edwardian high society with the

magical world of Faërie. This is an extraordinary clash: a world
built on incompatibilities – and our only guide is Bilbo Baggins,
an inexpert mediator with Faërie, both infantile yet a respect-
ably middle-aged, middle-class bachelor. For the folklorist Jack
Zipes, 'Traditionally the little hero is courageous, initiates the
adventure, and welcomes the chance to prove himself' – but not
Bilbo. Bilbo, 'and all hobbits for that matter', are typically 'non-
descript': they are examples of 'the ideal passive consumer who
would probably like to sit in front of his TV set, smoke a cigar,
drink a beer, munch on chips, and have his fantasies played out
for him on an electronic screen'.[26] In truth, this was effectively
Tolkien's claim for the book: in a long letter written in 1951 he
described it as 'the study of simple ordinary man, neither artistic
nor noble and heroic' if 'not without the undeveloped seeds of
these things'.[27] Yet Bilbo remains a very odd protagonist for a
children's book.

But we have begun in the wrong place. By the second edition of 1951, *The Hobbit* began with a bizarre preface that,
after noting the correction of a few discrepancies, refers to two
source texts – Bilbo's diary and the 'Red Book of Westmarch' –
neither of which actually exist. Having voiced anxieties over the
accuracy of the riddle-game, the (presumed) editor of the book
immediately proclaims that this 'does not, however, concern the
present story', and that first-time readers 'need not trouble about
it'.[28] An arcane point made via a minor inundation of eccentric
names and places – entirely incomprehensible – ends this short
text. Even a seasoned reader of *The Hobbit* would be flummoxed
by much of this, as the Preface was written before the publication of *The Lord of the Rings*, to which *The Hobbit* had belatedly
become a prequel. It only makes sense after one has studied
(not merely read) that later epic (if that is the right word . . .).
In any case, the first volume of *The Lord of the Rings* would not
be available for another three years. So, as I say, this is bizarre.

Tolkien is, in one sense, simply musing to himself; but I cannot help being reminded of the Jorge Luis Borges short story (if that is the correct term) 'Tlön, Uqbar, Orbis Tertius', that in just over a dozen pages creates an entire alternative world. That is Tolkien's unspoken aim: he is literary terraforming – and he is doing so in singular company, and at an epic level.[29]

With the canonical third edition of 1966, things began to reach strange new heights. The Preface was now titled

ᚦᛖ·ᚺᚪᚠᛒᛒᛁᛏ

ᚠᚱ

ᚦᛗᚱᛗ·ᚠᛏᛉ·ᛒᚠᛚᚻ·ᚠᚷᚠᛁᛏ

The first sentence in English is now 'This is a story of long ago', and the single page discusses the unconventional plural *dwarves* and the meaning of *Orc*, and the runes that stand at the head of the Preface, with a few more lines of runes cited, and a footnote to the now-published *Lord of the Rings*.[30] A children's book, then, with an opening statement on philology and Anglo-Saxon runes. But even this is not the beginning. If one turns from the title-page adorned with a stylized Celtic Dragon design (drawn by Tolkien himself), the first text is a two-colour hand-drawn map of 'The Lonely Mountain' with remarkably few landmarks save for two rivers, a few trees, and the edge of a forest, and more text in English and Anglo-Saxon runes. Three texts open the novel, then: a map (unreadable in parts), a preface (ditto), and a story that begins with a diminutive Bertie Wooster shooing away a Humpty-Dumpty sorcerer.

I have emphasized these clashes of style and mood because they are not only maintained but actually mushroom as the novel progresses, and, far from collapsing into absurdity, constitute a quintessential part of the book's idiosyncratic charm. Where else does the forlorn doom of the Anglo-Saxons unite with the gilded English manners of the careless years before the Great War on the enchanted ground of Elfland? Tolkien immediately capitalizes on the ludicrousness of his setting. Hospitality is a key theme of the book (and is also symbolic of Tolkien welcoming every imaginable source and reference into his tale), so Bilbo is straightaway faced with a succession of Dwarves, thirteen in all, arriving at his door. His social niceties of hospitality and courtesy oblige him to invite them inside and feed them, feed them all. This is an Edwardian house-call gone haywire: the Dwarves are visitors from another story, another set of narrative conventions, another world even – but Bilbo, conventional as he is, cannot refuse to entertain them. He is a victim of his own civilized values: like a Monty Python sketch, it is brilliantly daft. And Bilbo is not the only one to find a succession of Dwarves arriving: the book repeatedly reiterates and replays episodes. This opening scene is inverted with the Trolls: this time the hapless Dwarves arrive singly, or in twos or threes, and are easy picking for the Trolls who snatch them and bag them up for the cooking pot. The Dwarves arrive not in search of hospitality and food, but as a food delivery themselves, coming mighty close to being eaten by the Trolls, who turn out to be unlikely enthusiasts of a variety of home-cooking methods, eschewing raw food (fortunately for the Dwarves). Then, at Beorn's house, the Dwarves revert to their tactics at Bag End, arriving like the animals coming, more or less, two-by-two.[31] If their first arrival was staggered so as not to intimidate Bilbo (and also to create for the reader a comedic sequence of repetitions), this is replicated with more cunning at Beorn's house so as not to antagonize the dangerously irascible skin-changer, who 'can be appalling when he is angry' and admits that he is 'not over fond of dwarves'.[32] These arrivals are fraught with potential danger: to refuse hospitality not only insults and demeans the visitor, but actually reduces them to an object – to outcasts, even to fodder.

To return to the incongruities: what is fascinating about Tolkien's technique is the way he layers mismatched texts – from nursery rhyme to epic mythology – something that becomes part of the deep texture of *The Lord of the Rings* in much more subtle and complex ways through allusions to older stories and forgotten legends. This is something that Tolkien learnt from *Beowulf*: a sense of deep history combining with culture to form heritage and identity. The first sustained example of this is the song the Dwarves sing at Bag End – singing being one of the ways in which the different peoples of Middle-Earth distinguish themselves.[33] 'Far Over the Misty Mountains Cold' is a lament that encapsulates the hurt and heartbreak of Thorin's Company, and, for the astute reader, summarizes their plight through artful allusions; it was also set to music to stunning effect by Neil Finn (who appropriately enough founded the band Crowded House) in the film *An Unexpected Journey* (2012). So this is a serious moment, and Tolkien guides readers' responses through the transformative effects that the song and Thorin's subsequent clarification have on Bilbo. It lights a fire, and Bilbo is converted: the usually dormant 'Tookish' side of his character, inherited from his mother Belladonna Took, yearns for adventure. Then the Baggins side frantically reasserts itself and he shrieks 'like the whistle of an engine coming out of a tunnel', collapses, and goes into shock, repeating the meaningless phrase, 'struck by lightning'.[34] A lot is happening here, to a character we barely yet know.

Poetry is introduced into a prose novel at a key turning point, the stirring effect of song inspires action, Bilbo's identity is split (which foreshadows an ensuing, much more sinister split personality in the shape of Gollum), and he suffers a breakdown in his sense of self. Or possibly a traumatic rebirth: unlikely as it may sound, Tolkien read Carl Jung, and cites *Psychology of the Unconscious* (English translation 1916) in his work on fairy stories. In this study, Jung makes a passing remark that 'By means of a flash of lightning heroes were made immortal.'[35] Bilbo is about to become a hero of sorts (and, ultimately, immortal), and through this process facets of his previous character (such as worrying about pocket handkerchiefs, and hats, and walking sticks) will be seared away – by lightning.

But here there is also the utterly anachronistic image of a steam train, breaking into the scene of Dragon gold and Dwarvish conspiracy literally from nowhere. It turns out that Tolkien purposefully breaks his spell more than once with calculated anachronisms – or rather, the sudden appearance of an anachronism complicates and wrong-foots the reader. Just as we begin to believe we understand this world, this proto-Middle-Earth, we come up against tobacco, fireworks, tea and cake, barometers, and the game of golf; gunpowder in Goblin Town and the roar of Beorn on the battlefield being like 'drums and guns'; even fancy waistcoats.[36] It is also worth bearing in mind that the song of the Dwarves is also an anachronism. Despite being heavily alliterative verse with an Anglo-Saxon pulse, in reality it consists of a sequence of disguised limericks – that most celebrated style of nonsense poetry popularized in the nineteenth century by Edward Lear. Again, within a few lines Tolkien is heaping up miscellaneous incongruities.[37]

Bilbo's journey is therefore as much through diverse literary cultures as it is a trip through regions of the yet-to-be-named Middle-Earth. As I say, the full text of *The Hobbit* begins with Anglo-Saxon runes (known as *futhorc*), and runes play a key role in the plot: they are like riddles, and 'moon runes' are concealed in Thrór's map.[38] We are also told that *Orc* is not English – so immediately we are in the presence of two alphabet systems and (at least) two languages. Hobbits, meanwhile, are waistcoated and pipe-smoking *bons viveurs*, almost Chaucerian in their boisterous exuberance, yet Tolkien also emphasized that the atmosphere of Hobbiton is akin to Queen Victoria's Golden Jubilee in 'a quiet Warwickshire village: I think it engenders a particular love of what you might call central Midland English countryside based on good wall stones, and elm trees, and small quiet rivers, and so on, and, of course, sort of rustic people about'.[39] The Dwarves then move the story into fairy tale with their coloured beards and hoods and musical instruments, from fiddles to clarinets, but there is also a more ominous aspect to them – not least as the first, Dwalin, literally has a blue beard. Many of the Dwarves have names taken from the Old Norse poem the *Völuspá* (the 'prophecy of the Völva', or seeress) on the founding and the fate of the world.[40] The *Völuspá* is included in the Icelandic *Poetic Edda* (an anthology of Old Norse poems compiled between the eleventh and fourteenth centuries) that lists the names of various Dwarves: Dvalinn (Dwalin), Bífurr, Báfurr, Bömburr, Nóri, Þorinn (Thorin), as well as Durrin (Durin), Dáinn (Dain), and Þráinn (Thráin); the name Gandalf is also taken from the same source (Gandalfr, meaning 'wand Elf' or 'magic Elf'). Tolkien may also have heard of the Icelandic tradition of the Yule Lads: thirteen Dwarves (or Trolls) who arrive one-by-one during the thirteen days before Christmas to play pranks and pester the kitchen and larder. For Thorin and Company, however, thirteen is an unlucky number – which is the reason that they need an extra member (i.e. Bilbo); this superstition over the number thirteen arose in Britain historically comparatively late (in 1695), and referred to the thirteen seated at the Last Supper – which resulted in Christ's arrest and crucifixion and Judas' suicide.[41]

Bilbo, then, stands on the threshold of legendary history: take one step and he will become part of the tales of the Dwarves – of Thrór and Thráin, of Thrór's killer Azog who slew him in the

Mines of Moria, and of Gandalf's discovery of Thráin in the dungeons of the Necromancer. The Dwarves wish to reclaim their lost past, to retread their history – but in doing so they will also become part of the story of the Hobbits, and The Shire. It is, then, a dark and foreboding tale, and, by the close of the chapter, the words of the song are giving Bilbo 'very uncomfortable dreams': his world, his identity, have lost their stability and can no longer be relied upon.[42]

Telling Tales

The first serious problem the Company have to contend with are three knockabout Trolls named Tom, Bert, and Bill (William Huggins). They too are part of other stories and have their origins in such diverse sources as the Trolls of Old Norse myth and Edwardian music hall. Their language, for one, is not simply drawn from Tolkien's academic research into mediaeval dialect, but is clearly based on cockney London accents popularized by recordings such as Harry Champion's celebrated hit 'Any Old Iron' (1911).[43] But they are also within Tolkien's legendarium, for in their cave they have three ancient weapons. Elrond later identifies two of these blades as Orcrist and Glamdring, or, in the vernacular, Goblin-Cleaver and Foe-Hammer, or, to the Orcs, Biter and Beater – as with so many characters, both swords have more than one name. They were forged by the Elven smiths of Gondolin; indeed, Glamdring had been the King of Gondolin's sword. This means nothing to the reader, but Tolkien had been working on the 'Great Tale' of 'The Fall of Gondolin' – eventually part of The Silmarillion – since at least 1920 when he read a draft of the siege of the city to the Exeter College Essay Club (ominously, Dragons were instrumental in the destruction of the city-kingdom). Only much later was Elrond's connection with Gondolin made clear: Elrond's father was none other than Eärendel, who in turn was the son of Tuor, a Human who (like Ælfwine) had journeyed to the City of Elves, and his wife the Elf Idril; she was daughter of Turgon, the King of Gondolin.⁴⁴ So Glamdring is an heirloom of Elrond's house – his great-grandfather's sword (any old iron, indeed!). Moreover, Elrond is described in *The Hobbit* as having both Elvish and heroic ancestry: he is a Half-Elf, whose past lay in the ever-changing lands of the legendarium. Bilbo is now firmly in Middle-Earth – or is he? In Rivendell, the House of Elrond and the 'Last Homely House', Thorin refers to himself as the heir of Durin, the 'father of the fathers of the eldest race of Dwarves', which reaffirms the legendarium as a key frame of reference.⁴⁵ But Thorin also calls the Dwarves 'Longbeards', making them part of North European Gothic antiquity by hinting at a connection with the Lombards, known in Anglo-Saxon as *Longbeardan*. The 'Longbeards' were, moreover, not only an element of the mythic matter of England surveyed in mediaeval Gothic histories, but are also woven into Tolkien's own abandoned novel *The Lost Road*.⁴⁶ It is a vertiginous ride.

So the story is already veering from music-hall singalongs into grim Middle-Earthly and Gothic histories, before tumbling into British folklore with references to Midsummer's Eve and the crescent moon, clambering back into Middle-Earth with Durin's Day (the Dwarvish New Year – the first day of the last moon of autumn), and, in doing so, unexpectedly turning to Jewish culture. Even in the calendar there is a sense of deeper cultures and traditions: despite their Christian superstition of the number thirteen, the Dwarves follow a lunar calendar, so they effectively observe the Jewish year.⁴⁷ This multiplicity is true of the maps in the book as well, which are themselves distinctive texts. Thrór's map, for example, has east at the top, alluding to the mediaeval Christian belief that the Garden of Eden lay in the east and that therefore maps should be aligned to reflect divine order, while Tolkien's own map of Wilderland has north at the top. If maps are a way of ordering the world and imagining a shared communal identity, even a nation, here they are barely compatible and actually chart the *differences* between different peoples – and the different reasons that they have maps at all. Interestingly, cartography is also evident at a linguistic level in Hobbiton, where many place names are simply nouns given the definite article 'the': so we get 'The Hill', for example. This form is usually used when a reader or listener understands exactly what is being referred to (such as 'the Earth', or, in court, 'the burglar'); in Hobbiton, however, it has the opposite effect by implying that we *ought* to be familiar with the location but plainly are not – another deliberate disorientation. It is through such gambits that Tolkien repeatedly introduces sudden uncertainty: uncertainty of the world, uncertainty of the status of things in the world.

The capture of the Dwarves in *the* Misty Mountains and their entry into Goblin Town is a return to fairy tale, but the Goblins are far, far more menacing and violent than those in Tolkien's sugary fairy verse 'Goblin Feet' of 1915.[48] Although these Goblins are still potentially more comic rather than evil, these nasties are well on the way to becoming Orcs. Their brutal behaviour and aggressively triumphalist songs have fascistic overtones (although worse, much worse, is to come). Their dark origins are more reminiscent of the sinister poetry of Christina Rossetti's poem *Goblin Market* (1862):

> They trod and hustled her,
> Elbowed and jostled her,
> Clawed with their nails,
> Barking, mewing, hissing, mocking . . .[49]

However, rather than sing the sensual seductions of imperial capitalism, Tolkien's barking Goblins extol physical violence, and, ultimately, mechanized warfare: 'wheels and engines and explosions have always delighted them'.[50] What there is here, though, is a sense of Goblin culture: they chant, and joke, and celebrate themselves like loathsome Vikings. They also sing when burning the fir trees. First this is a threat as if they are cooking the Dwarves to eat them, but then, in the context of Tolkien's experiences on the frontline and later Nazi atrocities, their songs retrospectively become horrifying:

> Bake and toast 'em, fry and roast 'em!
> till beards blaze, and eyes glaze;
> till hair smells and skins crack,
> fat melts and bones black
> in cinders lie
> beneath the sky!
> So dwarves shall die . . .

It is chilling that Tolkien would later refer to the Dwarves as a 'semitic' people, their language having the sounds of Hebrew.[51]

At the heart of the novel is the key episode of the riddle-game; this is the scene that seems to be most reliant on earlier sources.[52] Riddles were an important feature of Anglo-Saxon poetic culture – described by Adam Roberts as an Anglo-Saxon ritual of power – and there are ninety-five riddles in the tenth-century manuscript of the *Exeter Book* (probably from an original hundred), as well as scattered examples elsewhere.[53] Riddles gave the Anglo-Saxons an opportunity to demonstrate wit and linguistic ingenuity, wordplay and the ambiguities of multiple meanings. Riddles reveal a poetic imagination rooted in metaphorical, symbolic, and allegorical thinking, and a taste for prosopopoeia (portraying an inanimate object as able to act and speak).[54] They also often bring disparate images and figures together – much as they do in *The Hobbit* by bringing Bilbo and Gollum together.[55] Anglo-Saxon riddles are, then, refreshingly different from the fateful and elegiac tone of much other verse of the time – although Tolkien immediately introduces an almost overpowering sense of threat by making Bilbo riddle for his life. In the hissing tones of Gollum, 'If precious asks, and it doesn't answer, we eats it, my preciousss' – undoubtedly the best line delivered by Andy Serkis in the Peter Jackson film *An Unexpected Journey* (2012).[56]

Before considering these riddles, however, it is worth considering Gollum, one of Tolkien's most memorable creations. Gollum already speaks in a riddling manner, speaking to himself as 'we', 'us', and 'my preciousss'. Furthermore, Constance Hiett has argued that in Old Norse, the neuter word for gold is *gull* or *goll*, and so 'gollum' is an inflection that could mean 'gold, treasure, something precious'; it could also mean 'ring' – indicating that Gollum absolutely identifies with the One Ring and that his identity is inextricable from it.[57] So Gollum does not have a singular identity but is a knot of mutually dependent and fragmented character traits that orbit around the Ring. In *The Lord of the Rings* he becomes a real oddity as Sméagol, but already in *The Hobbit* he is a freakish and fractured figure – if also darkly comic. So Tolkien's subsequent development of Gollum in *The Lord of the Rings* went hand-in-hand with his development of the Ring. This meant that most of the Gollum chapter was revised for the 1951 edition of *The Hobbit*, after *The Lord of the Rings* was effectively complete if not yet published. *The Hobbit* was not a fixed text but was reshaped by what came after it: history was rewritten.

Riddles are Gollum's game, much as they are in Old Norse among the gods, and Adam Roberts, for one, comments that Tolkien's own letters are 'full of ludic diversions, games, wit and puzzles, designed to divert and amuse his correspondents' – one could add also to hoodwink and mislead them.[58] Sources for the riddles that Bilbo and Gollum exchange have been found in Old Norse, the *Exeter Book*, mediaeval literature, and traditional nursery rhymes. Although Tom Shippey suggests that Gollum's riddles are mostly ancient and more sinister, and that Bilbo's are more domestic, it is true that definitive sources have not been established for all of the riddles of *The Hobbit*, and that the sources that have been proposed usually tend to be very different in tone.[59] For example, the four-line, nine-word riddle posed by Gollum beginning '*Voiceless it cries*' may be derived from a riddle in the *Exeter Book*; however, this source is a lengthy Anglo-Saxon riddle describing wind, rain, thunder, and lightning to which the answer is the Biblical Flood, so the answer 'wind' is only a part of the verse.

The riddles on darkness and the egg, meanwhile, may have sources in an Old Norse poem *Saga Heiðreks Konungs ins Vitra* ('the saga of King Heidrek the Wise'), which includes a riddle contest between King Heidrek, King of the Goths, and his challenger: a man ostensibly named Gestumblindi but who is in fact the god Odin in disguise. But again the riddles they exchange are rather different from any versions in *The Hobbit*. The darkness riddle, for instance, is supposedly based on a riddle to which the answer is not 'dark', but 'fog' – which Gollum would surely not have accepted as an adequate answer.[60] Besides, Bilbo composes one riddle on the spot by punning on Old English: the sun shining on daisies requires knowledge of the Anglo-Saxon term for the daisy flower: *dæges éage*, or 'day's eye'. The riddles, then, are a miscellaneous bag – but they are also a curious bag. Two riddles have similar answers (fish), and the second of these also has a classical source: it is derived from the riddle the Sphinx poses to Oedipus. Tolkien typically tied these together in *The Lord of the Rings* by establishing that Gollum acquired the Ring while angling: fishing became fate.[61]

So there is a very peculiar mix of sources and influences in the riddle-game. Tolkien himself (deliberately) muddied the waters by variously claiming or implying that all of the Bilbo–Gollum riddles had sources – and then maintaining that he had invented all-but two.[62] Again, the riddles are not only disparate in their range, deriving from recognizable categories such as folklore or nursery rhyme, but also elude the limitations of historical integrity by not having consistently Old Norse or Anglo-Saxon sources. I am (again) reminded of Jorge Luis Borges, himself an aficionado of Anglo-Saxon and of fantasy writing. In the essay 'John Wilkins' Analytical Language', Borges gives a clearly fictional account of a certain Chinese encyclopedia that thwarts, even outwits, the confines of conventional thinking. In this volume, animals are classified as:

(a) those that belong to the emperor; (b) embalmed ones; (c) those that are trained; (d) suckling pigs; (e) mermaids; (f) fabulous ones; (g) stray dogs; (h) those that are included in this classification; (i) those that tremble as if they were mad; (j) innumerable ones; (k) those drawn with a very fine camel's-hair brush; (l) etcetera; (m) those that have just broken the flower vase; (n) those that at a distance resemble flies.[63]

My point is that Tolkien is knowingly, if subtly, laying a series of red herrings in the riddle-game. What appears to be a single allusion to Anglo-Saxon culture is in fact a miscellaneous series of puzzles that range from the mead hall to the nursery – and one cannot help but recall again the language games of *Through the Looking-Glass* – a sort of 'over-play', to suggest an Anglo-Saxonist term. The calculated effect of this incessant play is to disorientate the reader as the identities of Bilbo and Gollum crumble – Tolkien intentionally creating a chaos of (non-)references and (non-)allusions from which he (the writer) can then try his hand at building some sort of order. At one notable point, Gollum recaptures a memory of teaching his grandmother to suck eggs, which Tolkien later used as evidence that Gollum originally grew up in a matriarchal society – although, in fact, Gollum's materfamilias is usually overlooked in accounts of the admittedly sparse female mentions in *The Hobbit*. (There's Belladonna Took, or Mrs Bungo Baggins – one of the three daughters of the 'Old Took' – the rumoured fairy wife, and arguably the Spiders of Mirkwood.[64]) But all that aside, these are clues – or further riddles – within the riddles, and so the biggest riddle of all in the riddle-game is, simply, what is going on here? And then, with the utmost neatness, Tolkien cleaves the Gordian Knot of confusion he has devoted pages to knitting up. Gollum makes a fatal error: rather than ask for a riddle, in his eagerness he says: 'It's got to ask uss a question, my preciouss, yes, yess, yesss. Jusst one more question to guess, yes, yess . . .' So Bilbo is free (if absent-minded enough in the face of being eaten alive) to ask a question rather than pose a riddle: 'What have I got in my pocket?'[65] And this is exactly the sort of question that concludes the riddling in *Heiðreks Konungs*. Gestumblindi (or rather, Odin) takes the initiative and asks what only the god Odin himself could know:

> Tell me this then after all, if you are wiser than any other king:
>   What said Ódin
>   in the ear of Balder,
>   before he was borne to the fire?[66]

The same question is posed in the *Vafþrúðnismál* ('lay of Vafthrúdnir'), the other renowned Old Norse riddle-game, in which Odin, again in disguise, competes in riddles with the

Jötnar (Giant) Vafthrúdnir. All three riddle-games thus end by wriggling out of the rules of the riddle. Besides, Bilbo's question is not only extremely difficult for Gollum, it is simply impossible for him to answer correctly as he believes that he has the Ring in his own pocket: he has pocketed it in a pouch kept in a hole on his island rock ('pouch' being a now obsolete meaning of the word *pocket*).[67] As we shall see, Bilbo is perpetually bending and breaking the rules to suit (and save) himself: he is one of the most amoral leading characters in children's literature.[68]

However, in the first published edition of *The Hobbit* the game runs rather differently. Gollum (not a Hobbit himself at this stage) creeps up to Bilbo, is apprehensive to find him armed, and is guardedly friendly. He straightaway suggests a riddle-game to buy time for him to learn more about Mr Baggins – he is, in fact, hospitable. Bilbo agrees to the game for the same reason. The terms of the game are: if Gollum wins, he can eat Bilbo, but if Bilbo wins, Gollum will give him a present. For the first time since Gandalf was good-morninged by Bilbo in the opening pages of the book we have two figures in conversation – and the dialogue is similarly wary. But riddle they do, until Bilbo is stumped and asks what he has in his pocket. Gollum cannot answer, weeps, and Bilbo demands his present. Off Gollum goes to retrieve his magic ring, shrieks at not being able to find it, and despairs that he has no present for Bilbo, a present that he had promised. He begs Bilbo's forgiveness – it was a wonderful ring of invisibility given to him on his birthday (some present! – although in fact this ring did not confer full invisibility as the wearer still cast a shadow). Bilbo, realizing that Gollum must have lost the ring he has just picked up, decides to keep quiet on the matter (finders keepers), and instead asks to be shown the way out. Gollum is happy to comply, and does so. And that is it: the decent, worthy, honourable Gollum would have willingly parted with his magic ring. As John Rateliff observes, in this original version Gollum had not only meant to give Bilbo the Ring for winning the game, but Bilbo actually 'demands a second prize (being shown the way out) in addition to the one he has quietly pocketed'.[69] Unsurprisingly, Tolkien had to rewrite this entire episode once the true nature of the Ring – and Gollum – became apparent to him.[70]

Tail Ends

Equipped with a mysterious ring that when the book was first published even the author did not recognize the significance of, Bilbo continues his journey and now enters the land of beast fable. There are intelligent Wolves, talking giant Eagles, an ursine skin-changer, talking giant Spiders, and, later, more talking birds – Ravens, this time – while Bilbo himself is repeatedly referred to as a rabbit, even, gallingly, a 'bunny' at one stage, as well as a 'descendant of rats'.[71] The Wolves are reinvented as 'Wargs' by Tolkien – a word of mixed heritage combining the Old Norse *vargr* meaning 'outlaw' or 'wolf', the Anglo-Saxon *wearg* meaning 'outlaw' or 'felon', and the Middle High German *warc* for 'monster'.[72] The talking birds recall Sigurd's ability to understand birdsong after he had tasted the Dragon Fafnir's heart, as well as being a staple of nursery rhymes such as 'Who Killed Cock Robin?' (which Tolkien had translated into Anglo-Saxon while at Leeds).[73] Beorn, the skin-changer, last of his race, sometimes appears as a great black bear, sometimes as a Human – he is based on the Viking 'berserker' or 'wolf-skin', a warrior who would enter an ecstatic psychotic state on the battlefield. The *Völsunga Saga* states that they 'went without armour, were as mad as dogs and wolves, they bit their shields, were as strong as bears or oxen, they killed everybody, and neither fire nor iron bit them; [this] is called going beserk'.[74]

So Beorn is another dual personality – indeed, as a Human,

Beorn appears to be a strict vegetarian, whose diet consists
mainly of bread and butter, clotted cream, honey, fruit, cakes,
and mead. He lives in a house modelled on Heorot, the mead
hall of *Beowulf*, sharing it with ponies, dogs, sheep, and cattle
who perform various household duties, such as lighting torches,
laying the table, and serving up food – and to whom he can
talk.[75] He also rallies the local wild bears and doubtless talks to
his bees as well – 'telling the bees' being an old English custom
of reporting important news to bees in the hive lest they take
offence and withhold honey: bees were considered not only wise
but also having a touch of divinity about them.[76] In contrast,
however, as a bear Beorn is ruthlessly bloodthirsty: he captures a
Goblin and a Warg, interrogates them to corroborate Gandalf's
account of the Dwarves' experiences in Goblin Town and their
subsequent pursuit by Wargs, and then executes his prisoners –
leaving the Goblin's decapitated head on a stake and the Warg's
skin nailed to a tree in warning. Beorn really is a singular case.
He mixes the gentle domestic delight of Dr Dolittle (the first
book in the series by Hugh Lofting, *The Story of Doctor Dolittle*,
had been published in 1920) with the maddened wrath of a
Viking intoxicated with bloodlust.[77] He is another example of
Tolkien challenging his readers by creating a unique and utterly
contradictory character.

While chattering birds and sly Wolves might evoke some of
the animals of Aesop's fables or Charles Perrault's *Mother Goose's
Tales* (1729); and the dexterous and conversant ponies conceivably allude to the rational horses of Jonathan Swift's Houyhn-
hnm Land in *Travels into Several Remote Nations of the World*
(more commonly known as *Gulliver's Travels*, 1726); and while
Beorn appears to be a displaced Viking were-creature, giant
Spiders – giant talking Spiders – do not have any obvious ante-
cedents. Spiders, like ants, are traditionally industrious workers and are usually treated as medicinal, or seen as bringers of

good luck – although Tolkien's own son Michael had arachnophobia, which is one reason Tolkien teasingly included these outsize creatures in stories such as *Roverandom*.[78] Alighieri Dante included Arachne in *Purgatorio* XII as a half-human half-spider, for which Gustav Doré produced a hideously inverted image, and the octopean Martians of H.G. Wells's *The War of the Worlds* (1897, 1898) move in spiderlike tripods.

Doubtless more germane, however, is Lord Dunsany, a writer of numinous fantasy tales familiar to Tolkien. Dunsany included giant Spiders in three Edwardian short stories. In 'The Fortress Unvanquishable, Save for Sacnoth', the hero Leothric, armed with the magic sword Sacnoth, is able to cut through the webs of a Spider 'larger than a ram' – so admittedly large enough to terrify a Hobbit or a Dwarf. The creature, which has human hair and even human hands, asks Leothric, 'Who are you that spoil the labour of years all done to the honour of Satan?', begins weaving a rope to hang him, and then takes fright at the named sword Sacnoth and scuttles away.[79] It may be a large Spider, but phrased through the misty and loquacious fancy of Dunsany, it is hardly a Mirkwood Spider. In the same collection, there is an hallucinatory tale 'Lord of Cities', in which there is another Spider who has woven a gorgeous black tapestry to decorate a ruined mill. The narrator dreams of the mill through the night, during which a river and the road debate between natural and man-made beauty; the Spider has the last word, stating that human cities are simply dilapidated sites in which Spiders can create exquisite art. Again, it is not a Mirkwood Spider.[80]

Instead, the most frightening Spider proper in literature before Tolkien is probably the one that frightens away little Miss Muffet. Preposterous as this might seem, a colour illustration to the nursery rhyme by Arthur Rackham (1867–1939), published in 1913, portrays a horridly oversized Spider behind the innocent Muffet, and Tolkien, an admirer of Rackham's spiky, unsentimental style, may well have seen the potential of giant predatory arachnids in the illustration. Despite Rackham's Spider doffing a rather natty top-hat, the origins of the Mirkwood clutter of Spiders, Shelob, and the alien demon Ungoliant probably began by a tuffet, among the curds and whey.[81]

As to their domain, Tolkien's unsettling giant talking Spiders inhabit the great forest of Mirkwood, which takes its name from William Morris's *The House of the Wolfings*, in turn an adaptation of the legendary Old Norse forest of *Myrkviðr*.[82] Despite the Nordic origins of the name, though, embedded in Mirkwood are Celtic legends, in which rivers of sleep and dreams run through the trees, and where, most of all, fairy tales proliferate. Because time and space are configured differently in Faërie, the clear (even Biblical) warning is 'DON'T LEAVE THE PATH' when you are in the woods; again: 'That you MUST NOT do, for any reason.'[83] This oft-repeated advice is not only reminiscent of retellings of 'Little Red Riding-Hood' and many, many later restrictions against children wandering, but is also a reminder of Tolkien's fascination with the lost road to Faërie (Valinor), lost through Human insolence, that can provide an escape from Middle-Earth at the end of *The Lord of the Rings*. The forest has deep roots, but variegated leaves.

Tolkien also knew the mediaeval poem 'Sir Orfeo', which he rather improbably taught to officer cadets during the Second World War. The lay tells of the kidnapping of a mortal queen by the King of the Fairies and her husband's pursuit of her through Elfland, occasionally glimpsing the fairy hunt:

> There often by him would he see,
> when noon was hot on leaf and tree,
> the king of Faërie with his rout
> came hunting in the woods about.[84]

The Mirkwood Elves share similarities: they too are hunting – although in 'Sir Orfeo' the fairies hunt, but never kill, their quarry – and the Elves of Mirkwood are in particular hunting a deer: a black hart and a white hind. White deer have mysterious and elusive mythological meanings: in Celtic mythology they seem able to move between different worlds – this world and the otherworld of Faërie – and were possibly ominous portents. Certainly in 'The Lay of Aotrou and Itroun', which Tolkien had translated from the Breton language a decade before he wrote *The Hobbit*, it is fatal to encounter the white deer. Aotrou makes a pact with the Corrigan (a Breton fairy-witch) so his wife Itroun will become pregnant. He subsequently pursues a white doe through a forest, which leads him back to the Corrigan. She demands his love as her fee; Aotrou refuses, and so dies – as does his wife after giving birth. This suggests that the white hind that the Dwarves watch is not exactly a propitious sight. On the other hand, in Anglo-Saxon (Germanic) culture the stag was a regal symbol that eventually became the badge of the white hart, particularly favoured by King Richard II and his supporters – even if it eventually proved ominous. Richard was deposed by his cousin Henry Bolingbroke (who then became Henry IV), a plot to restore Richard was mercilessly dealt with, and the former sovereign was confined in Pontefract Castle.[85] Within weeks he had died under mysterious circumstances, possibly through starvation. The white hart has, then, extremely troubling and contradictory associations – that is enough.

The Mirkwood Elves themselves are tricksy and abide by their own capricious laws – they are not the brethren and sustren of the Rivendell Elves, but blindfold the Dwarves when they are led to the caverns of the Elvenking (much as the Company of the Ring are blindfolded to be led into Lothlórien). These Elves are more grim than the pixie-ish Elves of Rivendell, and also get more drunk – in fact, drunkenness and the imported wine of Dorwinion becomes key to the plot. The ill will of the Elves towards the Dwarves is outlined here: it stems from a period of ancient history when the two peoples had warred against each other, which is a veiled reference to the politics of 'The Silmarillion' regarding the Elf King Thingol of Doriath.[86] The hero Beren had sought to marry Thingol's daughter Lúthien, but Thingol had demanded an impossible payment from Beren: a Silmaril. The Silmarils were three awe-inspiring jewels created by Fëanor, the greatest craftsman of Middle-Earth, in which he had caught the divine light of the two trees that originally lit the world. These trees were destroyed, and so the Silmarils were the remembrance of a lost time. But the Silmarils were themselves then stolen by Morgoth, paragon of evil, and so the 'Quenta Silmarillion' is, in essence, an epic account of the events surrounding the loss and recovery of these stones: despite (or, rather, because of) their exquisite, celestial beauty, the Silmarils provoked intense avarice, discord, conflict, and outright war.

Against every expectation, Beren succeeded in taking a Silmaril, and the Silmaril that Thingol duly received for his daughter was set in a necklace by the Dwarves. But they fell then under the curse of the gemstone and refused to return the jewellery. Thingol was waylaid and murdered by the Dwarves – who in the early *Lost Tales* are an evil folk – and the Dwarves and the Elves then fought at the Battle of the Thousand Caves. It is this history that lies behind the Elvenking's imprisonment of Thorin and the Dwarves – another example of the sudden depths that are momentarily glimpsed in this children's story. Yet in reappraising Dwarves in *The Hobbit* – most notably, perhaps, in the dying words of Thorin ('I go now to the halls of waiting to sit beside my fathers until the world is renewed...') – Tolkien rethought the entire role of the Dwarves and consequently repositioned them as one of the Free Peoples of Middle-Earth.[87] Bilbo's adventure therefore fundamentally changed the legendarium.

Escaping from the cells of the Elves, Thorin's Company then
enters a new phase: the Human settlement of Laketown. This is
based on such diverse influences as artist impressions of Neolithic
villages in the wetlands of the Somerset Levels, Robert Browning's description of Hamelin in his parable of child abduction
'The Pied Piper' (1842), and Tolkien's own poem 'Progress in
Bimble Town' (1931), which depicts a modern industrial town in
which the imagination, enchantment, and Faërie have no place.[88]
Both Browning's and Tolkien's poems dwell on changes brought
about by trade, and Laketown is a commercial centre – as the
neighbouring city of Dale, now in ruins, had been. This is somewhat unusual in Middle-Earth: there is little finance interest in
The Lord of the Rings, although there is some export of goods to
Mordor and Isengard – the latter becoming a significant part of
the final plot. Laketown is also, uniquely, an oligarchy and governed by merchants and business interests.[89] So the export and
import of wine and the mapping of trade routes become crucial
plot devices in *The Hobbit*. Furthermore, Tolkien's introduction
of economic realities questions the Dwarves' seemingly noble
quest to regain their home, recasting it, at best, as a treasure
hunt, at worst, as a reprise of the same greed aroused by the
Silmaril that led to thousands of years of hostility.

The anticipated riches that will follow the death of the Dragon
Smaug present another change of focus that is then refracted
through Tolkien's various lenses as rumours spread: from Bilbo
and the Dwarves, to Elves, the Humans of Laketown, and Goblins of the Misty Mountains and Gundabad. Monetary issues are
now ubiquitous. The Laketown people toast the Dwarves with
old songs foretelling 'the return of the King' whose 'wealth shall
flow in fountains/And the rivers golden run'. And now there is
another unexpected allusion here. This song, 'The King ... Shall
come into his own', recalls the late seventeenth-century ballad
'When the King enjoys his own again', referring to the Roman

Catholic Stuart monarchy of James II that was removed by the 'Glorious Revolution' of 1688, William of Orange taking the British throne in 1689.[90] The song was accordingly sung by Stuart and Catholic rebels – the 'Jacobite' supporters of King James (*Jacobus*) – during the next half-century of uprisings and rebellions, before the Jacobites were finally crushed at the bloodthirsty Battle of Culloden in 1746. Tolkien's covert Jacobitism is thus the second reference in *The Hobbit* to a deposed English (now British) monarch.

To the Dragon. Bilbo is the first witness to the hoard and is transfixed by the sight of it. Tolkien's instinctive philological response is to coin a new word: 'There are no words left to express his staggerment'. The experience is magical, and ignites Dwarvish passions: 'His heart was filled and pierced with enchantment and with the desire of dwarves; and he gazed motionless'.[91] Then Bilbo becomes more pragmatic and steals a golden goblet 'as heavy as he could carry'.[92] This response to fabulous wealth is not only entirely in keeping with the Hobbit's habitual thievery (stealing the Troll's purse, ransacking the larders of the Elvenking), but is also a direct reference to *Beowulf*, in which the theft of a gold cup wakens the sleeping Dragon. As Jack Zipes comments of Smaug, 'The dragon is a parasite' – it cannot make things itself – and he even adds that 'in socio-political terms, he is the picture-image of the capitalist exploiter'.[93] Hardly, I think – but we might wonder what, exactly, can a Dragon do with its treasure? It can gloat over it, and it can rant and rave if any of it is lost. So, as the story now encompasses desire, greed, avarice, and power, the Dragon hoard exposes the vanity and futility of accumulated wealth: this is not working capital, it is literally idle riches – but it confers status and underwrites power, which is why Smaug cannot have the integrity of his fortune cast into doubt by the loss of a single goblet. The result of Bilbo's theft in *The Hobbit* is exactly the same as the result of the theft in

Beowulf: the Dragon is roused from its dreams (or nightmares) and flies about in a fury. Bilbo's unnecessary act of larceny is a literary allusion that has potentially calamitous consequences for the Dwarves, for Laketown, and for Middle-Earth – if it also ultimately leads to the death of Smaug himself.

But before that, having lived up to his role of burglar, Bilbo then exercises his ingenuity and duplicity in a series of parleys and negotiations between various characters – there is much conferring in the final chapters. He returns to Smaug and, protected by his ring of invisibility, addresses the Dragon in a series of riddling sobriquets that summarize his adventures – essentially reducing the novel to a string of opaque kennings. Having already argued with himself about whether he should first go into the halls of the Dragon ('He fought the real battle in the tunnel alone'), he now actively reinvents himself in multiple ways – 'I am Ringwinner, and Luckwearer; and I am Barrel-rider.' The first of these epithets is, of course, of dubious veracity, which unfortunately casts doubt over his entire performance, but Bilbo is also careful to flatter Smaug – an instance of his deceit through insincerity (although perhaps conversing with dragons has its own rules – Bilbo certainly seems to think that conversing with Gollum freed him from usual rules of behaviour).[94] By adopting the different names of a shifting (and shifty) character, then, Bilbo's language is itself Dragonish. Moreover, Tolkien is again alluding to *Beowulf* and Anglo-Saxon culture. Bilbo's riddling self-narration is comparable to the refrains of oral epic poetry, and also conjures up the mood of the mead hall where untested heroes would boast of their feats and their exploits-to-come.

As for Smaug, Tom Shippey notes multiple voices here as well: Smaug begins by speaking in a contemporary if patrician style, before becoming colloquial and then – surprisingly – his diction grows increasingly archaic, even Biblical. This is in turn reflected in the way in which he is described by Tolkien, who perhaps drew on the depiction of Leviathan in the Book of Job.[95] The tone swings in little more than a page from Bilbo talking to himself about burglars and grocers to the Dwarves hearing the 'awful rumour' of Smaug's flight – *rumour* here meaning 'uproar, tumult, disturbance', which the *OED* notes as an obsolete meaning after the early nineteenth century.[96] Shippey, identifying more examples, regards this as characteristic of Tolkien's style: the measured clash between anachronism and everyday language – and while there is a disjuncture between different styles of speech, of conduct, and even of heroism, he nevertheless argues that 'there is a *continuity* between ancient and modern which is at least as strong as the difference'.[97] But I would argue that there is far more than that: language, characters, and action do not simply stand in both the ancient and the modern worlds – they flit restlessly from antiquity across the whole range of history, and society, and morality, and culture – and also of course draw on Tolkien's own, barely seen legendarium. They rarely balance or stabilize, but thrive on ambiguity, discrepancy, and contradiction throughout.

Inside the Lonely Mountain the Dwarves explore the hoard. Again there are echoes of the epic *Beowulf* here when Fili and Kili play harps, but one should not forget that, at Bag End, Fili and Kili played little fiddles, while it was Thorin who played the harp.[98] Yet this is not the hoard of the Dragon in *Beowulf*, for once more the atmosphere of the legendarium hangs over it (not least in Tolkien's famous illustration of Smaug in which a vast urn is inscribed with a Dwarvish curse emblazoned in Elvish letters). The fabled Arkenstone (derived from the Anglo-Saxon *eorclanstan*, 'precious stone' – like the swords, the jewel is named) is clearly analogous to a Silmaril, and Thorin covets it with a lust comparable to that of his murderous forebears.[99] The ghost of Sigurd is here too: Thorin stalks the halls of the Lonely Mountain, succumbing to the same sort of Dragon sickness that corrupted and transformed Fafnir; as Bilbo drily observes, the place still 'stinks of dragon'.[100] Smaug, meanwhile, who speaks in tongues and retaliates against the theft of a cup by razing a town, is slain by the heroic archer Bard, who is advised of Smaug's weak spot by a thrush, who has in turn eavesdropped on Bilbo, and who for his part hurled a stone at the bird. So we are back in a beast fable, with elements of Robin Hood, mass destruction, and bad temper – until the black arrow finds its mark and Smaug crashes like a warplane, destroying Laketown.[101]

If that is not enough, the quest of the Lonely Mountain is also haunted by other texts. The novel is bookended with bureaucracy: the legal contract that Bilbo signed (which Tolkien incidentally transcribed in Elvish letters) in return for a four-teenth share of the treasure, and the absent text of Bilbo's Will, when he is presumed to have died intestate.[102] Bilbo's Will has terminal shortcomings – it does not exist – but it has (or should have) the same purpose as the contract with the Dwarves: it is intended to establish ownership. The contract prepared by 'Thorin & Co.' already presumes ownership of Smaug's hoard, as if Thorin has power of attorney over the Dragon and is writing the wyrm's Will, but the shortcomings of contractual language become immediately apparent when Bilbo purloins the Arken-stone. He knows that trouble will come of it – another instance of Bilbo arguing (or parleying) with himself, with different aspects of his character – but he deliberately misconstrues the contract and gives the Arkenstone to Bard.[103] Bard, not unrea-sonably, asks if the gemstone is Bilbo's to give. Bilbo admits that, no, 'It isn't exactly' – but Bard takes it anyway.[104] Tellingly, the successive negotiations that Bilbo instigates become focused on the object and ownership of the Arkenstone. Moreover, at the summit before the Lonely Mountain between Thorin and Bard, the Elvenking, and Gandalf, Thorin is prepared to buy the stone back for the price set by Bilbo (one-fourteenth of the hoard)

– and so financial negotiations are taken up again, and the practicalities and pragmatics of monetary profit remain part of the narrative. Even the level-headed character Bard is attracted by the prospect of unguarded gold after he shoots down Smaug.

Talk of the Arkenstone passes between several characters, but the Arkenstone itself is only passed on four times in the book: from Thráin to Smaug to Bilbo to Bard (guarded by Gandalf), and thence to Thorin – who only receives it once he is already dead. It also physically travels very little compared with an equally iconic object such as the One Ring. However, the story of its possession is strikingly similar: Thráin inherits the Arkenstone; it is forcibly taken from him by Smaug, who is then killed; Bilbo finds it but lies about it; Bilbo then gives it to Bard, who returns it to the mountain in which it was unearthed. As for the One Ring, as we shall see Sauron forges the Ring, but it is forcibly taken from him by Isildur, who is then killed; Gollum finds the Ring and loses it; Bilbo finds it but lies about it; Bilbo later gives it to Frodo, who returns it to the mountain in which it was originally forged. Bilbo is central to both histories, and plays exactly the same part in each – a fortuitous, duplicitous, and yet decisive part. This is the key moral issue of the book: Bilbo lies and cheats over the Ring, and steals the Arkenstone. Is he justified in doing so?

To the end, then. Bilbo's return journey is something of an anticlimax. It is told very quickly, as quickly as Sir Gawain's brisk return to the court of King Arthur after his meeting with the Green Knight.[105] But there is a poignant moment of reflection in Bilbo's poem 'Roads Go Ever Ever On', which, when he utters it, causes Gandalf to exclaim that Bilbo is not the Hobbit he once was.[106] It is raining as Bilbo arrives back in Hobbiton, and even here Tolkien has a final unsentimental twist to add: there is another unexpected party of people in Bag End, mirroring the very first chapter. Having helped to take possession of a Dragon hoard, Bilbo is now in danger of losing all of his own belongings: being presumed dead, his assets are being auctioned off. If he was ever suspected of being 'queer' before he ran off with the Dwarves, he is definitely considered to be 'queer' thereafter.[107]

• • •

The Hobbit is a tall tale, made taller by the immense accumulation of disparate details and perplexing traces from sundry sources. This creates a teetering narrative full of jarring, discordant clashes that become more and more thrilling the less one tries to force order and certainty onto the text. It is a mash-up, a most unexpected journey. There are no anchors among all this chaos – no reliable narrator, no moral certainty, no God – so Bilbo becomes a free agent, free to express his own mass of contradictions. That is one reason why the One Ring is Bilbo's ideal object: he can pass (almost) invisibly, he can be anything he wants to be because he is ultimately blank. The one thing clear about the Ring is that it cannot be put to good: what moral utility does invisibility have? Bilbo quickly learns that it is suited to creeping about in the shadows and killing things (hardly making a fair fight – although he does, of course, famously pity Gollum), as well as theft on a quite industrial scale.[108]

C.S. Lewis, who anonymously reviewed *The Hobbit* twice, noted the characteristic motley tones of the book, writing that it begins like a children's story and ends like a tragic Norse saga – what Tolkien himself might have described as an anti-classical Northern elegy – and this is part of its attraction and strength.[109] It is not classically 'tragic' in the Aristotleian sense (which was in any case a category reserved for dramas), but it does have a rising sense of doom, and in his heroism, his problems of leadership, and his Dragon sickness, Thorin is in some ways a tragic character – and becomes more so once Smaug has been slain.

Character is expressed through action – we never really get inside Thorin's head, for example, and Bilbo is the only character we really know – and the plot hardly evokes pity and fear or the catharsis of those emotions. But Thorin can, in Aristotle's terms, be seen to fall into adversity 'not through evil and depravity, but through some kind of error [*hamartia*]', and there are key moments of reversal, recognition, and suffering: all three occurring at the parley over the Arkenstone – it is there that Thorin's fate is fixed.[110]

The novel is also pervaded with darkness. In the first chapter the Dwarves sing, *'In places deep, where dark things sleep'* and Bilbo listens as 'The dark filled all the room'; his unexpected guests muttering 'Dark for dark business!' The key chapter in the book, of course, is 'Riddles in the Dark'; Gollum is 'as dark as darkness', and the answer to one of the riddles (*'It lies behind stars and under hills'*) is 'dark'. At the Lonely Mountain, 'It seemed as if darkness flowed out like a vapour from the hole in the mountain-side, and deep darkness in which nothing could be seen lay before their eyes, a yawning mouth leading in and down.'[111] Many scenes are set at night (the Trolls, Rivendell, the death of Smaug), underground (the Misty Mountains, the Halls of the Elvenking, the Lonely Mountain), or simply in the dark (Mirkwood). The mood too is often dark: although the Trolls are comical they are also aiming to eat the Dwarves – although it has to be said that children's literature and fairy stories in general are full of cannibalism, such as the Brothers Grimm tale 'The Juniper Tree', itself quoted by Tolkien.[112] But the Trolls are not the only flesh-eaters here: Gollum wants to eat Bilbo, the Goblins threaten to eat the Dwarves, and the Spiders have them wrapped up to go as fresh meat. Meanwhile, there are dark episodes such as Beorn executing and mutilating his prisoners, and the wholly unexpected deaths of Thorin, Fili, and Kili – as well as the Master of Laketown, who, rather horribly, flees with his gold and dies of starvation in the wasteland, 'deserted by his companions'.[113]

Arrestingly, for a book about wizards and wizardry, the Ring is one of the very few instances of magic in Bilbo's adventures. The supernatural is significantly underplayed in *The Hobbit* – Gandalf can mimic voices, and create light and fire (and fireworks), but to summon the Dwarves to Bag End he simply vandalizes Bilbo's front door with a mark that Bilbo can neither read nor understand, and then pummels it out. By the time Tolkien wrote *The Lord of the Rings* it was evident that Bilbo had been selected to serve a higher purpose, but at the time of *The Hobbit* the experience will be 'very good for you – and profitable too, very likely, if you ever get over it'.[114] As we learn very little about the Necromancer, only the Ring itself is utterly supernatural, although it does not confer complete invisibility – so even here there is an uncertainty, a hesitancy in its powers. Although Tolkien is often accused of presenting absolutes of good and evil in his narratives, this book actually questions such reductive assessments at their roots: good and evil not only waver in *The Hobbit*, they happily swap sides. Gollum has a degree of honour, Bilbo is a recidivist thief, Thorin becomes a Dragon-sick tinpot tyrant. Smaug is certainly evil, but is also a shrewd wordsmith, if cunning, greedy, and vain – and only, in the end, acting just as Dragons do. And what of the oppressive Elvenking? Or the opportunist Dain?

If the Ring is not a supernatural panacea, it does, like the Arkenstone, fast-track character by encouraging Bilbo's career of crime and duplicity, and so is anything but an inanimate artefact. But then inanimate artefacts, objects, are often characterized in the book. Sting and the other blades are named, recognized, and feared, and the Troll's garrulous purse certainly has character. Riddles, which permeate *The Hobbit*, often employ personification, and if personification suggests that the Human (or at least the humanoid) is the measure of sentience and autonomy, it is also worth remembering that the Human is radically sidelined in *The Hobbit* from the very title (remembering the function of the definite article, 'the'). We do not meet any Human characters until Laketown (Gandalf, as a wizard, being a minor deity), and even there only the Bard and the Master are sketched out. Beorn is, as I have emphasized, a monstrous amalgam, his otherness rightly highlighted in the films *The Desolation of Smaug* (2013) and *The Battle of the Five Armies*. This relegation of the Human reflects the attitudes of the Anglo-Saxons – who, living among the mighty ruins of a vanished civilization, believed that the world was in terminal decline – but is also highly suggestive for today. Where does this leave us?

The short answer is: looking for more answers, which we may find in the sequel to *The Hobbit*, described in the following chapters. The longer answer embraces the removal of the Human and Human agency: what replaces the Human in Middle-Earth, and what does this mean for us today? Perhaps Tolkien himself was ultimately right when he wrote to his publisher Stanley Unwin in 1947: '*The Hobbit* was after all not as simple as it seemed'.[115]

THREE

The Ambiguity of Evil

And they shall look unto the earth; and behold trouble
and darkness, dimness of anguish; and they shall be driven
to darkness.

Isaiah 8:22

For all his 'literary terraforming', or 'world building', Tolkien's
works are full of loose ends, cul-de-sacs (literally, in 'Bag End'),
ambiguities, contradictions, undeveloped details, unexplained
elements, unsolved mysteries, and doubts. Often, things simply do not add up, or even make sense. This is in no way a
fault or a shortcoming; it is, rather, one of the great strengths
of Tolkien's work. Tolkien learnt from the anonymous author
of the Anglo-Saxon epic poem *Beowulf* that brief and elusive
references to a wider historical or legendary background can
create a highly suggestive texture, giving the impression of great
depth and substance. *The Lord of the Rings* in particular brims
with tantalizing references to earlier epochs and other realms,
unfinished tales of shadowy heroes and mysterious quests.

Sometimes the characters themselves ask for more information – nearly always fruitlessly. Much is forgotten in Middle-Earth, and key characters such as Gandalf and Sméagol forget even their own names; memory is unreliable, knowledge is inconsistent, truth is contingent on circumstances and interpretation. At deeper levels, world views of different individuals, even societies, are incompatible and irreconcilable, and some characters even seem to inhabit different worlds, tangential or independent of Middle-Earth, unbothered and unaffected by the pressing issues of the time. Again, this is a strength of the work: Tolkien has a capacity to describe different understandings simultaneously without insisting on the ultimate primacy of one version of events. Indeed, these deliberate incompatibilities could be described as Shakespearean, as Shakespeare characteristically presents his characters not only as holding different values but also, in consequence, making sense of the world in conflicting ways. If, typically, Tolkien dismissed Shakespeare, the two writers do share certain qualities and, as we shall see, there are also frequent references to Shakespeare in Tolkien's work.

The following two chapters will examine, then, how *The Lord of the Rings* was written, before charting the peculiar ambiguities of the text. It has to be said that for the vast majority of readers, *The Lord of the Rings* is anything but ambiguous: it is a quest narrative in which a variety of characters travel through a richly imagined and extraordinarily detailed landscape that, despite being in the realm of fantasy, bears a deep grain of authenticity. Tolkien meticulously describes flora and fauna, architecture and decor, language and culture, even the food and drink of the different peoples encountered. Histories, societies, and manners are underwritten by six appendices, and the geography of Middle-Earth is carefully mapped – all of which is relished by Tolkien's enthusiastic readers: *The Lord of the Rings* is an immersive reading experience. But the book is also in many ways unresolved, undecided, and indeterminate. It is not, to be accurate, a quest but an anti-quest, concerned with losing rather than finding; characters are complex, contradictory, and inconsistent individuals; places are riddled with questions and wreathed in mystery. The scrupulous attention to maps and timings and narrative logic is deft sleight of hand by the author, drawing conscious attention away from the inexplicable oddities of the text so that they compost down into a rich loam, a deep texture that teems with unexpected and beguiling dilemmas.

To take two examples of Tolkien deliberately disturbing the internal consistency of his work – one minor, one highly significant. When Frodo, Sam, and Pippin leave Hobbiton at dusk on an autumn evening they spend their first night sleeping beneath a fir tree. A Fox stops to look at them and sniffs. He thinks it odd, and all of a sudden we are in a beast fable: 'Hobbits! . . . Well, what next? . . . There's something mighty queer behind this.' But what is behind this, he never discovers. A narrator intrudes – 'He was quite right, but he never found out any more about it' – and that is the only thinking Fox in the entire novel, and the last we hear about it.[1] It is as if a brief glimpse is given of a thriving animal world scarcely affected by the Ring. Another, far more prominent and interventionist figure untouched by the Ring is the bemusing character Tom Bombadil (of whom more in the Conclusion). Bombadil plays a pivotal rule in the plot, but seems to be master of his own domain and is completely unmindful of the Ring. With telling perspicacity, Gandalf responds to the idea that Bombadil could guard the Ring as it has no power over him: 'if he were given the Ring, he would soon forget it, or most likely throw it away'.[2] After three hundred pages of growing anxiety and perplexity over the Ring that began the book, Tom Bombadil for one is utterly indifferent to it. Middle-Earth is not a comprehensive environment – at its edges are different concerns, other worlds of experience and reality.

The Fog of War

On 19 December 1937, Tolkien wrote to his editor at Allen & Unwin to inform him that he had written the first chapter of a new story about Hobbits. However, it would be over sixteen years before this sequel to *The Hobbit* was published – and even then only the first volume of a three-volume work. *The Fellowship of the Ring* was published on 29 July 1954, *The Two Towers* followed in the same year on 11 November, but it was little short of twelve months before the concluding volume, *The Return of the King,* left the press on 20 October 1955, having been delayed by its elaborate appendices. It was, then, almost a year and a quarter before the entire book – a single work – was fully available. It cannot be said too often that *The Lord of the Rings* is not a 'trilogy' in the strict sense of the word as the volumes do not stand alone: it is a three-volume novel, as Tolkien pointed out to his American publisher.[3] However, this misnomer has become inseparable from the book (and subsequently from Peter Jackson's films). Yet despite the lengthy wait for the story to be concluded, *The Fellowship of the Ring* won immediate public acclaim from Tolkien's close friend C.S. Lewis as 'lightning from a clear sky... an advance or revolution: the conquest of new territory', and in 1957 Tolkien was awarded the International Fantasy Award for the achievement.[4]

Why did *The Lord of the Rings* take so long to write? A pedant might point out that the author's level of productivity was under ninety words a day during those sixteen years – but of course Tolkien was, as ever, involved in many other things at the same time, and there was soon a world war to contend with as well. During these years, Tolkien unsurprisingly continued to teach and supervise, mark exam papers (including batches sent from New Zealand), and fulfil his burdensome administrative responsibilities at Oxford. In 1938, he was revising *Farmer Giles* and discussing how the illustrations in *Mr Bliss* could be printed, he scripted and recorded a programme for BBC radio ('Anglo-Saxon Verse' for *Poetry Will Out*, 14 January 1938), continued work on the revised translation of *Beowulf* (taken over by C.L. Wrenn before the end of the year), and assisted two colleagues on editions of Middle English texts. He continued to attend meetings of the Inklings and regularly attended dinners of The Society, a club for Oxford academics of which he had been a member since about 1935, as well as the Catenian Association, a support group for Catholic men. He also dressed as Geoffrey Chaucer for a gala at the Oxford Playhouse and recited 'The Nun's Priest's Tale' from memory. But by now he was suffering from overwork and dealing with financial worries brought on by the health issues and the educational needs of various family members, and was forced to rest under doctor's orders; he duly wrote more of *The Lord of the Rings* and started a Celtic fairy story 'King of the Green Dozen' (never finished).

The next year war loomed ever more threateningly, and Tolkien spent four days training as a codebreaker for the Foreign Office at the Government Code and Cypher School. Although he was considered 'keen', he was informed in October that he was not, at present, required.[5] He delivered his much-admired lecture 'On Fairy-Stories' at the University of St Andrews (later published in 1947), resumed work on his collaborative edition of the *Ancrene Wisse*, and was now earning extra money by marking Civil Service exams. His gala performance this year was Chaucer's 'Reeve's Tale' in Northern dialect, again from memory (if abridged), and again dressed as the poet. Despite continuing in poor health due to a head injury and concussion – and with Edith also unwell and later in the year requiring an operation – he continued writing and rewriting *The Lord of the Rings* and began to map out episodes. Thousands of words were written, and revised, and discarded as he felt his way through the story, but he eventually succeeded in producing a recognizable text of volume one. Then Britain declared war on Nazi Germany, and the University of Oxford quickly became a centre of operations: Pembroke College, for example – Tolkien's own college – was partly requisitioned by the Army and the Ministry of Agriculture. Meanwhile, at some point in the year he went with Lewis to see Disney's version of *Snow White and the Seven Dwarfs*, which had been released in Britain in 1938.

Being forty-seven years old at the outbreak of war in 1939, Tolkien himself was ineligible for military service (conscription was ordered on men between the ages of eighteen and forty-one), but he served as an air-raid warden, probably from 1940 when he learnt that he would not be needed as a cryptographer. His university duties rose steeply as a result of the war – not least by having to overhaul the English Faculty education programme to provide 'War Degrees' – but he was nevertheless finally able to finish his lengthy preface to the 'Clark Hall' *Beowulf* (published in July 1940) – for which he received welcome payment. He also worked steadily on *The Lord of the Rings* from mid-1940 through 1941, the years in which Britain suffered a succession of terrible air raids against civilian targets – although Oxford (like Cambridge) escaped being targeted. He wrote his novel without a clear plan, instead discovering as he wrote the shape of the story, the threads of narrative, and the role of characters – and by January 1942 the Company of the Ring had found refuge in Lothlórien. Because of wartime paper shortages, Tolkien would often draft in pencil, and then rewrite in ink and erase his earlier version. His vision for how the story could progress also became clearer, and drafting, redrafting, and redrafting again, by mid-1942 he had reached Isengard, where he found himself mystified by the appearance of the *palantír* (later finding it to be one of the seven 'Seeing Stones' of Númenor). Remarkably, at the same time he was also revising his translation of 'The Lay of Aotrou and Itroun' and composed 'Leaf by Niggle' – an allegory that seems to express anxieties at not being able to finish either *The Lord of the Rings* or his manifold scholarly projects (both the 'Lay' and 'Niggle' were published in 1945).[6] He settled his account at Blackwell's Bookshop in Oxford by giving Basil Blackwell his translation of *Pearl* on the understanding that Blackwell would publish it; there was still talk of *Mr Bliss* and *Farmer Giles* being published by Allen & Unwin; and Tolkien continued to write the occasional poem. Most significantly, though, by the end of 1942 he was looking forward to finishing *The Lord of the Rings* in early 1943. Meanwhile, the privations of rationing were somewhat alleviated when the family acquired a brood of chickens to provide fresh eggs – as well as giving Tolkien an additional tedious job in hen husbandry.

In 1943, he began editing and then translating another Middle English poem, 'Sir Orfeo', which the next year he taught to officer cadets taking academic courses at Oxford alongside their training; he also became an external examiner for Allied prisoners-of-war studying in Germany and Italy. By this time his son Michael had distinguished himself in the Royal Air Force before being invalided from the service following the failed Dieppe Raid of 1942, and his younger son Christopher was in basic training – again for the RAF. In April 1944, Tolkien returned to *The Lord of the Rings*, determined to finish it in moments between his teaching of students and cadets, his unremitting administrative burdens, and his air warden duties. By May, Frodo and Sam were in Ithilien, at the borders of Mordor. He read the drafts to Inkling friends Lewis and Charles Williams – Lewis blinking back the tears when he heard the chapter 'The Choices of Master Samwise'. Tolkien, believing that the end was now in sight, worked increasingly late into the night – but in fact he was only two-thirds of the way through the book. Work stalled for a number of months; months became years.

The war with Germany ended on 7 May 1945; his friend

and confidant Charles Williams died unexpectedly a week later; just over a month after that Tolkien was elected to the Merton Professorship of English Language and Literature (which unfortunately doubled his lecture load for a year until a replacement was found for his previous position). Then, at the end of 1945 he started writing *The Notion Club Papers*, a philosophical novel that continued the themes of *The Lost Road*, but as a series of discussions based on the conversations and characters of the Inklings. *The Notion Club* is an odd, mixed-genre book, equally influenced by the scholastic disputation of the mediaeval poem *The Owl and the Nightingale* (c.1189–1216) and Thomas Carlyle's zany and unconventional novel *Sartor Resartus* (1836).[7] *The Notion Club* is doggedly discursive; the non-linear narrative proceeds by digressions along very peculiar lines: at one point, for example, the club archivist Nicholas Guildford drolly observes that 'The Moon is very parochial'(!).[8]

The Notion Club took Tolkien back to his story of 'The Fall of Númenor' and not only inspired various related poems and revisions of earlier verse, but even a new language – Adûnaic – and a new perspective on the inundation of Númenor: 'The Drowning of Anadûnê'; but this was all effectively an evasion of *The Lord of the Rings*. Due to years of overwork his health remained poor, and his doctor recommended a term's leave – which Tolkien considered simply impossible in the understaffed and straitened university of post-war Oxford, with the result that his ensuing years were dogged by ill-health. Instead he took a three-week break in Stonyhurst, Lancashire, and continued to tinker with his Númenórean texts. It was not until September 1947 that he returned to *The Lord of the Rings* – but only briefly. Writing the last third of the book promised to be an extremely demanding and intricate task; it also required him to make changes to *The Hobbit* – something that Rayner Unwin, his publisher's son, had noticed was necessary after reading a draft of Book I of *The Lord of the Rings*. So he busied himself with meeting the many other demands regularly made on him.

However, in August 1948 an opportunity arose to complete his novel. Tolkien's son Michael and his family went on holiday, and Tolkien was able to spend a month on writing retreat in their house, Payables Farm in Woodcote, located eighteen and a half miles south of Oxford. Free from teaching, marking, the English Faculty, correspondents, and chickens, he focused singlemindedly on his book, and before he returned to Oxford on 14 September he had completed the first full draft of *The Lord of the Rings* – it was some half a million words long and, with supplementary material, it would become even longer. The exhilaration of finishing the first draft gave his work a momentum that carried him through the lengthy process of revision and adding auxiliary material such as 'The Tale of Years'– his chronicle of events in the Second and Third Ages of Middle-Earth. Gratifyingly, back in Oxford he received a set of sample illustrations for *Farmer Giles* of which he approved; they were drawn by Pauline Baynes who would go on to provide cover designs and poster-sized maps for *The Lord of the Rings*. Tolkien was still extremely busy with professional academic concerns, but work now accelerated on *Farmer Giles of Ham*, and although he still had very little time to authorize the layout and correct proof sheets, this slim volume was nevertheless published in October 1949.

That year Tolkien was granted his first sabbatical leave after nearly two decades of full-time academic service, and he took the opportunity to rationalize his commitments. He relinquished the Clarendon Chaucer and committed to revising the edition of *Sir Gawain and the Green Knight* he had first completed with E.V. Gordon, as well as bringing to press his late friend and colleague's edition of *Pearl*. He visited the Republic of Ireland for the first time – twice in the same year, in fact

– as an external examiner, and he returned regularly over the next few years. But most importantly, he finished typing out *The Lord of the Rings* (which he had to do himself) and gave the draft to Lewis, who read it in less than a month and judged it to be 'almost unequalled in the whole range of narrative art known to me'.[9] At the same time, news of *The Lord of the Rings* had reached the ever-open ears of other publishers, and Collins were now angling for the book. Tolkien struck up a special relationship with Milton Waldman, an editor there, and wrote to him at length about the legendarium. Tolkien was frustrated that Allen & Unwin had all-but rejected the various versions of 'The Silmarillion' and associated tales he had discussed with them, and now saw an opportunity to publish *The Lord of the Rings* and *The Silmarillion* together (even though, realistically, this would probably have meant adding at least another decade to the date of first possible publication...). Indeed, in one letter Tolkien was uncharacteristically dismissive of his original publisher's long-term patience and forbearance – but then he had remained in what amounted to genteel academic poverty for all of his working life and yet nevertheless completed an unparalleled work of fiction. Waldman's guarded enthusiasm and Tolkien's conviction that the 'Quenta Silmarillion' was effectively complete created something of a false hope for both of them. Predictably, Tolkien started to rewrite comprehensively the text of the legendarium rather than finalize *The Lord of the Rings*.

Tolkien now wished to be released from what he saw as a moral obligation to publish *The Lord of the Rings* with Allen & Unwin, so began pressing for the simultaneous publication of 'The Silmarillion'; Stanley Unwin reasonably pointed out that they had never been sent a full and complete manuscript of 'The Silmarillion'. Relations soured, and the situation was exacerbated by Tolkien's poor health at the time (having had all of his teeth extracted). At Collins, meanwhile, Waldman airily told Tolkien to cut *The Lord of the Rings* and then disappeared to Italy, leaving Tolkien adrift at Collins where there were no other comparable supporters of his work. As for Tolkien, in correcting proofs for the American edition of *The Hobbit* he was encountering various misunderstandings in revisions he had requested three years previously. Moreover, he was now pondering the relationship between this book and its effective sequel – the now-dormant *Lord of the Rings* – and whether his changes to *The Hobbit* were justifiable in a book that already had an enthusiastic readership. Untangling these problems would help to repair relations with Allen & Unwin, who were now also interested in Tolkien's translations of *Sir Gawain*, *Exodus*, and *Pearl*. In addition to this, Tolkien was also helping Ida Gordon edit the text of her late husband's edition of *Pearl*, which was published in 1953 under Gordon's sole name – despite his extensive work for the edition, Tolkien refused to be credited as co-editor. He gradually returned to rewriting the legendarium and getting 'The Silmarillion' into a publishable state – which in turn entailed minor changes to *The Lord of the Rings*.

The second edition of *The Hobbit* was published in July 1951, and at the end of the year Tolkien tried to renew his negotiations with Collins by writing at great length to Waldman – not least as Allen & Unwin remained interested in publishing *The Lord of the Rings*. By April 1952, however, he became uncomfortably aware that Waldman was the only real advocate of his work at Collins, who were baulking at the length of *The Lord of the Rings* (in part due to the post-war paper shortage) and who therefore had no intention of taking 'The Silmarillion' as well. He was wholly disheartened, on top of which he still had taxing university duties, and bouts of illness – including fibrositis and neuritis of his arm that severely slowed his writing. He apologetically approached Allen & Unwin again in the hope that at least *The Lord of the Rings* could be reconsidered, despite his misguided courtship of Collins and repeated insistence that 'The Silmarillion' needed to be published simultaneously. He abandoned reworking 'The Silmarillion' and started revising *The Lord of the Rings* – a book begun some fifteen years earlier – paying particular attention to its internal consistency in the chronology, and having the brilliant idea of including both versions of Bilbo's fateful encounter with Gollum as evidence of the Hobbit's deceitfulness prompted by the Ring. The revised version was collected by Rayner Unwin, son of Stanley Unwin who, aged ten, had read and written for his father a reader's report of the nascent *Hobbit*. Rayner Unwin immediately began preparing a budget for publishing the book, but wrote frankly to his father that it would be a gamble and might lose the firm £1,000 (equivalent to over £30,000 today); his father replied, '*If* you believe it is a work of genius, *then* you may lose a thousand pounds.'[10] Rayner Unwin calculated costs and offered Tolkien a profit-sharing deal rather than an advance, planning for three hardback volumes. Tolkien was euphoric at the offer; he had four months to deliver the final version of the first volume, which, appropriately enough, was due on 25 March 1953: Ladyday, the date on which the One Ring was destroyed and the 'Fourth Age' of Middle-Earth began. The two of them now treated the manuscript of the book with extreme care, reluctant to trust it to the Royal Mail and preferring to transport it themselves: it had become an artefact, precious to them.

Tolkien did not, of course, meet the deadline. In addition to revising *The Lord of the Rings* he spent time finishing his translation of *Sir Gawain* and prepared a version for a radio broadcast, and had also finally submitted his article 'The Homecoming of Beorhtnoth Beorhthelm's Son' to an academic journal, published in 1953. This was a dramatic dialogue 'on chivalry and common sense' set in the immediate aftermath of the Battle of Maldon (fought in 991) and the subject of a celebrated Anglo-

Saxon poem on the nature of heroism and courage that colours the mood of the battle scenes in *The Lord of the Rings*.[11] His administrative workload remained high, he was moving house, and Edith had been unwell again. Nevertheless, it is noticeable how often Tolkien was thanked in academic publications on which he had commented and advised – he was extraordinarily conscientious in assisting research students and colleagues, and was not only acknowledged in assisting with Anglo-Saxon and mediaeval works, but was also thanked in studies such as B.L. Joseph's *Elizabethan Acting*.[12] Yet on 12 April he did send the first two books (volume one of *The Lord of the Rings*) to Rayner Unwin. He was less than a month late – a mere heartbeat in the Tolkien calendar. Tolkien received the first proofs at the end of July, but was dismayed to discover that the printers had taken it on themselves to correct his characteristic spellings of 'dwarves' and 'elven' to 'dwarfs' and 'elfin', which led to further delays – but it was nevertheless nearly ready for the public.[13]

Tolkien proofed, revised, drafted and redrafted his illustrations, and also discussed titles for each volume – although he was never entirely happy with these, stating that they were 'a fudge thought necessary for publication'.[14] The maps, which Tolkien knew were essential, had proved impossible to complete to his satisfaction and in the end were redrawn by his son Christopher over Christmas 1953. The completed second volume was delivered on 1 September 1953, and on the same day Tolkien visited the BBC to discuss his translation of *Sir Gawain and the Green Knight*, broadcast in four parts between 6 and 30 December of that year and oft repeated. It was a desperately frantic time: on 27 January 1954, for instance, he was sent no fewer than eighty-six pages of proofreader's queries concerning *The Fellowship of the Ring*, and more queries arrived within the week. A design for the dust jacket was overdue, as was another map and the blurb for the back cover; the proofs of the second volume had begun to arrive and the final volume needed to be completed, but Tolkien did take the time to show off the proof sheets of the first volume at meetings of the Inklings.[15] Volume three was indeed delivered on 8 May 1954 – but without the 150 pages of appendices covering dates, languages and alphabets, family trees, and minutiae. Much of this (such as Samwise Gamgee's ancestry) was really only of interest to Tolkien himself – and some of it distracted him in fruitless digressions – but its necessary inclusion underlines the increasingly experimental nature of *The Lord of the Rings*. In any case, the appendices also contained remarkable supplementary material such as ten heartrending pages on the love between Aragorn and Arwen. More importantly for a twentieth-century audience, these appendices are the core of the Amazon Prime Video TV series in their outline of the history of Númenor. It is unsurprising, then, that Tolkien probably briefly returned to his history of Númenor among all his other commitments in order to incorporate these changes.

On 14 June 1954 Tolkien received an advance copy of *The Fellowship of the Ring*: 'It was', he wrote to his editor, 'a great moment'.[16] He was exhausted – 'nearly run out' – but he still had to complete the appendices. This was thorny work as it had consequences for *The Hobbit* as well, and it took him another six months of a 'crushingly laborious year'.[17] But the publication of *The Fellowship* was a turning point after which there was no going back for *The Lord of the Rings*; Tolkien even subscribed to a newspaper cutting service in September 1954 to stay abreast of reviews and comments on his work. On 11 November, the appendices to the third volume still unfinished, the second volume – *The Two Towers* – was published, and within a few months both *The Fellowship of the Ring* and *The Two Towers* had gone into second printings (in hardback, premium price volumes). It was 1955 and the reading public was eagerly awaiting *The Return of the King*, but bizarrely, Tolkien briefly returned to one of the stories of the legendarium – undoubtedly a displacement activity as the completion of *The Lord of the Rings* was imminent, whether the author could accept it or not. He prevaricated over the appendices as fans of the first two volumes sent letters inquiring into the background of Middle-Earth, and was in danger of being overwhelmed by the detail of his imagined world. Yet at the same time he busied himself with almost pointless minutiae, such as adding a reference to *The Lord of the Rings* to the Preface of *The Hobbit*. Yet it was, perhaps, a significant concession: in print at least, the two works were being drawn ever closer together. Work on the appendices consequently continued into 1955, alongside Tolkien's relentless university commitments, such as his election as Sub-Warden of Merton College. Time had all-but run out, and readers were desperate to know of the plight of Frodo and Sam, Merry and Pippin, and the rest of the Company of the Ring. So it was that by the end of March 1955, Tolkien was, reluctantly, finishing what was his lifetime *magnum opus*, and on which his son Christopher was again engaged in a twenty-four-hour feat of cartography for yet another map.[18]

The Homecoming was broadcast by BBC radio on 3 December 1954 (after the first two volumes of *The Lord of the Rings* had been published), following a translation of *The Battle of Maldon* poem itself. This was read by Michael Hordern – the consummate Shakespearean actor who went on to play Gandalf in the 1981 BBC radio version of *The Lord of the Rings* – and the whole production was considered accomplished enough to be re-aired in June 1955.[19] Tolkien was (perhaps predictably) disappointed by the actors' (not Hordern's) delivery of alliterative verse – nevertheless, it is here that Middle-Earth on the radio really begins. Thus it was that on 25 January 1955 the BBC wrote to Tolkien proposing a radio version of *The Fellowship of the Ring* in six parts. Tolkien considered the proposal 'with deep misgivings', but was prepared to follow his publisher's advice and even assisted with the script.[20] The six-part production was broadcast in half-hour episodes in November, and was praised by the *Observer* newspaper. By now *The Return of the King* was, thankfully, in press but its proofing, especially of the appendices, cost Tolkien hours of sleep – indeed, anyone familiar with the tables of Elven script in the appendices will appreciate the complexities of trying to typeset this in the 1950s as part of an experimental novel.[21] Tolkien carried on regardless, finally sending the corrected proof sheets back on 25 July, before going on holiday to Italy – or 'Gondor', as he called it, Middle-Earth having engulfed his imagination.[22] *The Return of the King* was published on 22 October 1955. His work was complete.

So, that is why it took so long to finish. Tolkien was anything but idle, but he was profoundly over-committed in multiple areas. In the face of almost insurmountable and unceasing difficulties it is a miracle that *The Lord of the Rings* was ever finished at all, and then ever published. One cannot but help feeling that the lines of 'Northern Courage' quoted in the Anglo-Saxon poem *The Battle of Maldon* and which form the heart of his drama *The Homecoming of Beorhtnoth Beorhthelm's Son* had a peculiar bearing on Tolkien's life at this time:

Hige sceal þē heardra,   heorte þē cēnre,
mōd sceal þē māre,   þē ūre mægen lȳtlað

'Will shall be the sterner, heart the bolder, spirit the greater as our strength lessens'.[23] But the final, protracted push had drained him. He was back in the tumult of university term, and although Allen & Unwin had immediate plans to publish 'The Silmarillion', Tolkien could not find the strength to embark upon another marathon.

Ancient Modernisms

The story begins in darkness. A murmuring voice tells of the forging of the Great Rings, and the One Ring. Or the story begins in idyllic sunshine with a discovery on a riverbed of a ring, the One Ring. Three films (*The Lord of the Rings*, 1978; *The Fellowship of the Ring*, 2001; and *The Return of the King*, 2003) begin with the Ring, the One Ring, but the book itself does not. Tolkien's *Lord of the Rings* begins with a purposefully pompous and indeed rather Dickensian announcement of a birthday party, while the story of the forging of the Rings of Power and the succeeding account of the loss and rediscovery of the One Ring in the River Anduin is buried in the second chapter. Tolkien's concern in the first chapter is with echoing and inverting the opening of *The Hobbit*, from 'An Unexpected Party' to 'A Long-Expected Party', in which the Ring plays only a cameo – if conspicuous – part in Bilbo Baggins's celebrations and stratagems. The story begins, in other words, in village festivity, among flowers and fireworks and the conviviality of the leisured classes.

But *The Lord of the Rings* does not in fact begin with Bilbo's eleventy-first birthday. Before the first page of the narrative there is a map of 'A Part of The Shire' printed in two colours in the hardback editions and, as mentioned, drawn by Tolkien's son Christopher. Preceding that is a 6,500-word prologue on the ethnography of Hobbits, the history of pipe-smoking, the governance of The Shire, and a highly abbreviated account of the events of *The Hobbit* (focusing on Bilbo's apparent acquisition of the Ring).[24] Preceding the Prologue in the first edition is an almost impenetrable Foreword in which Tolkien ruminates on his (fictitious) sources; in the second and subsequent editions this Foreword was expanded to become less opaque in its reflections, and in the course of which Tolkien abruptly dismissed any suggestions that the novel was allegorical. The note on sources was itself expanded and added to the Prologue. But that is not all: preceding the Foreword is the eight-line verse on the Great Rings, and preceding the verse is the title-page designed by Tolkien and bordered with his idiosyncratic calligraphy of angular Dwarvish runes and flowing Elvish script.[25] Where does the book begin? Tolkien even devised the book's dust jacket and had a hand in the design of the gold blocking on the spine, which places the title within a stylization of the One Ring.

These are 'paratexts': framing or supplementary texts, sometimes provided by another hand. Although the word 'paratext' itself was not coined until a year after Tolkien's death, it is a common feature of two sorts of publications: academic editions and children's books. Mary Salu's translation of the mediaeval spiritual manual the *Ancrene Riwle* ('guide for anchoresses'), which appeared in the same year as *The Return of the King* (1955), begins with a preface by Tolkien himself, followed by an introduction by Gerard Sitwell, and a note by the translator. A.A. Milne's *Winnie-the-Pooh* (published in 1926, the year that Tolkien returned to Oxford), meanwhile, has a decorated title-page, a dedicatory poem, an introduction, and a map (drawn by E.H. Shepard) before the first chapter, which then begins with a brief framing scene. Likewise, the second edition of *The Hobbit* (1951) has Thrór's map, a runic title-page, and a philological and orthographical note before the first chapter.

Tolkien's evident love of paratexts is evident in his other works such as the Chaucerian *Farmer Giles of Ham*, which has a Latin title-page and a 'translator's' foreword, and his book of fairy verse *The Adventures of Tom Bombadil*, which has an 'editor's' preface.[26] But it is at the end of *The Lord of the Rings* that these paratexts make their presence most dramatically felt in no fewer than six appendices that not only provide numerous additional passages on the characters and dynasties that feature in the main text, but also a detailed chronology (containing

yet more supporting detail), genealogies, calendrical information, phonetic and orthographic tables, and a linguistic essay
that concludes with its own postscript. Many of these appendices encourage readers to re-read and re-evaluate the narrative
they have just finished because they provide new information
and fresh perspectives on characters and events. Moreover, the
linguistic essay, 'The Languages and Peoples of the Third Age',
includes a section on translation, in which Tolkien 'admits' to
having translated the proper nouns of his story from Westron
(the 'Common Speech') into a more familiar English idiom: he
has, in other words, 'Englished' all the names.[27] So The Shire is
not really The Shire, but *Sûza*; Sam (short for Samwise, from
the Anglo-Saxon *samwîs*) is not really Sam but Ban (*Banazîr*);
and Gamgee is really *Galbasi* – all words based on the ancient
Gothic language. In the final pages of *The Lord of the Rings*, then,
Tolkien completely inverts the reader's experience of The Shire,
Sam, everything, by revealing the alien unfamiliarity of what
for nigh-on fifteen hundred pages has become recognizably
familiar. It is a stunning, almost literal *mise-en-abîme*: a sudden
and infinite regress. Middle-Earth is, it transpires, unreachably
remote after all and abruptly recedes into the primal uncanniness of a mysterious lost language:

> Atta unsar þu in himinam weihnai namo þein·
> qimai þiudinassus þeins· wairþai wilja þeins·
> swe in himina jah ana airþai·[28]

Then there's the index prepared by professional indexer Nancy
Smith and Tolkien's secretary (and later daughter-in-law) Bail-
lie Klass for the second edition (1966), and finally Christopher
Tolkien's particoloured maps, which in the hardback editions
unfold to up to eight times the size of a page. While nearly all
scholarly works have indices and many have appendices as well,

among the very few novels with indices most are comic novels (Isaac D'Israeli's *Flim Flams!*, 1805), or ironically scholarly
(Virginia Woolf's pseudo-biography *Orlando*, 1928), or – again
– children's books, such as Lewis Carroll's *Sylvie and Bruno*
(1889–93 – a book much admired by Tolkien).[29] Maps also
occasionally feature in English novels: they supplement John
Bunyan's Puritan handbook *The Pilgrim's Progress* (1678) and are
integral to Robert Louis Stevenson's *Treasure Island* (1881–3),
among others. But while several speculative fiction novels
published since *The Lord of the Rings* have included appendices, they are very unusual before Tolkien's work – and perhaps
the most significant is an analogous contemporary critique of
totalitarian oppression and surveillance. George Orwell's *Nineteen Eighty-Four* (1949) is a novel that is both footnoted and
includes a 4,000-word linguistic appendix on 'The Principles of
Newspeak'. One of the oddest things about finishing reading
The Lord of the Rings, then, is to discover that it does not finish – and in the fifty years since Tolkien's death, twenty further
volumes of his texts of Middle-Earthiana have been published.

What all this amounts to is that Tolkien is a writer of experimental fiction – but not in the tradition of the satirical or playful
(or even 'postmodern') textual games of authors and poets such
as François Rabelais, Alexander Pope, Laurence Sterne, and
Thomas Carlyle (and, latterly, Georges Perec). Rather, Tolkien's
paratexts (often, moreover, footnoted) are a defining part of his
genre of 'feigned' history.[30] This is fiction written as if it were a
translated, edited, and annotated historical text: indeed, in the
original Foreword, Tolkien states that his role was 'translating
and selecting the stories of the Red Book'.[31] Samuel Richardson had presented his novel *Clarissa* (1747–9) as an authentic
correspondence of nearly a million words of which he, Richardson, was supposedly merely the editor – but that is an epistolary
novel of contemporary manners and social conduct. Tolkien's

work, in contrast, is an epic work of Faërie. A dozen years after first publication Tolkien rewrote the Foreword and did now appear to be more candid in accepting authorship – except that, as with *The Hobbit*, he still seemed determined to mystify his readers. The first paragraph of the Foreword now claimed that Tolkien's interest in the history of the 'Elder Days' was 'primarily linguistic in inspiration and was begun in order to provide the necessary background of "history" for Elvish tongues'.[32] This appears to be a wholly perverse claim and a stupendous act of misdirection for *The Lord of the Rings*, in which the Elves are fairly marginal. But it was repeatedly maintained by Tolkien that his three-volume novel was simply a backdrop to his invention of Elvish languages, 'largely an essay in "linguistic aesthetic"'.[33] Notwithstanding this, however, Tolkien's abiding sense of historical veracity did remain with him for the rest of his life. His biographer Humphrey Carpenter recalled visiting in 1967 and finding that in response to a reader's query, 'he seems to see himself not as an author who has made a slight error that must now be corrected or explained away, but as a historian who must cast light on an obscurity in a historical document'.[34]

The later Foreword raises other issues. Tolkien firmly distances his work from the Second World War and its aftermath, and critics have usually followed his lead. In his first, pioneering critical study of Tolkien, *The Road to Middle-earth* (1982), Tom Shippey argued against contextualizing Tolkien as a post-war writer, building on his earlier comment that 'The idea of putting Tolkien in the 1950s literary scene with Huxley, Orwell, and Golding ignores Middle-earth's enormous gestation period'.[35] Instead, Shippey recommended focusing on linguistic influences and Old and Middle English sources – although he has subsequently revised his position.[36] Was Tolkien a writer of the 1950s? Barely: he had finished the first full draft of *The Lord of the Rings* by 1949. The immediate context for *The Lord of the Rings* – the Korean War (1950–53), Operation Hurricane (Britain's first atomic weapons test, 1952), the coronation of Elizabeth II (2 June 1953), and news of the ascent of Everest by Hillary and Tenzing reaching London (also 2 June 1953) – is therefore largely irrelevant. But the wider context of the 1930s and 1940s – the rise of totalitarianism, nationwide mobilization, the requisition of buildings and supplies, global conflict, atomic weapons, the privations of the 'home front', rationing (post-war rationing did not end in Britain until 4 July 1954), and the twilight of the British Empire – is surely addressed by *The Lord of the Rings*. It is a novel set during the 'Great War of the Ring' and is saturated with questions of leadership and government, power and oppression, individualism and community, identity and freedom of action.[37] More specifically there is criticism of the dubious policy of the appeasement of tyrannical regimes at the Council of Elrond, and the painful chapter 'The Scouring of The Shire' (cut from the film versions) covers repressive and bureaucratic authorities, food shortages, urban sprawl, and cheap prefab housing.[38] We must certainly bear in mind that the first stirrings of Middle-Earth and the legendarium went back to Tolkien's convalescence during the Great War and, as he himself stressed, *The Lord of the Rings* itself was begun in December 1937 as a follow-up to *The Hobbit* and well before the renewal of international hostilities in September 1939. But Hobbits and the Ring and the whole history of the Third Age were a product of the 1930s and 1940s – none of this material originated in Tolkien's decades-long recrafting of 'The Silmarillion'.

The 1966 Foreword also emphatically denies that *The Lord of the Rings* is in any way an allegory of recent political events. Tolkien tersely declares, 'I cordially dislike allegory in all its manifestations'.[39] This frequently quoted remark is another smokescreen: if Tolkien disliked allegory so much, 'in all its manifestations', why did he write so many allegories? 'The

Monsters and the Critics', his watershed essay on *Beowulf*, contains two allegories; 'Leaf by Niggle' (1945) is clearly an allegorical story; he even described 'The Tale of Aragorn and Arwen' in the appendices to *The Lord of the Rings* as an 'an allegory of naked hope'.[40] In a letter drafted in April 1956 he commented, 'Of course my story is not an allegory of Atomic power, but of *Power* (exerted for Domination)' – strongly suggesting that it is, then, an allegory of power.[41] In the introduction to his planned translation of the intricately allegorical poem *Pearl*, Tolkien had defined allegory very precisely as a set of consistent and detailed correspondences between the object of the allegory and the expression and imagery of the allegory itself: 'To be an "allegory" a poem must *as a whole*, and with fair consistency, describe in other terms some event or process; its entire narrative and all its significant details should cohere and work together to this end.'[42]

According to this strict definition, George Orwell's *Animal Farm* (1945) would thus qualify as an allegory in narrative prose, but hardly *The Lord of the Rings*.[43] It is not an allegory, but it does contain symbolism – which, according to Tolkien again, is 'the use of visible signs or things to represent other things or ideas'.[44] The One Ring is a symbol of authoritarian power and domination, then, not an allegory of the atomic bomb. Moreover, the Ring's sentience links it to Tolkien's interest in science fiction, to robots and artificial intelligence. It is an object crafted using state-of-the-art technology (or magic) that has acquired some limited but independent consciousness and ability to act, and is not subservient to the mastery of its wearer. Interestingly, Isaac Asimov's Laws of Robotics were formulated in 1942 when Tolkien was in the middle of writing *The Lord of the Rings*, and were in part a response to the mechanized warfare and remote killing of the Second World War – but the Ring was not, of course, forged in accordance with these laws.[45] Perhaps more generally, by 1966 (or, doubtless, by 1956) Tolkien had probably become vexed by semi-literate commentators seizing on the word 'allegory' to describe his novel. As he put it himself, 'I much prefer history, true or feigned, with its varied applicability to the thought and experience of readers. I think that many confuse "applicability" with "allegory"'.[46]

The Lord of the Rings therefore probes post-war, post-imperial English identity through various symbols and metaphors rather than as an extended allegory, and is, in a sense, a 'state of the nation' study. It encompasses travel literature in which the sea (central to island identity) plays a mysterious and ineffable role – the western sea of Middle-Earth representing the transit to an afterlife – and the stunning effects of malevolent forces threatening the state. These may be physical threats, such as the collapse of communal order and ensuing bloodshed, or psychological threats – such as Frodo's temptations by the Ring and his supernatural confrontations with the Eye of Sauron, as well as the hazardous encounters with the *palantíri* (the Seeing Stones). In this sense, *The Lord of the Rings* presents political microcosms, focusing, as a reviewer of the second edition suggested, on 'the group as a political unit, on the interaction of political units, as well as on the means and ends of political systems' – which presents a compelling contrast to individualistic Orwellian heroes who attempt to defy such systems.[47] As such, despite focusing on an unlikely political group – Hobbits – the book explores the internal dynamics of group identities, which in twentieth-century theatres of war are discovered to be founded on male intimacy in friendship and camaraderie, loyalty and love – evident in the tenderness and devotion that Sam shows towards Frodo.[48] It is an assertion of the humane standing against industrialized slaughter.

If Tolkien is indeed a writer of the 1930s, this might – daringly – place *The Lord of the Rings* alongside Modernist works such as Virginia Woolf's *The Waves* (1931), T.S. Eliot's *Collected*

Poems (1936), Samuel Beckett's *Murphy* (1938), and James Joyce's *Finnegans Wake* (1939). With one exception, though, Tolkien seems not to have read these contemporaries. However, the connection with Joyce is proven: Tolkien wrote notes on *Finnegans Wake* and 'stream of consciousness', and seems to have been attracted to Joyce's experiments in sound, form, and meaning.[49] Yet as the critic Margaret Hiley argues, ultimately Tolkien was disappointed in Joyce's invented language – not because Joyce was too radical, but because he was not radical enough.[50] Tolkien's invention of the Elvish languages should perhaps really be seen as a Modernist feat *par excellence* – a more accessible, if uncompromising, version of Joyce's linguistic gymnastics.[51]

Nevertheless, this, at least on the face of it, does place Tolkien among the Modernists, and while it is conventional to read Tolkien's Middle-Earth writings as an extreme form of mediaevalism largely inspired by his professional research and publications on texts such as *Beowulf, Sir Gawain and the Green Knight*, and *The Canterbury Tales*, this is drastic pigeonholing. Tolkien does have Modernist tendencies. Extending or foreshortening time is common in Modernist works, as are different and overlapping time schemes. *The Lord of the Rings* is fashioned like a pocket watch when it comes to timeframes: Tolkien took considerable pains in ensuring that his multiple narrative threads were locked into a stable calendar, and even checked that the phases of the moon were correct. Yet even within this careful structure there are deliberate time slips – most noticeably in Lothlórien where, as is common to Elfland or Faërie, time stalls. In the traditional ballad of 'Thomas the Rhymer' (quoted by Tolkien), Thomas is taken to Faërie by the Queen of Elfland; he stays there for forty days, but when he returns to his own world finds that seven years have elapsed.[52] Time also wavers in the dark when the Company of the Ring travel through Moria, or in taking the Paths of the Dead, and the Ring clearly plays tricks with time in extending the lifespan of its bearers. Characters are frequently confused about the passage of time, trying to calculate dates as a way of keeping hold of reality but feeling it slip away.

What is equally noticeable is Tolkien's constant shifts in perspective that erode the realist conventions of the narrative, especially his arsenal of stories-within-stories. Some of these appear as interpolated poems and songs, sometimes from different traditions – prompting Sam (a habitual poet) to speculate, with preternatural canniness, about the sorts of songs in which he and Frodo will be celebrated. The narrative is often self-reflexive, drawing attention to its status as story, to competing and alternative narratives, to the unreliability of writing and fragmentary texts (such as the burnt and bloodstained Book of Mazarbul discovered in Moria, or Barliman Butterbur's failure to send a crucial letter), and to the profusion of different (often untranslated) languages in Middle-Earth – Elvish itself being rarely translated.[53] These extra texts, some of which plumb the depths of the unpublished 'Silmarillion', provide characters with complex networks and memories of intertextual allusion that create their own extraordinary *mise-en-abîme* that add to Tolkien's own commentary through paratexts, footnotes, and appendices. Characters, particularly Frodo, also dream, hallucinate, and suffer psychological trauma. Both Sméagol and Frodo are profoundly damaged by the Ring as their identities fracture and collapse. In the case of Frodo, his ravaged mental topography is repeatedly exposed – whether on Amon Hen as he surveys the mobilization of Middle-Earth in a hyper-real delirium, or on the slopes of Mount Doom where his being is condensed to a martyr facing a wheel of fire. Even the steadfast Gimli suffers an unexpected breakdown on the Paths of the Dead – almost uniquely, we enter his consciousness and share his anxieties as we walk with him step by deathly step. In contrast, other characters

are imperturbable blanks – most notably Legolas, whose disin-
terest in the Hobbits is uncomfortably evident on their journey
from Rivendell to Lothlórien; he says virtually nothing to them.

So Tolkien explores multiple narrative positions and especially unreliable narrators – the extreme example of the unreliable
narrator being Bilbo who lies, lies, and lies again about his acquisition of the Ring. In a moment of inspired bravado, Tolkien
integrated Bilbo's incompatible stories about the Ring told in
different editions of *The Hobbit*, a text that pre-dated *The Lord
of the Rings* by almost twenty years, to expose the dangers of the
object. Many characters tell stories about themselves that expose
their lies and delusions: from rhetoricians such as Saruman to
fantasists such as Gollum, while Gríma Wormtongue poisons
the ear of Théoden. The verse taxonomy of the Free Peoples
that Treebeard recites omits the Hobbits – effectively writing
them out of history. When Frodo arrives in Bree he claims to
be writing a book, and with Faramir he simply refuses to speak
and then tricks Gollum (albeit ostensibly to save him). Even Elf
magic is unreliable: the Mirror of Galadriel does not offer true
reflections but 'shows things that were, and things that are, [and]
the things that yet may be'.[54]

In common with Modernist writing, Tolkien also resists
a definitive ending to his novel. Several commentators have
remarked how the book seems to end several times: the destruction of the Ring, the crowning of Aragorn, the return to The Shire
(or *Sûza*), the dispatch of Gríma and Sharkey, the restoration of
The Shire, and the voyage from the Grey Havens. Frodo, for
example, observes that 'This is the ending' when Arwen arrives
in Minas Tirith – which, of course, it is not.[55] But that is by no
means all: then follow the appendices that, among many other
things, add more to the story of Gimli and Legolas in '*one of the
last notes in the Red Book*' – the narrative of *The Lord of the Rings*
now deferring to another, unpublished text.[56]

Like Modernist poets, Tolkien also mixes personal intertextual references into his work in, for example, his use of the Gothic language in names and his adaptation of the Anglo-Saxon poem 'The Wanderer', which is half-quoted by Aragorn at the borders of Rohan. And like writers such as Virginia Woolf and D.H. Lawrence, Tolkien was also attracted to contemporary psychology and developed his ideas on fairy stories from Carl Jung's *Psychology of the Unconscious*.[57] Characters in *The Lord of the Rings* play back memories, dream, and hallucinate (which, weirdly, also happens in 'The Wanderer'), often connecting across time and space through premonitions and even telepathy.[58] Frodo dreams of Gandalf imprisoned at Isengard in the House of Tom Bombadil and Merry dreams of archaic warfare in the barrow of the Wight. Wearing the Ring shifts Frodo and Sam into an alternative reality where their senses are altered. For Frodo on Weathertop, the Nazgûl come into sharp focus, no longer shrouded in black but pale, death-white figures in grey and silver. His night vision too becomes sharpened, as if he is becoming more intrinsically a creature of shadows and the dark.[59] For Sam in Shelob's Lair – at the threshold of Mordor – the Ring's power is greatly magnified: everything changes and 'a single moment of time was filled with an hour of thought'.[60] He is in a vaporous otherworld but can hear keenly and even comprehend the alien language of the Orcs.

But it is in ambiguity and uncertainty that Tolkien is at his most distinctive – a characteristic he once more shares with Modernist writers, while developing the contrasts he had deployed in *The Hobbit*. His prose style shifts from domestic comedy to apocalyptic tragedy, and his mix of characters too is a clash of styles. When Pippin meets Denethor, the Steward of Gondor, two worlds collide: the most Woosterish of the Hobbits in the impossible company of a menacing ruler of ancient Númenórean lineage whose sanity is in imminent collapse. But then Pippin, that 'fool of a Took', has in the *palantír* already glimpsed Sauron – the most devastating power of evil in Middle-Earth.[61] Likewise, it is Merry, the connoisseur of pipe-weed, who helps to defeat the stalking undead nightmare that is the Witch-King of Angmar. Both also feast among the wreck of Isengard after it has been shattered by the Ents, drawing dry laughter from both Legolas and Gimli. It is Sam, meanwhile, whose thoughts are more commonly on gardening or rabbit stew or fish 'n' chips, who delivers the most grievous wound to the hideous monster Shelob. Indeed, Sam is a notably complex character who becomes many things: a poet, a father, seven-times Mayor of Hobbiton, and, ultimately, the true hero of the tale.

Let us take a step back here. Tolkien's influences, like his Middle-Earths, are myriad, but some of the richest areas of research into Tolkien's work are in tracing the influences of Anglo-Saxon, Icelandic, and mediaeval literature on his fiction and poetry.[62] Tolkien's professional life, as we have seen, was dominated by these fields, and many commentators suggest that the Middle-Earth writings are effectively an introduction to this early Northern literature. Tolkien's work does appear to sit very comfortably with Old English epic, Norse saga, and Arthurian romance, and his enthusiasm in reworking this legendary material to make it relevant for contemporary audiences. This connects him with writers such as Edmund Spenser, John Bunyan, William Blake, and William Morris: from *The Faerie Queene* (1590–96) to *The Pilgrim's Progress* (1678), from *Jerusalem, The Emanation of the Giant Albion* (1804–20) to *News from Nowhere* (1891). This is a powerful tradition in which to place Tolkien, as it addresses the activity of allegory and fantasy in literature; moreover, these writers describe visionary landscapes that are nevertheless quintessentially English, from Spenser's 'Garden of Adonis' to the moral topography of Christian's *Progress*, from Blake's mystic visions of London and 'England's mountains green' to Morris's utopian socialist mediaevalism. Tolkien's own landscapes, encompassing the parochialism of The Shire, the very English wilderness surrounding the Withywindle, and the deserted plains of Rohan (reminiscent of Exmoor, Dartmoor, and Bodmin Moor) are part of a long literary tradition in defining Englishness.[63] The Shire is often considered as an English idyll, but England is not confined to The Shire. Instead, *The Lord of the Rings* presents a 'territorialization' of national identity: England is reflected in aspects of The Shire and Rivendell, Rohan and Gondor, even Isengard and Mordor. Travel through Middle-Earth is therefore a succession of scenes that juxtapose diverse Englands: the eighteenth-century-styled Hobbits (with their waistcoats and pipes and handkerchiefs) encounter otherworldly Elves who emerge from the twilight of the Dark Ages, the equestrian Anglo-Saxon Rohirrim, and the high Roman classicism of Gondor.[64] Together they face the industrial revolution of Saruman and the pandemic fascism of Sauron. This is one area that the films perhaps inevitably simplify, unifying the differences between, for example, Rohan and Gondor – the films are less fluid and more static in their representation of national identity, whereas the novel has a more prismatic sense of character and nationhood, history and place. For Tolkien himself, this was a deliberately 'mixed culture' of familiar and unfamiliar elements to enable readers 'simply to get inside this story'.[65]

But there is more. Tolkien's fiction offers nothing less than a history of English literature from *Beowulf* to Virginia Woolf: *The Lord of the Rings* is a panoramic celebration of more than a millennia of literary creativity, the culmination of an extraordinarily diverse canon of work. To take Tolkien's literary cartography mentioned above as an example. In addition to *The Pilgrim's Progress* (which he had taught at Leeds), *Treasure Island* (which he cited), and *Winnie-the-Pooh*, there are maps in Jonathan Swift's satirical travel narrative *Gulliver's Travels* (also cited in Tolkien's work), Charles Dickens's *Little Dorrit* (1855–7), and Thomas Hardy's 'Wessex' novels, as well as in children's books such as Kenneth Grahame's *The Wind in the Willows* (1908, again cited).[66] The leading literary critic of Tolkien, Tom Shippey, suggests that the first three books of *The Lord of the Rings* are a kind of complex map of his world, but it is really cartography – proper, drawn maps – that secure Middle-Earth.[67] Like Joyce's Dublin, Middle-Earth has a physical geography – in fact, in an interview Tolkien said, 'You must have a map, no matter how rough.'[68] Tolkien's letters and drafts bear this out to an almost obsessive degree: he had to map the landscape as accurately and as authentically – and, it seems, as frequently – as possible. It is no surprise, then, that for Sally Bushell, author of *Reading and Mapping Fiction* (2020), Tolkien is 'the ultimate creative literary cartographer'.[69]

There are maps of Middle-Earth, The Shire, and Gondor and Mordor in *The Lord of the Rings*. The map of The Shire (the first that readers encounter) is an expression of the orderliness of Hobbit society, visualizing the physical dimensions of the community neatly arranged into the four 'Farthings' – north, south, east, and west. Maps – like genealogies, archives, and museum collections – are ways of imagining a shared identity and bringing it into being as a homeland or nation-state, and such building blocks are evident across Middle-Earth, from the family trees of well-to-do Hobbits to the inscrutable archives of Minas Tirith where Gandalf conducts his research into the lore of the rings.[70] Pippin wishes he had studied maps in Rivendell – another place of libraries and preserved ancient artefacts – which is a clear instruction for the reader to do the same.[71] At the end of the novel, the Mouth of Sauron similarly offers precise details of territorial gains and governance as the terms for negotiating a peace: Mordor too has paid careful attention to cartography. For readers such as Shippey, these features make *The Lord of the Rings* an 'antiquarian' work, rooted in archaic literature and culture, but really Tolkien is exploring how identities and communities are socially constructed through various institutions – in effect, through a simulated ethnography.[72]

This makes the geographical journeys across Middle-Earth as much a survey of English history as a tour of landscapes. Rudyard Kipling layers English history in just this way in *Puck of Pook's Hill* – a book that influenced Tolkien's unfinished novel *The Lost Road*.[73] But it is too easy to suggest that Aragorn, for example, has aspects of various English champions and heroes through myth and history: King Arthur (armed with a legendary sword), King Alfred (a monarch uniting a nation), St George (a hero battling against impossible odds), or Robin Hood (first encountered as a disreputable semi-outlaw on the edges of society). Likewise, to claim that Gandalf is descended from the nation-building wizard Merlin. Such parallels are loose and, frankly, unconvincing and do not bear sustained scrutiny. Aragorn does not have a Round Table or a band of Merry Men, neither does he rescue a maiden from a Dragon; Gandalf is not a half-demon trapped by the magic of a Morgan le Fay or infatuated with the Lady of the Lake, and in fact a more direct source for Gandalf was the German mountain spirit, 'Der Berggeist'.[74]

Instead, Aragorn walks the paths of exile, connecting him with the unnamed subjects of Anglo-Saxon poems such as 'The Wanderer' and 'The Seafarer' – but he is exiled not only in space but also in time: from his memories, ancestry, and destiny. Aragorn's recovery of his history becomes a major theme of the book. History and genealogy turn out to be unquenchable. Aragorn thus emerges from the past to confront Sauron, and is described as a dream or a legend quickening into life from the ground.[75] The Hobbits (*Holbytlan*) too are fabled folk, legendary creatures from songs and children's stories, leading the Rohirrim again to wonder, 'Do we walk in legends . . . ?'[76] Repressed history is, in fact, irrepressible. The Barrow-Wights show that history may be entombed but refuses to die – and this undead agency helps to plait the plot together: the ancient blade with which Merry stabs the Lord of the Nazgûl was forged for precisely that confrontation hundreds of years earlier in a forgotten war fought against the Witch-King of Angmar. History similarly explodes from the depths of Moria, in which the Dwarves delved too deeply and awoke (or released) a Balrog, *de profundis*. In early drafts, Tolkien figured the Balrog as an avenger sent from Mordor, but he rewrote this passage to make the fiend part of the hidden history of the Mines of Moria, the 'Dwarrowdelf'.[77] History breaks into the contemporary. The shadow of the past is not only inescapable but defines and motivates the present. Gildor warns the Hobbits that The Shire is not a country retreat but is caught up in global politics too: 'The wide world is all about you: you can fence yourselves in, but you cannot for ever fence it out.'[78] As Roger Sale has pointed out, although experience of the Hobbits in *The Fellowship of the Ring* is of 'a world that is expanding and becoming more resonant and understandable', it is 'at the same time becoming more dangerous' – far more dangerous: the 'Black Riders' becoming 'Ringwraiths' and then the ominously alien 'Nazgûl'.[79] The historical has an inexorable momentum – hence Tolkien's memorable declaration that he preferred history, 'true or feigned', and the increasing historical reality of his creation: 'I am historically minded. Middle-earth is not an imaginary world.'[80] But interestingly, although Tolkien lays claim to a historical mind and 'feigned' history, this is a history of high emotions, drama, ambiguity, and, most importantly, artistry.[81]

Neither does history in *The Lord of the Rings* flow smoothly. Not only are there unreliable narrators aplenty as I have suggested, but Tolkien admits these competing versions into his text, learning to relish the contradictions and to multiply historical uncertainties.[82] The completely straightforward account given of Bilbo's acquisition of the Ring in the first edition of *The Hobbit* is, as I have argued, exposed as a tissue of lies by the time we get to *The Lord of the Rings* – the second edition of *The Hobbit* already having revealed that Bilbo's story and actions are suspect. Bilbo lies to Gandalf, to the Dwarves, and even lies in his own book; he only shamefacedly admits to lying when he gives another version in Rivendell – a different version to that he had originally told Glóin and the rest of the knot of Dwarves.[83] All of which "'twas strange, 'twas passing strange' to Gandalf.[84] But it is more than that: it is sinister, as Gandalf confides to Frodo before he leaves after Bilbo's birthday party. Tolkien thus turns an inconsistency between his first novel and its sequel into a key piece of evidence that the Ring is a malignant influence: it has, in other words, disrupted history.

Tolkien's technique here is to decipher and reinterpret his own texts as if they are made up of clues and traces. Gandalf does the same thing in his interrogation of Gollum, extrapolating crucial information from Bilbo's half-true report of Gollum's speech, written under entirely different circumstances for an entirely different occasion. Thus Gollum's answer to a riddle ('teaching his grandmother to suck – "Eggses!"') is made a riddle itself from which Gandalf deduces that Gollum (or rather, Sméagol) was raised in a matriarchal society.[85] The text therefore becomes a re-creation of historical research.

A side-effect of this virtual historicism is that it deepens the historical texture of Middle-Earth in general and *The Lord of the Rings* in particular. In his British Academy lecture on *Beowulf* (delivered 1936), Tolkien had argued that the apparent historical detail in the poem was aesthetically crafted, creating 'the illusion of surveying a past, pagan but noble and fraught with a deep significance – a past that itself had depth and reached backward into a dark antiquity of sorrow. This impression of depth is an effect and a justification of the use of episodes and allusions to old tales, mostly darker, more pagan, and desperate than the foreground.'[86] The relationship of *Beowulf* to those older, darker, more pagan, and more desperate tales – now lost – is analogous to the relationship of *The Lord of the Rings* to the unfinished 'Silmarillion': in the epic elegy of the Anglo-Saxons Tolkien found an evocative echo of his own work, both published and unpublished.

Temporal echoes reverberate through the plot: words and scenes are repeated and replayed, events are foreshadowed, and characters unexpectedly recur.[87] The whole of *The Lord of the Rings* is foreshadowed by *The Hobbit*: the Company travels literally on the same roads, stays at Rivendell, and encounters comparable threats – Goblin Town and Moria, the Mirkwood Spiders and Shelob, Orc armies and hopeless battles. Both groups of travellers meet the same Trolls (before and after petrification) and explore their cave, which has already been turned into fiction with Sam's droll 'Troll' song – a song that dated from Tolkien's days in Leeds and which appears in his *Songs for the Philologists*.[88] So there is effectively a movement here from history to legendary folklore, although unanswered questions remain. The quarried pit in the Trollshaws, for instance, remains a passing, enigmatic detail, like the perplexing and unsettled features of Joseph Conrad's *Heart of Darkness* (1899) – unexplained, perhaps inexplicable.[89]

The maverick character Tom Bombadil is unexpectedly known to both Farmer Maggot and Elrond, and Gandalf spends the penultimate chapter in his unlikely company rather than returning to The Shire.[90] Frodo callously cries that it is a pity that Bilbo did not stab Gollum when he had the chance. Gandalf responds with the wisdom of ages: 'Pity? It was Pity that stayed his hand', and goes on to muse over whether Gollum still has a part to play in the history of the Ring – in which case, 'the pity of Bilbo may rule the fate of many'.[91] Over seven hundred pages later Gollum is captured by Frodo and Sam, and Frodo hears this very conversation he had with Gandalf, 'quite plainly but far off, voices out of the past' – he has become his own double, a Frodo governed by an earlier incarnation of himself.[92] Gollum himself keeps turning up like the proverbial bad penny as if he is the avatar of the Ring, a presence inseparable from its power. Isildur's heir (Aragorn) returns to confront Sauron in the *palantír* with the very sword that maimed him, and the undead Oathbreakers return to their allegiance with ancient Gondor. Even the appearance of the Eagles at the Battle of the Black Gate prompts Pippin to recall Bilbo's tale of 'long long ago' – but 'This is my tale, and it is ended now.'[93] As he approaches the climax of *The Lord of the Rings*, then, Tolkien draws an explicit connection between the two tales, the one echoing the other, in the mind of a character and consequently in the mind of the reader. *The Lord of the Rings* blurs into the earlier story which we know to have been embroidered, overlaying the immediate danger of battle with an old fireside tale for children. Finally, Frodo's mutilation by Gollum is an eerie repeat of Sauron's mutilation at the hands of Isildur – and both are thus robbed of the Ring. Or conversely, Frodo's amputated finger, bitten off by the broken teeth of Gollum, has already been foreshadowed by Sauron's finger being sliced off by Isildur wielding a broken sword – is Frodo's loss of the Ring the repetition of a prior event or is Sauron's loss the anticipation of what is yet to come?[94] These maimings are also synecdoches of the decapitation of hands suffered in *The Silmarillion* by characters such as Beren and Maedhros, but they also have a deeper significance. The nine fingers of 'Nine-Fingered Frodo' number the Company of the Ring, which was itself modelled on the Nine Nazgûl.[95] None of Frodo's wounds heal: he remains nine-fingered and falls ill on the anniversaries of being stabbed with the Morgul blade and being poisoned by Shelob: the wounds are recurrent reminders of his past failures.

Darkness Visible

This uncanny sense of déjà-vu helps to give *The Lord of the Rings* a fatedness. Characters refer back to the events of *The Hobbit* – indeed, questions of prophecy and luck are raised right at the end of *The Hobbit*, when Gandalf first hints that loftier forces are at work: 'Surely you don't disbelieve the prophecies, because you had a hand in bringing them about yourself? You don't really suppose, do you, that all your adventures and escapes were managed by mere luck, just for your sole benefit?'[96] Indeed, Gandalf frequently (and cautiously) refers to fate. When Frodo is recovering from being wounded by the Morgul blade, he comments that 'fortune or fate have helped you' – but which of these two guided Frodo and misguided the dead hand of the Witch-King: one or the other, or both, or neither?[97] Gandalf is hesitant, undecided. A few pages later the mystery deepens when Gandalf starts to tell the Council of Elrond of the treachery of Saruman: the Ring was discovered in the same year that Sauron, in the guise of the 'Necromancer', was expelled from Mirkwood: 'a strange chance, if chance it was'.[98] Gandalf keeps pondering the riddle of fate, which remains just beyond his grasp; Galadriel warns that the 'tides of fate are flowing', yet nevertheless harbours the Company of the Ring for four weeks.[99] Middle-Earth is swayed by unfathomable powers that even semi-divine characters are unable fully to comprehend – in fact, the Morgul blade is itself an instance of the unknown menaces that pervade Middle-Earth; it is never quite made clear to the reader what sort of danger it poses.

Later, Gimli suggests that Pippin was lucky in escaping from the Uruk-Hai when they were attacked by the Riders of

Rohan and the Hobbit was able to cut his bonds with a discarded blade. It is both luck, but, as Gimli admits with a flash of wordplay, was also made possible through Pippin's presence of mind under desperate circumstances: 'you seized your chance with both hands, one might say'.[100] This in turn had led to a riddle as the Hobbits left no tracks when they were carried by the Orc Grishnákh to the edge of Fangorn Forest. Pippin is again saved by 'good fortune' forty pages later when he gazes into the *palantír* – a turning point in the plot as it preoccupies Sauron who has yet to learn of the fall of Saruman and thus proves hugely distracting to him.[101] A similar fortunate fate is invoked when Sam inadvertently reveals the covert purpose of Frodo's journey to Faramir. Faramir takes pity (that word again) on the hapless Sam: 'be comforted, Samwise. If you seem to have stumbled, think that it was fated to be so.'[102]

Perhaps, but tied in the knot of luck, fortune, and fate is another term: doom. Doom lays heavy on *The Lord of the Rings* – it is literally the aim of the anti-quest, the end of the road: to Amon Amarth, Orodruin, or Mount Doom, and, ultimately, inside the Mountain of Fire to the very Cracks of Doom. Gandalf is troubled by doom, realizing after the Battle of Helm's Deep that doom is inevitable, and that much enchantment will consequently pass from Middle-Earth; Galadriel has already foreseen this, saying to Frodo, 'your coming is to us as the footstep of Doom'.[103] This is the enigma of the three Elven Rings, for although Sauron did not touch them, they are still bound to the power of the One Ring, and so the Elves do not know what will happen if the Ruling Ring is destroyed; according to Elrond, 'It would be better if the Three had never been.'[104]

Likewise, the last march of the Ents is accompanied by bellowing song:

To Isengard with doom we come!

With doom we come, with doom we come!

Treebeard knows that 'we are going to *our* doom'; yet if the Ents did nothing, doom would in any case come to them.[105] Frodo too finally understands that the Ring, his burden, is his doom, and that Sam cannot come between him and his doom.[106] Luck and chance have darkened into fate and doom: 'we've trusted to luck,' says Frodo, 'and it has failed us'.[107] Sam is more positive: luck is all they have left as they symbolically ascend Mount Doom.[108] But as Gandalf reluctantly admits to Pippin on the walls of Minas Tirith, 'There never was much hope ... Just a fool's hope'.[109]

The Anglo-Saxon word for 'doom', *dóm*, has its origins in the old Germanic languages – including Old Saxon and Gothic – and originally referred to laws, before gaining the more ominous meaning of 'Fate, lot, irrevocable destiny ... rarely in [a] good sense'.[110] The *OED* notes that the phrase *crack of doom* is archaic, referring to 'the thunder-peal of the day of judgement' – the thunder that so terrifies Macbeth when in the mirror of the Witches' cauldron (a baleful forerunner of the Mirror of Galadriel) he sees Banquo's royal line 'stretch out to th' crack of doom'.[111] The *crack* is, then, a crack of thunder, but Tolkien transforms it into a place – an elemental yet liminal fissure where earth and fire combine, and a place whose name can only explode into its true meaning – its destiny – through being destroyed.[112] Although the Quest of Mount Doom is doomed to fail and *does* fail – Frodo does not truly fulfil the task assigned to him – this inevitably is a consolation as it confirms that the struggle is against oppression, domination, and tyranny. Fighting on the side of the gods against chaos was, as the Anglo-Saxons recognized, doomed to fail, but failure did not mean defeat – instead, it was the heroic exertion of will over desperate adversity: chaos will come, but must still be resisted. And miraculously in a twist that Tolkien would describe as 'eucatastrophic' (blissful and unforeseen consummation, rather than luck or chance), of the joyous calamity of Gollum's final intervention, the Ring is itself doomed.[113] It disappears into the fiery depths, the volcano erupts, and the 'skies burst into thunder seared with lightning': that is the true 'crack of doom'.[114] As Peter Schakel has put it, '*Eucatastrophe* does not deny the existence of sorrow and failure. Rather, it denies universal final defeat.'[115]

The hesitancy and randomness of the plot of *The Lord of the Rings* was in part due to Tolkien feeling his way through, discovering the story in the process of writing it. So, in initial versions Aragorn was a Ranger Hobbit who wore wooden shoes and was called Trotter, and Treebeard was originally an evil creature – much as is his alter-ego, Old Man Willow in the Old Forest (see the beginning of Chapter Four for further details of these changes). But as he felt his way through the knotted plotlines, Tolkien began to be governed by some sort of direction, contradictory and problematic, which resonated with ancient esoteric sources.

Tolkien explicitly references mediaeval rather than classical or Renaissance philosophy in his work, combining, as Tom Shippey has convincingly demonstrated, two key philosophical theories of evil in developing his ineffable model of fatedness.[116] In particular, the thinking of Anicius Boethius (*c*.AD 475–7 d. 526?) is central. Boethius was a Roman living under Gothic rule in the sixth century; his work *De Consolatione Philosophiae* (*The Consolation of Philosophy*) became a core philosophical text for Anglo-Saxon and mediaeval thought, possibly translated by King Alfred and certainly by Geoffrey Chaucer (under the title *Boece*), as well as influencing Anglo-Saxon poems. *The Consolation of Philosophy* marks a transition from paganism to Christianity: it was a sort of non-Christian Christian work focused on the questions of evil and freewill that emphasized the virtues of suffering and otherworldly ideals – and it saturated English intellectual life for half a millennium.

Boethius, in dialogue with an imagined allegorical lady – the personification of 'Philosophy' – contemplates his reconciliation with the necessity of suffering to achieve a state of grace in the afterlife. The philosopher wrote his treatise while in prison and under sentence of death, lamenting how his fortunes have declined – to which the lady Philosophy responds by showing how philosophy can offer comfort and relief in the very worst of circumstances. First, she shows that true happiness and spiritual wealth lie in virtue, self-sufficiency, and values such as friendship, rather than in material possessions, before arguing that these aspects of perfect goodness are 'not merely in God: they *are* God'.[117] 'God', in Boethius' terms, 'governs the entire universe with the rudder of the good . . . all things obey him, and . . . evil has no existence in the world.'[118] God does not intervene in worldly affairs, but, because the world is divinely ordered, virtuous acts harmonize with this order and hence seem to attract providence or luck: chance being defined as 'an unexpected event due to the conjunction of its causes with action which is done for some purpose'.[119] As the philosopher John Marenbon puts it, 'Philosophy explains that events are said to happen by chance when they are the result of a chain of causes which is unintended or unexpected'.[120] Freewill exercised for the good and to further happiness will therefore appear to be favoured by chance – although absolute freewill is actually seriously questioned by the omniscience of the Boethian God.[121]

Despite Boethius never once mentioning Christ, his thinking had a crucial and abiding impact on Christian thinking for centuries. Boethian morality seems to guide the longed-for consolation in the Anglo-Saxon poems of exile 'The Wanderer' and 'The Seafarer', in which those enduring loss and loneliness can make sense of their earthly predicament by looking forward to an eventual divine salvation. Evil is consequently an instrument that enables one to ascend to a higher realm of being. In 'The Wanderer', then, the exiled speaker rises above the changeable world to find consolation, whereas in the partner-poem 'The Seafarer' the speaker finds that the changeable world can itself be a route to the divine. The choice is the Augustinian distinction between making use of this world for higher purposes as opposed simply to enjoying its transient pleasures, mixed with the doomy Anglo-Saxon fortitude of 'Northern Courage' in enduring inescapable hardship.

St Augustine compared Christian life to travelling through a landscape – 'through what is corporeal and temporal we may comprehend the eternal and spiritual' – and Tolkien was fascinated by the idea of exile and with pilgrimage literature in general.[122] Aragorn, for example, comes out of exile to claim his kingship and then takes Arwen with him to the exile of the mortal grave, sundered from her Elvish kin in Valinor. The Elves of Middle-Earth are already in exile – especially Galadriel, who needs to prove herself to return to the Undying Lands of Faërie. Frodo, meanwhile, finds himself increasingly exiled from friends and home and eventually from his own world of Middle-Earth.[123] It is worth bearing in mind how many of the leading characters unexpectedly sail across the western seas to Valinor, Tolkien's Elfland, with the departing Elves and Gandalf: Bilbo, Frodo, then Sam, and even Gimli. All four are given an afterlife divorced from their 'natural' state.

But it is the question of evil that is central to Boethian thinking and Tolkien's ambivalent use of it.[124] Boethius is told by the lady Philosophy that there is really no such thing as evil, rather, evil is the absence of good – 'evil is nothing' – and even that which appears to be independently and actively evil is part of a larger pattern of divine fortune or order.[125] Such evil does not have an independent existence: it is parasitic and cannot create

– a point that is repeated throughout *The Lord of the Rings* –
and while Boethius allows that there are wicked beings in the
world, they should be pitied rather than punished. What is seen
as evil is only the consequence of Human freewill turning from
good, but good will always prevail. As the lady argues, 'So dry
your tears. Fortune has not yet turned her hatred against all
your blessings. The storm has not yet broken upon you with too
much violence. Your anchors are holding firm and they permit
you both comfort in the present, and hope in the future.'[126] The
image of the storm was taken by Tolkien and given to Gandalf
when he reunites with Aragorn, Gimli, and Legolas: 'We meet
again. At the turn of the tide. The great storm is coming, but
the tide has turned.'[127] And again to Théoden: 'For behold! the
storm comes, and now all friends should gather together, lest
each singly be destroyed.'[128] And again, when he sights an air-
borne Nazgûl: 'The storm is coming . . . Ride, ride! Wait not for
the dawn! Let not the swift wait for the slow! Ride!'[129] Other
translated Boethian phrases also murmur through Tolkien's text:
'at the end of all things'.[130]

Boethius' thinking thereby chimed with early Christian
theology that combined with idealist Platonism into Neo-
Platonism. Boethius, who wrote the *Consolation* in the face of
death before being ultimately tortured and executed, was ele-
vated to the status of a martyr.[131] Yet a lingering doubt hangs
over *The Consolation of Philosophy*: it is a dialogue, a form often
used in satire, in which Philosophy speaks in the pagan terms
of ancient Greek thinkers – possibly a deliberate manoeuvre to
expose the limitations of classical philosophy when faced with
Christian grace. So Boethian thinking too draws attention to its
own ambiguities and shortcomings.

Yet it is clear that the fraught temperament of fate and, more
strikingly, the impenetrable nature of evil – particularly in *The
Lord of the Rings* – are not even straightforwardly Boethian.

Attempts to explain evil and evil creatures are strangely un-convincing because evil itself is multifaceted. Were the Orcs originally Elves who were corrupted by Morgoth? But if Orcs are Elves tempted or twisted or tortured to the dark side, why is there no mercy or redemption afforded to them? Elrond declares that nothing is evil at its origin, but this seems like opinion or faith rather than fact.[132] Similarly, Frodo says to Sam in the chapter 'The Tower of Cirith Ungol' that 'The Shadow that bred them can only mock, it cannot make: not real new things of its own', but how does he know this (unless he is merely repeating Elrond), and what gives Frodo authority to speak of the ancient origins of Orcs in any case?[133] Gandalf, meanwhile, dismisses Orcs as being 'spawned'.[134] Much information is imparted in Middle-Earth by unreliable sources – such as Treebeard, who, as we have seen, has not even heard of Hobbits. Treebeard also claims that Trolls are 'counterfeits', made 'in mockery of Ents, as Orcs were of Elves'.[135] In *The Hobbit* the three Trolls are pet-rified, becoming the 'stuff of the mountains they are made of' – but made they nevertheless were, and from stone too to create some of the most powerful war machines in Middle-Earth.[136]

The problem here is that evil in Middle-Earth often seems to be not only tangible, but active and powerful, with the ability not only to corrupt and destroy, but to create – if only in 'mockery'. This presents an alternative to Boethian philosophy: a dualist way of thinking in which good and evil, light and dark, are en-gaged in a constant struggle. In this intellectually systematic and cosmogonical thinking, typified by Manichaeism, evil is as manifest as good, warring with it through different realms, prin-ciples, and states. This is as plausible a reading of good and evil in Middle-Earth as the Boethian claim that evil is simply the absence of good in a good world. The numinous complexities of *The Silmarillion*, in which the evil divinity Melkor (later named Morgoth) takes an active and inventive role in challenging the

creation and the celestial harmony of Middle-Earth and dis-
rupting the sacred lands of Valinor, certainly seem to fit a dualist
model, and Sauron, originally the lieutenant of Morgoth, shares
his master's malevolent ingenuity and creativity. Sauron created the Black Speech, built Barad-Dûr, bred the Olog-Hai and
the Uruks (genetically modified Trolls and Orcs), and forged
the One Ring – an object of subtle beauty and maddening
desire.[137] As such, there are in Middle-Earth at least two major
(and incompatible) philosophical systems in play.

Manichaeism is named after the teachings of the third-
century Persian prophet Mani (or Manes). It too had a long and
enduring influence, but as a religion was condemned as heret-
ical by the Christian Church if nevertheless tied to Christian
thinking and embraced by radical Christian sects such as the
twelfth-century Cathars in the south of France – themselves
ruthlessly suppressed by a crusade, no less. Mani, 'The Apostle
of Light' who numbered earlier prophets such as Zoroaster and
Jesus among his intellectual lineage, proposed a universal religion based on a dualist theory of good and evil that was indebted
to Gnostic thinking. Humans are Fallen and in exile, and so life
on earth was a condition of alienation and pain in an inher-
ently evil world enmeshed in the wickedness of sensual delights.
But believers could transcend this sinful material existence and
return to paradise through strict asceticism. Evil therefore does
undisputedly exist in Manichaean theology: it is not only active,
creative, and dynamic, but is the very stuff of material reality
and mortal experience. Good and evil have equal and manifest powers in such thinking, and the world is in consequence
the arena in which they eternally war – although, in reality, it
was the established religions of the East and West that warred
against Manichaeism. But despite its eradication in the Middle
Ages and the almost complete destruction of its scriptures, by
the mid-sixteenth century Manichaeism had become a byword

for a dualist philosophy that balanced good with evil.[138]

This is why there is much confusion over evil – especially in the early chapters of *The Lord of the Rings* – and terrible uncertainty over luck and fate, providence and doom throughout the book. The Black Riders are agents of Sauron, but what of Old Man Willow or the Barrow-Wight? At one point Tolkien considered placing both of these under the control of the Nazgûl – or even making the Wights Ringwraiths without steeds. But the mystery of the Barrow-Wight is in the unknown capacity and countenance of evil.[139] As Aragorn says, 'There are many evil and unfriendly things in the world that have little love for those that go on two legs, and yet are not in league with Sauron, but have purposes of their own.'[140] So Sauron does not define evil, but is just one example of the chaotic spectrum of forces inimical to the Free Peoples. Gimli too observes that 'Caradhras was called the Cruel, and had an ill name ... when rumour of Sauron had not been heard in these lands.'[141] The Watcher in the Water outside Moria lives by its own slimy laws, yet seems almost wilfully attracted to Frodo, the Ringbearer – as Gandalf notices. Tolkien is, then, intriguingly ambivalent about theories of evil and the extent to which evil follows freedom of choice. It becomes clear that the Orcs of Mordor, for example, are little more than slaves living under martial law brutally enforced by the Nazgûl – even the elite Uruks Gorbag and Shagrat would rather 'slip off and set up somewhere on our own with a few trusty lads'.[142]

Furthermore, Tolkien was a devout Catholic and it is perhaps surprising that *The Lord of the Rings* lacks the overt Christian allegory or symbolism of, say, C.S. Lewis's *The Lion, the Witch and the Wardrobe* (1950), not to mention any unequivocal clarity in the treatment of evil. There are only glancing references to Christianity in *The Lord of the Rings*, buried so deep as to be almost invisible: the Company of the Ring leaves Rivendell on 25 December and the One Ring is destroyed on 25 March, which was traditionally the day of the Crucifixion and the beginning of the New Year.[143] But Tolkien's thinking on evil is deliberately undogmatic and resistant to reductive formulations. Some characters are essays in temptation and straying from virtue – however briefly. Boromir, a representative of an embattled country under persistent attack from Mordor, sees the Ring as the salvation of his people and in a moment of madness fuelled by the Ring itself he tries to seize it. His rage has been brewing during a lifetime spent as heir to the leadership of a country under persistent threat of invasion, and in resistance to the annexation of its border territories: his is not a coolly calculated decision, not a choice made of freewill. Saruman too is tempted – tempted to retain the wonder of Middle-Earth. The destruction of the Ring will, he argues, change the world irrevocably and for the worse: all enchantment will disappear. This decision is a considered exercise of freewill by one of the wise, indeed, a semi-divinity – it turns out to be a very bad decision, but, at least initially, his reasons are comprehensible. Denethor also makes bad decisions – under siege both mentally and physically, and on the brink of insanity. In these cases freewill can clearly be compromised by extreme circumstances, which surely further confuses the nature of evil. This is what W.H. Auden persuasively argued in an enthusiastic review of *The Return of the King* for the *New York Times* – that the good characters can imagine becoming evil, but evil can only perceive deeper evil: 'Evil ... has every advantage but one – it is inferior in imagination. Good can imagine the possibility of becoming evil – hence the refusal of Gandalf and Aragorn to use the Ring – but Evil, defiantly chosen, can no longer imagine anything but itself.'[144] Sauron's key failure of imagination is that the mission of the Company that leaves Rivendell is to destroy the Ring: the Ring-bearer's task is really that of Ringbreaker.[145] Boromir, Saruman, and Denethor all fall prey to temptation – and if the Ring symbolizes anything more than authoritarian power or domination, it is surely this: the power of temptation, the temptation of power. It is the same power that Satan uses to lure Eve in the Garden of Eden, the same force that compels the sinner – but this is not Biblical temptation within a Christian theology that leads straight to Hell and damnation. Rather, it is temptation as surrendering to the command and dominion of another. It exposes the failure of *will* – and that sort of failure is, precisely, disgraceful, degrading, and dehumanizing.

As to pity, it is a word that recurs through *The Lord of the Rings*. Without Bilbo's pity for Gollum the anti-quest would have foundered on the banks of the Anduin, and Frodo thus learns to pity Gollum too. Saruman (Sharkey) is also pitied by Frodo on the threshold of Bag End, even after he attempts to knife the Hobbit. This is Frodo at his most Christ-like: 'No ... Do not kill him even now ... He was great once, of a noble kind ... He is fallen, and his cure is beyond us; but I would still spare him, in the hope that he may find it.' Saruman is sickened: 'You are wise, and cruel. You have robbed my revenge of sweetness, and now I must go hence in bitterness, in debt to your mercy.'[146] Pity, like resisting temptation, is an integral aspect of freewill and virtue. It is an act of will that does not seek dominion but rather defers to another, weaker, failed will. It is merciful, and, by being so, underscores the freedom and the supremacy of, literally, goodwill.

*   *   *

The Lord of the Rings was written during a global conflict under the most pressing and dire circumstances. It was composed alongside a plethora of other things and repeatedly abandoned. It took over a decade to write and another half-decade to get into print. It is a triumph of the will and endurance of its author.

As a literary work, it is a titanic experiment in fiction, history, and myth; it contains multitudes, from ancient philosophy to beast fable, from paratexts to invented languages. It has created an entire culture of its own and a multi-billion-dollar industry, but before turning to that, I will outline how the plot was 'discovered' by Tolkien – paralleling the chronicle that began this chapter with a history of the narrative itself. The deep and diverse ambiguities and dramatic impasses suggested in this chapter emerged in part from the untrammelled composition of the novel: it was begun again and again, hundreds of pages were written and revised and rewritten and revised once more before being rejected. There was no real plan, just a need to find out about the One Ring – and, as the following chapter argues, the story of Tolkien writing *The Lord of the Rings* is replicated in the book itself. Its artistry is, in part, in the artistry of its composition. *The Lord of the Rings* is a reflection, then, of its own process of coming into being: it is an acute example of a text that, more than anything else, dramatizes its own genesis.

FOUR

The Hesitancy of Good

In winter's tedious nights sit by the fire
With good old folks, and let them tell thee tales
Of woeful ages long ago betid.
>William Shakespeare,
>*Richard II* (*c*.1595)

Tolkien wrote *The Lord of the Rings* with little sense of plot or character, direction or development, meaning or significance. He had two anchors during the long and difficult process of writing: the tales of his legendarium, which provided a remote background atmosphere to this supposed sequel to *The Hobbit*, and his friends in the Inklings to whom he read the work as it was written. This was a shrinking circle, consisting principally of C.S. Lewis and Charles Williams, together with Tolkien's youngest son Christopher.[1] But Tolkien was really his own staunchest ally and fiercest critic. Lewis wrote of his great friend that 'No one ever influenced Tolkien – you might as well try to influence a bander-snatch. We listened to his work, but could affect it only by encouragement. He has only two reactions to criticism; either he begins the whole work over again from the beginning or else takes no notice at all.'[2] The *bander-snatch* refers to a creature in Lewis Carroll's nonsense poems 'Jabberwocky' and *The Hunting of the Snark* (1876), elegantly defined by the *OED* as a 'fleet, furious, fuming, fabulous creature, of dangerous propensities, immune to bribery and too fast to flee from'. Lewis's comparison indicates the wayward independence of Tolkien's creative genius, his haphazard energy, the fitful way in which he proceeded. But in fact, Lewis was instrumental in getting Tolkien to finish *The Lord of the Rings* as a *narrative* rather than pursuing the proliferating archives of 'The Silmarillion', acting as a 'mid-wife' to the process.[3] As Walter Hooper, Lewis's secretary and later editor, recalled, Tolkien said to him, 'You know Jack [i.e. Lewis]. He had to have a *story*! And that story – *The Lord of the Rings* – was written to keep him quiet!'[4]

It is, then, worth charting the extraordinary ebb and flow of the work as it was written: the innumerable false starts and dead-ends, the abrupt changes in the action and the key figures, and the long periods in which the book was all-but abandoned. What will emerge from this is not only Tolkien's supreme achievement in actually finishing *The Lord of the Rings*, but also, I suggest, that the work is a profound reflection on its own composition – a dramatization of the act of writing, a celebration of its own literary existence. If it symbolizes anything, it symbolizes itself.

How to Begin?

In the very first manuscript pages of the first draft of *The Lord of the Rings* – titled 'A long-expected party' – Bilbo declares his intention to go away and get married, the idea occurring to him (and to Tolkien) spontaneously. He then quietly, rather than spectacularly, disappears from his birthday celebrations using the Ring, leaving his possessions labelled for distribution among his family and friends.[5] He had run out of money, and the adventurous (Tookish) side of his personality had suddenly woken up again: this would be another adventure for Bilbo. He wants to see a Dragon again and there is even a hint that he will visit Britain: 'Far west where the Elves still reign. Journey to perilous isle.'[6] Of course, that was not to be, and the story was gradually revised to include Gandalf and to focus on Bilbo's son Bingo (!). Bingo in turn became Bilbo's nephew (Bilbo was still the central character at this very early stage) and personages such as Gaffer Gamgee began to be fleshed out.

The Ring, however, was the thing. Its possible connection with the Necromancer was alluring to both Bingo and to Tolkien – Tolkien even called it 'ring-lure', as compared with 'dragon-longing'.[7] He knew it meant something, but what, exactly? Tolkien could only find out by writing the book. So Bingo sets out with two or three relations and they find themselves in a landscape Tolkien had already described in his poem 'The Adventures of Tom Bombadil', published in the *Oxford Magazine* in February 1934 – Tolkien typically mining his own work.[8] 'The Adventures of Tom Bombadil' thus provided the idea that Bingo, Odo, Frodo, Vigo, and/or Marmaduke (the names were very fluid until the book was eventually completed) would go into the Old Forest, meet 'Willow-Man' and the Barrow-Wights, and be rescued by Tom Bombadil. All of these four places or characters are present in the poem. The story then, as Tolkien put it in a letter to his publisher Stanley Unwin, took an 'unpremeditated turn' with the sudden appearance of the Black Riders.[9] What began as an encounter with Gandalf on horseback (Gandalf even sniffing the air) quickly became something far more menacing: the creeping, snuffling dread of the Ringwraiths.[10]

The core of the opening chapters set in The Shire – the unfathomable threat of the Black Riders, the meeting with Gildor and the Elves, the visit to Farmer Maggot (originally a comic interlude) – form part of these early drafts, but the nature of the Ring is still a mystery, Gandalf is remote, and Sam has yet to make an entrance. But Tolkien had already started speculating about the Ring in disconnected passages, noting that the Ring can overcome its bearer and make them permanently invisible, inhabiting a world of 'grey ghost pictures against the black background in which you live'.[11] There were many of these Rings of Power given to different peoples, but they were all under the command of the Lord of the Rings. Yet one ring had been lost – and that was the one that Gollum, a Hobbit sort of creature, had found: it was a 'queer fate'.[12] Reading these drafts, one can perceive Tolkien thinking through the story in a dialogue between Gandalf and Bingo – Bingo asking questions, Gandalf doing his best to answer them and keep hold of his narrative thread, at one point musing, 'for the moment I am trying to explain Gollum', and commending Bilbo for his pity.[13] He also sketched out rough maps of the route being taken, and sketches of the terrain.

Tolkien then began to feel that he was already losing control of the book and that it was getting 'quite out of hand' and progressing towards 'quite unforeseen goals'.[14] The Hobbits had entered the Old Forest, and now there was certainly a sense that Tolkien was exploring the landscape in search of meaning – the only plot certainty being the pursuit by the Black Riders, who in early drafts may well have ventured to Tom Bombadil's very doorstep.[15] Following a difficult transit of the Barrow-Downs, aided by Bombadil, the Hobbits rejoin the road, arrive at Bree (first a mixed town, then a Hobbit town), and meet a Ranger or wild Hobbit who wears wooden shoes. His name is Trotter, and Gandalf vouchsafes him to the travellers in a letter left with the Hobbit landlord.[16] Trotter was obviously dramatically recast as Aragorn (variously renamed Ingold and Elfstone), but many elements survived from these drafts and were revised into virtually finished forms. Bingo sings a song at the inn and inadvertently slips on the Ring, Trotter recites parts of the song of Beren and Lúthien on Weathertop – thereby locking *The Lord of the Rings* into the 'Great Tales' of the legendarium – and the Ringwraiths attack Bingo while he is wearing the Ring.

Once the Hobbits had arrived at Rivendell and reunited with Gandalf, Tolkien made further rough attempts to plan the story. It was clear that Rivendell would have to be some sort of watershed with Elrond and Gandalf offering explanations of events, and he was also wondering who Trotter really was – so he started posing queries. Bingo Bolger-Baggins he felt was a 'bad name'; Frodo would be better, but 'I am now too used to Bingo'.[17] The name 'Sam Gamgee' appears as a potential companion to Bingo – but he felt that there were too many Hobbits now. Tolkien also entertained the idea of the Elves retaining their rings, which would become a meaningful theme. He was then struck with the importance of Bilbo's ring, which is desired by the 'Dark Lord' because 'if he had it he could see where all the others were, and would be master of their masters' – the idea now being that the lesser rings were scattered throughout Middle-Earth in the possession of Dwarves and Dragons, Elves and Men.[18]

These multiplying queries initiated what Christopher Tolkien describes as the fifth version of the story, with his father returning to the opening party in Hobbiton and producing 'an exceedingly complicated document'.[19] Much detail was added concerning Hobbitlore, Sam emerged as Bilbo's gardener, and, crucially, the 'Long-Expected Party' was now immediately followed by a chapter originally titled 'Ancient History', in which Tolkien began to explain the saga of the Rings of Power, weave it into the legendarium, and speculate on the future role of Gollum.[20]

Tolkien also wrote the verse on the rings – although the number of rings forged varied – and at one point suggested the existence of 'elf-wraiths'.[21] Having got to the Old Forest he again went back to the beginning, thankfully renamed Bingo (who was now Frodo Baggins) and juggled the other Hobbit names (now Folco, Merry, Odo, and Sam), and began with a foreword 'Concerning Hobbits'. This section, which of course became the Prologue, considers Hobbits to be more akin to Humans than to Elves or Dwarves, but although they are a little people and disappearing from the countryside they are not fairies – not at all magical.[22] There is some useful attention to architecture at this stage, later expanded into the section on smials, but no explicit connection is yet made between The Shire and England.[23]

At Bree, Trotter remains an outlandish Hobbit – 'grim and wild and rough-clad' – and Tolkien tried rewriting the episode to include the arrival of Gandalf with Odo.[24] This led him to the realization that in addition to maps of the territory, once characters began to weave in and out of each other's stories a clear chronology was necessary.[25] This is a recognizable feature of the eventual novel: Tolkien went to great trouble to establish an accurate day-by-day calendar of events, including the correct phases of the moon, and the characters in *The Lord of the Rings* repeatedly check their own timelines. This reassures the characters themselves, the reader, and Tolkien himself by establishing some stability as an anchor of certainty and precision against the swirling ambiguity that surrounds them.[26] According to Shippey, the formula 'x days / nights ago', for example, is used over thirty times in the novel, which parallels eighteenth-century clock-watching realist novels such as *Tom Jones* (1749) in which Henry Fielding pays assiduous attention to timekeeping.[27] The chronology in Appendix B of the finished book, 'The Tale of Years', is therefore a fitting coda to the recital of time in the novel. Moreover, Tolkien seems to have felt that accurate dating was one of the features of the impression of historical depth that he was so entranced by in *Beowulf*, and he even tried to work out a timeline for that poem.

Tolkien once again got his characters to Rivendell, and once again had a series of issues to address. He considered radically changing the plot to make Bilbo the hero throughout, or Frodo (now renamed Folco) a comic character (!). In August 1939, he also drafted out a plan of the entire novel after the Hobbits leave Rivendell: the snowstorm on the Misty Mountains, an adventure with 'Giant Tree Beard in Forest', a journey through Moria, and a description of the land of Ond (Gondor) and the siege of its principal city. Bingo/Folco/Frodo then arrives in Mordor where Gollum pursues him disguised with a new ring of invisibility, there is a 'Cavalcade of evil led by seven Black Riders', a searching 'Eye', and the eruption of the 'Fiery Mountain' destroying the 'Dark Tower'.[28] Notably absent from this summary are Saruman and Isengard, Galadriel and Lothlórien, Théoden and Rohan, Faramir and Ithilien, and Shelob and Cirith Ungol, as well as the major battles. Moreover, here Treebeard was an evil character who had imprisoned Gandalf in Fangorn Forest, and who later captures Frodo.[29] Nevertheless, a shape was emerging, and Tolkien also had in mind Frodo's inability to destroy the Ring and Gollum taking it, before falling into the fire.

In rewriting the Rivendell chapters Elrond and Gandalf comment on the Old Forest, Barrow-Wights, and Bombadil – but Tolkien's central task was to establish what was to be done with the Ring, and how to do it. He organized his characters for the next phase: Frodo and Sam would undertake the anti-quest, along with Gandalf (early seen as a welcome, if unexpected, companion), Trotter (now a Human character), and Boromir – soon joined by the Hobbits Faramond and Merry. But the membership of the Company was highly fluid, and Tolkien kept rethinking it; he also now began to wonder if Treebeard should be supporting the mission.[30] Neither could he resist slipping his own private references into the narrative. His poem 'Errantry', later published as a Tom Bombadil song, was the source for Bilbo's verse 'Eärendil was a Mariner', which he recites to Elrond and the Elves. 'Errantry' itself is based on 'I hae nae Kith, I hae nae Kin', which begins with the line 'O what's the rhyme to porringer?', a ranting Jacobite song dating from the late seventeenth or early eighteenth century. The third verse of the original calls for the Protestant king William III to be hanged and 'James to have his ain again' – James being the deposed Catholic monarch James VII and II.[31] So, as with *The Hobbit*, there is an unexpected trace of rebel Jacobitism in *The Lord of the Rings*, and Aragorn, who helps Bilbo with the poem, is, of course, a returning king coming to claim his own again – he even has the healing hands that were associated with the Stuart kings.[32]

The Company manage to leave Rivendell and embark on the next stage: 'The Ring Goes South'. Even in the early drafts there are tensions within the Company: Boromir was shaping up as a traitor, Legolas and Gimli rehearse the ancient enmity between Elves and Dwarves, and Gandalf and Trotter are at odds. These frictions remain in the final version, where it is noticeable that Legolas does not speak directly to Frodo until they arrive at the edge of Lothlórien as well as rebuking Pippin, while Merry is more often than not a silent traveller. It is a bleak affair, undertaken in the depths of winter, driven by despair.[33]

The Company fail to cross the Misty Mountains and to enter the Mines of Moria, Tolkien writing a memo to himself that the Dwarven halls of Moria should be very different from those of the Lonely Mountain in *The Hobbit*.[34] Gandalf has the same trouble in gaining entrance as he does in the final novel, the Watcher in the Water makes a brief appearance, and once inside they find their way through the dark to Balin's tomb and, in a passage added later, discover a journal of the attempted resettlement of the Mines.[35] Tolkien then resorted to notes: the Company are attacked by Goblins and a Black Rider as they seek to leave, Gandalf struggles with the Black Rider (later revised to a Balrog), and the two of them fall from the broken bridge into the abyss below. In parentheses Tolkien immediately added, 'Of course Gandalf must reappear later – probably fall is not as deep as it seemed.' [36] Unlike much else, then, Gandalf's return was planned from the earliest draft of the scene.

In the Foreword of the second edition of *The Lord of the Rings* Tolkien claimed that at this point, in the dark days of the Second World War, he then abandoned the narrative for nearly a year, from late 1940 to 1941 – although Christopher Tolkien queries the dating, determining it to be December 1939 when his father paused, and in or around August 1940 when he recommenced his writing.[37] Tolkien then paused again until 1942, and although he abandoned the story once more for over a year until April 1944 he did start to rewrite the first chapters and once again tinkered with the chronology.[38] Unsurprisingly, the chapter that required most work was 'Ancient History' (published as 'The Shadow of the Past') and Gandalf's account of the Rings of Power. Tolkien still did not understand the full nature of these rings, their relationship to the account of the Ring given by Bilbo in *The Hobbit*, and how the Ring would govern the subplot of the novel through Aragorn's accession to the throne of Gondor as the heir of Isildur, an earlier Ringbearer. Strangely, Tolkien was also attentive to the dreams that Frodo has in the House of Tom Bombadil and at Bree, as if he hoped that these were intimations of the plot to come – clues to as-yet undisclosed events.

Saruman was at last brought in as a fallen wizard, enabling a rich new narrative thread that would begin with the incarceration of Gandalf and ultimately culminate at Bag End in the penultimate chapter of the novel. But all that was to come

– Tolkien was now wrestling with the immediate implications of the lengthening history of the Ring that extended the open debate at Rivendell. Eventually this wrangling led to a new version that began with 'The Council of Elrond'. In one daring step forward Tolkien was able to rethink the summit at Rivendell: he introduced Saruman, in all his colours and disguises. Saruman's wiles explained Gandalf's absences and delays, paved the way for all his mechanized machinations in the new industrial society of Isengard, and created a new landmark in the plot. Through the dramatic possibilities of Isengard, *The Lord of the Rings* not only began to shake off the familiar locations and atmospheres of *The Hobbit*, but now hinted at a whole world of diverse cultures. We have moved from Hobbiton through the sweet and safe haven of Rivendell, but now there was a dark and bitter tang brewing, and it was what lay beyond the familiar that beckoned.

The first of these new innovations was the Balrog of Moria. Its description has been much contested: does it have wings or not? Tolkien's description is beautifully equivocal, and reveals his subtlety. Recently, the philosopher Graham Harman has identified a comparable quality in the horror writer H.P. Lovecraft (1890–1937) – the laureate of the Cthulhu Mythos of monstrous and terrifying inter-dimensional entities and Tolkien's contemporary. The key to understanding Lovecraft's work, according to Harman, is that it is non-anthropocentric, and that Human understanding and knowledge cannot come close to making sense of his alien reality. Lovecraft is a 'productionist' writer (as opposed to a reductionist writer) who finds 'new gaps in the world where there were formerly none'.[39] Harman explains this by comparing Lovecraft's writing to the Cubist paintings of Pablo Picasso and Georges Braque: 'No other writer is so perplexed by the gap between objects and the power of language to describe them, or between objects and the qualities they possess ... Lovecraft echoes cubist painting ... by slicing an object into vast cross-sections of qualities, planes, or adumbrations, which even when added up do not exhaust the reality of the object they compose.'[40] This means that 'Lovecraft's major gift as a writer is his deliberate and skilful obstruction of all attempts to paraphrase him',[41] and Harman demonstrates this by showing just how difficult (and ludicrous) paraphrases of his descriptions are. As an example he takes Lovecraft's representation of a statue of Cthulhu:

> If I say that my somewhat extravagant imagination yielded simultaneous pictures of an octopus, a dragon, and a human caricature, I shall not be unfaithful to the spirit of the thing ... but it was the *general outline* of the whole which made it most shockingly frightful.

Plainly, this cannot be paraphrased as 'It looked like an octopus, a dragon, and a human, all rolled into one.' So Lovecraft's language is 'the paraphrase of a reality that eludes all literal speech'.[42] This, for Harman, is '*weird realism*'.[43]

In fact, there are (to my mind) better examples in the Edwardian ghost stories of M.R. James (with which Tolkien was familiar).[44] In 'Canon Alberic's Scrap-Book' (1895), James describes a picture that includes a hideous humanoid creature:

> At first you saw only a mass of coarse, matted black hair; presently it was seen that this covered a body of fearful thinness, almost a skeleton, but with the muscles standing out like wires. The hands were of a dusky pallor, covered, like the body, with long, coarse hairs, and hideously taloned. The eyes, touched in with a burning yellow, had intensely black pupils, and were fixed upon the throned King with a look of beast-like hate. Imagine one of the awful bird-catching spiders of South America translated

into human form, and endowed with intelligence just less
than human, and you will have some faint conception of
the terror inspired by the appalling effigy.[45]

The key words here are not in the physical description, but in
the mental trauma it produces: *imagine* 'one of the [for there are
many] awful bird-catching spiders of South America' that was
translated 'into human form' – a fearful parody of the translation, or movement, of holy relics – and *somehow*, unnervingly,
'endowed with intelligence just less than human'. Yet even that
awful feat of imagination would only provide a 'faint conception'
of the 'terror [it] inspired'. This, as Harman would suggest, is a
reality that is impossible to describe, in which 'numerous bizarre
or troubling features of a palpable thing are piled up in such
excessive manner it becomes difficult to combine all these facets
neatly into a single object'.[46]

   To return to the Balrog. In the first draft of Tolkien's description, the Balrog does have an almost Jamesian etiolation, with
yellow eyes and a red tongue; 'its arms were very long' and its
'streaming hair seemed to catch fire'.[47] But in the published
version it has lost this sharpness of definition and become a
darkness of power and terror. It is first described as something
that 'could not be seen': a 'great shadow' enveloping a 'dark form,
of man-shape maybe' – that undecided 'maybe' is perfect – yet
with a 'streaming mane' of fire, then a 'fiery shadow'; the shadow
about it 'reached out like two vast wings'. As Gandalf three times
declares, 'You cannot pass', the Balrog 'drew itself up to a great
height, and its wings were spread from wall to wall'.[48] The metaphorical wings of shadow thus coalesce into something more
tangible – or do they? The appearance of the Balrog is deliberately unresolved, flickering like fire, flaring between different
realities. We are left in doubt, cowering like Gandalf, 'a wizened
tree before the onset of a storm'.[49]

Having cast Gandalf into the abyss, Tolkien took stock and produced a detailed plan that included dates of events: Lothlórien, Boromir's threats against Frodo, Frodo's escape with Sam, and their capture of Gollum. Gollum leads them through the Dead Marshes before betraying them; Frodo arrives at the Crack of Doom but cannot cast in the Ring; they are surrounded by Black Riders mounted on giant vultures. Tolkien then tried various ideas, pondering the role of Sam: 'Is he to die?'[50] He wondered whether Gollum should take the Ring and be seized by Sam, who throws them both into the fire. He considers a glen of giant Spiders, Sam disguised as an Orc, Frodo's capture by Orcs and his hatred of Sam who has taken the Ring – and some of these ideas, here sketched in embryo, did indeed appear in the final version. He then turned to the other characters, bereft at the loss of Frodo. Merry and Pippin get lost in Fangorn and meet Treebeard, Aragorn and Boromir go to Minas Tirith, Legolas and Gimli determine to go home but then they meet Gandalf, returned from the dead. '*He is now clad in white*': he has returned as a greater power.[51] The notes gathered momentum: Tolkien planned battles, more of Boromir's treachery (perhaps he joins with Saruman, perhaps he is killed by Aragorn), and the return journey during which Isengard is given to the Dwarves. But now there is also the brooding question 'What happens to Shire?'[52] However, his immediate concern was to get Frodo and Sam to Mordor, and then to work on what would become the proliferating subplots that began with Merry and Pippin being separated from their companions, and which only rejoined the main narrative twenty-two chapters later after the Battle of the Black Gate.

As he wrote the first versions of the chapters concerning Lothlórien and Galadriel, Tolkien continued to muse over the origins of the Rings of Power. His idea now was that they had been forged by the great Elvish artist Fëanor, who had also crafted the Silmaril jewels, but, like the Silmarils themselves, had been stolen by Sauron's master, Morgoth. Fëanor – the central figure of *The Silmarillion* and the prime mover of the ceaseless and violent attempts to recover the gems – haunts Galadriel in unexpected ways. When Galadriel distributes gifts among the Company of the Ring, Gimli is first given her brooch and named Elfstone – a name that Tolkien then immediately bestowed on Trotter as his true name, before wondering whether Elf-Friend, Elfspear, or Elfmere would be more suitable.[53] Nevertheless, this decision was to have a lasting impact on Aragorn, as it steered his destiny towards marriage with the Half-Elf Arwen. As to Gimli, he eventually requests – and receives – three strands of golden hair from Galadriel's head, which he proclaims will be set in crystal as an heirloom of his house. Galadriel herself avows that 'none have ever made to me a request so bold and yet so courteous'.[54] And yet Tolkien saw meaningful potential in this gift. After he had finished *The Lord of the Rings* he intermittently returned to 'The Silmarillion' and added Galadriel to the legendarium as the 'greatest of the Noldor, except Fëanor maybe, though she was wiser than he, and her wisdom increased with the long years'. Fëanor was Galadriel's half-uncle and older than she, and it was Fëanor who asked for a lock of her hair three times; three times she denied him a single strand, and so they were 'unfriends forever'.[55] It was Galadriel's refusal that led Fëanor to make the Silmarils, bringing about all the consequent ills of the 'First Age'. Tolkien thus created a retrospective background for Gimli's heirloom that not only makes Galadriel's gift all the more momentous, but also entwines it in the whole history of the Elves. Moreover, the light of the Silmarils is also reflected in the phial of radiant water that Galadriel gives to Frodo, so gleams of the legendarium flicker through these scenes as well.

The introduction of Lothlórien also allowed Tolkien the

opportunity to complicate his depiction of the Elves, who otherwise would have been barely present in *The Lord of the Rings*.[56] Lothlórien is not maintained by singing or by Elf archery, but by fighting against Sauron: it is not an oasis of calm, but a citadel on permanent alert.[57] The Elves have their own capricious laws, such as blindfolding their guests – or, rather, they intend to discriminate against the Dwarf Gimli and blindfold only him.[58] They almost come to blows until Aragorn persuades the whole Company that they should all be blindfolded – creating a metaphor for the progress of a book that has little overall plan but which stumbles blindly on. So apt was this motif that it is later repeated when Faramir blindfolds Frodo and Sam before taking them to his hideout.[59] Indeed, many important episodes take place in the dark or underground: Old Man Willow, the Barrow-Wight, Moria (in which Gandalf descends beneath the Mines to prehistoric depths), Helm's Deep, Shelob's Lair, the Paths of the Dead, and Mount Doom. In the attack on Helm's Deep, moreover, Saruman's use of explosives – 'a blasting fire' – could, as Théoden points out, be used to 'seal up those that are inside', transforming the refuge into a living tomb.[60]

Tolkien also began to understand that the fate of Lothlórien – indeed of all the Elves – was bound to the One Ring. The power of Galadriel's ring Nenya, the Ring of Adamant, would disappear if the One Ring was destroyed. It became apparent that this would not only precipitate the emigration of the Elves of Lothlórien from Middle-Earth but also the permanent exile – effectively a death sentence – for Galadriel herself as she would not be able to accompany them. As a rebel Elf Queen Galadriel has been banished from Valinor – until she resists the One Ring and is allowed to be repatriated.

Tolkien now had a clearer conception of the plot. Boromir tries to take the Ring, Frodo and Sam escape, Orcs take Merry and Pippin, and Boromir dies defending them – but leaving some doubt as to which Hobbits have been taken. Aragorn leads Legolas and Gimli after the Orc band, but he questions his decision to do so again and again.[61] There are incomplete versions of the encounter with Éomer and the Riders of Rohan (not nearly so fraught as the meeting later became) and of the Orc captors, and then the arrival of Treebeard. Despite the malignancy of Willow-Man (Old Man Willow) and Tolkien's early sense that Treebeard was to be a similarly malevolent arboreal being, he later wrote that he had known 'for years' that Frodo [sic] would 'run into a tree-adventure somewhere'. Moreover, he had 'no recollection of inventing Ents'. Instead, he 'came at last to the point, and wrote the "Treebeard" chapter without any recollection of previous thought; just as it now is'.[62]

While Christopher Tolkien agrees that the chapter 'did indeed very largely "write itself"', Tolkien had surely had Ent-like trees on his mind not only since the Hobbits' trouble in the Old Forest, but since he first read *Macbeth* at school. Some months before the publication of *The Return of the King* he wrote to his friend and admirer W.H. Auden, noting that he did not 'consciously' invent the Ents at all, and that the Treebeard chapter 'was written off more or less as it stands'. Tolkien mulled over this in the letter, suggesting that Ents had emerged from his unconscious and are 'composed of philology, literature, and life', the name being derived from the Anglo-Saxon phrase *eald enta geweorc* ('work of Giants').[63] But he then complained about the Dark Ages Scottish play *Macbeth*, and his 'bitter disappointment and disgust from schooldays with the shabby use made in Shakespeare of the coming of "Great Birnam wood to high Dunsinane hill": I longed to devise a setting in which the trees might really march to war'.[64] So Shakespeare's apparent shortcoming, cultivated by Tolkien for decades, helped to inspire the march of the Ents on Isengard when the Forest rouses itself to war.

He had other diverse sources too. In the Gospel of St Mark there is a tantalizingly brief account of Jesus curing a man of blindness by rubbing spit onto his eyes; when Jesus asks if he can see aught, the man looks up and says, 'I see men as trees, walking.'[65] Algernon Blackwood's mysterious tale 'The Man Whom the Trees Loved' (1912) includes the suggestive idea that 'behind a great forest . . . may stand a rather splendid Entity that manifests through all the thousand individual trees', and also speculates that 'trees had once been moving things, animal organisms of some sort, that had stood so long feeding, sleeping, dreaming, or something, in the same place, that they had lost the power to get away' – which is how Treebeard defines the Ents that have become sleepy and 'tree-ish'.[66] Likewise, the idiosyncratic work of artist Arthur Rackham is characterized by bristly, twisted, anthropomorphic trees that appear as the guises of Elves and other supernatural beings, or simply as the animated nature in the background of his scenes; his trees are key characters of Faërie. More frivolously, in 1932 the Disney animation studios produced a *Silly Symphony* episode of 'Flowers and Trees' that has trees actively moving about, falling in love, and then being threatened by a rotten stump who ignites a fire and then catches alight. The film was highly acclaimed: it was the first Disney cartoon to be made in full colour, was the first to have an all-classical score (including excerpts from Beethoven's sixth symphony and Schubert's 'The Erl King'), and even the first to feature the death of a character; it also won the first Academy Award for Animated Short Subjects. 'Flowers and Trees' was a milestone in film-making and a renowned success.

Tolkien had been planning a role for Treebeard for some time, and his notes before he wrote the chapter reveal an ambivalent attitude to the Ent, who is 'In some ways rather stupid'.[67] Moreover, initially Treebeard admitted to knowing Tom Bombadil and the Old Forest, creating a continuity between the woodlands and nature spirits of Middle-Earth that Tolkien then removed: disjuncture and discontinuity being more telling. Treebeard as he eventually appeared does indeed know less than he seems to: he has no idea what Hobbits are, for example, as they were left out of the old versified lists that, for him, constitute the harmony of the natural world – so his old view is incomplete and distorted.[68] More seriously, the Ents have lost the Entwives, a fatal oversight that condemns their species to extinction.[69] The Entwives were associated with gardens rather than forests, and rather pathetically Treebeard asks if they have been seen in The Shire. Attentive readers will recall that in the second chapter of *The Fellowship of the Ring* Sam is drinking in The Green Dragon and claims that his cousin had seen a 'Tree-man' on the North Moors of The Shire, as 'big as an elm tree, and walking'.[70] Yet this is another calculated dead-end, and is never connected with the Ents or their Entwives, and in any case Treebeard is vague about the lands beyond Fangorn. Strangely, Gandalf (much favoured by Treebeard as he is the only wizard who truly cares about trees – so what of Radagast?) seems to have been charmed by Treebeard and claims that he is 'the oldest living thing that still walks beneath the Sun' in Middle-Earth – which begs the question: what of Tom Bombadil, or even Sauron?[71] For his part, Treebeard does not tell Merry and Pippin that he saw Gandalf in Fangorn just a few days prior to finding them, so he knows that Gandalf did not die with the Balrog.

It is at this stage worth referring to what was believed to be the work of Giants in Anglo-Saxon England: Roman remains. The landscape through which the Company has been travelling is persistently layered with strata of ruins. At the borders of The Shire there are the Barrow-Downs, littered with ancient burial mounds; a few miles from Bree there is Weathertop, the ruined watch-tower of Amon Sûl. The travellers frequently find overgrown paths and broken steps, silent and perplexing remnants. The lands of *The Lord of the Rings* are ruinous. The Anglo-Saxons believed that they inhabited a broken world, abandoned by a race of Giants who had constructed fortresses and amphitheatres, dead-straight roads lined with ornate columns and richly decorated villas – but these people had passed and their architectural skills and secrets had been lost. Tolkien had included ruins in *The Hobbit* in the broken city of Dale, but in *The Lord of the Rings* almost the whole of Middle-Earth seems to be littered with inscrutable remains, defined by relics of the past and providing the opportunity for moments of reflection on temporal change.

At vital junctures, Tolkien then audaciously introduces unexpected key-changes in this topographical itinerary. As the Company leave Moria with the memory of Gandalf's fall into the abyss still horribly fresh in their memories, they pass by the pool of Kheled-Zâram, and in a moment of heritage tourism Gimli takes Frodo and Sam to see the reflection of the mountains there. It moves Sam to silence – an incommunicable experience.[72] Later, Gimli and Legolas agree to visit together the Glittering Caves of Helm's Deep and the depths of Fangorn Forest.[73] Although these visits do not take place until the return journey, they are not tit-for-tat exchanges – or, for that matter, more heritage tourism: rather, they are attempts to share the values and aesthetics of one species (the natural rock art valued by the Dwarves) with another (the organic beauty of trees prized by the Elves) – a shared environmental communion.[74] Legolas does not have words to describe the experience of the Caves: the Elvish languages falter in the face of alien beauty. Conversely, when Aragorn sees the stupendous monumental statuary of the Argonath – giant statues of his forebears Isildur and Anárion on the River Anduin – he physically changes. His identity, like his sword, is reforged. He speaks in a 'strange voice'; Frodo, cowering in fear at the bottom of the boat,

sees that 'the weatherworn Ranger was no longer there'; Strider
has become Aragorn, and has now – if only briefly at present –
found his voice of sovereign authority.

To continue with the drafts, returning to Gandalf and his
meeting with Aragorn, Gimli, and Legolas. There is more unexplained mystery here. The three companions see an old man
by their fire – is it Saruman?[75] Gandalf confesses that it was
not him and seems to suggest that it was Saruman, and one
of Tolkien's early notes indicates that it is in fact Saruman –
yet Aragorn observes that the Horses were not made uneasy
by the figure, suggesting that they would have panicked in the
presence of a fallen wizard.[76] So who was it? A figure glimpsed
at the edge of a fire in the dead of night, neither the disgraced
Saruman nor Gandalf the White; in the draft, Gandalf suggests
it was 'a vision' (deleted) or perhaps 'some wraith of [Saruman's]
making'.[77] Evidently Tolkien himself was unsure, but is there
another possibility: is it the shadowy figure Gandalf the Grey –
the ghost of Gandalf past, a memory subliminally shared among
friends? Gandalf the White, meanwhile – initially mistaken
as Saruman to the extent that Legolas looses an arrow at him
– is an enigmatic figure who speaks in riddles, and so 'white'
does not indicate any greater clarity over his previous incarnation as 'grey'. From the earliest drafts he has 'forgotten much
that I knew, and learned again much that I had forgotten' – a
remark made even more ambiguous in the final text by Gandalf
admitting he has forgotten much of what he *thought* he knew
– including his own name.[78]

On their arrival at Edoras, the golden hall of Théoden,
the four travellers are challenged by the guards who, in this
early draft, literally speak in Anglo-Saxon, echoing lines from
Beowulf.[79] Gandalf the White begins to take on a more active
role as one of the few characters who seems able to command the
plot, manipulating and misleading others, refusing to surrender

his staff before his audience with Théoden and then using it to exorcize the king.[80] It is here too that Aragorn meets, and, perhaps, falls in love with Éowyn, 'a stern amazon woman', as she serves him wine at their meal and their eyes meet.[81] Tolkien was not sure: he jotted down a series of notes stating that Aragorn and Éowyn wed, then that Aragorn is too old, then that Éowyn should die to avenge Théoden, then that Aragorn did love Éowyn and never married. Further notes show a darker turn to the end of the story: on returning to Rivendell and homeward bound, the Hobbits learn that the Nazgûl have razed Lothlórien and that Galadriel has been lost, or left to wander in Middle-Earth.

The chapters on the defeat of Saruman and the destruction of Isengard show how extensively Tolkien was prepared to rewrite his novel. In the first versions, for example, Théoden was ambushed on his way to the Hornburg and loses many of his guard before he succeeds in getting inside; Saruman's Orcs and Wild Men then attack, and Théoden rides out again to engage them. Saruman's forces batter down the doors of the stronghold and Aragorn is beaten to the ground before the Rohirrim win the day. Other elements were, however, apparently in place from the outset, such as the strange and lethal forest of Huorn trees that appears, the diversion of the river to drown Isengard, as well as Merry's reflections on pipe-weed amidst the wreckage. Tolkien was not at all sure how the whole Saruman episode might be developed. In one draft Aragorn comments on Gandalf's plans, but his words are equally applicable to Tolkien's own writing and composition: 'Gandalf's plans are risky, and they lead often to a knife-edge. There is great wisdom, forethought and courage in them – but no certainty.'[82]

The first version of Gandalf's parley with Saruman is inconclusive – Saruman's staff is not broken and the crystal globe hurled from the tower by Wormtongue simply shatters. Tolkien later claimed that he recognized the 'Orthanc-stone' as a *palantír* straightaway and realized its significance, but it was only in Tolkien posing himself a series of questions about the object that both Gandalf and he gradually recognize it as a Seeing Stone, and also only in further drafting that Pippin retrieves it and so falls prey to temptation. He also pondered whether Saruman had deliberately thrown the *palantír* to goad Gandalf into using it and perhaps expose his plans to Sauron. Such were his deliberations throughout composition, and, as with many characters, objects, and events, things only came into focus little by little – in the case of the *palantír* it took over a year of refinements before its role was made clear.[83] Treebeard, meanwhile, states that the Ents will guard Saruman for seven times the years he tormented them.[84] In fact, Treebeard guards him for less than six months before letting him go – a very poor decision with calamitous consequences.[85] Again, the judgement of Ents is drawn into question: despite his formidable confidence and unquestioned authority, Treebeard is in fact worryingly unreliable.

Tolkien's stamina faltered and he ceased work on the book. He knew he had to get Frodo and Sam to Mordor, and had already written a version of the Minas Morgul episode and capture of Frodo, possibly to give the earlier stages a target episode. He also reminded himself that 'Minas Morgul must be made more horrible. The usual "goblin" stuff is not good enough here.'[86] Eventually he resumed the Hobbits' journey in the Emyn Muil (at the threshold of the Dead Marshes) in scraps of dialogue and notes – but rather like Frodo and Sam he could not see how to negotiate this forbidding landscape of stone crevasses and crags, and the ever-present threat of Gollum's pursuit of the Ring. He drafted and redrafted – 'A few pages for a lot of sweat', as he put it in a letter of 1944.[87] The wanderings of Frodo and Sam mirror Tolkien's writing process: frustratingly slow progress, retracing steps and going around in circles, and pursued by an obscure malice from another, earlier story. Yet it is by looking back into the past that enabled Tolkien to find a way forward. Frodo recalls his conversation with Gandalf in Bag End – that it was a pity that Bilbo did not kill Gollum when he had the chance. Tolkien realized that the relationship of Gollum to the Ring – indeed, to the whole story – was far more deeply enmeshed than he had earlier envisaged. He rewrote the earlier conversation and then quoted it as Frodo stood among the rocks of the Emyn Muil: Gollum's destiny was bound to the Ring, and thereby to Frodo.

So Gollum now joined Frodo and Sam as a guide rather than stalking them as his quarry. The doubled personality of Gollum was elaborated: Sam overhears him holding 'colloquies' with himself – 'a sort of good Smeagol [sic] angry with a bad Gollum'.[88] Gollum's character was becoming increasingly complex – as were his relationships with the Hobbits – and in a letter describing the progress of the work, Tolkien compared Sam's treatment of Gollum as analogous to Ariel's treatment of Caliban in Shakespeare's play The Tempest.[89] They pass through the Dead Marshes, arrive at the Black Gate, and thence through Ithilien where they are seized by Faramir (originally Falborn). It is here that Tolkien later added the passage in which Sam is confronted with a dead Southron warrior whose troop is ambushed by Faramir's Rangers: he wonders what his name was, where he came from, whether he would have rather stayed at home.[90] Sam's thoughts run along the same lines as do Paul Bäumer's in Erich Maria Remarque's First World War novel All Quiet on the Western Front (1929) when he shares a fox-hole with a dying French soldier. The anonymous enemy is given an identity, only for it to be immediately snatched away: 'Why do they never tell us that you are poor devils like us, that your mothers are just as anxious as ours, and that we have the same fear of death, and the same dying and the same agony . . . ?' In fact, Sam is glad he could not see the dead man's face, and should not think about his name: for Remarque, the dead man's name would have 'the power to recall this for ever, it will always come back and stand before me'.[91] It is a sobering moment.

The Hobbits' talk with Faramir allowed Tolkien the chance to fill in much of the background of Númenor and Gondor and was rewritten several times as it became unwieldy and overly digressive – including at several stages, for example, a disquisition on the history of languages, later wisely cut. But the point here was to draw a sharp distinction between Boromir, who was intoxicated with the Ring, and his brother Faramir who, having learnt of it, does not even wish to see it. As Gandalf says, the 'blood of Westernesse' (Númenor) runs 'nearly true' in Faramir, yet it did not in Boromir, which explains not only their different responses to the Ring, but also the ability of Aragorn – himself of Númenórean descent – to resist it.[92] It is a clear example of the legendarium buttressing the new story.

Tolkien worked hard on the book as Frodo and Sam approached the walls of Mordor – 'wrote and tore up and rewrote most of it a good many times' – but he was encouraged by Lewis and Williams and intrigued by the complexity of Gollum.[93] Originally he planned to have several Spiders in Kirith Ungol (spelt thus at this stage), but that would have been too much like The Hobbit, so he reduced them to a single Spider, Ungoliant – Morgoth's fearsome ally from 'The Silmarillion' (and considerably more powerful than a Balrog) – before settling on Shelob, last of the brood of Ungoliant. The action remained fairly stable: Frodo is stung and effectively left for dead by Sam, who takes the Ring; however, it is first Gollum who leads a band of Orcs to Frodo, then Orcs arriving to investigate the commotion who chance on Frodo's body. Sam puts on the Ring: it is so powerful at this stage that he can see through rocks and understand the Orcs, but Tolkien emphasized that 'the ring does *not* confer courage on Sam'.[94] Sam attempts to follow the Orcs, but the doors of Kirith Ungol slam shut – and at this point Tolkien paused for two years.

Where to Go?

It was 1946 before he resumed the book. He returned to the subplot by reworking the later chapters on Rohan, tried to finish the chapter on Pippin's arrival in Minas Tirith, and planned the final volume of the book. In this version, Éowyn slays the Lord of the Nazgûl in battle before Minas Tirith but is herself mortally wounded, and Gondor invades Minas Morgul and takes the war into Mordor. In another version, Théoden is shot dead charging into Osgiliath (the abandoned Gondor city at the border with Mordor) and the Lord of the Nazgûl's steed – a giant vulture-like creature – tears at his flesh with its talons before being decapitated by Éowyn with a sword blow that mysteriously dispels the Witch-King himself. The story ends with the fall of Sauron and the ensuing ruin of Lothlórien, and there are some odd ideas – such as Gandalf tossing the *palantír* of Minas Tirith from its tower and accidentally killing a Gondor captain. Much of the writing involved getting the characters to Minas Tirith for the imminent conflict there: Pippin with Gandalf, Merry (secretly) with the Riders of Rohan, and Aragorn through the mountains – making three distinct, and intricate, subplots (and, in doing so, comprising elements of the conventionally stated seven basic plots).[95] In addition to the action of the plot and details of setting, Tolkien was extremely careful to get the dating right for the plot and each subplot, drafting and revising the time schemes, as well as referring to his maps and calculating relative distances travelled on foot and on horseback – he even worked out a system of measurement ('Long Measures') for Hobbits to determine the length of their stride.[96] His account of the war was, in other words,

planned with military precision. In addition, Tolkien now had
materials for the appendices in mind and started drafting 'The
Quest of Erebor', a text that tied *The Hobbit* more closely to *The
Lord of the Rings* by describing Gandalf's meeting with Thorin
at The Prancing Pony in Bree.[97] It is remarkable that even as
Tolkien was piecing together his hugely ambitious mosaic of
plotlines for his work-in-progress he was simultaneously drafting supporting storylines and further subplots – although in the
event 'The Quest of Erebor' was not included due to problems
with length and remained unpublished until it was included in
Unfinished Tales (1980). The relationship between these various
plots has helpfully been described as 'interlaced', although knotted, tangled, or 'elfed' (to use a Shakespearean neologism) might
be a better term, and although these entwined plots confuse
both characters and readers, this is because both characters and
readers are contending with them at ground level: we are stuck
inside multiplying narratives.[98] The apparent symmetry of the
plot – Pippin in Gondor, Merry in Rohan – is merely incidental,
and belied by the mass of asymmetrical material. This sense of
readers having to deal with the same issues that confront the
characters is again comparable to Shakespeare, in which nearly
all we have on page or stage are individual perspectives spoken
by different characters.[99] The difference in *The Lord of the Rings* is
that Tolkien himself is confused, and finds his way not by means
of a masterplan or long-decided or familiar plot structure but –
to quote *King Lear* – 'feelingly'.[100] Sam, who has a keen critical
perspective, describes being in Lothlórien like being '*inside* a
song', and the predicament that he and Frodo find themselves
in as they enter Mordor as being 'in a story', adding that he
wonders 'what sort of a tale we've fallen into'.[101] The answer is,
a fearsomely tortuous one.

   The siege of Minas Tirith includes the notable confrontation between Gandalf and the Lord of the Nazgûl. In an early

version, Gandalf bars the way of the Witch-King with the same words he used against the Balrog: 'You cannot pass . . .'[102] The Witch-King laughs, but then a cock crows, 'caring nothing for battle or death, welcoming the morning, and at the same moment . . . the horns of the Riders of Rohan are heard echoing on the sides of the mountains'.[103] Tolkien later said that this was one of the scenes that had stayed in his mind after finishing the book, and that it still moved him. The scene in fact echoes Shakespeare's *Hamlet*, in which the Ghost of Hamlet's father starts and leaves when the cock crows:

> It faded on the crowing of the cock.
> Some say that ever 'gainst that season comes
> Wherein our saviour's birth is celebrated
> The bird of dawning singeth all night long;
> And then, they say, no spirit can walk abroad,
> The nights are wholesome; then no planets strike,
> No fairy takes, nor witch hath power to charm,
> So hallowed and so gracious is the time.[104]

The crowing cock held a revered role in English folklore, as the antiquary Henry Bourne recorded in 1725, noting that it is 'a received Tradition among the Vulgar, That at the Time of Cock-crowing, the Midnight Spirits forsake these lower Regions, and go to their proper Places'.[105] Bourne saw this as a form of divine consolation, relating it to the Nativity and an old belief that Christ was born at cock-crow – the cock crowing all night – and that at the same time the Angels sung carols to the shepherds; cock-crow was also the time of the Resurrection. Hence, 'as the Saviour of the world was then born, and the *heavenly Host* had then descended to proclaim the News . . . the Angels of Darkness would be terrified and confounded, and immediately fly away', thus, 'the Spirits of Darkness, having always in

Memory that fatal Hour, are startled and frighted away as the Cock proclaims it'.[106] The belief was recorded as early as the fourth century by the Roman Christian poet Prudentius.

Tolkien still planned to have Minas Morgul overrun by the combined armies of Rohan and Gondor and the Rangers, who would then march into Mordor; now they would be joined by the Elves of Lothlórien and the Ents. They call forth Sauron, but he sends a minion bearing Frodo's coat of *mithril* as proof that they have captured him, and who then attempts to negotiate a peace that would enforce punishing terms on Gondor and Rohan. Gandalf, realizing that Sauron cannot have recovered the Ring, rejects this treaty; the combined army is then ambushed by the forces of Mordor, but at that moment the Ring is destroyed. As Sauron falls his final act of revenge is to detonate the Orthanc *palantír* in the hope that it will kill Aragorn.

Perhaps Tolkien felt that this pluralistic army was too reminiscent of the Battle of the Five Armies at the end of *The Hobbit*, and that an exploding *palantír* was rather too sensationalist. In the final version, the triumph of Gondor and Rohan in the Battle of the Pelennor Fields is tempered by the fact that Sauron has not been defeated, just stalled, and still commands vast military forces. Their resolution to meet Sauron's army at the Black Gate is consequently an utterly futile advance doomed to inevitable defeat – yet which could at least occupy Sauron's attention and provide the tiniest of hopes that Frodo will succeed in his anti-quest. Bearing this in mind, any full frontal assault on Mordor would appear to be overly exultant, which is why it was ultimately replaced by the venture of despair to the Black Gate.

Meanwhile, Éowyn's confrontation with the Lord of the Nazgûl, the Witch-King of Angmar, now developed along the lines of Shakespeare's confrontation of Macbeth with Macduff:

> *Macbeth:* I bear a charmèd life, which must not yield
> To one of woman born.
> *Macduff:*   Despair thy charm,
> And let the angel whom thou still hast served
> Tell thee Macduff was from his mother's womb
> Untimely ripped.[107]

The Witch-King, of course, cannot be killed by any living man. In the first version of their duel Éowyn has cropped hair so she could disguise herself as Dernhelm, but at the last minute Tolkien changed this and had her cinematically revealing her long, golden tresses. Merry's role in slaying the Lord of the Nazgûl also began to emerge as Tolkien drafted the scene: he wounds him with a sword actually forged to combat the Witch-King that he has been carrying since being waylaid by the Barrow-Wight. The wound unknits the power of the Witch-King, making him vulnerable to Éowyn's deathblow.

Merry, grievously sick, 'wandering half blind and witless', finds his way to Minas Tirith and is found by Pippin, and then healed by Aragorn – the company of travellers, sundered since their brief reunion at Isengard, begins to reform again, the sub-plots resolving themselves into a single thread.[108] The story began to gain momentum once more. Tolkien also added sentences looking back to Rivendell and the formation of the Company of the Ring, highlighting Merry's part in the destruction of the Lord of the Nazgûl, thereby justifying his inclusion among the Company. Tolkien also considered how the Ring could be used against Sauron, outlined in a draft of the chapter on the council of war, 'The Last Debate'. A powerful person (Aragorn, Elrond, Gandalf) could wield the Ring and become the deathless Ringlord. He would dominate the minds of all, sucking the power and thought from them, even from Sauron himself and his servants, who would now worship the Ringlord as a god. Sauron would indeed be toppled and annihilated, 'but behold, there would be Sauron still...'[109] This chapter also originally included the passage of the Paths of the Dead, told mainly by Gimli and eventually moved earlier in the book to become Gimli's internal monologue; he later refuses to talk of the experience. The combined army of the Host of the West then goes to confront Sauron at the Black Gate; Merry and Pippin are at first left behind, then Pippin is permitted to accompany the doomed force.

Frodo and Sam are of course at the same time making their painfully slow progress across Mordor. Tolkien was determined that Frodo should be captured by Orcs, and he drafted that incident as early as 1944. The Orcs then take his *mithril* coat and other possessions to Sauron in Barad-Dûr, who then passes them to his ambassador for the negotiations at the Black Gate – this was a critical point of connection between the plot and subplot, and also placed Frodo and Sam in dire peril. But Frodo also had to be able to escape and continue his journey, and it was not until three years later that Tolkien tried to extricate him.[110] The eventual solution was that, once his belongings had been taken, the Orcs would start squabbling, fighting, and then killing each other – all of which is seen from the viewpoint of Sam, who discovers Frodo's whereabouts by singing and listening for a response. This idea was taken from a legend of Richard the Lionheart, imprisoned by the Duke of Austria, and the attempts of his minstrel Blondel to trace him. Blondel visits a castle that confines a single prisoner:

he sat directly before a window of the castell . . . and began to sing a song in French, which king Richard and Blondel had sometime composed together. When king Richard heard the song, he knew it was Blondel that sung it: and when Blondel paused at halfe of the song, the king, *began the other half and completed it*.[111]

Songs play many parts in *The Lord of the Rings*: they accompany travel and convey history, they may be elegiac laments or comic nonsense; they are weaponized as battle hymns or, as here, they are an intimacy among comrades, the salvation of the lost.

The Hobbits then descend to the plain of Mordor, reluctant explorers of this hellish land. But explorers they are, and Tolkien surveyed the geography and the infrastructure of the region with a realist's eye, while characteristically paying keen attention to dates, distances, and supplies of food and water. So the Land of Darkness is not presented as a nightmarish figment of the imagination, but has roads and water cisterns for troop movements and Orc camps – the terrain is horribly tangible as they approach Mount Doom. Once there, however, there will be no return as their own food and water is exhausted.[112]

At this point, the plan was that Sam, having been tripped up by Gollum and broken his leg, would be left on the slopes of Mount Doom while Frodo climbs alone, pursued by Gollum. Once within the Chamber of Fire inside the mountain, Frodo cannot complete his task, Gollum attacks him and seizes the Ring, but Sam has by now made his own way inside; he wrestles with Gollum, and the two topple into the Crack of Doom.[113] This plan soon developed: Frodo is tempted by Sauron who offers to share in his power; his indecision 'remains immovably balanced between resistance and yielding' before he resolves to claim the Ring for himself and become 'King of Kings' making 'great poems' and singing 'great songs' so that 'all the earth should blossom'.[114] Gollum arrives to shatter this illusion and breaks Frodo's finger in wrenching off the Ring, but while he cavorts in triumph Sam has crawled in and pushes him over the edge. Then Tolkien thought that Gollum should perhaps repent and commit suicide in the fire with the Ring – not unlike Victor Frankenstein's Being immolating himself in the frozen wastes. Strangely, a Ringwraith then appears before Frodo and murmurs to him, 'Here we all end together'; nevertheless, Frodo and Sam escape and are rescued by Eagles.[115] Tolkien worked over this idea several times, apparently missing the vital point that Gollum would have to be able to see Frodo – or at least have a good idea of exactly where he is – in order to snatch the Ring; nevertheless, the sequence of events was coming into focus, and the ensuing rewrites sealed the scene. A particularly significant development – evidently one of the last revisions to be made – is in Frodo's declaration of his title to the Ring. Tolkien's focus until now had been that Frodo could not throw away the Ring: 'I cannot do what I have come to do.' But then he revised this to the much more sinister line 'I *do not choose now to do* what I have come to do'.[116] Frodo's failure to complete his task is the result of his own freewill (albeit swayed by the Ring), rather than an exhausted inability to act in the face of immense forces.[117]

The Ring destroyed, the Hobbits rescued, they reunite with their six fellow travellers in Minas Tirith. Tolkien still continued to think and rethink even at this stage. A rather tender moment in which Gandalf places two slender rings of *mithril* on Frodo's fingers, on either side of his lost finger, was cut. Some issues, such as Éowyn's marriage to Faramir (Éowyn having survived after all), were resolved straightforwardly; Arwen was introduced as Aragorn's betrothed, and several of the scenes surrounding his coronation in Gondor were written with little hesitation or need for revision. Other issues, however, remained unclear. Even at this stage Tolkien was still musing 'What happens to Shire?', and even when the Hobbits meet the beggarly Saruman on the road home the extent of the changes in The Shire have not yet been imagined – at the most there is a hint of some mischief among the residents.[118] The encounter with Saruman was carefully framed with details of geography and dates that Tolkien aimed to get meticulously accurate, and the episode only assumed its final shape in the second printed edition of 1966.[119]

The end was in sight, and as the Hobbits passed from Riven-dell and approached their home, Tolkien now wrote of the liberation of The Shire in a single, swiftly written first draft, many aspects of which were retained into print – at least until the four Hobbits are cornered by ruffians at Farmer Cotton's house. They come out fighting, Frodo immediately stabbing Sharkey dead before the Hobbits kill six of his henchmen and then rouse The Shire. However, details of the first stages of industrialization, urbanization, and needless tree-felling in The Shire are already included in this first draft, although the Party Tree is still standing, if forlornly. The miller Ted Sandy-man appears as an outspoken advocate of such modernization, dismissing Sam's 'Babyland' of Elves and Dragons.[120] Tolkien then had second thoughts and installs Sharkey the Boss at Bag End – although he is not yet Saruman; the former occupant the turncoat Hobbit Cosimo (later Lotho) Sackville-Baggins has been strangled. Frodo then challenges Sharkey to a duel and effortlessly slays him, and the ruffians make their last stand at the Battle of Bywater. This order of events was reversed, and Sharkey became the self-righteous Saruman, who eventually has his throat cut by Wormtongue – a fitting revenge. In these first drafts, then, Frodo is a very different Hobbit from the one who in Mordor had abandoned any use of weapons. By the final draft, however, he draws no sword and is merciful.[121] The pen becomes mightier, and so Frodo all-but finishes Bilbo's book in the closing pages – Tolkien trying out different titles, and only making the final decision at proof stage.[122] The story was complete.

As in *The Hobbit*, the sentimentalized presentation of The Shire is deliberately broken down at the end, but in *The Lord of the Rings*, this 'desentimentalization' is far more brutal, exposing a pitiless cruelty – if somehow done with a certain amount of wit in the ridiculing of the Shirriffs, Merry and Pippin's gung-ho

confidence, and Saruman's sardonic vengeance. It is a particularly wretched homecoming for Sam, who suffers the most
through the novel as Frodo becomes ever more otherworldly.
But it is a daring move for Tolkien to create an idyll kept alive
in memory in the darkest moments of the story, only to mar
it in the most callous way – crushing the dreams and hopes
of his favourite characters. Gandalf's knowing abdication of
responsibility does not help either, cryptically remarking that
the Hobbits must settle the troubles in The Shire themselves –
'that is what you have been trained for' – before unexpectedly
going off to see Tom Bombadil.[123]

In one sense, 'The Scouring of The Shire' reflects the bitterness of victory felt in Britain after the Second World War.
There is rationing in The Shire, as well as movement orders and
new rules enforced; in post-war Britain food rationing, as noted,
continued until 1954.[124] The walk to Bag End is 'one of the sad-
dest hours in their lives': Bagshot Row has become a quarry
and the Party Tree has been chopped down.[125] 'This is Mordor,'
murmurs Frodo: evil is not limited to a place or an individual
(or individuals): it is a taint, a pollution, a poison that can seep
into a Hobbit as much as it can into a wizard.[126] The ultimate
disgrace is only hinted at – that Wormtongue has eaten Lotho
Sackville-Baggins.[127] So, the Hobbits have not only been subjugated and tyrannized, but also reduced to foodstuff. Orcs are
cannibals, Trolls (in *The Hobbit*) devour Humans and Dwarves,
and there are ghoulish rumours of Gollum supposedly taking
and eating babies – a Hobbit eating a Human; now it appears
that Humans will eat Hobbits to degrade their opponents and
demonstrate their absolute political power. It is no wonder that
Frodo is too deeply hurt to remain in Middle-Earth, and to
quote the philosopher Eugene Thacker, it might be said that
the horror of his continued existence as a deeply wounded and
damaged individual 'has less to do with a fear of death and more

to do with the dread of life'.[128] That is Frodo's predicament at
the end of the book.

But the book is an open text even through the final chapter,
and then as graphically shown by the appendices that scrupu-
lously keep the story moving within ever-widening contexts – a
metafictional emphasis that confirms Sam's intuition, 'Don't the
great tales never end?'[129] Frodo almost bungles his last farewell
by not inviting Merry and Pippin, and at the end Gandalf is
revealed as the bearer of the third Elvish ring.[130] Frodo has
undeniably killed the things he loved – the Elves, Rivendell,
Galadriel, and Gandalf: his enduring legacy is the failure of
Faërie. The final words are left to Sam, who, having come to
the very brink of an immortal afterlife, is told to return home:
'Well I'm back' – a wonderfully contemporary, colloquial verse
of scripture.[131] Sixty years of profound thinking are distilled into
three words. The phrase is a statement of being and identity,
being in Middle-Earth and not the undying Elflands beyond
the western seas. Perhaps it is what Tolkien said to Edith (or at
least thought) when he returned from Mass. After communion
with the infinite grace of God, I'm back to the cares of the world
and it is nearly mealtime . . .

What Just Happened?

Tolkien was well aware of his method of composition, writing
on 14 January 1956, 'I have long ceased to *invent* . . . I wait till
I seem to know what really happened. Or till it writes itself.'[132]
His uncertainty and tentativeness about the plot – or rather,
plots – as they unfolded before him, his doubts and hesitancies
about his characters, his digressions into marginal detail and the
distractions of tangential stories and even unrelated narratives is
reflected not only in the successive stages of the composition of
The Lord of the Rings, but in the entire finished book. As Tolkien

wrote of the 'author' in the Foreword to the first edition, 'Bilbo was not assiduous, nor an orderly narrator, and his account is involved and discursive, and sometimes confused'.[133] So much is left unexplained and unexplored, and as the critic Tom Shippey points out, this is Middle-Earth's 'density, its redundancy, and consequently its depth'.[134] The story is filled with stories, found texts, stories-within-stories that do little to confirm the narrative.[135] Bilbo's stories are doubted by his fellow Hobbits, but he is nevertheless writing them up in his book. Gandalf tells Frodo the history of the Rings of Power, which is authenticated by the engraving on the One Ring and is part of the verse that readers have already encountered as the epigraph to the book: a quotation from a source given before the narrative begins. Frodo lies to his Hobbiton neighbours about where he is going, and the Hobbits then travel under a cover story in which Frodo is now supposedly writing a book. A story goes with every place they visit – the Old Forest, the House of Tom Bombadil (what Tolkien might have considered the cottage of lost tales), the Barrow-Downs, the Trollshaws. At Bree, Barliman Butterbur tells tales about Strider that are almost immediately contradicted by Gandalf's letter. Aragorn tells his own tales, and sings songs of ancient times. Gandalf later leaves an almost invisible and inscrutable message on Weathertop that is only meaningful to Aragorn. Even the most credulous reader must see that he reads a great deal into a few thin scratches on stone – that Gandalf was here on the 3rd of October – and then admits that 'the marks might mean something quite different, and have nothing to do with us'.[136] The Council of Elrond is a feast of storytelling, in which Gandalf quotes from an ancient manuscript he discovered in the archives of Gondor. The Mines of Moria provide a fund of new stories, from the inscription on the Moria Gate, which is a tiny riddle, to Gimli's sonorous song and Gandalf's and Aragorn's reminiscences of travelling through the

Mines before – although Gandalf has forgotten the way. There are more texts inside: Balin's tomb and the fragmentary Book of Mazarbul tell the tale of the attempt at resettling the Mines.[137]

Histories, stories, poems, songs, rumour, talk abound over the next thousand pages, leading Sam to conclude, 'What a tale we have been in', and, as I have noted, whether the 'Great Tales' ever end – thus fictionalizing the entire experience.[138] And it does increasingly appear to have been a dream, especially to the Hobbits. The world has changed for Aragorn and Arwen, Gandalf and Galadriel, but the reader does not accompany them – instead, we return with the Hobbits. Even before they reach The Shire they expect to return to an everyday life, and the dramatic events of the War of the Ring rapidly recede – the Ring is history – even though the War is suddenly and literally brought back home to them in the shape of Saruman: history, these stories and tales, are inescapable and define the present. This too is the experience of reading: the sequence of imagined events really has been like a dream, a voyage through strange worlds, and if now we are beginning to wake up and will one day close the book it will nevertheless continue to haunt us.

Along the way there have also been hints of the future made by a shadowy narrative voice: we are told, for example, that Frodo never again visited Lothlórien, which not only introduces longing and loss to his life, but also at the time implies that he will fail.[139] These reverberations and repetitions of the past and past stories are not only exacerbated by the hesitancies and undecidedness of the characters, but by Tolkien's unreliable narrator – which was partly a tactic to excuse any contradictions or anomalies that remained in the book after its long, slow process of composition and revision. Aragorn, for instance, is riven with doubt because Tolkien is unsure of his character development, and from the outset his identity has been fraught with ambiguity. At The Prancing Pony in Bree, Strider's legitimacy is confirmed

THE HESITANCY OF GOOD   169

by an unfortunately unsent letter from Gandalf that gives his real name as Aragorn, and also includes a riddle that begins with a traditional proverb used by both Chaucer and Shakespeare: '*All that is gold does not glitter*'.[140] As noted in Chapter One, in the course of the narrative Aragorn is variously named Longshanks and Wing-Foot, and takes the name Telcontar for his dynasty, but even by the time he meets with Éomer, he can declare himself in three lines of names as he brandishes the sword that was broken. Aragorn renaming himself thus introduces a new mood that amazes Gimli and Legolas and he immediately grows in stature.[141] His constellation of names – often bestowed by different characters – situates him in not one but many stories, reassuring Tolkien of his roles both here and now, and to come.

Aragorn's plural identities underline Tolkien's fascination with names, many of which – notably Frodo (Bingo) and Strider (Trotter) but also of minor characters such as the Orc leaders – took months, even years to be resolved. While one of Tolkien's solutions to this was to relish the multiple names, resisting clear-cut designations of characterization, issues of nomenclature run much deeper into the book and reveal a fundamental truth about Tolkien's writing that presents another connection with Shakespeare. The characters of Shakespearean tragedy repeatedly question their identities, seek affirmation and definition, and endeavour to control their sense of self through language – which often does the opposite in slipping away and undermining individual stability. To take an example at random: King Lear asks, 'Who is it that can tell me who I am?'; his Fool mordantly replies, 'Lear's shadow', and the whole play documents the searing obliteration of Lear's nature.[142] Despite Tolkien's frequent dismissal of Shakespeare he did lecture on *Hamlet* and was deeply moved by a performance of the play in 1944, finding Ophelia's mad scene almost unbearably poignant.[143] The recognition that Éowyn is not dead – her breath mists Prince

Imrahil's steel vambrace (forearm guard) – is derived from *King Lear*, in which Lear vainly hopes that Cordelia's breath will mist a looking glass, and Ioreth, the lowly female commentator who reports on Aragorn's coronation, is a typical Shakespearean figure.[144]

Tolkien's characters often, then, seem unsure of who they are, give and receive names, and frame themselves in language – often in poetry or song. One of the first complications that the Hobbits face as they set off is deciding under what name Frodo should travel. The Black Riders know the name of Baggins, having tortured it out of Gollum, and so Gandalf recommends leaving Baggins in The Shire and adopting the name 'Mr Underhill'. Frodo then meets the exiled Elf Gildor Inglorion and his company in Woody End, and Gildor christens him 'Elf-Friend' – giving him a fourth name to join Frodo, Baggins, and Underhill.[145]

Gollum's case is more complex: he has four given names – Sméagol and Gollum, and Slinker and Stinker – and only refers to himself as Gollum after accepting the name from Frodo and Sam, which helps to generate his fantasy about 'Gollum the Great' and '*The* Gollum'.[146] He habitually and narcissistically refers to himself as 'precious' or 'my precious', and these terms of self-endearment evolve into 'sweet one' and 'Most Precious Gollum'.[147] Of course he also addresses the Ring in these same terms, suggesting that his identity is not simply inseparable from this talismanic object but that he is what I have described as the avatar of the Ring. Gollum is obviously a highly uncanny character with a double or split identity – or rather, perhaps, antagonistic identities. This is primarily in the flux between Gollum and Sméagol – these two aspects not only act and speak differently, but bring riddles of existence back to Gollum's consciousness. When Frodo calls him Sméagol, the change in his name produces a change in Gollum's character that leads to language games.[148] Yet his uncanniness is even more compellingly felt in his relationship with the Ring.[149] Physically he is the Ring's shadow – wholly reliant on it for his own insubstantial being; he is a severed limb or the puppet of an object – an object that should be inanimate but which has attained will, a force that can trigger coincidence and inflame passions. He should be dead, he is a half-wraith who speaks to himself in hectic and fractured and nonsensical repetitions – an idiolect with which Tolkien would have been familiar from his time spent in military hospitals: these are the traumatized ravings of the shell-shocked. In short, Gollum is a ghost of anguish past (not of anguish passed) – an inescapable torment that all-too vividly brought back the sufferings of the Great War as the world went to war a second time while Tolkien was writing. Frodo endures a comparable collapse. Like King Lear, who is 'bound / Upon a wheel of fire', he has his selfhood utterly eclipsed at the feet of Mount Doom: he cannot recollect the most elemental memories of food or water, tree or flower, moon or star. He is 'naked in the dark' before the 'wheel of fire'.[150]

The text is full of other doublings and confusions of identity – if not so relentlessly dramatic as Gollum's. The usually level-headed Sam debates with himself when Frodo's corpse appears to be at his feet, uncannily paralleling the Gollum/Sméagol duality.[151] Frodo speaks to himself when he is planning to leave The Shire, and Sam debates with himself again on Mount Doom – so perhaps this is a Hobbitish trait, meaning that the split between Gollum and Sméagol is to be expected. All the Hobbits also experience loneliness and isolation. Frodo makes the decision to leave the Company on his own (a decision thwarted by Sam), and Sam endures the most extreme estrangement when he is alone in Mordor; Merry misses Pippin when he leaves Rohan for Gondor, and Pippin misses Merry when he is taken to the Houses of the Healing and Pippin fears that he will die there.[152] Significantly, Merry and Pippin have already been doubled: the Uruk-Hai have orders to capture the Halflings, but seize them rather than searching for Frodo and Sam – Saruman is too hasty.[153] In this plot twist, then, Merry and Pippin become doubles or decoys for Frodo and Sam – and the elegant logic of having nearly half of the Company of the Ring composed of Hobbits neatly falls into place.[154] This is the beginning of the vast strategy of misdirection that comprises the subplot. This narrative sweep begins in disaster and accident with the death of Boromir, who fails to protect the Hobbits. It is then driven by another calamity when Pippin is lured into staring into the depths of the *palantír* and is beheld by the Eye of Sauron – but these missteps are advanced into a considered policy of opposing Mordor, which ends with the Host of the West assembled at the Black Gate while Frodo creeps towards his goal. Aragorn looking into the *palantír* is consequently a shortcut to confronting Sauron as the heir of Elendil bearing the sword that took the Ring from him, now reforged; the effect is to force Sauron's hand.[155] It is unclear whether Denethor has seen Pippin in the *palantír*, but it is likely that he has seen Frodo in Cirith Ungol, meaning that the Ringbearer's mission has failed and that he is a prisoner of Sauron.[156] The Seeing Stone, an object with an almost radioactive power (see the Conclusion), deceives both Denethor and Sauron.[157]

The closest that any other character comes to addressing themselves in such an exposed way is when Gimli walks the Paths of the Dead: unusually, we enter Gimli's thoughts and share his fears. As suggested, this technique of self-revelation is usually reserved for Hobbits, but in the case of Gimli it arose out of the writing process. Tolkien in part cannibalized an earlier draft of the journey along the Paths of the Dead recounted by Gimli himself, but in doing so saw the opportunity to add an unexpected perspective through internal monologue.[158] Powerful

characters such as Galadriel, in contrast, are able to speak directly
to the minds of others. When the Company arrive in Lothlórien
Galadriel reads their minds – Sam blushes, feeling himself to
be naked: 'She seemed to be looking inside me'.[159] She tempts
Sam to return to his garden in The Shire – that much we know
– but the remaining members of the Company refuse to say
what she had found deep within their desires: these are secrets
that are never disclosed in the text, if some may be guessed at.
There are other unspoken secrets. Aragorn, for example, does
not divulge Boromir's last words to him regarding Frodo, which
is not unlike Odin's unanswerable question to King Heidrek and
to the Giant Vafthrúdnir, quoted above:

> What said Ódin
> in the ear of Balder,
> before he was borne to the fire?[160]

The most powerful figure in the text, Sauron, is also ever probing
the minds of others, yet as Gollum claims he cannot yet see all
things all at once – so even the mightiest have shortcomings and
Sauron does indeed make pivotal errors in his campaign tactics.[161]
Meanwhile, Sam makes a curious comparison between Faramir
and Gandalf, noticing a resemblance that Faramir attributes to
his Númenórean heritage.[162] This is a highly confusing likeness
as Gandalf only appeared in Middle-Earth some thousand years
after the fall of Númenor; moreover, only shortly before Faramir
has said 'We are a failing people' – a decline that Sam unwit-
tingly implies will envelop Gandalf too.

The book is filled with such indeterminate relationships and
limited perspectives. Gwaihir the Windlord, Lord of the Eagles
no less, informs Gandalf that Rohan sends Horses to Mordor
('or so it is said' – note the qualifier), but Aragorn and Boromir do not believe this and when Gimli makes the accusation

against Éomer he angrily denies it: six characters are involved in ascertaining the truth of this rumour.[163] For his part, Éomer is highly suspicious of the snares of Galadriel, the 'Lady in the Golden Wood', which rouses Gimli's passions to the extent that they nearly come to blows.[164] In contrast, Treebeard and Gandalf expect to meet at Isengard – 'Treebeard might almost have been loitering about near the gates on purpose to meet him' – but this too remains an unexplained and opaque relationship.[165] Merry and Pippin, meanwhile, feel uncomfortably superfluous and insecure during Gandalf's meeting with Saruman – there is even a social hierarchy expressed through Saruman's mellifluous tones: the Hobbits feel shut out, 'listening at a door to words not meant for them' – like children or servants.[166] Saruman's eloquent pleading here is also characteristic of Tolkien's ability to present radically different perspectives of apparently straightforward encounters. As Saruman's stirring fluency swells, Gandalf is presented as wilfully misconstruing his charming tones – what in the Middle Ages was known as *gramarye* – to be so skilful with words that they could literally cast a spell over listeners.[167] Frodo too lacks perspective among the treacherous rocks and precipices of the Emyn Muil, echoing Aragorn's despair: 'All my choices have proved ill.'[168] Again, one feels that this could be Tolkien trying to move his narrative forward. Sam makes the wrong choice in leaving Frodo to be captured by Orcs – another potentially ruinous decision.[169] The Phial of Galadriel fails at the Crack of Doom, quashing her hope that it will be a light 'when all other lights go out'.[170] Then Frodo fails, spectacularly fails, and places the entire world of Middle-Earth in the most extreme peril.[171]

Such failure is not only inevitable, it is the very stuff of the Anglo-Saxon mind. Anglo-Saxon literature is steeped in failure, and this failure pervades *The Lord of the Rings*. As Tolkien observed in his lecture '*Beowulf*: The Monsters and the Critics', the pagan gods of the North are destined to wage war against the monsters of chaos and in the final battle (Ragnarök) the gods will lose, but there is glory in their downfall. They will fail, but this failure will not be defeat: rather, it is a declaration of indomitable, invincible will. And Humanity will be their allies in this fight against insuperable odds. So in *The Lord of the Rings* the Free Peoples of Middle-Earth join with godlike figures (Gandalf, even the immortal Elves) knowing that they will fail. The Last Alliance against Sauron ends in failure because the Ring is not destroyed and Sauron rises again as the Necromancer. So it may be of some comfort, if cold comfort, that Frodo does finally succumb to the temptation of the Ring and thus fails – it is the only possible outcome. Denethor calls the anti-quest a 'fool's hope', Gandalf repeats that there never was much hope, and at the very climax of the Battle of the Black Gate the Nazgûl bear down on the Host of the West and 'all hope was quenched'.[172] They know that all will fail, but still they fight. And of course even the destruction of the Ring leads to irrevocable failure: the poisoning of The Shire and the disappearance of the Elves, of the wizards, of enchantment; the disappearance even of Hobbits. For Tolkien, *Beowulf* is 'not an "epic", not even a magnified "lay". No terms borrowed from Greek or other literatures exactly fit: there is no reason why they should. Though if we must have a term, we should choose rather "elegy".'[173] *The Lord of the Rings* too is an elegy, a lament for what is irreversibly lost, for the irretrievable past, for the everlasting dead.

It is also a lament for the beauty and enchantment that has been condemned – the Ring, ironically, being both the embodiment and guardian of enchantment, but also disturbing proof of the treacherous powers and abysmal depths of the imagination. Despite the Ring being able to confer invisibility, it is actually used very little in the book. Certainly it is a temptation and corrupts characters as different as Gollum and Boromir, and on both of these the Ring exerts a fascination without them actually possessing or wearing it – initially in the case of Gollum, and never in the case of Boromir. Yet Sam does bear it for a while, even puts it on for no real reason except that of desperation, or loneliness, or futility, or hopelessness, and, after a brief fantasy of turning the wasteland Gorgoroth into a garden, is able to return it.[174] Bilbo too gives it up – if under some duress from Gandalf. Meanwhile, although the other members of the Company seem unaffected by its presence and proximity, the nebulous and inexplicable Watcher in the Water is drawn to the Ring.[175] But then if the Ring is the quintessence of enchantment it is, like the Elves, capricious, and even, like Tolkien's labyrinthine creation of Middle-Earth, chaotic – those are its only abiding laws. It exists beyond other powers of fate or providence, and even its supposed powers are invisible and indiscernible.

The Ring also wields power over death. The Ringwraiths are undead, existing in a phantasmic, twilight state; Gollum is the walking corpse that Bilbo and Frodo may become.[176] Bilbo becomes wraithlike – not spectral, but spread too thin. Although Bilbo and Frodo do not become actual wraiths, they can only exist in another world – the Undying Lands of Valinor – and so do not die. The image of the walking dead is also, perhaps disquietingly, reflected in Tolkien's ability to continue writing *The Lord of the Rings*. The plot would waver, he would abandon the novel, then months, sometimes years, later, he would resurrect it. It would not rest, would not die. This becomes a central theme: the beginning of what became *The Two Towers* has three characters thought to be dead returning to life: Merry, Pippin, and most spectacularly Gandalf, who returns invulnerable: 'none of you have any weapon that could hurt me'.[177] Gandalf raises Théoden from a death-like stupour, and in the last march of the Ents inert trees become an active force.[178] The Dead Marshes are still filled with the phantasmic dead persisting after thousands of years, and at the end of the volume Frodo too is thought to be dead. In *The Return of the King* the first to return are the dead Oathbreakers, led by Aragorn; Denethor believes his son Faramir to be dead; Éomer believes his sister Éowyn to be dead (and she herself was seeking death); Merry is also believed to be dead.[179] Denethor becomes a metaphorical wraith, a 'living ghost', by taking control of his own death as one of his corrupted ancestors, the Númenórean 'heathen kings'.[180]

The Lord of the Rings is a study in failure and death. But there is also hope, manifested through 'eucatastrophe' – Tolkien's term for a sudden, blissful reversal of fortune. This is not the effect of *Deus ex machina*, where a plot is resolved by the unforeseen and contrived arrival of a new character or intervention, but the refashioning of providence. Frodo's strength of will takes him as far as Orodruin, Mount Doom, and to the very edge of Doom, but no further. Yet despite failing, his proximity to the Cracks of Doom enables fate to be recast.

•   •   •

Despite all that I have written in the past two chapters of the literary sophistication of *The Lord of the Rings*, you, dear reader, will find that Tolkien's work is not included in slick overall surveys of literature, particularly of twentieth-century litera-ture, particularly of Modernism. Some of the reasons for this are described in the following chapters. However, for the pres-ent, this rejection unfortunately makes it too easy for critics to ignore Tolkien and relegate his work to a crank fringe. One of the most shocking points made in Tom Shippey's ground-breaking book *J.R.R. Tolkien: Author of the Century* is how many supposedly professional critics, whether teachers or lecturers or critics or reviewers, are content to dismiss his work without hav-ing read it – despite his books having been translated into some forty languages. The other way of phrasing this is to consider how James Joyce's *Ulysses* and *Finnegans Wake* would have fared if they were judged by so-called critics who had not read the books, or who were incapable of engaging with their literary and linguistic challenges.

The philosopher Timothy Morton has recently considered *The Lord of the Rings* in the context of 'Romantic irony': 'Consider Schlegel's idea of Romantic irony. It manifests in narratives in which the narrator becomes the protagonist, unnervingly aware that the world he or she has constructed is a fiction . . . Irony involves distancing and displacement, a moving from place to place, or even from homey place into lonely space.'[181] Surprisingly, he then denies that *The Lord of the Rings* has such qualities. But surely this is precisely what Tolkien is doing – his characters doubt the reality of their experiences, fictionalize it into tales and songs, are aware that they are in stories, and consequently recognize that they are mere characters.[182] Tolkien's perspective moves from omniscient narrator to first-person experiences in the mind of Gimli, in the split personality of Gollum, and in the self-doubting reflections of Sam and other characters. The book is a dramatization of Tolkien's own process of composition, and after publication he wrote that 'It is not "about" anything but itself.'[183] He objected to Auden's suggestion that the book symbolized his own inner struggle: 'The story is not about JRRT at all, and is at no point an attempt to allegorize his experience of life'.[184] It is perhaps revealing, though, that in these notes he refers to himself in the third person – and in any case he did, inevitably, put parts of himself into the book – not as the ambiguous narrator, but in Faramir's dream, which is Tolkien's dream, and which he believed he had inherited. Tolkien dreamt of an inundation, a 'Great Wave, towering up, and coming in ineluctably over the trees and green fields'. This 'Atlantis complex', as he termed it, led to a lifelong fascination with Atlantis, which he incorporated into his legendarium as Númenor, and which in turn formed the background to *The Lord of the Rings* in the figures of Aragorn, Denethor, Boromir, and Faramir, and in the heritage of Gondor. Tolkien 'bequeathed' his dream to Faramir, who represents Tolkien's own presence in the text.[185]

But more than 'Romantic irony', is Tolkien's mediaevalist fantasy really a bizarrely idiosyncratic Modernism, uneasily poised between the distantly remote ideals that sent young men to fight in the Great War (typified by Théoden), and the diffident laconicism that characterized the Second World War (Sam)?[186] Indeed, the more closely one scrutinizes *The Lord of the Rings*, the more extraordinarily metafictional it appears: a story about stories, a fiction about fictions, a text about texts. It exposes literary conventions, plays with form, and persistently draws attention to the nature of narrative. It teems with unreliable narrators and multiple perspectives, fragmented and perplexing meaning, the ruins of a broken and hostile world. Middle-Earth has no stable moral compass; is unexplained and inexplicable; is swarming with dreams, the irrational, the supernatural, and the chaotic; and is so alienating that nearly all of the central characters have to leave it for another world. Thus it took a polymath cultural commentator to identify any similarity of style between Tolkien and his contemporaries: the pioneering writer George Steiner. Steiner, in an obituary for Tolkien published in *Le Monde* (6 September 1973), wrote that

> In England, in contrast to France, the Celtic, Irish, Scottish, and Saxon myths and the Arthurian cycle have made their presence felt in a number of the most significant works of contemporary poetry and prose. It is impossible to appreciate the lyrical genius of Robert Graves, the novelistic force of John Cowper Powys or William Golding, the bestiaries of Ted Hughes whose violent tones current[ly] dominate English poetry, without recognizing

the enduring and obsessive presence of ancient epics and legends in the current intellectual climate.[187]

This positions Tolkien as a writer of the twentieth century more as a revivalist of Old English and Old Norse, Anglo-Saxonism and mediaevalism precisely because twentieth-century literature was dominated by ancient myth. He should find his place alongside writers such as James Joyce, Jorge Luis Borges, Ted Hughes, and Angela Carter: not only among the Modernist innovations of the fragmentary, the transient, and individual consciousness, but in byzantine language games, fantastical textual conceits, mythic reinventions, and the magic realism of true fairy tales. Despite his oft-quoted distaste for technology, urbanization, and the modern world, and his considered sartorial conservatism (waistcoats and tweeds, in contrast to the mannered style of a contemporary writer-artist such as Wyndham Lewis), Tolkien's thought was pioneering. Adam Roberts comments that he 'bridges old Anglo-Saxon fascinations with heroism, doom and catastrophe with modern fascinations with guilt, desire, power, compromise and the hidden springs of psychological life'.[188] But it is more, far more than that. The ancient tales were, for Tolkien, a springboard, enabling him to leap way beyond history, far beyond the present.

He was not the only writer concerned – or, one might reasonably say, obsessed – with this at the time. George Orwell (1903–50) mirrors Tolkien's warnings against the destruction of the English countryside and English character in books such as *Coming Up for Air* (1939), a novel that overlaps considerably with the critique of technological progress in the chapter 'The Scouring of The Shire'.[189] Tolkien and Orwell, in so many ways so different, in fact share deep concerns about the rise of Fascism, the spread of urbanization, and the politics of language. In *Nineteen Eighty-Four*, Orwell warned of totalitarian society through thoughtcrime, 'Big Brother', and the all-seeing 'tele-screen'; as Tom Shippey has pointed out, Tolkien voiced these same fears in *The Lord of the Rings* through the Rings of Power, the *palantíri*, and Sauron's malevolent and all-seeing Eye.[190] Tolkien's faith, however, is finally embodied in the individual who will sacrifice all – even their afterlife – to save their fellows; it is a faith that has few, if any, equals.

After *The Lord of the Rings*, Tolkien published little else – and, sadly, not 'The Silmarillion'.[191] The grand themes of the legend-arium had become impossibly tangled in the minute details of *The Lord of the Rings* and would not be disentangled to form a single text in his, or any other, life. One imperfect version of *The Silmarillion* was edited by Christopher Tolkien, assisted by the fantasy writer Guy Gavriel Kay, and published in 1977. In 1980, Christopher Tolkien edited *Unfinished Tales*, which included alternative versions of some of the legendarium stories as well as background episodes to *The Lord of the Rings*. Between 1983 and 2002 the twelve volumes (plus an index volume) of *The History of Middle-earth* were published, and there have since been a succession of further books, such as the 'Great Tales'. This means, for example, that there are now multiple ver-sions of, for example, 'The Children of Húrin' and of 'Beren and Lúthien' available.

Although Tolkien retired in 1959, his academic publications continued into the 1960s. He had written short prefaces to the *Ancrene Riwle* (edited by Mary Salu, published in 1955) and the Anglo-Saxon text of *Apollonius of Tyre* (edited by Peter Goolden, 1958), and his edition of the English text of the *Ancrene Wisse*, an edition first discussed in 1936, was finally published in 1962. Unfortunately, when he was sent the proofs in 1960 they coin-cided with a printers' strike and required much work, seeming to stall a renewed enthusiasm for 'The Silmarillion'.[192] Yet there was a gentle tide of other works. *The Adventures of Tom*

Bombadil, a quirky collection of poems – some of which had already been printed – appeared in 1961; *Tree and Leaf* gathered together his 'On Fairy-Stories' and 'Leaf by Niggle' and was published in 1964; and the adult fairy tale *Smith of Wotton Major* came in 1967; he also continued to write and publish poetry. By this time, Tolkien also had some prominent admirers. In 1965, he wrote to his son Michael to say that he had met Burke Trend, Cabinet Secretary to the UK government, who informed him that he and most of the Cabinet were fans of *The Lord of the Rings*, as were many on both sides of the House of Commons. Moreover, he had also received what he described as 'a warm fan-letter' from the novelist and philosopher Iris Murdoch.[193] As A.N. Wilson wrote in his memoir *Iris Murdoch as I Knew Her*, '*The Lord of the Rings* she read and reread, enjoying detailed conversations about it with its author, or with Christopher Tolkien, the author's son' – Christopher being by then a colleague of Murdoch's husband John Bayley at New College, Oxford.[194]

Unsurprisingly, in 1968 Tolkien was the subject of a lengthy BBC documentary, which drew attention to his scholarship and his writing, and his fanbase and his critics.[195] Tolkien was not at all keen to be involved. Joy Hill, who worked for Tolkien's publishers Allen & Unwin and who became his secretary, noted that 'Professor Tolkien has something of an ingrained hostility against the BBC because of the way various of his books have been serialised'.[196] Nevertheless, Tolkien was paid 250 guineas for his participation (about £4,670 today), and the programme was aired on 30 March 1968 (repeated in 1973). Tolkien was again unimpressed by the 'bogosity' of the BBC, its 'world of gimmickry and nonsense', and the producer's 'BBCism', which he felt had led to him being presented as 'a fuddy not to say duddy old fireside hobbitlike boozer'.[197] Fifty years on, however, *Release – Tolkien in Oxford* (1968) has become a fascinating document of Tolkien's attempts to explain, if not justify, his writing to a wider audience.

In the same year he and Edith moved to Poole, near Bournemouth. They had holidayed in Bournemouth for many years, and the move seemed right for Edith. Tolkien remembered how excited she was by their new house; sadly, however, she was not to enjoy it for very long. Edith died in 1971. Tolkien (in some relief, it has to be said) returned to Oxford to live in rooms in Merton College. He died in 1973 during another visit to Bournemouth.

The years that followed publication of *The Lord of the Rings* were, for Tolkien, then, relatively fallow; they were not, however, dormant years for the book itself. Even before *The Two Towers* was in print a version of *The Fellowship of the Ring* had been broadcast by BBC radio. The next chapter accordingly turns to the decades that followed publication and the turbulent fortunes and misfortunes of Middle-Earth in adaptation – the very apotheosis of both the sublime and the ridiculous.

FIVE

Lucid Moments

All books are either dreams or swords,
You can cut, or you can drug, with words.
Amy Lowell,
'Sword Blades and Poppy Seed' (1914)

The protracted confusions, doubts, hesitancies, and changes of mind that characterized Tolkien's composition of *The Lord of the Rings* give, I have suggested, a highly distinctive atmosphere to the book. In the ensuing radio, film, and television adaptations, however, this is hardly the case. The directors of these adaptations are barely interested in how Tolkien's novels were *composed* – their concern is in how the drama of the works can best be recreated in a different medium: as film theorist Linda Hutcheon notes, adaptation is 'a *process of creation*' that 'always involves both (re)interpretation and then (re)creation', both 'appropriation and salvaging, depending on your perspective'.[1] These adaptations obviously have the books as sources (and, arguably, Tolkien's other Middle-Earth writings) – but they also, crucially, have previous adaptations to work from. The cinema in particular is a highly collaborative creative industry and is critically aware of previous film adaptations as these have faced the same problems of translating a complex work into a different medium. So new films are not simply drawing on earlier versions and alluding to them, they are effectively new variations of old adaptations. There was a rich canon of radio and film for Peter Jackson to draw on in his six films, and they are indebted to earlier onscreen and audio versions: primarily the Ralph Bakshi-directed *The Lord of the Rings* (1978), the Rankin/Bass animation *The Return of the King* (1980), Brian Sibley's BBC radio dramatization of *The Lord of the Rings* (1981), and Rob Inglis's unabridged audiobook reading (1990). Similarly the Amazon Prime Video TV series is clearly influenced by – and may be in part a homage to – the preceding six Peter Jackson movies. In this way, adaptation is (Hutcheon again) a 'form of intertextuality: we experience adaptations (*as adaptations*) as palimpsests through our memory of other works that resonate through repetition with variation'.[2]

It is in hands other than Tolkien's own, then, that the many ambiguities of *The Lord of the Rings* (and, to a lesser extent, *The Hobbit*) have been resolved into some sort of clarification. Steadying this textual instability leads to occasional disjunctures between the various versions of *The Lord of the Rings* in different media. The Tom Bombadil episode, dear as it was to Tolkien's heart, is cut from nearly every reworking – only the original BBC radio broadcast of 1955 and the American National Public Radio version of 1979 retain anything of Bombadil (although – and somewhat surprisingly – he does appear in the computer game of *The Fellowship of the Ring*).[3] Possibly this rejection is due to an outmoded sense of English pastoral that he seems to represent, or his utterly incongruous mood of blithe joviality in the face of impending evil. Whatever the case, he is an experiment that very few have dared to repeat since the publication of the first volume. Other absences, such as 'The Scouring of The Shire', are more controversial, although in the Jackson films a vestige of this episode is glimpsed in the Mirror of Galadriel – an allusion that could only be recognized by those who had studied the book, and which was bound to create disappointment among that part of the audience when it failed to materialize fully onscreen.

Film and radio scripts inevitably streamline characters, scenes, episodes, and plots in ways that simplify or settle an author's measured undecidedness. That is the prime difference between the literary original and versions in other media. Even a series of films as exuberant as Peter Jackson's *The Hobbit*, which takes such extraordinary liberties with the text and seems to spin out in many different directions, still conforms to the conventions of twenty-first-century cinema – each major character, for example, is on a personal journey of self-discovery. Nonetheless, these various adaptations do often cast light on the texts' complexities: they are lucid moments in the ongoing history of the Rings of Power.

Middle-Earth Media

During his academic career, Tolkien himself had occasionally dabbled in radio work. As noted, he had been recorded for a Linguaphone course on English in 1930; part of his translation of the poem *Pearl* was broadcast by BBC radio in 1936, and two years later he recorded a BBC radio programme on Anglo-Saxon verse. As *The Lord of the Rings* was being finalized his translation of *Sir Gawain and the Green Knight* was aired in December 1953, and a year later his radio drama *The Homecoming of Beorhtnoth Beorhthelm's Son* was broadcast in December 1954 (with Michael Hordern's reading of *The Battle of Maldon*).

Both productions were repeated, although Tolkien himself was dissatisfied with the performances in *The Homecoming*; he had already recorded his own version in his study, complete with sound effects – such as the creaking of a wagon being achieved by dragging his furniture around – and thought this version superior to that eventually broadcast.[4]

The appearance of the first volume of *The Lord of the Rings* in the bookshops was therefore bookended by Tolkien's most active period as a 'media don', and almost immediately, in January 1955, the BBC proposed a radio dramatization of *The Fellowship of the Ring*. Shortly afterwards, Silvia Goodall abridged *The Lord of the Rings* for the BBC Home Service as part of the *Adventures in English* series, in which each episode was followed by an educational activity; this series was broadcast in spring 1956.[5] Although Tolkien was somewhat ambivalent about the dramatization, recent discoveries by Tolkien expert Stuart Lee have shown that he took an active role in editing his work and correcting producer Terence Tiller's scripts, although the recordings themselves – in which Gandalf was played by veteran radio actor Norman Shelley – appear to have been lost.[6] Despite the texts being dramatically reduced they still required a narrator, and while *The Fellowship of the Ring* was covered in six thirty-minute episodes (cut from an original forty-five minutes) and included the whole chain of events covering Old Man Willow, Tom Bombadil, and the Barrow-Wights, the second series somehow squeezed *The Two Towers* and *The Return of the King* into just six half-hour episodes. But despite the broadcasts receiving media attention as well as good reviews, notably in the *Observer*, Tolkien himself was unfortunately not particularly impressed, especially with the portrayal of Bombadil.[7] Yet he did agree to the brief continuation and even, surprisingly, the necessity to cut major elements such as the first half of *The Two Towers*, covering Rohan and Saruman. He also remained

polite to Tiller, even while criticizing such unnecessary changes
as making Old Man Willow an agent of Mordor on the basis
that Mordor was not the sole adversary to the 'humane'.[8] In
other words, even in a drastically curtailed form Tolkien wanted
to retain a sense of the mysteries, ambiguities, and loose ends
of his work. Whatever his misgivings, though, Middle-Earth
had moved into a new medium, and now film-makers began to
take notice.

Negotiations for a film version of *The Lord of the Rings* began
within two years of the publication of *The Return of the King*.
Rayner Unwin wrote to Tolkien in May or June 1957, and
Tolkien replied on 19 June that he would 'welcome the idea of
an animated motion picture' – despite his 'heartfelt loathing'
of Disney expressed thirty years earlier – going on to say that
'I think I should find vulgarization less painful than the sillifi-
cation achieved by the B.B.C.'.[9] Tolkien's hopes, agreed with his
publisher, were rather blunt: '*Art or Cash*', meaning either 'very
profitable terms indeed', or 'absolute author's veto on objection-
able features or alterations'.[10] An approach was duly made by
the science fiction writer, editor, and agent Forrest J. Ackerman
to the film and television producer Al Brodax. The treatment is
worth noting as Ackerman was proposing a hybrid film: a mix
of live action, animation, and miniature models (a movie-buff,
Ackerman had procured the original threadbare model dinosaurs
from the pioneering 1925 film *The Lost World*). So the production would have had a characteristic texture, blending media
and cinematic effects – and it is tempting to see this innovatory
style of film-making in a sense reflecting the 'mixed media' of
Tolkien's text of fiction, history, travel writing, linguistics, cartography, and so forth. But it was not to be – thankfully so,
when one realizes the outrageous liberties that Morton Grady
Zimmerman took with the text in his script – Tolkien was
never going to approve it, as his exasperated and frankly livid

responses clearly show.[11] For example, Zimmerman introduces
many more Eagles – first an early bird alighting in The Shire,
and then as mounts for the 'Nine Walkers'; Rivendell becomes
a fairy wood and Lothlórien a fairy castle. Then there are Orcs
with beaks and feathers (auks?) and a levitating Faramir. There
were dozens of unnecessary changes in diction, setting, geography, timescale, and plot. 'The canons of narrative art in any
medium', in Tolkien's opinion, 'cannot be wholly different', but
poor films unnecessarily exaggerated source material and introduced unnecessary matter, 'owing to not perceiving where the
core of the original lies'.[12] Zimmerman had completely missed
the tone of the work, mangled the plot, as well as ignoring 'Practically everything having moral import', such as the temptation
of Galadriel.[13]

The producers Samuel Gelfman and Gabriel Katzka had
first approached Tolkien and his publisher (George Allen &
Unwin) in 1967 to buy the film rights to *The Lord of the Rings*
for United Artists (UA). Those who would be angling for permission to film the novel before the decade ended ranged from
major studios such as Metro-Goldwyn-Mayer (MGM) and
Disney to the cult American folksinger Arlo Guthrie. Moreover, in 1968 there was a gambit by Denis O'Dell, one of the
directors of Apple Corps and a producer on *A Hard Day's Night*
(1964) and *Magical Mystery Tour* (1967), to have The Beatles
star in a film version. O'Dell pitched the idea to UA – coincidentally, it transpires, as they had handled *A Hard Day's Night*.
UA agreed on a Beatles *Rings* movie, on condition that a major
director was involved: they suggested David Lean, Michel-
angelo Antonioni, or Stanley Kubrick, among others. Lean
had already started work on *Ryan's Daughter* (1970), so O'Dell
sent the books to Kubrick and then flew out to India where the
band were practising transcendental meditation with Maharishi
Mahesh Yogi – and actually considering a film on the subject.

Ringo Starr, unimpressed by the Maharishi, left India as soon as O'Dell arrived, and then, bizarrely, O'Dell split Tolkien's book between the remaining Beatles for them each to read a volume: Paul McCartney *The Fellowship of the Ring*, John Lennon *The Two Towers*, and George Harrison *The Return of the King*; they were also encouraged by the hippy folksinger Donovan who also happened to be present at the Academy of Transcendental Meditation. As O'Dell points out, 'Beatles mythology offers several versions of who was supposedly earmarked for which character in the book', but he thinks none of them are correct – the only certainty was that John Lennon was very keen to play Gandalf and said 'it would be no problem to get "at least a double album" of musical material together for the project'.[14] Unfortunately, however, Kubrick declared the book 'unmakable', and so, despite a preliminary meeting with Lennon and McCartney, the project was dropped.[15]

But evidently the sixties counterculture had fully embraced Tolkien, combining flower-power with Frodo-mania on American university campuses, pipe-weed with pot – meaning that there was a readymade young audience for any film. This popularity was in a large part due to a pirated paperback edition of *The Lord of the Rings* published in 1965 by Ace Books at 75¢ per volume.[16] Tolkien's publishers, Allen & Unwin in the UK and Houghton Mifflin in the US, had dragged their feet in publishing a paperback, but then who in the 1960s would buy a three-volume paperback novel? There were very few multi-volume novels published in the twentieth century, and the true multi-volume novels rather than episodic series, such as Tolstoy's *War and Peace* (published in two paperback volumes by Penguin in 1957), were established classics or, in the case of Anthony Powell's *A Dance to the Music of Time* (1951–75), appearing over many years. Cheaper printing costs had led Tolkien's publishers to decide on an authorized paperback edition published by Ballantine Books, but the Ace paperback trumped the Ballantine edition, captured the student market, and sold some 100,000 copies in its first year – of which Tolkien received nothing. When it did appear, the Ballantine edition was only 20¢ a volume more expensive than the Ace edition and there was a strenuous campaign by fans to blacklist the Ace publication and compensate Tolkien's lost royalties. When he was finally paid, the sums involved and consequent tax incurred may well have confirmed his decision to sell the film rights; he also blamed the case for distracting him from completing *The Silmarillion*.[17]

Suddenly, then, *The Lord of the Rings* was no longer a rarefied three-volume hardback book experience, but a cheap, pocket-sized softback. For many of the new generation it became a shared point of reference, a touchstone. Within five years the critic C.N. Manlove could comment:

The trilogy came just when disillusion among the American young at the Vietnam war and the state of their own country was at a peak. Tolkien's fantasy offered an image of the kind of rural conservationist ideal or escape for which they were looking (it also could be seen as describing, through the overthrow of Sauron, the destruction of the U.S.). In this way *The Lord of the Rings* could be enlisted in support of passive resistance and idealism on the one hand and of draft-dodging and drugs on the other. A second factor may have been the perennial American longing for roots, a long tradition and a mythology: these things are the fibre of Tolkien's book, where every place and character is lodged at the tip of an enormous, growing stem of time.[18]

It also became huge in Britain. The heart of the London underground music scene from summer 1967 was Middle Earth, a club located at 43 King Street in Covent Garden. This venue saw the debut of Tyrannosaurus Rex, later T. Rex, with Marc Bolan on vocals and guitar, and Steve Peregrin Took (i.e. Pippin) on percussion. The early and often manically whimsical songs of Bolan and Took were vaguely infused with a Tolkienesque atmosphere, and their first album had the decidedly Elvish title *My People Were Fair and Had Sky in Their Hair... But Now They're Content to Wear Stars on Their Brows* (1968). Pink Floyd also played at Middle Earth – their songwriter Syd Barrett having written a Hobbitish ditty 'The Gnome' about a little man named Grimble Grumble who eats, sleeps, drinks wine, wears green and red, and has an adventure (*The Piper at the Gates of Dawn*, 1967). Donovan (present when The Beatles had read Tolkien), meanwhile, planned a whole suite of songs inspired by *The Lord of the Rings*, recording 'Poor Love' (including a reference to Faramir) at a live performance in 1967 (released as *Donovan In Concert*, 1968), before rewriting the lyrics. On 19 May 1968, Middle Earth hosted the Gandalf's Garden Benefit with Tyrannosaurus Rex and David Bowie performing – *Gandalf's Garden* being a spiritual wellbeing magazine to which DJ John Peel contributed.[19] After police raids Middle Earth moved to promoting live gigs and happenings at the Round House in Chalk Farm, Camden, which included hosting the British debuts of The Doors and Jefferson Airplane (later supported by Lighthouse, a Canadian band featuring one Howard Shore on saxophone – the same); they also held benefits for *Oz* magazine, the controversial and much-prosecuted voice of the underground.

In America, meanwhile, things went to extremes. An early, eerie track was 'Ring Thing' by folk psychedelia group Pearls Before Swine (*Balaklava*, 1968), in which Tolkien's verse is intoned over random bagpipe drones. In contrast, Leonard Nimoy recorded the frantically jaunty 'The Ballad of Bilbo Baggins', neatly connecting Mr Spock of *Star Trek* to Mr Baggins of

The Hobbit (*Two Sides of Leonard Nimoy*, 1968). But more reput-
able musicians added more subtle touches of the rich and varied
textures of Middle-Earth. Canadian-American folksinger Joni
Mitchell adopted the word 'Wilderland' for her song 'I Think
I Understand' (*Clouds*, 1969), and it has since been taken up by
later artists.[20] Back in Britain, Jack Bruce, formerly of the super-
group Cream, included 'To Isengard', a track split between an
acoustic folk song and a virtuoso bass solo coda, on his debut solo
album *Songs for a Tailor* (1969). Later folky renditions include
the busy chimes of Sally Oldfield's 'Songs of the Quendi' hymn-
ing the three Elven Rings, and the rather more vivacious laments
of Mostly Autumn's folk-Goth set, *Music Inspired by The Lord of
the Rings* (2001).

The sixties music album most profoundly influenced by
Middle-Earth was unquestionably *Poems and Songs of Middle-
Earth* (1967), consisting of recordings of Tolkien's own readings of his Tom Bombadil poems and Donald Swann's musical
cycle *The Road Goes Ever On*, sung by William Elvin and accompanied by Swann on the piano. Yet few listen to it now. The
score was published in the same year in an edition lavishly decorated with Tolkien's extensive Elvish calligraphy and including
his notes on the Elvish languages and even some comments
on Middle-Earth religion. Swann, best known as part of the
musical revue Flanders and Swann, was a composer and pianist,
and worked on the settings for a dozen years before refining
them in close collaboration with Tolkien – who, for example,
suggested revising 'Namárië', the Elvish song of farewell, to
make it a monophonic plainchant. The style is perhaps best
described as aesthetic mediaevalist operetta, the cycle of pieces
linked through the common theme of travelling: journeying
through different landscapes and through light and dark. While
this recording has hardly had an impact comparable to the folk,
rock, and pop songs of Middle-Earth, Tolkien seems to have

felt that it was worth contributing to a musical statement that resisted mainstream popularity – as ever, he was creating alternatives that challenged expectations. But Middle-Earth had already escaped him and was now common, popular property – the realm of studied guitar picking rather than elegant piano playing, for strobed clubs rather than Oxford college gardens, for Notting Hill and Haight-Ashbury hippies rather than erudite philologists. In time, all of these would come together, but in the 1960s they presented the many paths you could go on.[21]

Assuredly oblivious of the light classical inflections of *The Road Goes Ever On*, something of a Middle-Earth subgenre developed in rock music. The first two Led Zeppelin albums were released before the end of the decade and marked a watershed in rock music. In 'Ramble On' (from the band's second album, familiarly known as *Led Zep II*), the guitarist Jimmy Page characteristically combines energetic acoustic arrangements with sudden explosions of insistent electric riffing that lead into lyricist Robert Plant singing a strange verse about being cuckolded by Gollum in Mordor; the music pauses as if to allow the reference to sink in, then the final heavy chorus. Two albums on, it was on *Led Zep IV* (variously titled as it has no given title) that the Tolkien references peaked. In 'Misty Mountain Hop' the Misty Mountains offered a refuge from a drug bust, and 'The Battle of Evermore' mysteriously dramatized a battle between Elves and Ringwraiths (both named). But this was only a prologue to 'Stairway to Heaven' – a stunningly transcendent song that remains the seminal rock achievement of the 1970s, and then some. This is a song of Middle-Earth, if the references are (as ever with Robert Plant) occluded through his vocal inflections and personal moods. The second line – 'all that glitters is gold' – proverbially refers back to Aragorn, and thence to Shakespeare and Chaucer. Ambiguities multiply with words having more than two meanings (characteristic of Tolkien, as

I have argued in earlier chapters), before the singer feels the yearning of the Elves looking Westwards, but instead goes with Faramir through the smoke that Sam has inadvertently left to smoulder. There are paths and winding roads, and forests filled with faint sounds. Robert Plant, again not unlike Sam talking of tales, then considers the value of song, haunted by Galadriel in shining white, and haunted further by the tall shadow of Frodo. While the song is impressionistic and critics have found many other meanings in it, it surely bears the deep imprint of Middle-Earth: Robert Plant is thinking through Tolkien and the imagery of *The Lord of the Rings*, refashioning it for a seventies rock audience – he even had a dog called Strider.

Geezer Butler, lyricist and bassist with another heavy rock band, Black Sabbath, was reading *The Lord of the Rings* while they were writing and recording their first album (1969, released under their own name in 1970), most clearly shown in 'The Wizard'. Indeed, in the extreme reaches of the black metal subgenre, bands like Cirith Ungol mine the Black Sabbath back-catalogue for riffs and shuffles, with some groups such as Summoning devoting entire albums to Middle-Earth (*Minas Morgul*, 1995), or the foreboding ambient soundscapes (often in Orcish) recorded by Swedish concept group Za Frûmi. Also in 1970, Swedish musician Bo Hansson recorded the instrumental rock album *Sagan Om Ringen* (1970), a major hit in Sweden released in the UK as *Music Inspired by Lord of the Rings* (1972), and in 1975 Canadian progressive rock trio Rush reprised the opening tones of 'Stairway to Heaven' on their second album, *Fly By Night*, as 'Rivendell'. More inventively, the jazz musician John Sangster had by then recorded a diverse set of pieces, *The Hobbit Suite*, in 1973. 'The Knockabout Trolls' is an excuse for a deft vaudeville percussion solo, 'Runes by Moonlight' is reminiscent of cocktails at twilight, the loose blues progression 'Smaug's Lair' owes more than a little to 'The Pink Panther Theme', while

'Hippity Hoppity Hobbit' is good for any children's party. He followed this with three volumes covering *The Lord of the Rings* (1975–7) and another two albums *Double Vibes: Hobbit* (1977) and *Landscapes of Middle-Earth* (1978). Some of Sangster's cuts become ever less likely: 'Sam the Man' reinvents Samwise Gamgee as a cool hustler, 'The Uruk-Hai' sounds like a police squad cruising the shadier parts of town, whereas 'The Balrog' slinks along with a super-sleazy wiliness; even 'Tom Bombadil' is way more New Orleans swing than Olde Englyshe madrigal. It may be cool jazz music, but it seems worlds away from Tolkien – the cult-classic 'Balrog Boogie' by the Swedish avant-garde rock band Diablo Swing Orchestra (*The Butcher's Ballroom*, 2006) better shows how the two might actually be creatively combined. Similarly, perhaps, Chris Thile's brilliant bluegrass album *Not All Who Wander Are Lost* (2001) includes 'Riddles in the Dark' – a hyper-charged banjo/mandolin duet in which the instruments quiz and challenge each other.

There is also an orchestral and classical repertoire, such as Johan de Meij's brilliant prize-winning Symphony No. 1, inspired by *The Lord of the Rings* (premièred 1988); this acclaimed work was recorded by the London Symphony Orchestra in 2001, alongside the cinema release of Peter Jackson's *The Fellowship of the Ring*. Other contemporary classical work includes the remarkable Symphony No. 7, *The Dreams of Gandalf* (1996), by Finnish composer Aulis Sallinen, who had already written an opera, *Kullervo* (1988), based on the Finnish legend from the *Kalevala* – which Tolkien himself translated and used as a source for his 'Great Tale' of 'The Children of Húrin'. *The Dreams of Gandalf* began as a ballet, and has been reviewed as 'full of captivating tunes cloaked in absolutely magical orchestration'.[22] Finally, official endorsement has been given to the Tolkien Ensemble, a Danish collective that grew out of the Royal Danish Academy of Music and who have recorded all of the songs and poems of *The Lord of the Rings* across four acclaimed albums (1997–2005). The compositions vary in style from British folk to neo-Romantic classical and include readings by Christopher Lee, offering more plaintive and elegant soundscape than the rousing refrains of the film soundtracks. Likewise, a musical of *The Lord of the Rings* was licensed to be produced by Kevin Wallace Ltd and directed by Matthew Warchus; it premièred in Toronto in 2006 and moved to the West End in 2007. The music of Middle-Earth composes a broad church.

Meanwhile, the film deal took two years to finalize, but eventually on 8 July 1969 Tolkien sold the film rights to both *The Lord of the Rings* and *The Hobbit*, along with rights to merchandizing and ancillaries, to UA.[23] The price agreed was $250,000, which Tolkien apparently required to pay a tax bill.[24] It was an unusual deal: Tolkien retained a 7.5 per cent royalty on future adaptations (once an 'artificial payment level' of 2.6 times the final productions costs was reached), allowing for royalties to continue to be paid rather than this being an outright transfer of property. Equally unusually, the rights were sold in perpetuity. Perhaps most significantly, though, the contract allowed for the works to be rewritten:

The sole and exclusive right . . . to freely adapt, change, transpose, revise, rearrange, add to and subtract from the Work or any part thereof and the title, theme, plot, sequences, incidents and characterizations thereof, to make interpolations in and substitutions for any part or parts thereof, to make sequels to and new versions or adaptations of the Work or any part thereof, to use any part or parts of the Work or of the theme thereof or any incidents, characters, character names, scenes, sequences or characterizations therein contained in conjunction with any other work or works, and to separately or cumulatively

do any or all of the foregoing, to such extent as the Pur-
chaser, in its sole discretion may deem expedient in the
exercise of any of the rights, licenses or privileges herein
conveyed and to interpolate in said motion picture photo-
plays music compositions, gags, lyrics, and music of all
kinds, to set to music any verse, lyric, prose or part or parts
of the Work and any characters thereof.[25]

In November of that year, UA announced that they would be
making a film of *The Lord of the Rings*.

Pre-Production *Rings*

UA looked set to make a version of *The Lord of the Rings* that
would appeal to the counterculture, and remain with these young
radicals as they mellowed into middle age in the 1970s and
1980s. The movies of the time were exemplified by rock 'n' roll
capers (exemplified by *A Hard Day's Night*); sex, drugs, violence,
and philosophy (*Performance*, 1970); and folk horror (*Witch-
finder General*, 1968); while the fantasy genre was dominated by
the special effects of Ray Harryhausen (*Jason and the Argonauts*,
1963, and *One Million Years B.C.*, 1966). UA approached the
edgy British film-maker John Boorman.[26] Boorman, who had
directed the cult crime classic *Point Blank* (1967) and would go
on to hit the big time with *Deliverance* (1972), had just made
Leo the Last (1970), a social satire dramatizing the Marxist class
struggle in a contemporary London street, for which he had
won Best Director at the Cannes Film Festival. United Artists
asked him what his next project would be, and Boorman sent
them a script for *Merlin*, an Arthurian fantasy. UA responded
by inviting Boorman to write a treatment for the newly acquired
Lord of the Rings – according to Boorman, UA had bought
the film rights 'without having any idea what to do with it';

Boorman, who knew the book already, found it 'a heady, impossible proposition'.[27]

Boorman accordingly spent the end of 1969 and much of 1970 planning *The Lord of the Rings*. He invited Rospo Pallenberg, an aspiring scriptwriter, to stay for three months at his home in County Wicklow in Ireland. According to Boorman, Pallenberg 'pasted every page of *The Lord of the Rings* on to four walls in a room in my house' and they worked 'in that room, literally inside the book'.[28] They made charts and chronologies and card indexes, moved counters across maps, and even corresponded with Tolkien, eventually drafting the full script three times. Boorman's plans were for a single live-action film with innovative special effects – to the apparent relief of Tolkien, who, according to Boorman, had a 'dread' of animation.[29] Yet despite their immersion in Middle-Earth – the hills of Wicklow being as close to Middle-Earth 'as you can get in this depleted world' – Boorman and Pallenberg drastically rewrote the novel.[30] It was Pallenberg's idea to make the adaptation a single film rather than three separate films, and to identify explicitly with the sixties counterculture. This not only led to the suggestion that Ringo Starr should be cast, but also that Sauron was to be 'a combination of Mick Jagger and Punch', who performs (like Jagger himself in the film *Performance*) his own theme song.[31] Pallenberg also proposed that there should be explicit sex onscreen, including scenes of erotic horror set in a brothel. They even discussed casting Tolkien himself in a framing device to supply the backstory. These ideas are pointedly self-aware and richly allusive, positioning the film in the tradition of international arthouse directors such as Sergei Eisenstein and Akira Kurosawa, as well as, closer to home, film-makers Donald Cammell and Nicolas Roeg. Some of these brainstormed suggestions, such as the dark psychedelia of a rubber-lipped Sauron and the appearance of Tolkien, did make it to the finished script

– although whether Tolkien would have actually played himself in such a film is highly doubtful. Others were, however, toned down: Frodo is gently seduced by Galadriel rather than having the Company take him to a whorehouse.

While the bald description of these changes makes them appear preposterous, even laughable, Boorman in fact spent a great deal of time and creative energy trying to solve the challenges of turning a half-million-word book into a two-and-a-half-hour epic war movie. He did so by drawing three interwoven storylines from the plot: 'the supernatural – Gandalf, Elrond, the evil eye; the noble – Aragorn, King Théoden, etc.; and the hobbits – Frodo, Samwise, Merry, Pippin'.[32] He even addressed the practicalities of making the film, 'only one possible way to deal with casting ... No stars or big names – go for bizarre physical types in many cases nonactors – perhaps dub every player with a voice other than his own to emphasise the other world quality'.[33] Having said that, both Vincent Price and Christopher Lee were in the frame for roles – the latter of course ultimately appearing with magnificently measured menace as Saruman in five of Peter Jackson's films.[34] Boorman even budgeted the projected production, planning to film on sound stages in England, on location in Ireland, and, for the battle scenes, in Spain. Moreover, he revisited the script in the 1990s, intending to downplay the warfare in order to focus on the contrasting relationships between Frodo and Sam, and Gandalf and Saruman, as well as developing the role of Gollum.

Boorman felt that the 176-page treatment 'carried the spirit of Tolkien', the 'spirit rather than the letter of the book'.[35] However, by the time Boorman and Pallenberg delivered the script, their commissioning executive at UA had left and apparently no-one else there had even read *The Lord of the Rings*. The treatment was duly rejected by UA; other studios (including Disney) were approached, but to no avail. Boorman did not give up and continued to pitch the film for over twenty years, and in a sense, then, it is remarkable that he did not find backers for it. Meanwhile, his fascination with 'Romantic realism' found its ideal in *Excalibur* (1981) – perhaps the best mediaevalist fantasy film outside Middle-Earth ever made.[36] Gandalf, Boorman wrote in *The Emerald Forest Diary* (1985), 'filled my life. He was, after all, Merlin in another guise.'[37] Expanding on this in an interview, he said, 'Fundamentally, Gandalf is Merlin and Frodo is the young King Arthur'.[38] Unsurprisingly, then, ideas for locations and special effects developed for *The Lord of the Rings* were utilized in *Excalibur* and later films. In *Excalibur*, for instance, Mordred impales Arthur with a lance, but Arthur still advances, driving the shaft of the lance through his body; in Boorman's script for *The Lord of the Rings*, Théoden is similarly impaled, yet swings the lance around to unhorse the Lord of the Nazgûl. The unmade *Lord of the Rings* and the ideas it encapsulated, then, haunted (even dominated) Boorman's film-making for years.[39] In other words, John Boorman too was thinking through Tolkien: Middle-Earth provided the realm of his imagination.

Boorman and Pallenberg's script begins in Tolkien's study before the scene changes to Mordor and the verse of the Rings of Power being chanted by old men and children, across a widening panorama of Middle-Earth. In this way, like later versions the film would have begun with the Ring, not Bilbo's birthday party. But then we do get the Hobbiton celebrations (including the 'Proudfeet' joke), before Gandalf appears and, against a background of fireworks, insists that Bilbo should depart The Shire for Rivendell. He does so, leaving the Ring for Frodo; already there is a Black Rider watching. Straightaway the four Hobbits are off to Rivendell themselves, eating hallucinogenic mushrooms along the way – an early sign that this Middle-Earth will be chic, druggy, and wild. Encountering Humans (reapers in a field) who are hunting Halflings, Frodo teases them with his invisibility, but the Hobbits then hide from another Black Rider who tries to sniff them out – a prototype of the iconic movie scene in which they hide by the road under the roots of a tree. A Black Rider pursues them into the Old Forest, but is caught in the thick undergrowth; however, the Forest is also wary of the Hobbits and becomes animated until Sam chants garden spells to calm it. As they emerge from the Old Forest there are now three Black Riders chasing them – the pursuit out of The Shire is urgently insistent in Boorman's script – until Aragorn comes to their aid and they stand and fight the Riders, Aragorn himself battling with the two halves of his broken sword. Frodo puts on the Ring and now attracts all nine Black Riders; the Ring slows down time, but Frodo is speared when he removes it. All five survivors then mount Aragorn's Horse and gallop towards the Ford of Rivendell, where Elvish knights charge down the Black Riders in the river, and they dissolve into slime.

In the Great Hall of Rivendell, a crystal palace, there is ritual chanting led by Elrond to heal Frodo, who is fast becoming a transparent wraith: 'The bone is quite clear beneath the translucent skin.'[40] A thirteen-year-old Arwen surgically removes the splinter of the Ringwraith's weapon from Frodo, with Gimli ordered to 'strike off the arm' if she cries out.[41] Gandalf quells the impatience of Boromir by telling him that her struggle to heal Frodo is symbolic of the struggle of the Elves against Sauron. Frodo now recovered, Elrond then introduces the history of the Rings of Power, which is acted out in a kind of stylized Kabuki play or masque. Jugglers juggle the appropriate number of rings for Elves, Dwarves, and Humans, with Sauron indeed appearing as a cross between Mr Punch and Mick Jagger, while a wilful mongrel dog tosses around a transparent ball banded with gold representing Fate and the One Ring. The drama continues with the confrontation between the Last Alliance and Sauron, and the Ring rolling into the river to be found by Gollum. Sauron,

Saruman, and Gandalf then perform a sinister dance, in which Saruman tries to entice Gandalf to join with him and establish an alternative power-bloc to Mordor, before a Bilbo character appears, takes the Ring from Gollum, and skips off. *Finis.* The question now is: what is to be done? Bilbo, then Frodo, each offer to take the Ring, the Company of the Ring is quickly formed – although Gandalf doubts its wisdom, murmuring, 'Is it madness to send this Hobbit?' – and Arwen is appointed as a spirit guide; she also provides Elven cloaks and waybread (*lembas*) for them.[42] Thus they leave.

Merry and Pippin lark about with Boromir, but Frodo dreams of Bilbo who had given him Sting and then wanted to see the Ring again, feeling 'growing revulsion for the old man'.[43] By morning, the Ring has slipped off its chain from Frodo's tunic and is being contemplated by Boromir; Frodo wrenches himself away from him.[44] Instructed by the ethereal Arwen, Aragorn and Boromir divide Isildur's broken sword between them, she kisses the blades and with bloody lips kisses each of them on the mouth, making them blood brothers; Aragorn and Boromir then kiss each other. In the Misty Mountains the Company is attacked by Wargs – 'furry-white mutants of men and animals, ferociously savage' – and Gandalf doses his companions with an inebriant and wraps them in a glacier to escape.[45] At the Gate of Moria, Gimli's ancestral memory of the password to the Mines is recovered through primal scream therapy, accelerated by Gandalf mercilessly beating him. Gollum is already in Moria and can be heard; also audible is a sound of beating drums. The Company soon find that the ground is littered with inert Orcs, humanoid creatures with 'reptile and bird-like features' and covered in organic armour – and the noise is not drums but the beating of their hearts.[46] The Orcs start into life, rise up, and give chase. The Company have reached the Bridge of Khazad-Dûm (a rope bridge) when the Balrog appears, producing a paralysing effect until Gandalf and the demon plummet into the abyss together, while the remaining Company flee.

Outside, the companions strip and bathe in a magical lake. Galadriel rises from the waters (the lady of the lake) and bewitches them. Legolas starts to perform a bird-like dance, while Gimli, Boromir, and Aragorn all gaze in lust at her 'sparsely clad' body.[47] Boromir embraces and kisses Galadriel; she ignores him and takes Frodo into her pavilion. There, she seduces the Hobbit while outside the Company wait jealously. Having consummated his relationship with Galadriel, Frodo can now gaze into her mirror (although we are not told what, if anything, he sees), and when he returns to the Company they notice his 'new assurance'.[48] The Company navigate down the river in Elvish boats, are ambushed by Orcs, and Merry, Boromir, Sam, and Gimli are all wounded. At this point, the film pauses with an intermission – fashionable at the time, and indicating that the production was to be about three hours long.

Resuming the plight of the Company on the banks of the Great River, Frodo tries to decide on his course but is stalked by Boromir. Here, the action remains close to the book: Frodo escapes by slipping on the Ring and, half in a vision, sees Middle-Earth spread before him while the Eye of Sauron searches like a spotlight. The Company miss Frodo, then miss Boromir, and seek them; Orcs attack and Boromir is slain defending Merry and Pippin, who are taken; and Aragorn promises the dying Boromir that he will go to Minas Tirith. A key difference here, however, is that Aragorn has, from afar, seen Frodo and Sam leave. The remaining three companions bury Boromir and, despite Aragorn's promise, pursue the Orcs.

The scenes now switch between plot and subplot, often very rapidly: Frodo and Sam traversing the Emyn Muil, trailed by Gollum, and then capturing him; the three companions chasing the Orcs and finding their corpses piled on a pyre by the Riders of Rohan. After meeting the riders, the companions then resolve to go to Minas Tirith, abandoning Merry and Pippin to Fangorn Forest. The passage of the Dead Marshes is faithful enough to the novel, although the Sméagol/Gollum conflict takes place between his right hand and his left hand. Not so in Fangorn, though, where Merry and Pippin immediately meet Saruman – or rather 'as Saruman should have been' – an otherworldly wizard 'attempting to break through from a different plane of consciousness'.[49] The Hobbits seize his sword, try to stab him, tumble over, and Gandalf – for it is he – is laughingly restored to himself. He summons a hawk that functions as a *palantír* (of which there are none in this script), allowing him to see reflected in its eye how the other members of the Company fare, and to summon the Horse Shadowfax. Together these three go to 'Théoden's Castle' (Edoras) where Gandalf rides into the throne-room (!) to confront the king, who has succumbed to the decadence of 'Silks and Satins'.[50] At this point, Gandalf tells of his battle with the Balrog in Tolkien's own, powerful words combined with Boorman's own, poetic vision, in which Gandalf reflects that it was the 'silly voice' of the Hobbits that called him back. He dreamt of Halflings: 'They were sore afraid, yet braver than many kings; they were foolish, yet wiser than many wizards; they lived in despair yet they found hope. Their spirits drew me back from the everlasting night.'[51]

This is an extremely effective narrative plunge that one could easily imagine being adopted by later adaptations. Boorman brilliantly withholds Gandalf's abysmal combat until the very last moment: in doing so, he makes the visit to Edoras supremely significant – even though, in the book, of course, all has already been explained to Aragorn, Gimli, and Legolas. Gandalf rouses Théoden, the Hobbits rather cruelly trip the hunchback Wormtongue, and the King of Rohan throws his sword into the air – the very image, if in a different context, with which Ralph Bakshi was to end his own film version. But this treatment continues: Théoden and Gandalf, with Merry and Pippin respectively, go by separate ways to Minas Tirith. Switching attention now to Frodo and Sam, the Hobbits discover that the roots of an ancient tree have breached the walls of Mordor and they manage to cross the border under its dead branches. However, chased by screaming Orcs they jump into a canal and are swept to Barad-Dûr where they meet the Shelob [*sic*], who after battling with Frodo stings him with her tongue in his moment of confidence. Sam duly stabs the vile arachnid from below and, very reluctantly, takes the Ring: 'So I'm the last.'⁵²

Boorman then gathers his forces for the battle of Minas Tirith. He converges his armies, with Aragorn leading a regiment of the Risen Dead raised from an ancient battlefield, and Legolas and Gimli rallying their kinsmen for the fight. At the same time Gandalf and Pippin are refused entry to Minas Tirith by the mad steward Denethor, who begins to will himself to die in a grotesque parody of the siege of the city, until Pippin describes the fall of Boromir. The Lord of the Nazgûl declares himself in the siege of Minas Tirith. These scenes are cut against Sam in Barad-Dûr: Frodo is imprisoned naked in Barad-Dûr and guarded by Saruman, no less, but Sam, wearing the Ring, explodes through the dungeons of the Dark Tower – the effect of the Ring is agonizing to the Orcs that surround him, but eventually he collapses, exhausted. Pippin becomes court jester to Denethor, Denethor is mad (very like Shakespeare's King Lear) and Pippin goes down to the battle dressed in the torn costume of a slaughtered Fool (again, very like *King Lear*) where he hears the cock crow.⁵³ The advent of the Riders of Rohan empties the city of Minas Tirith as all who can prepare to fight:

> CIVILIANS and WOMEN as well as SOLDIERS swell the
> ranks bearing any kind of weapon that comes to hand. They

are ragged and dirty, the fires have blackened their faces. The SOLDIERS have not shaved for days. Many of them are weak from lack of food. It is an undisciplined rabble that empties out of the garrison city on to the Pelennor Fields. The ORCS flee before this crazy onslaught.[54]

Oddly, Éowyn and Merry slay the Lord of the Nazgûl without reference to his invulnerability to living men, but, that aside, the battle is familiar territory apart from the ravings of Denethor. Now the Orcs rally and renew their attack and then Aragorn arrives, leading an army of Rangers, Legolas's Elves, Gimli's Dwarves, and the Risen Dead, who are all disguised as a gigantic hundred-yard-long serpent. They counter-attack the Orcs, Aragorn accidentally kills Denethor – who was on the verge of committing suicide anyway – but revives Éowyn by lying on her, embracing her, and kissing her passionately; his sword spontaneously repairs itself and, now resplendent as King of Gondor, he leads the advance on the gates of Mordor.[55] The party of the 'Chosen' – King Aragorn, his Queen Éowyn, King Éomer, Gandalf, the Hobbits, Gimli and Legolas, and the remaining warriors – then meet with the Mouth of Sauron, who is the ubiquitous Saruman. Gandalf and Saruman duel with words, countering the images each conjures up with its nemesis, characteristic of Anglo-Scottish ballads such as 'The Two Magicians'.[56] Saruman wavers, but then Wormtongue produces an effigy dressed in Frodo's clothes and the Chosen recoil in horror. Frodo himself, meanwhile, is being tortured by having the Lord of the Nazgûl's helmet clamped over his skull, before being rescued by Sam, then being recaptured and only escaping again by putting on the Ring, which continues to have an excruciating effect on the Orcs; Sam also brandishes it. In the presence of the Eye the effect of the Ring is almost nuclear, 'bleaching everything into a white translucency', but they get away and approach Mount Doom, the scenes cutting between the painful ascent of Frodo and Sam, and, within their sight, the desperate, last-ditch stand of the Chosen.[57] Gollum finally reappears, Frodo claims the Ring, Gollum bites off his finger and falls into the mountain. The battle suddenly ceases and the sun comes out. The Orcs, now repentant, slough off their armour, like snakes, underneath which they are more Human – if slug-white – and all join in cheering Frodo and Sam from the mountain until they reach Gandalf: 'You did it! You . . . you . . . you Hobbit!'[58]

There is a carnival quality to these closing scenes, although affairs of state rapidly occupy Aragorn and Éowyn (waited on by Pippin and Merry) and so distance the former companions from each other. Through the crowds and debris the five remaining comrades pass Saruman, now an itinerant trickster, and arrive with uncanny rapidity at The Shire. But only Sam, greeted by his 'buxom girlfriend', stays there.[59] Frodo cannot tarry and walks on with Gandalf, Gimli, and Legolas. They arrive at sand dunes, where Arwen beckons to Frodo, and then he and Gandalf walk across the beach, through the surf, and board a boat to join Arwen, Elrond, Galadriel, and Bilbo. Gimli and Legolas remain on the shore as the boat sails west, exchanging gnomic utterances and deciding to stay where they are: 'It is not quite leaving, nor is it yet remaining,' says Legolas, 'for a beach is between, like the twilight.'[60] They hear Frodo's laughter as the boat fades from view and a rainbow rises, 'Only seven colours. Indeed, the world is failing . . .'[61]

Boorman and Pallenberg's script was never filmed, and has been much vilified, but is that completely fair? I have described it in detail as only the more outré and radically reworked episodes tend to be cited, but in the context of the entire film that was projected, it is surely a vivacious rendering of a three-volume novel into a single long film. I, for one, admit to liking it: it is imaginative and insightful, very fast-paced, and anyone who reads the treatment will be struck with how sensitively it cites some of the most memorable lines of the book, such as the crowing of the cock. Yes, there are huge cuts: no Old Man Willow, Tom Bombadil, or Barrow-Wights (but no surprise there, perhaps); no Bree or Weathertop; no Lothlórien, or Ents, or Helm's Deep, or Isengard, or Cirith Ungol; no Faramir, no Eagles – in fact, no flying creatures at all (on the grounds that they were too distracting); and no 'Scouring of The Shire'. But some details are certainly striking: the Lord of the Nazgûl, for instance, is mounted on a flayed Horse rather than the Fell Beast, and among the defenders of Minas Tirith are masked bee-keepers in leather with 'bees swarming around their gloved hands' – a wonderfully restless and disconcerting folk horror image.[62] These features, together with the insistent physicality – characters embracing, kissing, making love, or simply being naked – and the strange pageantry that accompanies Aragorn's accession and Frodo's victory (such as Pippin in tattered Fool's garb) introduce a strange and sinister air comparable to later cult films such as *The Wicker Man* (1973). Extreme as these rewrites were, then, Boorman's ambition was to make the mythic and archetypal elements of the narrative fully cinematic through 'radical adaptation': to put myth 'in all its mysterious, irrational glory' onto the screen.[63]

I have, then, tried to communicate not only the idiosyncrasies (which have annoyed various commentators), but also the frequent precision, insights, and the sheer excitement of the script – some scenes of which could easily be mistaken for Peter Jackson's. Indeed, key points are reflected in Jackson's films. First, in significant cuts: Jackson also dispensed with Old Man Willow (in fact, the whole of the Old Forest), Tom Bombadil, Barrow-Wights, and 'The Scouring of The Shire'. Following his brief authorial frame, Boorman reworks the opening to make it immediately cinematic – as does Jackson. Identical too are the dramatic pursuit of the Hobbits, the concision of the Council of Elrond, Frodo's disgust at Bilbo (in the book Bilbo is instead pathetic, and Frodo wants to strike him), and Frodo (rather than Merry) solving the riddle of Moria Gate. More significant is the gratuitous, if wholly cinematic, introduction of an Elvish army: Legolas's Tree Elves by Boorman, the Elves of Lothlórien at the Hornburg by Jackson. Boorman also juxtaposes the ebb and flow of the War of the Ring with the final movements of Frodo and Sam in Mordor with deft precision – in the book they are firmly separated by many chapters. Most strikingly, though, the portrayal of Boromir is markedly similar in both film treatments: his initial impetuosity and impatience succumbing to a playfulness with the Hobbits on the road, and then his temptation when the Ring slips from Frodo's tunic. In Jackson's hands, the Ring actually falls into the snow and Boromir holds it up for a moment on its chain – none of this character-building is in the book. Even the gluttonous feast scene in Boorman's previous film *Leo the Last* anticipates Denethor's disgusting meal in Jackson's *The Return of the King*, in which birds' legs are gnawed apart – a warning that Denethor himself will fall. In other words, the aborted Boorman–Pallenberg script was a source on which Peter Jackson could – and surely did – build.

Halflings Half-Filmed

In 1976, no films having yet been made, the rights to *The Hobbit* and *The Lord of the Rings* were bought from United Artists by Saul Zaentz, and UA was then in turn bought by MGM. According to their website, the Saul Zaentz Company 'acquired these rights in 1976 in an arrangement with United Artists to produce an animated version of *The Lord of the Rings*'; the company also acquired trademarks for the characters, places, and objects included in the books – although distribution rights for *The Hobbit* remained with MGM/UA.[64] The first fruit, however,

was a TV film of *The Hobbit* made by Rankin/Bass, an established production company that had already become a Christmas
institution in America thanks to their seasonally saccharine
stop-motion animation of *Rudolph the Red-Nosed Reindeer*,
which has aired every Christmas since 1964. The Rankin/Bass
Hobbit, animated by Japanese animation studio Topcraft, was
first broadcast in 1977 (see Chapter Six).

The Middle-Earth movie landmark of the 1970s was, however – for better or worse – Ralph Bakshi's controversial film of
The Lord of the Rings, premièred on 15 November 1978. Bakshi
was an *enfant terrible* of the animation world. His career had
begun with Terrytoons and Paramount in the 1960s, and in 1969
he became a director at CBS when he was only twenty-nine,
but he was best known for *Fritz the Cat* (1972). This was an
X-rated underground sensation based on Robert Crumb's sleazy
feline comic character, which in the first ten minutes includes
swearing, racial politics, drug use, group sex, exploitation, and
irresponsible urination – and continues in much the same vein
for the next hour and a quarter: as the poster boasted, 'We're not
X rated for nothin', baby!'[65] It is worth noting that *Fritz the Cat*
appeared in the same year as such notorious and offensive films
as *Deep Throat* and *Pink Flamingos*, and if sexploitation flicks
were not exactly mainstream, they had become a recognizable
part of the geography of popular contemporary film and could
potentially make vast profits – from a $700,000 budget *Fritz*
grossed over $90 million.[66]

By 1976, however, Bakshi had moved on from the sleazegrind
of *Fritz* and had released *Wizards*, a post-apocalyptic future
fantasy and a barely disguised allegory of the Jewish people,
Israel, and the Holocaust. *Wizards* mixed idiosyncratic animation with rotoscoping for the final battle scenes – rotoscoping
being a technique of painting over live-action footage to blend
photographic material with animation: in other words, 'living

animation'.[67] While earlier uses of rotoscoping such as Disney's *Snow White and the Seven Dwarfs* (1937) aimed to make these different film textures seamless, later examples such as the performance of 'Supercalifragilisticexpialidocious' in *Mary Poppins* (1964) made a virtue of the mismatched media to create playful, carnivalesque, and incongruous effects. Bakshi characteristically made his rotoscoped scenes dark and dirty, solarized (reversing tones) to smear them with fluorescence, disorientated through strobing chiaroscuro, and set against lurid and fantastical backgrounds.[68] Perhaps there is a nod here to Gene Deitch's expressionist landscapes of his short film of *The Hobbit*, although it is also worth bearing in mind that Bakshi adopted the technique in part because his funding had run out. Both John Boorman and Ralph Bakshi were darlings of the counter-culture, then, but Bakshi remained a dazzling – if flawed – artist: unafraid (if recklessly) of mashing up erotic cartoon Elves with Nazi reportage as trippy as the album cover of Cream's *Disraeli Gears* (1967). In fact, Bakshi may well have had a rock soundtrack in mind for his rotoscoped *Lord of the Rings*, and has since claimed that he contacted Led Zeppelin to score the film, and even that Mick Jagger (again) had wanted to voice Frodo.[69] In the event, however, the soundtrack was composed by Hollywood stalwart Leonard Rosenman who had received an Academy Award for the music to Stanley Kubrick's *Barry Lyndon* (1975), and who gave the film a somewhat incongruously martial air.

It should be emphasized, then, that Bakshi was a radical innovator, not a pornographer. *Fritz the Cat* was an anti-establishment sex cartoon with a provocatively infantile style – both content and form were a shock; *Wizards* was a fantasy allegorizing the Jewish experience by using mixed-media techniques previously again associated with children's films – and again, both content and form were potentially a shock. Hence

Bakshi treated his *Lord of the Rings* film as a serious animation project, saying 'I am trying to produce an adult animated
fantasy which is not a cartoon but is realistically drawn': as he
claimed, 'This is live action with the *design* of animation . . . The
thing about the movie – why the technique will be different –
is that it's not a cartoon but rather the first realistic painting
in motion.'[70] Moreover, he was 'not going to alter the story'.[71]
Bakshi disagreed with Boorman's approach of making do with
one film – ideally there should be three: 'I'd rather do the books
as close as we can, using Tolkien's exact dialogue and scenes.'[72]
He also claimed to have discussed his version with Priscilla
Tolkien, the author's daughter.[73] One may not appreciate the
final results, but one cannot doubt Ralph Bakshi's sincerity:
'Why would you want to tamper with anything Tolkien did?'[74]

The second half of the 1970s had already seen a retrench-
ment of Tolkien: in 1977 *The Silmarillion* was finally published,
edited from Tolkien's voluminous notes by Christopher Tolkien
and Guy Gavriel Kay. At the same time, *The Sword of Shannara*
(1977) by Terry Brooks was published to a mixture of undeserved
praise and outright condemnation for, according to influential
fantasy writer and editor Lin Carter, ruthlessly ripping off *The
Lord of the Rings*, while veteran science-fiction and fantasy writer
Michael Moorcock was moved to attack the renewed enthusiasm for Tolkien in a misguided essay, 'Epic Pooh'.[75] Moorcock,
whose own idiosyncratic fantasy writing is exemplified by the
Wagnerian despair of his anti-hero Elric of Melniboné, criticized Tolkien (as well as Lord Dunsany, C. S. Lewis, and Richard
Adams) as a celebration of Anglican [*sic*!] Tory petit bourgeois
sentimentalism that produced a 'corrupted romanticism', deciding that 'anyone who hates hobbits can't be all bad'.[76] While
Moorcock's essay is obviously designed to provoke, it is revealing
that despite championing the apparently disregarded 'proles', he
seems completely to overlook the rural labouring-class character

Sam. Moreover, he states that 'great epics dignified death, but they did not ignore it', and that this is 'one of the reasons why they are superior' to *The Lord of the Rings*.[77] Yet Moorcock seems oblivious not only to the last chapter of *The Lord of the Rings*, or to the extraordinary meditation on mortality in 'The Tale of Aragorn and Arwen' in Appendix A of *The Return of the King*, but also, essentially, to Tolkien's entire vision of Middle-Earth, which is fundamentally concerned with facing death.

Moorcock, then, builds a straw man of Tolkien in order to knock him down. It is naïve reading: criticizing Tolkien for over-simplification of complex Human issues is achieved by over-simplifying Tolkien's exploration of those same issues. Another example: Moorcock criticizes Tolkien (and his ilk) for refusing 'to face or derive any pleasure from the realities of urban industrial life' – the same Tolkien who said in a BBC interview when asked about motor cars, 'Love them! Love riding them, love driving them!' and had carefully gauged ideas about industrialization.[78] In other words, Moorcock has confused the attitude of the Hobbit characters with Tolkien's own position. But Moorcock's antipathy goes deeper: he was a key figure in the London underground culture of the late sixties centred around Ladbroke Grove, and performed with and wrote lyrics for the psychedelic rock band Hawkwind. At the same time he was writing fiction prolifically to the extent that he is (unfairly) perceived as a pulp writer – a disparaging term that does not do justice to his finest creations: Elric and Jerry Cornelius, both aspects of the 'Eternal Champion'. But Moorcock's fantasy was not part of the countercultural *Zeitgeist* in the same way that Tolkien's Middle-Earth was, and he was not celebrated in music or art to the same degree, and so there is an intense sense of frustration in his treatment of Tolkien: simply put, why the Oxford don, why not the radical young hippy Moorcock?[79] In fact, the Ladbroke Grove scene can be viewed as the underground of the counterculture – an alternative to the dominant Carnaby Street chic of Swinging London. It was dark, unstable, moody – just the sort of revolutionary counterculture that Ralph Bakshi had celebrated – except that Bakshi was now lauding Tolkien, whose work he described as 'Brilliance. Absolute brilliance.'[80] Tolkien appreciation – obsession – now represented the rift between UK and US fantasy. But by the early 1980s, Moorcock's allies Hawkwind were happy to quote Frodo's chilling words at the Crack of Doom on their album *Choose Your Masques* ('Dream-worker', 1982) – a sample taken from Ian Holm's BBC radio performance; gallingly, Moorcock had also provided lyrics for the recordings.[81]

Bakshi's film version was bankrolled by Saul Zaentz after a deal with MGM fell through (once again due to a change in personnel), and took just two years – a short time for a long animation.[82] Chris Conkling was the first scriptwriter, and Peter Beagle then rewrote Conkling's script, reverting to Tolkien's dialogue and dropping the more outlandish structural changes. There were, however, major changes in the interests of rationalizing the narrative for a cinema release: no Bombadil or associated episodes (again), but no Arwen either, no gifts from Galadriel, and no relationship between Aragorn and Éowyn – which, since there was no Faramir either, meant that Aragorn's only possible future bride could have been Éowyn. Treebeard, meanwhile, appeared onscreen for barely a minute. There are further oddities: rather curiously, Saruman's name was (inconsistently) changed to Aruman to avoid any audience confusion with Sauron. There are also narrative non-sequiturs and odd interjections from a narrator, and a wholly unsuitable ending. The film finished with the victory at Helm's Deep as Frodo and Sam were led into Shelob's Lair. Bakshi, of course, had envisaged this as the first of two films, but UA refused to publicize it as *The Lord of the Rings: Part One*: it was *The Lord of the Rings*, period. So although the film was technically a commercial success (grossing over $33 million from a $4 million budget), the crucial second part was never made. Bakshi was, understandably, furious. And yet his work was not completely overlooked by award panels: *The Lord of the Rings* was nominated for a Saturn Award (Best Fantasy Film, 1979), a Golden Globe (Best Original Score, 1979), and a Hugo Award (Best Dramatic Presentation, 1979), and won the Golden Gryphon at the Giffoni Film Festival in 1980.[83]

Any assessment of Bakshi's film must therefore be made under the weighty proviso that this is merely one half of a film, and runs to just 133 minutes (Jackson's *Fellowship of the Ring* runs to 178 minutes in the theatre release and 228 minutes in the extended DVD release). But there are certainly shortcomings. The Hobbits are too cutesy, Sam is a rustic dolt, and Merry and Pippin are barely characterized; even the Hobbits' feet are wrong – huge, barely furred appendages rather than being Tolkien's 'leathery soles' with 'thick curling hair, much like the hair of their heads'.[84] The rest of the Company are barely better: Aragorn and Boromir are stock fantasy heroes who seem disdainful of clothing and are well on the way to emulating the barely clad Conan the Barbarian, and Legolas seems to have minced out of an Oscar Wilde comedy of social manners. Gandalf, however, has gravitas, Galadriel – mixing mystery and magic – is finely portrayed, and Saruman is efficiently evil. The Ringwraiths are crippled horrors who today would be seen as demonizing disabilities; the Orcs, all rotoscoped and red-eyed, are very effective; the Balrog is a complete disaster.

So much for the studio's execution, and it is difficult to see beyond the visualization. But it would be an injustice not to do so: the script is a triumph, and there is some striking voice acting dubbed onto the animation, including the acclaimed Shakespearean actor William Squire as Gandalf, and John Hurt – shortly to become a household name in *Midnight Express* (also

1978), *Alien* (1979), and *The Elephant Man* (1980) – as Aragorn. Firstly, the film retains much of Tolkien's own dialogue and in the mouths of the correct characters – unlike Jackson, it has to be said. Second, Bakshi introduces major structural revisions that nevertheless seem so natural as to be Tolkien's own: readers and viewers simply do not notice these changes, and many have almost seamlessly been carried into Jackson's versions.[85] In the opening seconds even the lettering of the titles of both the Bakshi and Jackson *Rings* is similar, whereupon Bakshi begins with the forging of the Rings of Power, and the Ring being cut from Sauron's finger before being lost and then rediscovered in the River Anduin. Although the style of these scenes is terribly dated in Bakshi (badly acted silhouettes against hessian), the pacing is spot-on. Bakshi front-loads his movie with the whole story of the rings. Jackson virtually does the same, mirroring Bakshi sometimes shot-by-shot – the major difference being that Jackson reserves the sequence showing the discovery of the Ring by Déagol while fishing, Sméagol's murder of Déagol, and his refuge under the Misty Mountains until the opening of his third film. But the congruity of the films is not simply remarkable: Jackson's *Rings* can be seen not only as an homage to but almost a remake of Bakshi's *Lord of the Rings*.

So there are effective moments in Bakshi: as Janet Brennan Croft points out, the intercutting between Frodo's ridiculous song in The Prancing Pony and Merry's encounter with the Ringwraiths is effective visual cinematic drama and also eventually influenced Peter Jackson; likewise, Sam joining Frodo in the boat on the River Anduin and paddling against him is retained. But the main structural change involves cutting between scenes of the Hobbits leaving The Shire with those of Gandalf visiting Saruman, the confrontation between the two wizards, and Gandalf's imprisonment at the apex of Isengard. This sequence includes the iconic encounter with the Ringwraith on the road out of The Shire, when the Hobbits cower under the roots of an ancient tree and the Ringwraith's influence is felt in the sudden appearance of creepy-crawlies and Frodo's almost irresistible desire to put the Ring on his finger.[86] Again Jackson is effectively reshooting from Bakshi's script, from spectacular tracking shots such as Gandalf riding into Isengard to tiny details such as Saruman's long nails: these are Bakshi's innovations, canonized in Jackson's films – even if other elements, such as the painful and crippled lurching movements of Bakshi's Ringwraiths, Jackson wholeheartedly rejected for a far more robust physique. But this whole sequence of the Hobbits and Gandalf's defiance of Saruman makes it into Jackson's *Fellowship of the Ring*: it is not from the published novel, which simply has the Black Rider passing and sniffing as the Hobbits cower, with the whereabouts of Gandalf at this stage a complete mystery.[87] That demonstrates the significance and influence of Bakshi's film. But most importantly, perhaps, Bakshi raised the idea of filming *The Lord of the Rings* to aspire to be a serious work of cinema art. As the science fiction critic Andrew Butler has commented, 'Whatever the faults of the compressions and omissions of the adaptation, it is clear that Bakshi took his source seriously and offered an adult rather than juvenile version'.[88] Once *The Lord of the Rings* was recognized as an adult film, things would never be the same. So why did it take so long for the film to be remade: twenty-three years from release-date to release-date?

The main reason for the lack of enthusiasm for Bakshi's *Lord of the Rings*, innovatively filmed and structurally resolved as it was, is that the previous year had seen the first of George Lucas's *Star Wars* films (now retrospectively titled *Part IV: A New Hope*). Combining a simplified version of Boorman's mythic struggles with a deliberately dilapidated sci-fi futurism, *Star Wars* presented space travel, robotics, and computing as hand-me-down technology – fallible and therefore recognizable – swiftly enabling the film and its franchise to become a runaway global blockbuster, with, importantly, the promise of more and more films to come. Kids wanted spaceships that looked like their parents' washing machines – they could relate to that. In contrast, Bakshi's violently collaged, out-of-this-world animations unfortunately looked like dated and overwrought examples of sixties drug culture – which is precisely where Bakshi headed next.[89] Following *The Lord of the Rings*, the director returned to his rock roots with the deranged, ultra-cool *American Pop* (1981), a history of the US through popular music as experienced through successive generations of a Russian-Jewish family (Bakshi's own background), again rotoscoped to sometimes hyper-real effect. But Bakshi would also continue to make fantasy epics, creating *Fire and Ice* in 1983, another cult classic – this time in collaboration with iconic artist Frank Frazetta (the 'Godfather' of fantasy art), and drawing on the formidably rich tradition of Frazetta's swords and sorcery paintings, instantly recognizable from the book jackets of Conan the Barbarian paperbacks from the 1960s and 1970s, and the covers of *Heavy Metal* magazine. *Fire and Ice*, while remaining indomitably Bakshi, is way less chaotic than his earlier left-field extravaganzas, but (or, consequently) he remains proud of it.[90]

Elsewhere in fantasy film, Disney were foundering in the early 1980s. The studio only really caught up with this darker, more adult market in 1985 with the Celtic fantasy animation *The Black Cauldron*. The film took inspiration from both Bakshi's *Lord of the Rings* and former Disney animator Don Bluth's ambition to create depth and complexity in these new animations – what Tolkien himself had described as the 'subcreation' of a 'Secondary World'.[91] But this was so different from the usual Disney format that it is known as 'the film that almost killed Disney': it very nearly bankrupted the studio.[92] So the harnessing of authenticity comes at a price, and at a risk. John

Boorman, Ralph Bakshi, and Peter Jackson were prepared to pay the price and take the risk. Boorman has never had the chance to realize his vision before the public; Bakshi got halfway there with rotoscoping and his fractured influence lives on; Jackson nailed it with *The Lord of the Rings* and its expansive fusion of the material culture of real swords and actual locations with saturated CGI (computer-generated imagery) and 'mo-cap' (motion-capture) effects.

Hot on the heels of Ralph Bakshi's film came the 1979 American radio version of *The Lord of the Rings*; this was broadcast on National Public Radio, and scripted by Bernard Mayes – a radio dramatist and originally a BBC broadcaster; he also played the part of Gandalf. This was an ambitious adaptation that ran to nearly twelve hours across twenty-four episodes – even Tom Bombadil was included. On the downside, however, despite (or perhaps because of) the script's fidelity to Tolkien's text, the production curiously often lacks the pace and drama necessary for radio; moreover, Mayes favoured child actors (or at least infantile-sounding actors) for most of the Hobbits and the Elves. The next year Mayes adapted *The Hobbit* in six hours, using some of the same actors. But, as we shall see, these US radio versions were dwarfed by the later BBC adaptation.

Before then, though, 1980 saw the release of the Rankin/Bass film *Frodo, The Hobbit II* under the title of *The Return of the King*. The Rankin/Bass strategy for a second TV film is sometimes considered a sequel to Ralph Bakshi's unfinished film of *The Lord of the Rings*, but according to an advert in *Variety* magazine, *Frodo* was in production by 3 May 1978, six months before the release of Bakshi's movie. It eventually aired on 11 May 1980 on the ABC network as *The Return of the King*.[93] As Ned Raggett puts it, 'With Bakshi's *Lord Of The Rings* leaving the story hanging, and while the sequel's production wasn't directly tied in with Bakshi's effort at all, Rankin/Bass ended up doing the still strange but almost logical thing of, essentially, finishing Bakshi's work for him, but doing so with the cast, animation style and general approach of their own *Hobbit*.'[94] But this is not quite right: Rankin/Bass had started their second film before Bakshi's unfinished epic was released, and, without evidence to the contrary, they really seem to have identified a 'Hobbit 2' film. Topcraft were again the animators, and several of the same actors were retained from the Rankin/Bass *Hobbit*. The 1980 *Return of the King*, then, attempts to recount the narrative of the final volume of *The Lord of the Rings*, aided by a framing narrative of Bilbo's 129th birthday party in Rivendell (on the return journey to The Shire) – and countless cuts to try to keep the running time to ninety minutes (it is, in fact, ninety-eight minutes). Although there is much original dialogue, there are almost constant, highly questionable additions such as an Orcs' marching song, and expanded passages such as Sam's dreams of glory as Samwise the Strong, as well as an extra character in the shape of a Gondorian minstrel played by Glenn Yarbrough, composer of the score and formerly singer with sixties band The Limeliters. One peculiar consequence of this is that the Bakshi *Lord of the Rings* does not actually segue into the Rankin/Bass *Return of the King* – not least as Shelob is lost in the gap between the two films. Yet it perhaps exercised some influence on the Jackson *Rings* in the depiction of the masked and cadaverous Mouth of Sauron – although in the Rankin/Bass movie he serves no role as he has none of Frodo's possessions with which to taunt Gandalf's delegation.

In the meantime, the BBC contacted the Saul Zaentz Company to seek permission for a radio adaptation of *The Lord of the Rings*, until learning that the Zaentz Company did not own those rights; they accordingly approached the Tolkien Estate. By chance – if chance it was – at exactly the same time that the Corporation was negotiating the rights Brian Sibley, an aspiring radio writer, approached the BBC with a proposal to dramatize the book. He was duly commissioned to script the drama, paired with the more experienced radio dramatist Michael Bakewell – first Head of Plays at the BBC who among many productions had in 1969 edited the BBC serialization of *War and Peace* and dramatized several Sherlock Holmes cases for radio. Bakewell generously allowed the younger Sibley to lead the relationship, although Bakewell was indispensable in writing, for example, extra verses to the 'Ride of the Rohirrim' and scripting the more complex battle scenes. The production was co-directed by Jane Morgan and Penny Leicester, with Elizabeth Parker of the BBC Radiophonic Workshop adding special effects. Sibley and Bakewell went through many rewrites with Morgan and Leicester, assisted by Christopher Tolkien, who offered generous advice from his home in France – providing, for example, an audio cassette to guide pronunciation.[95] This means that the BBC radio *Lord of the Rings* has the most accurate pronunciation of any recorded version and can be taken as authentic in its renderings of names – although, to be honest, this remained a challenge even for Tolkien himself, who was even sometimes uncertain how to pronounce the name of a major figure such as Sauron.

Sibley realized (or perhaps gathered from Christopher Tolkien) that Tolkien himself had not mapped out the story in advance: it was not planned, but discovered. So the person who was writing the narrative did not in fact know how it was going to end – something that gives the tale its immediacy. *The Hobbit* was not written with an eye to publication but, like much children's literature, was told to children, so as Sibley suggests in an interview, 'what you're experiencing is the process of the writer experiencing the story'. This process becomes epic in a work as ambitious as *The Lord of the Rings*. Literary shortcomings are 'totally and utterly compensated for by this sense of discovery that you the reader discover the next moment at the point when the writer himself discovers it as he is writing it down'. Thus at nearly every turn we feel poised with the characters – and with the author too – uncertain which direction to take. So as I have suggested, there are many points where Tolkien does not have everything tied up, and this draws readers back to the book again and again: 'Each time we read it', Sibley observes, it has this fresh sense of 'I'm living this'.[96] This is what Sibley and Bakewell communicate in their adaptation. They do not try to solve every crux but allow the story to be its own, uncertain self – so Sauron, for instance, is presented with doubts and fallibility, not as a simplified implacable force of evil.

Having said that, Sibley was faced with the serious problem of turning a three-volume novel into thirteen hours of radio drama. Although Sibley had much more time in which the plot and subplots could develop, this was arguably a far more serious challenge than the earlier film-makers faced as there can only be speaking parts on radio – otherwise characters are effectively invisible. So recognizable and distinctive voices and active roles had to be found for nine key characters (the Company) plus the numerous supporting characters. This problem was partially solved by the music, composed by Stephen Oliver who had scored 'essentially English' productions of *Alice Through the Looking Glass* (not dated), as well as the RSC's *Romeo and Juliet* (1976) and *Nicholas Nickleby* (1980), and who used Wagnerian refrains to track the characters and action superbly.[97]

Each of the twenty-six parts also had to have an internal consistency and integrity, and each episode had to end with a cliffhanger. Sibley decided that a narrator was necessary for a story of this complexity, although he later tried to dispense with narration in his adaptations of *Gormenghast* (1985, featuring Sting as Steerpike) and *The Once and Future King* (2014), and would apparently like to try *The Lord of the Rings* without a narrator. Nevertheless, for the 1981 series the narrator, Gerard Murphy (versatile enough to play King Lear and also appear in the TV comedy series *Father Ted*), provided an important anchor and, where necessary, significantly helped to give structure to each episode.

How to begin? There were undoubtedly flaws in Bakshi's film, but Sibley liked the silhouetted history of the Ring with which it began. Yet he could hardly reprise this sequence right at the start of his own version, as it would instantly brand it a radio remake of a recent film. Instead, Sibley sought permission from Christopher Tolkien to use the account of the 'Hunt for Gollum' from *Unfinished Tales*, which enabled him to establish Gollum – Sibley's favourite character – at the very outset of the story. So, after a brief introductory narration, the first episode begins with Gollum being tortured in Mordor: a startling and immediately arresting opening to the series – and surprising too for readers already familiar with the book, promising an imaginative and resourceful series to come. Thereafter, Sibley relied on 'The Tale of Years', Tolkien's scrupulous chronicle of day-by-day events that comprises Appendix B of the novel, for shaping the plot, rather than basing his chronology on the text itself. In Sibley's opinion, Tolkien was not a novelist: 'and therein lies the strength of the book'.[98] This brilliant point not only underlines the repeatedly unexpected quality of *The Lord of the Rings*, but importantly acknowledges Tolkien's radical and experimental writings and readings, revisions and renditions that I have described in previous chapters. So, although this radio series appears to follow Tolkien's structure this is in fact deft sleight of hand, as there is subtle and creative redrafting to satisfy the requirements of episodic radio drama.[99]

As to cuts, sadly Tom Bombadil and the associated scenes of the Old Forest, Old Man Willow, and the Barrow-Downs are (perhaps inevitably) absent, but Sibley had no regrets about this, knowing that Bombadil in any case pre-dated *The Lord of the Rings*. He felt that the appearance of the Black Riders drives the first part of the story, and that these rather leisurely scenes dissipate the initial momentum that has been building up.[100] Once the Hobbits arrive in Bree, however, most of the remaining scenes are incorporated. 'The Scouring of The Shire' is particularly striking as it provides much-needed drama to the last episode, which otherwise would have had the quality of a rather superfluous coda. As it is, Saruman, intimidatingly played by Peter Howell (prison governor in the film *Scum*, 1979), brings a simmering cruelty and prophetic doom to the last scenes that makes the final journey to the Grey Havens a more purposeful cadence. The recording demonstrates how this ending is a marked counterpoint to the central action of the subplot (the War of the Ring) in refocusing the traumas at a domestic and personal level, and finally bringing the manifold narratives together, before the characters are again separated.

The cast assembled for the BBC's recording was extraordinary. It included the veteran Shakespearean actor Michael Hordern as Gandalf, Robert Stephens as Aragorn (helping to revive his illustrious career), national treasure John Le Mesurier as Bilbo, Ian Holm (fresh from *Alien*, 1979) as Frodo, and Bill (then 'William') Nighy as Sam. The revered Michael Hordern had been the reader for the BBC broadcast of *The Battle of Maldon* in 1954, but he had never read *The Lord of the Rings*; Ian Holm, however, was a great fan. Peter Woodthorpe, who had played Estragon in the first English version of *Waiting for Godot* (1955), was cast as Gollum, playing him for the second time: Woodthorpe had already appeared as the voice of Gollum in Ralph Bakshi's movie, establishing a meaningful continuity between the two versions. Neither was Woodthorpe alone: Michael Graham Cox also reprised his role in the Bakshi film as Boromir (he also voiced Bigwig in *Watership Down*, 1978).

The use of actors whose voices were already familiar to the audience of Bakshi's film was another reason, then, why Sibley had to make his own radio version distinctive. But at the same time there was an acknowledgement of the increasing canon of Middle-Earth adaptations that positioned the BBC radio series as the heir to Bakshi's film. Woodthorpe's performance, played with spine-tingling conviction – Sibley describes it as 'physical' – is one of the high points of the series.[101] Moreover, his portrayal of Gollum laid deep foundations for later characterizations, notably Rob Inglis's audiobook rendition and ultimately Andy Serkis's justifiably acclaimed role in Peter Jackson's films. Serkis's Gollum did seem strangely familiar to those who had heard the BBC drama or listened to the audiobook because Serkis manifested a tangible Gollum (or so it seemed) through the magic of CGI. He gave expression and shape and movement and, crucially, interaction to a creature that had already been given its own unique voice and unmistakable mode of behaviour some two decades previously – although he did add the strangled noises his own cat made when vomiting up a fur-ball, drew inspiration from the paintings of Otto Dix and Francis Bacon and from his observation of drug addiction, and ultimately had to reshoot many scenes when the mo-cap technology was perfected by Wētā Workshop, enabling Serkis to marry his movements to his voice.[102] Thus these different versions share ideas and actors from one generation to the next: Gollum is also part of Ralph Bakshi's legacy, while Ian Holm graduated from playing Frodo in these BBC recordings to playing Bilbo in Jackson's *Rings*. The novel becomes, in a sense, the sourcebook for later, related adaptations.

The BBC radio *Lord of the Rings*, the first of the twenty-six parts being aired on 8 March 1981, also had an abiding afterlife as a set of cassette and later CD recordings. According to Sibley, Peter Jackson had the programmes on cassette and listened to them as a student, so the inclusion of Ian Holm in the films is actually in part a deliberate homage to the influence of the BBC radio version. Indeed, when Sibley visited Wētā during the filming of *The Lord of the Rings* the BBC radio version was playing in the background.[103] It is also rumoured that Jackson provided the actors with the recordings to listen to on the flight to New Zealand. It is no surprise, then, that Jackson's films of *The Lord of the Rings* are structured like the Sibley and Bakewell radio episodes, from the backstory told by Gandalf in 'The Shadow of the Past' to the concluding episode with Frodo's last words to Sam.[104] Ironically, Sibley was initially doubtful of Jackson's films, but was convinced they would work when he was shown a preview, including the scene of the Hobbits hiding beneath the tree root – a scene that itself quotes directly from Ralph Bakshi. Middle-Earth in audio and moving image is most successful, then, as a collective enterprise.

How Many *Rings*?

While the Tolkien industry did not go exactly into hibernation after the BBC radio dramatization – there was a Russian TV film of *The Hobbit* in 1985, and a distinctive Finnish TV mini-series of *The Lord of the Rings* broadcast in 1993, and more *History of Middle-earth* volumes appeared regularly off the press – the next major international event was not until 2001 with the release of Peter Jackson's pioneering film *The Fellowship of the Ring*.

Jackson was not an obvious choice to remake *The Lord of the Rings*. He was best known for cult splatter movies such as *Bad Taste* (1987) as well as the more rarefied *Heavenly Creatures* (1995).[105] In any case, it appears that he had only read the book once when he was seventeen.[106] However, he had been inspired to do so by the Bakshi film; furthermore, he had read it in an edition that had artwork from Bakshi's film on the cover.[107] If nothing else, Bakshi's unfinished, thwarted movie showed that there was a potentially international cinema market for *The Lord of the Rings*. *Heavenly Creatures* had been distributed by Miramax, who had an option on Jackson's follow-up film, *The Frighteners* (1996), for which he was spearheading remarkable CGI effects, inspired by *Jurassic Park* (1993). Jackson had suddenly become a hot property and was being courted to remake *Planet of the Apes* as well as *King Kong* – which he duly began scripting before considering a more ambitious project. He approached Saul Zaentz for the Tolkien rights, and pitched *The Hobbit* and a two-part *Lord of the Rings* to Miramax. Miramax had coincidentally just financed Zaentz's *The English Patient* (1996) which then won nine Oscars, so in 1997 the Saul Zaentz Company accordingly optioned the film rights for *The Lord of the Rings* to Miramax Films (while retaining the underlying trademark and service mark rights).

Jackson worked with his partner Fran Walsh on one script for two *Rings* films, to be filmed back-to-back; they were soon joined by playwright Philippa Boyens. Miramax boss, the now-disgraced (and convicted) producer Harvey Weinstein, invested some $12 million in the project, but became concerned at the escalating costs of the projected films and insisted on reining back to one two-hour film adaptation. Jackson would not even consider something that was 'literally guaranteed to disappoint every single person that has read the book'.[108] Weinstein was also trying to meddle with the script and artwork, Jackson comparing his idiotic advice to the grandiose pretensions of a phony mafia don: 'Look, ya gotta kill one of the Hobbits. One of the Hobbits has to die.'[109]

Weinstein then demanded a new deal, including his investment back, and royalties and a credit on any future project. He gave Jackson and Walsh four weeks to find new investors, during which time they controlled the rights to *The Lord of the Rings*. Jackson and Walsh made a thirty-minute film presentation outlining their plans, flew to Los Angeles, and approached PolyGram and New Line Cinema. Famously at their meeting with New Line, chairman Bob Shaye asked, 'I don't get this at all – why would you make two films when there are three books?'[110] Unbelievably there was suddenly a three-film deal on the table, with New Line prepared to pay $90 million per film.

New Line had profited enormously from the franchises of *Nightmare on Elm Street* (1984) and *Teenage Mutant Ninja Turtles* (1990) and seemed to see *The Lord of the Rings* as 'branded property': the project was a merchandizing franchise and a movie with built-in sequels that, being filmed simultaneously, would be unlikely to disappoint audiences.[111] Concurrent shooting in New Zealand would economize further on locations, crew, and even negotiations over actors' fees, saving an estimated $100 million and completing the films for a fraction of their cost in Hollywood.[112] The downside was that Jackson proposed to extend a series of connected and interdependent plots across three films shot simultaneously, meaning that New Line would be committed to a succession of releases even before the first film had been released and reviewed. But for a limited time Jackson was controlling the rights to *The Lord of the Rings* and so could deliver them to New Line. The deal was struck. Miramax sold the rights to New Line, with both Zaentz and Miramax slated to bank 5 per cent of the gross profits of the projected films.[113]

From the off, Jackson was influenced by Ralph Bakshi's treatment and his early experience of the Bakshi *Rings* also seems to have had a formative influence on his own later version, and it is telling how many scenes and also plot sequences are based on Bakshi. Indeed, Jackson has admitted that 'the first time he read the book it was a tie-in effort featuring Bakshi's film art on the cover', and has since 'freely said' that 'at least one of his scenes paid specific homage to the earlier film's approach'.[114] Well, certainly at least one: the entire opening sequences of *The Fellowship of the Ring* and *The Return of the King*, for example, appear to be direct quotations from Bakshi's film, as are the scenes of the Hobbits on the road intercut with Gandalf confronting Saruman, the first encounter with Strider at The Prancing Pony, the Black Riders trying to murder the Hobbits in their beds, the crossing of the Midgewater Marshes, Gollum skulking through the rocks of the Emyn Muil on the trail of Frodo and Sam, the flashback to Gandalf and the Balrog plummeting like a fireball into the abyss, and Saruman rallying his forces at Isengard before the attack on the Hornburg.[115] Likewise, Jackson makes the same cuts: no meeting with Farmer Maggot, no Old Forest, no Old Man Willow, no Tom Bombadil or Goldberry, no journey across the Barrow-Downs, and no Barrow-Wight. None of this diminishes Jackson's achievement one whit; rather it knits the cinema of Middle-Earth together – much as the respect afforded to the BBC radio drama by Jackson adds levels of richness and allusion to his films. As one of Jackson's two co-writers, the playwright Philippa Boyens, said, 'I like to think of it that we chose to leave some things untold, rather than left out. Unsaid.'[116]

Peter Jackson's script, treatment, and editing of *Rings* clearly worked (to the tune of nearly $3 billion), but even in addition to the changes that had already become customary following Bakshi and the BBC radio series, Jackson makes many changes. The beginning of *The Fellowship of the Ring*, after the prologue on the Ring and Bilbo's birthday party, introduces more immediate tension with the arrival of the Black Riders and the suggestion that Bag End has been ransacked – in fact, it is Gandalf inside; similarly, Strider initially appears to be working with the Black Riders. Inevitably, the long, explanatory chapter of the Council of Elrond, full of stories-within-stories, is hugely cut, but it also became far more confrontational, even violent.[117] In the book, debate is measured, voices are not raised; in the film, though, Gimli tries to smash the Ring with an axe blow (his 'energetic ferocity . . . that the film needs', as actor John Rhys-Davies put it), Boromir's temper flares (again, influenced by Bakshi), Gimli vehemently argues with Legolas, and the whole assembly straightaway collapses into bitter quarrelling – the rancorous discord reflected in the featureless gold of the Ring.[118] Frodo then has to repeatedly make his offer to take the Ring before he is heard, which he states only once in the book during a long and cheerless silence. The formation of the Company of the Ring also takes time and discussion in the book; in Jackson's film it happens almost immediately, spontaneously repairing the conflicts. Nevertheless, the central point – that the decision of the Council is an act of freewill – remains clear, and this is actually enhanced by the Company instantly uniting.

Other scenes, such as the Falls of Rauros and Frodo's departure, are also significantly rewritten. In the book, Gandalf's little homily on pity for Gollum, time, and on Frodo being meant to have the Ring, is given across a dozen pages at Frodo's fireside in Bag End; in the film of *The Fellowship of the Ring*, Gandalf speaks the words to Frodo under the Misty Mountains, while he is deciding which route to take through Moria.[119] The words on time then return to Frodo shortly afterwards at the end of the film when, on the banks of the River Anduin, he decides to take one of the boats and leave the Company. In the book, there is a comparable flashback in which, again at Bag End, Frodo muses that it was a pity that Bilbo did not kill Gollum, the words returning a volume later when Gollum is tamed and Sméagol begins to resurface (see above, pp. 117–18). More remarkably, Gandalf's heartfelt words of pity for Éowyn – 'who knows what she spoke to the darkness, alone, in the bitter watches of the night, when all her life seemed shrinking . . .' – are in the film given to Gríma Wormtongue, as if he has eavesdropped on her lamentations and construed them as exposing her disloyalty to Théoden, twisting them into a sexual threat.[120] Philippa Boyens, co-writer on the screenplay, suggests that in the films, the very geography of Middle-Earth mirrors the emotional state of the characters, the darkest moments occurring in the dark – Moria, Shelob's Lair, the Paths of the Dead.[121] This further explains why dialogue was revised and even switched from the original novel: cinema is a medium of light in the dark, so scenes of darkness heighten moments of crisis and give prominence to characters' words. Unexpectedly, however, the critic Brian Rosebury actually criticizes Jackson's films for being 'too arrestingly beautiful, since they are composed in terms of the formal constraints exacted by the flat, rectangular canvas of the moving image', being too painterly compared with Tolkien's very immersive, three-dimensional descriptions. But films (at least Jackson's first three Middle-Earth films) are by their nature flat, rectangular canvases – it is what the space is filled with that matters, and in the case of the *Rings* it is filled with wonder.[122]

Meanwhile, despite the vast resources of Tolkien's book, Jackson nevertheless adds extra (often melodramatic) scenes: notably, the films often resort to the apparent death of key characters – Frodo falling at the Ford, Frodo being speared by a Cave Troll, Arwen's decision to go to the Grey Havens – whereas Tolkien is more sparing of the effect: Gandalf falling to the Balrog, Frodo being stung by Shelob.[123] One sequence added to *The Two Towers* has Aragorn, Gimli, Legolas, and the Rohirrim attacked by Warg riders. During the mêlée, Aragorn is unhorsed, dragged along the ground by a maddened Warg, disappears over a precipice, and is missing, presumed dead. This is shortly after Aragorn has met Éowyn – who has fallen in love with him – and so a barely coherent Gimli breaks the tragic news to her that he has been lost. Aragorn, however, is rescued by his Horse, rides across the plains like the last of the Western heroes, arrives at Helm's Deep to the wonder of all, and, entirely oblivious of Éowyn, readies for battle. Having created this Aragorn–Éowyn–Arwen love triangle – Éowyn having glimpsed Legolas returning to Aragorn the Evenstar necklace of Arwen – Jackson then had to resolve Éowyn's character 'journey'. He did so by making Faramir more fallible. In the book, Faramir is in stark contrast to his brother Boromir: Boromir is fatally tempted by the Ring and drives Frodo (and Sam) away on their lonely journey to Mordor. Then, when they meet Faramir, Sam blurts out their mission – but Faramir effortlessly resists the Ring and they are allowed to go on their way. In the film, however, Faramir does decide to take them to Minas Tirith and deliver the Ring to his father, and they actually get as far as the ruined city of Osgiliath (former capital of Gondor) before Sam persuades him to let them go. The marriage of Éowyn to Faramir consequently seems less perfunctory: both are troubled, both disobey their rulers (who are also close family), both feel that they have failed, and both almost die: there is a cinematic logic to this even if it may not be how things are resolved in real life. It is also worth pointing out that, off the screen, both Éowyn and Arwen appeared on posters publicizing the film.

Other changes: in *The Two Towers*, again, the Elves of Lothlórien join with the Rohirrim to fight against Saruman. This is a startling anachronism, as Jackson's *Fellowship of the Ring* begins with the Last [*sic*] Alliance of Elves and Humans against the common enemy Sauron – but seeing a well-drilled Elvish army in action was too much of a temptation for the film-maker, and, in any case, otherwise there would only have been a handful of photogenic Elves in the entire movie. For good measure, Jackson then killed off Haldir, the leader of the Elvish forces, who dies in Aragorn's arms as he gazes over the piled bodies of his dead kinfolk. However, the tragedy of the War of the Last Alliance and the Battle of Dagorland was that by the end of it the Elves were devastated and were never again able to field an army. That campaign lasted a total of twelve years and ended the Second Age; Jackson's portrayal of another final alliance culminating in battle inevitably lacks the protracted apocalyptic intensity of Tolkien's original conflict and, naturally, subordinates it to Sauron and the fate of the One Ring.

In fact, the film of *The Two Towers* extends the single book chapter of Helm's Deep into a forty-minute spectacular. The movie magazine *Empire* placed the Battle of Helm's Deep at number two in its list of twenty-five 'Greatest Battles', noting the influence of earlier classics such as *El Cid* (1961) and *Zulu* (1964) on its staging, while *Total Film* magazine placed it at number one of 'The 10 Greatest Middle-Earth Moments', judging 'This is Middle-Earth's finest hour'; even before the film was released, Richard Taylor, head of props and special effects at Wētā Workshop, described it as 'a scene simply beyond comprehension'.[124] The battle is, consequently, full of additional material, from Legolas's notorious skateboarding stunt, careering down the battlement steps on a discarded shield while briskly loosing arrows, to Gimli being 'tossed' by Aragorn into the midst of the Orcs – after having earlier refused to be tossed across the Bridge of Khazad-Dûm. Such incidents add levity and humour to the horror of war, while also humanizing these non-Human races. But they also appealed to a definite demographic of younger film-goers, and much of Jackson's editing was in toning down the violence of battle scenes. There were allegedly twenty hours of battle footage shot over 120 days and nights for Helm's Deep, but instances of, for example, the hacking of corpses by the Orcs were cut in the interests of film classification, tempering the bloodshed to achieve the intended censorship rating of 12A.[125] The fight scenes also look forward to video games – again with a younger audience in mind.

In contrast, the material on the Ents in *The Two Towers* was compressed and simplified: Treebeard's authority is never questioned or compromised, and he is presented as formidably well informed and reliable – leading Adam Roberts to reflect, 'Tolkien loves trees more than battles; where Hollywood loves battles more than trees'.[126] In a similar vein, Brian Rosebury suggests that the films are 'too reluctant to dramatise rhetorical conflict [such as that between Saruman and Gandalf] when physical conflict can be substituted'.[127] Yet what is really happening here is in deference to the medium: close-ups and cuts, camera angles and perspectives, colour and sound, special effects and spectacle comprise the rhetoric and artistry of films, not language and text – cinema adaptations of Shakespeare, for instance, would never rely on a single fixed camera mimicking the view from the auditorium. Moreover, many of Jackson's revisions show how lines of prose on the page can be concentrated into a handful of words on the screen – as Jackson himself said, 'the language of cinema is different to the language of the written word'.[128] Viggo Mortensen, for instance, identifies Aragorn's defining moment as leading the Host of the West into their final, doomed battle with the simple, softly spoken, and overwhelming call to arms, 'For Frodo'.[129]

In addition to the necessary changes demanded by the medium of film – shorter, more dynamic scenes; a streamlined, chronological narrative; the interplay between plot and sub-plots – Peter Jackson's films are, then, notable for their radical divergences from the book. This is one reason for Christopher Tolkien's utter denunciation of Jackson's achievement, telling the French newspaper *Le Monde* on 9 July 2012 that

Tolkien has become a monster, devoured by his own popularity and absorbed by the absurdity of our time ... The chasm between the beauty and seriousness of the work, and what it has become, has overwhelmed me. The commercialisation has reduced the aesthetic and philosophical impact of the creation to nothing. There is only one solution for me: to turn my head away.[130]

But Jackson knew that he was not only making the films for diehard Tolkien fans (and no-one knew more about Middle-Earth at the time than Christopher Tolkien) – he also had to attract an audience of cinema-goers who had perhaps never read the book. He stated this quite plainly: 'Our adaptation can't be faithful. You can't just take the book and go and shoot it.'[131] Yes, he took liberties with the text, but he also visualized Middle-Earth with a spectacular brilliance, and populated it with unforgettable characters. Jackson cast established stage actors (Ian McKellen) against unknowns (Orlando Bloom), stars of horror (Christopher Lee) with family favourites (Sean Astin) to create a mix of acting styles and experience. Likewise, he promiscuously shifted tone, register, and genre – fantasy and bromance, war films and comedy – alluded to martial arts movies, Biblical epics, and video gaming, and blended extraordinary CGI monsters with expressive close-up characterizations – quite literally so, in the case of Gollum – as well as being 'the culmination of all the films I have made'.[132] There are candid references to other films too: Tolkien scholar Verlyn Flieger, for example, has shown that Jackson quotes from the film *The Wizard of Oz* (1939) in scenes such as the arrival of the Hobbits at Bree, where, like Dorothy and her companions entering the Emerald City, the four travellers are confronted by a closed door and have to knock to be allowed in.[133] Other references perhaps reach even further, by luck or design. Théoden's defining moment in *The Return of the King* occurs when his lieutenant Gamling says that the armies of Mordor cannot be beaten; Théoden's reply reverberates with the Anglo-Saxon 'Northern Courage' exemplified in the poem

The Battle of Maldon: 'No, we can't, but we will meet with them nonetheless'.[134]

In any case, Jackson's films could also have been even more radically different. Sceptical as one might be of John Boorman's innovations, Peter Jackson not only story-boarded, but actually filmed many scenes, later deleted and kept from the extended DVD editions.[135] In *The Fellowship of the Ring* these include Pippin playing in a band as Hobbits leisurely 'strip the willow' (a beautifully distinctive folk dance step); Gandalf portrayed as having given up smoking and instead eating toffees, lapsing and resuming the habit – only then to discover that Rivendell is a non-smoking establishment; Sauron forging the Ring by holding gold that melts in his palm and then piercing it with a blade to mix his blood into the molten metal; and flashback footage to a young (i.e. clean-shaven) Aragorn and Arwen 'frolicking together in the woods'.[136] Moreover, one ending of *The Fellowship of the Ring* filmed was of an Uruk-Hai Orc rising from the Anduin as Frodo attempts to escape in a boat, pulling him into the river, and the two fighting underwater. The Ring then slips from Frodo's neck to disappear back into the depths, the Uruk dives down to get it and drowns in the attempt, before Frodo and Sam somehow retrieve the Ring and escape. On the other hand, for Frodo's vision from Amon Hen 'we originally shot exactly what's in the book'.

For *The Two Towers*, this deleted footage includes Arwen herself arriving at Helm's Deep to meet Aragorn and fight alongside the Elves of Lothlórien, making her more of a warrior figure. Éowyn, too, had more combat scenes, making her more assertive, but less complex: in one, she helps to deliver a baby in Helm's Deep, whereupon Uruks burst the gate and she fights them off without armour, displaying extraordinary instincts of female sisterhood – and, it must be said, Miranda Otto's commitment to passionate fighting is equal to that of Viggo Mortensen;

she then vents her fury on Aragorn for taking the Paths of the Dead. Faramir, for his part, has a vision of Frodo being phys- ically transformed into Gollum. Likewise in *The Return of the King*, Aragorn duels with Sauron at the Black Gate; and Frodo and Gollum brawl over the Ring at the Crack of Doom *and both fall in*. Parts of 'The Scouring of The Shire' were also filmed, and even the intelligent Fox that remarks on the Hobbits al- most got into the film, albeit transformed into a deer or a rabbit. Although Peter Jackson often reverted to the novel in editing, that was not always the case, and in fact the extended DVD editions of the films (analogous perhaps to Tolkien's abundant appendices and subsequent supplementary material) not only add extra footage but in many instances use different takes of scenes included in the original theatrical release. Fans have since re-edited the various *Lord of the Rings* films on YouTube and Vimeo and spliced together sequences to create other Tolkien works, and there are much-admired independent films available for free such as *The Hunt for Gollum* (2009) and *Born of Hope* (2009).

Jackson's films as filmed, edited, and released remain momen- tous achievements. Characteristic of Jackson's technique in *Rings* is his emphasis on material culture, the physical texture of the *mise-en-scène*. Sets and locations are palpable, weapons and armour are tangible and were forged in a specially made metal foundry, and some items such as Théoden's breastplate had engravings inside them to inspire the actors – Viggo Mortensen wore his costume off set when riding and was even rumoured to sleep with his sword (Andúril) and also did many of his own fight scenes, which resulted in a broken front tooth.[137] Wētā wanted the films to have 'a historical rather than a fan- tasy feel', so comparable attention to detail was paid not only to the paraphernalia strewn about in Saruman's chambers and to the accuracy of Elvish scripts and runes in scenes, but even to the anatomy of the Fell Beast, whose wings were made large enough to ensure they could carry both it and the fully armoured Lord of the Nazgûl.[138] Astonishingly, the arrows of the Elves of Loth-lórien were individually crafted to an advanced design that is more accurate than the primitive arrows of other species: the flights are goose or swan feathers that make the arrows spiral when they are loosed.[139] Other props were made in different versions so that they could 'act' in the films in different ways and from different perspectives – notably the One Ring, of which over thirty versions were crafted in different weights and sizes so they could be handled differently, and of course one highly polished ring reflects the rancorous arguing at the Council of Elrond.[140] Such material details may be only barely noticeable, but they are there nonetheless.

At the same time, film critic Bob Rehak has pointed out that 'not a single performance' in these films is 'untouched in some way by visual or practical special effects'. This includes forced perspective, duplicate sets and props in different scales, green screen techniques, and body doubles – either a digital agent shadowing the real actors or a human double digitally enhanced with the original actor's face – as well as, most notably in the case of Gollum, mo-cap animation and CGI. Notably, after trailblazing stop-motion animator Ray Harryhausen's death in 2013 Jackson acknowledged another debt: 'The Lord of the Rings is my "Ray Harryhausen movie". Without that life-long love of his wondrous images and storytelling, it would never have been made – not by me at least.'[141] Virtually no part of Jackson's Middle-Earth is not enlivened by the state-of-the-art CGI and the more traditional effects such as wigs and prosthetics – wigs, in the case of Gríma Wormtongue's, with added fake dandruff (potato flakes).[142] What all this amounts to, in the words of another film critic, Mark Langer, is 'The End of Animation History': the 'collapse of the boundary between animation and live-action ... the destruction of the border separating simulation and reality, or the one that exists between the non-material world and the material world' – the consequence of 'an ever expanding cultural anxiety about the fact that it is no longer possible to distinguish between representations of real events or simulations of those events'.[143]

These disparities, so much a feature of Tolkien's novel, are particularly evident in Andy Serkis's stunning performance of audience-favourite Gollum/Sméagol. Although the perform-ance has its roots in Ralph Bakshi's animation, Peter Wood-thorpe's film and radio voicings, and Rob Inglis's audiobook reading, as well as in Tolkien's own depiction of mental disin-tegration – itself inspired by sharing a military hospital ward with the victims of shell-shock – Serkis's Gollum is nevertheless a 'breakthrough performance'.[144] For this dazzling composite role, Jackson and his team combined Andy Serkis's live on-set acting for 35mm footage, with mo-cap, ADR (automated dia-logue replacement), and animation.[145] The result, as Bob Rehak puts it, is that Gollum 'provides a means of deconstructing our conventional wisdom about performance and authenticity, and hence about the way movies themselves deliver the world to us' – the role is, in other words, revolutionary, going beyond the confines of the films themselves into a new realm of fantasy.[146] It is wholly fitting that it should be Gollum in this role. Gol-lum is beyond Tolkien's control: he is like Shakespeare's Mer-cutio, except that Tolkien suspected that he would play a part in the future of Middle-Earth and so mercifully did not kill him off in *The Hobbit*. Bilbo does not stab him, although he so eas-ily could – he kills Spiders without a second thought and even stones birds, lest we forget – but there's a sense of the world shift-ing with Gollum. Gollum comes to embody the experimental quality of Tolkien's writing, Sam musing whether Gollum would be the hero or the villain in a tale, and then directly asking him that very question – although by then Gollum has disappeared.[147]

A child reading *The Hobbit* (second edition) gathers that there is something afoot, as did Tolkien in writing the character – even if it took him some years to work it out.

Jackson's creative exuberance comprehensively modernizes Ralph Bakshi's rotoscoping, but it also replicates its mixed media (as well as Tolkien's own dazzling syntheses of sources and styles) in what can be seen as a 'chaos of borrowings, translations, substitutions, and simulations'.[148] In fact, Jackson actually out-Tolkiens Tolkien at one point: in the book, Aragorn recites to the Hobbits the story of Lúthien, which he has translated from Elvish (a translation for which there is no original); in the film, however, Jackson has had part of the tale translated 'back' into Elvish – so Aragorn now recites lines that only Frodo (and not the audience) can understand: 'Tinúviel elvanui'.[149] Like Tolkien too, Jackson also included personal cameo roles in the films: for example, he plays one of the Corsairs of Umbar, while artist and art director Alan Lee is one of the Nine Mortal Men in the prologue. More pointedly, one of the Orc masks was specifically designed to look like producer Harvey Weinstein who had caused Jackson so much trouble in getting the movies greenlit; Weinstein's film credit also appeared on a page featuring a troll.[150] Tolkien himself, meanwhile, is echoed in *Rings* by Ian McKellen: he based Gandalf's voice on the author's – a decision that itself alludes to W.H. Auden's comment that it was an 'unforgettable experience' to hear Tolkien recite *Beowulf* in a lecture hall: 'The voice was the voice of Gandalf.'[151]

There are subtleties and inflections in the action of the films too. While the film was marketed as family viewing, it plays with gender relations such as the androgyny of Galadriel, the relationship between Boromir and Aragorn (which has attracted much interest on websites such as DeviantArt), and distorted family dynamics from Bilbo to Denethor.[152] The appearance of Gandalf the White and the uncertainty over his name – 'I was

Gandalf' – is highly effective onscreen as the difference between Gandalf the Grey and Gandalf the White is more evident, a constant reminder that this is an estranged Gandalf, no longer the familiar Gandalf the Grey, now more otherworldly.[153] Gandalf's character arc is to become, in very different ways, a parental figure to Frodo, Aragorn, and Pippin – much as Ian McKellen was, in particular, perhaps, to Elijah Wood.[154] Aragorn's own journey is to find himself, as Mortensen played the role, rising to the status of a leader rather than hiding and operating in disguise – and this too was acknowledged off-screen as he became the leader of the cast during shooting. [155] The most subtle and enduring innovation, however, was, as the plot lacked a singular villain, to make the Ring a central character. In the novel it has a weird sentience, but this becomes more harrowingly palpable in the film – even in scenes where it is not actually visible (thus effectively invisible). It was filmed in different ways, often in extreme close-up, 'filling the entire screen,' said Jackson, 'to give it a kind of presence' – a 'sense that the Ring is alive and can almost be heard breathing!'[156]

For the actors, the three films were shot simultaneously over fifteen months with 350 different sets and a crew of 2,000, often working fifteen-hour days and six-day weeks. Walsh and Boyens had worked on the script daily for over a year, but come filming Jackson was constantly revising and rewriting the script every day, and shooting some fifteen minutes of footage for each page of the script – the usual practice being a minute a page – to capture dozens of variations.[157] His style was spontaneously improvisational, and several of the actors involved have commented on the 'nearly constant revisions' of the script.[158] As Ian McKellen (Gandalf) observed: 'He's really particular, unlike a lot of directors, as to what he wants, and mainly what he wants is a variety of things to choose from … He wants a number of alternatives.'[159] From the masses of footage the films were made in the editing suite. This meant that actors were unclear about how the plot and their own characters might develop; what is more, the shooting schedule meant that actors could perform in scenes from three different films in the same day, or, conversely, some scenes were completed months apart: the exchanges between Frodo (Elijah Wood) and Sam (Sean Astin) on the stairs of Cirith Ungol, for example, were filmed a year apart. This uncertainty over characterization and action is, in fact, a strength of the films: no-one – not the writers, actors, or even the director – knew how the finished films would be plotted, or, with so much CGI painted in later, how they would look. A notable instance of this is the casting of Viggo Mortensen as Aragorn, who was a late addition to the cast after it was decided that Stuart Townsend was not quite right. Mortensen arrived after shooting had already begun, stepping into filming 'almost as unexpectedly', Brian Sibley suggests, 'as his character, the mysterious, unknown Strider, appears in the story'.[160] In other words, it is not only the Hobbits who do not know who Strider is, neither do the actors – or indeed anybody else on the set. Howard Shore, meanwhile, approached the score as an operatic work, inspired in part by Richard Wagner's Ring cycle in his use of dozens of individual refrains or *leitmotifs* that echoed the settings, characters, and action.[161] Again the effect was of disparate individual elements coalescing into symphonic harmony.

Filming was, then, experimental, provisional, contingent – precisely the peculiar qualities that typified Tolkien's composition: a chaos of abandoned creativity was only gradually harnessed into order. As Brian Sibley said of Tolkien's own manner of writing, so with Jackson: there is a sense that what audiences experience is the process of the actors, the director, the whole crew experiencing the story as it happens. The characters discover Middle-Earth in real time and at the very same time as we do, sharing in the blossoming of the narrative, living the film.

• • •

A year before the first of the Jackson *Rings* films was released, eminent American critic and man-of-letters Harold Bloom rather unfortunately opined, 'I suspect that *The Lord of the Rings* is fated to become only an intricate Period Piece'.[162] Within twelve months the first online trailer for *The Fellowship of the Ring* (April 2000) gained a record 1.7 million downloads in twenty-four hours; two years after that *The Return of the King* won eleven Oscars, equalling *Ben-Hur* (1959) and *Titanic* (1997) for the highest number of awards. The success of *The Lord of the Rings*, book and film, went stratospheric. *Empire* magazine reviewed the final film as 'a landmark in cinema history', not only in the CGI, mo-cap, and sheer realized ambition of a serious fantasy epic, but for three films made simultaneously, outside California, and then re-released as extended editions with DVD extras that defined box-sets.[163] Jackson and his team created a worldwide movie phenomenon without relying on A-list celebrities, established New Zealand ('Wellywood') as a world leader in cinema, and, as VHS video began to fade, helped to launch the global DVD market: seeing the movies was not enough – viewers wanted to own them for repeated watching. In the period 1997–2001 the films also generated 3,200 person years' employment in New Zealand and created a whole new tourist industry, prompting Prime Minister Helen Clark to announce that 'The Lord of the Rings has been like one big rolling tourism promotion for New Zealand'.[164] Peter Jackson's primary aim had been to make 'three good movies, as opposed to making three movies that are totally faithful to the books', but 'almost without exception, all those things that are memorable and vivid from reading the books are there in the movies'.[165] His success ensured that cinema would never be the same again.

SIX

Just War

Th'artillery of words.
> Jonathan Swift,
> 'Ode to Dr William Sancroft' (1689)

In 1962, William L. Snyder negotiated with Allen & Unwin for
the rights to film *The Hobbit*, planning to produce an animation;
the agreement was made in April 1963 and Snyder then had
a limited timeframe in which to make a film before the rights
expired in 1966. He engaged his go-to director Gene Deitch,
an Oscar-winning animator (awarded for Best Animated Short
Film, 1961) and a previous director of Terrytoons. Deitch worked
on a script for a year with his friend Bill Bernal, but at the time
neither Dietch, Bernal, nor Snyder realized *The Hobbit*'s connection with *The Lord of the Rings*, which had not yet appeared
in paperback in America and so had only a limited readership.
Despite his assurances to Tolkien to the contrary, Deitch felt
free to change whatever he felt like, including introducing a
fairy-tale princess who marries Bilbo – his not unreasonable

excuse being that Hollywood routinely and liberally rewrote books to be made into movies. But with the popularity of the paperback *The Lord of the Rings* Deitch realized the potential of his developing plot and began to complicate his script to make way for an eventual sequel.[1] He also had an innovative production idea: 'I had proposed an impressive visual effect, combining cel-animated figures over elaborate 3D model backgrounds. I know that Max Fleisher had once tried something like it, but I intended to take the idea to greater heights and atmosphere. I even attached a special name to the technique: "*ImagiMation!*"'[2]

Snyder, however, failed to secure a deal from 20th Century Fox, and Deitch's script was abandoned. Then, with the publication in America of a pirated paperback edition of *The Lord of the Rings* and the sudden explosion of enthusiasm for Middle-Earth, Snyder realized he could retain his now-lucrative property if he could only get a film into a theatre by his two-year deadline of 30 June 1966. He accordingly asked for a one-reel colour movie from Deitch within a month, consisting of just twelve minutes of animation. Deitch based the new version on his full-length screenplay, cutting it to the bone. He worked with cut-outs created by illustrator Adolf Born, while another friend, the American radio broadcaster Herb Lass, read the narration. Having finished the film at breakneck speed, Deitch arrived in Manhattan with the edit and the film was screened in a tiny theatre. With no time for advertising, Deitch stood in the street and charged passersby 10¢ to attend – in fact, he gave these bystanders a 10¢ coin which they simply handed back to him. Snyder and Deitch then gathered a few testimonials from members of the audience to prove that the screening had taken place. The upshot was that Snyder was able to sell back the rights at a substantial profit. The film immediately disappeared, but has since become available online and is worth a dozen minutes of anyone's time . . .[3]

Deitch's version begins in Dale, telling of the Arkenstone and a Dragon named Slag. Only three survive the Dragon's attack – a watchman, General Thorin (or Torin), and Princess Mika; they go to seek help from Gandalf, a wizard living in a ruined tower. The four then visit Bilbo, a Hobbit, whose destiny it is to slay Slag. Reluctantly, and having left Gandalf behind, Bilbo leads them through fantastical expressionist landscapes until they meet the 'groans' (treelike trolls) who roast Bilbo's three companions on a spit until Bilbo's mimickry enrages them and they fight until caught by the dawn sun, whereupon they are turned into dead trees. Bilbo then falls down a crevasse in the mountains and encounters Gollum (pronounced 'gholloume'), who possesses the Ring of Power – which Bilbo instantly finds already on his finger, makes off with, and rejoins his companions. They pass through Mirkwood without incident, arrive at Lonely Mountain [*sic*], and Bilbo goes to the sleeping Dragon Slag and steals the Arkenstone. He then builds a giant crossbow from old mining tools, fixes the Arkenstone as its arrowhead, and shoots Slag dead. Bilbo and Princess Mika duly marry and rule Dale before returning to Hobbiton.

At one level this is a preposterous car-crash of an adaptation that viewers will find at best risible, at worst an unforgiveable affront. It is highly doubtful that Tolkien ever saw it – but surely Peter Jackson or one of his crew knew of it. Jackson's first *Hobbits* film, *An Unexpected Journey*, likewise begins in Dale – unlike the novel – and the Arkenstone is straightaway established as a totemic object. The Ring is emphasized and Deitch's Gollum has clear affinities with the Andy Serkis portrayal. Mirkwood is an LSD-inspired technicolour forest and there is the spurious introduction of a female character and love interest – both innovations of the later Jackson movies. Most strikingly, the four adventurers kill Slag with a contraption made from discarded mine workings in Lonely Mountain, much as Jackson's

Dwarves do in *The Desolation of Smaug* – and although the
Dwarves are ultimately unsuccessful in their attempt to immo-
bilize Smaug in gold, neither episode has any precedent in the
novel. In the space of a twelve-minute animation, then, there
are several key deviations from the plot that Jackson either capitalized or independently chanced upon. It has to be said that
with its idiosyncratic stylings, and despite his outlandish revisions, Gene Deitch's designs would have made a striking movie
if his full-length screenplay had been filmed; it may even have
been a landmark production – if typical of the sixties – had it
appeared in 1967. But the *Hobbit* film rights were bought back
and subsequently formed part of the UA film deal for *The Lord
of the Rings* – it appears that protracted litigation to determine
whether the twelve-minute animation constituted a *de facto* film
was felt to be more expensive than simply regaining and then
re-marketing the rights.

In 1968, BBC radio broadcast *The Hobbit* in eight parts
between 29 September and 17 November, dramatized by
Michael Kilgarriff and produced by John Powell.[4] The production is notable for referring to Middle-Earth (a term that
does not appear in the book), and for a very accurate opening
in which Bilbo and the narrator (the 'Tale Bearer') debate the
initial paragraphs. Then Gan*dalf* appears (strangely accented
thus) and the thirteen Dwarves, led by 'To*reen*' (Elrond also
later describes the kingdom of Gondo*leen*), but, pronunciations
aside, the opening is wonderfully accurate and brisk until the
Dwarves' song, which is, like much of the soundtrack, a study
in cod-mediaeval dissonance – sadly, nearly any contemporary
songwriter could have lifted this to cult status. Thenceforth, the
episodes are increasingly reworked, although the overlapping
dialogue is both dramatic and efficient in communicating much
detail. The Goblins speak in an electronic dialect that would bear
upon the tones of the Witch-King in the 1980 Rankin/Bass film

production, and Gandalf becomes gratuitously invisible under the Misty Mountains. However, Gollum is an impressively affective creature and Bilbo's frank discussion with him about being eaten may have influenced Martin Freeman's hapless Bilbo in *An Unexpected Journey*. The production has inevitably been deemed a 'classic', and it was repeated at the time as part of the BBC's 'Radiovision' scheme – educational film strips that were keyed to radio programmes broadcast during the school day – and rebroadcast in 1991. Whatever its standing, the series impressively demonstrates *The Hobbit*'s ascent to the accepted canon of children's literature and the classroom.

Meanwhile, the film and television rights for *The Hobbit* had become part of the UA deal, and then in 1976 the property of the Saul Zaentz Company; almost immediately, a ninety-minute TV film of *The Hobbit* was in production, made by Rankin/ Bass Animated Entertainment. For *The Hobbit*, Arthur Rankin Jr (designer, co-producer, and co-director) claimed, 'There is no material in this picture that did not come from the original Tolkien book.'[5] Film heavyweights such as John Huston (Gandalf) and Otto Preminger (the Elvenking Thranduil) lent their voices to the film, and the images were in part inspired by Arthur Rackham's illustrations. One innovation of this version was that while Rankin/Bass developed the conceptual art, the production was handed to the Japanese animation house Topcraft, which later morphed into the hugely successful animation studio Ghibli, which for many Western audiences defines Japanese anime film through works such as Hayao Miyazaki's *Nausicaä of the Valley of the Wind* (1984). Like so many adaptations of Tolkien's work, then, studios saw an opportunity to challenge the dominance of mainstream style – in this case Disney animation – with an innovative Pacific Rim fusion. The film is generally faithful to the book, although Bilbo is a willing participant in the Quest of Erebor, Smaug is noticeably corpulent, Bard is promoted to Captain of the Guard, there is a higher body count among Thorin and Company (only seven Dwarves survive), and, surprisingly, there is no Arkenstone. The film did, however, include Tolkien's beloved songs – much music was provided by Glenn Yarbrough, together with Maury Laws, house composer for Rankin/Bass – and the beginning (like Jackson's film) is almost a musical; it also ended in expectation of a sequel based on the Ring. It is a concise adaptation, nevertheless, squarely aimed at children, and did possibly have some influence on Peter Jackson's *Hobbits* in the pre-Smaug scenes of the grandeur of Erebor and the mining and smelting activities within the Lonely Mountain, the emphasis on Bilbo being held by his toes by the huge trolls (which receives only the briefest of mentions in the book), Bilbo's fall into the depths of Goblin Town, and the discovery of the keyhole in the Lonely Mountain.[6] With a budget of $3 million, *The Hobbit* was, according to the *New York Times*, 'the most expensive animated television show in history'; it was first broadcast on 27 November 1977.

Hobbits and *Hobbits*

As with the filming of *The Lord of the Rings*, though, it was to be decades before *The Hobbit* achieved the status of a cinema blockbuster. Peter Jackson's *Rings* was completed twenty-five years after Ralph Bakshi's frustrated attempt, but it was to be a thirty-seven-year wait between Rankin/Bass's TV movie and the three-film epic *Hobbits* (2012–14) – and again it was Peter Jackson who masterminded the adaptation.

With *Rings*, Jackson had achieved the apparently impossible, and with dazzling results – but it had been a gruelling project; *Hobbits*, likewise, was to prove an arduous undertaking. Jackson, now Hollywood royalty but remaining loyal to New Zealand, had followed *Rings* with a powerful remake of the quintessential movie classic *King Kong* (2005), as well as a more modest take on Alice Sebold's novel *The Lovely Bones* (2009), and was also working with Steven Spielberg on *The Adventures of Tintin* (2011). New Line Cinema certainly had plans to make *The Hobbit*, but legal disputes had damaged their relationship with Jackson in the aftermath of *Rings* and they were looking for a new director. By the end of 2007, however, the rift had been repaired and New Line announced that the Oscar-winning Mexican film-maker Guillermo del Toro, best known for the surreal parable *Pan's Labyrinth* (2006), would direct two *Hobbits* films, with Jackson as writer and executive producer. In the event del Toro did not continue with the project due to time delays (although he is credited as a co-writer), Jackson and his team assumed full control, and expanded the series to three films.

The decision to turn a children's book into a 'trilogy' (although again, none of the films are stand-alone productions) was more of a creative decision than simply a way of capitalizing on a lucrative franchise. As Jackson shot the film, he and his co-writers – once more Fran Walsh and playwright Philippa Boyens – simply felt that they could not lose the extra footage. Consequently, the project well underway, Walsh and Boyens had to pitch the proposal to Warner Bros. to move up to three films. For Boyens, it was an opportunity 'to tell part of the story that will never get told if you don't tell it now'.[7] The new three-film version was announced in August 2012 – just four months before the release of the first film – and in June 2013 there were ten weeks of additional shooting in New Zealand to provide further scenes.[8]

This expansion of the plot took different forms. Much of the material was rooted in Tolkien's original book, but developed at far greater length – in part to tie the developing *Hobbits* to *Rings* as closely as possible. Boyens, for example, took the hint that Trolls should not have been marauding in the Trollshaws as an indication that a more pervasive evil power was growing.

Likewise, the wizard Radagast the Brown (briefly mentioned by Gandalf in the book, while speaking to Beorn) is developed from scattered references in *The Lord of the Rings*, and he in turn sees the Mirkwood Spiders as evidence that the forest is being poisoned. The writers immersed themselves in the books for insight: as Boyens suggested,

> If you read *The Hobbit*, the arrival of the orcs at Erebor [*the event that kickstarts the Battle of the Five Armies*] is very random. But if you go deeper into the canon of Professor Tolkien, you realise they didn't appear out of nowhere. It's quite a specific, visually exciting way that they manage to take the mountain by surprise. Erebor holds this incredibly strong strategic position – if someone else was to take it, it would leave everything open to attack . . . [9]

Even Radagast's rabbits of Rhosgobel have a source in Tolkien: there are sixteen references to rabbits in the book (and one mention of a 'bunny') – so this too is an artful nod towards the text, if exuberantly absurd. [10]

There was, then, no reason not to include additional material from *The Lord of the Rings* in fleshing out characters and plot: details were taken from 'Durin's Folk' (Appendix A) and the chronology 'The Tale of Years' (Appendix B), allowing three linked subplots to be developed: the rise of Sauron as the Necromancer; the blood-feud between the Dwarves and the Orcs of Moria, led by Azog (the Defiler, the 'Pale Orc'); and the intervention of Gandalf in Thorin's quest to reclaim Erebor, which began when they met at The Prancing Pony in Bree. These three subplots also cover the plight of the Dwarves Thrór and Thráin (grandfather and father of Thorin Oakenshield, respectively), while richly enhancing the plot focusing on the Dragon Smaug. Indeed, Tolkien himself recognized these connections and tried to develop them himself – but never entirely satisfactorily. The most marked elaboration of Jackson, Walsh, and Boyens, though, is the gigantic expansion of the handful of fleeting references to the Necromancer in the films. These were written up as a major storyline to corroborate that the Necromancer is Sauron resuming power, chronicling his mounting strength, binding him to the Orcs of Moria as well as to the ever-present and explosive threat of Smaug. Gandalf's barely explained absences in the book of *The Hobbit* thus provided opportunities to advance this subplot, just as a passing comment made at the Council of Elrond in the text of *The Lord of the Rings* – that the White Council had driven the Necromancer from Dol Guldur – could be literalized as a battle between wizards and wraiths in the ruined fortress. Moreover, the Necromancer's later actions in declaring himself as Sauron, rebuilding his strength in Mordor, and launching the War of the Ring could be grounded by adding details such as the raising of the Ringwraiths in a plausible (and chillingly filmed) sequence that explains where they have been for centuries, revealing Sauron's growing power in being able to release them to serve him again.

Jackson confirmed this approach: 'We're not just adapting *The Hobbit*; we're adapting a lot of the additional material that Tolkien added to the appendices of *The Lord of the Rings*. So we're able to get a lot more into what was going on in the world outside of Bilbo and the dwarves – which is really why it's ended up being two movies.'[11] In fact, although critics were quick to point out that the films only had a 300-page children's book of material, there are fifteen concisely written pages of 'Durin's Folk', many succinct entries in 'The Tale of Years', and references throughout *The Lord of the Rings* itself (mainly occurring in the first volume), and although the film-makers were not permitted to use Tolkien's own twenty-page attempt to unite his two novels, 'The Quest of Erebor' (originally destined to be another appendix but not published until it was included in *Unfinished Tales* in 1980), this connecting text nevertheless further influenced the shape of the films. Jackson really felt that the movies could illuminate Middle-Earth: 'You read the books, the Appendices, the letters and the interviews that Tolkien gave ... and you realise you are dramatising some of the things he was hinting at.'[12] This, then, justifies the inclusion of the Elf Legolas, whose background as the son of Thranduil, the Elvenking of Mirkwood, is given at the Council of Elrond. The Dwarves' journey in barrels out of Mirkwood and down the Forest River, meanwhile, is an uneventful page-long transit in the book; in *The Desolation of Smaug*, however, it becomes an epic action scene – a spinning maelstrom of flight and pursuit, of breakneck skirmishing and impossible acrobatics, of drenched Dwarves tumbling through precipitous rapids. As Boyens commented on the film, 'the story grows in the telling'; she was perhaps unconsciously echoing Tolkien himself, who begins the Foreword to *The Lord of the Rings*, 'This tale grew in the telling ...'[13]

Alongside this fascination with joining the two grand narratives, however, was the need to make the film appealing to a twenty-first-century cinema audience. First, by having stronger female characters; secondly, by adding a typical Hollywood subplot of thwarted love; and thirdly – more subtly – by imparting a sense of impending doom. Galadriel was the obvious choice for a powerful female figure – her brief but memorable appearance in *Rings* presented her as an awe-inspiring presence, astutely perceptive and keen-witted. In *Hobbits*, she would become a warrior again – as she had been in her youth – to battle the forces of darkness. But one strong female was not enough: the writers needed an Éowyn figure too. Enter Tauriel. Galadriel has astonishing depths, but in *Rings* she veils these beneath a divine tranquillity; Tauriel, however, is no passive Elf maiden. She is essentially Éowyn: the next generation. Evangeline Lilly, the actor who played her with such zeal, saw her as psycho-pathic: 'She has no problem killing; that is what she does. She is a killing machine.'[14] In fact, the Elves of *Hobbits* are much darker – more like the honour/shame rebels of 'The Silmarillion' tales. Lee Pace accordingly plays Thranduil as a sadist, basing him on Shakespeare's Oberon (*A Midsummer Night's Dream*) and The Fisher King.[15] 'There is something sadistic about the Elf people that I have always enjoyed,' he remarked during filming, adding that Thranduil 'doesn't just want to kill the Orcs, he wants to cut them, slice them, torture them'.[16] Of these reinvented Elves, Fran Walsh commented, 'Tolkien had a wonderful phrase for it . . . Less wise . . . More dangerous.'[17]

Tauriel then created the opportunity for another subplot: the love triangle between her, Legolas, and, perhaps improbably, the Dwarf Kili – inter-species affairs in Tolkien's Middle-Earth being confined to Elf–Human (although Orcish cross-breeding is also hinted at). This opened up a whole new world, a new Middle-Earth. Jackson's reasons? Describing *The Desolation of Smaug*, in which Tauriel makes her first appearance, he remarked, 'I am enjoying deviating from the book . . . We introduce a lot of Appendices material, more than in the first film. We intro-duce Legolas and Tauriel, who are not characters from the book. In fact, Tauriel is not even a character from Tolkien. But as a filmmaker that is a refreshing thing.'[18] The extra *Hobbits* mater-ial was, with ironic understatement, a way of 'Opening up the mythology'.[19]

So at the same time as the writers were dissecting *The Hobbit* for as much information as they could find and mining *The Lord of the Rings* for any supporting details, they were also unafraid to invent. In addition, when it came to filming – and as with scripting and directing *Rings* – Jackson had an almost wilful yet Tolkienesque instinct to explore, experiment, and extemporize the story as it was being told: 'Some of the stuff you've seen today', he told a reporter, 'we're literally making it up as we go along.'[20] He let his imagination run riot in *Hobbits*, often to great success. The deep level of detail, the introduction of disparate elements of *The Lord of the Rings*, the amplification and exaggeration of events, the effervescent inventiveness and bristling vivacity – this is invigorating stuff. It is *The Hobbit*, but not as we know it; it is a *Hobbit* for the twenty-first century: bold, cheeky, and playful – a spirited retelling.

At least it is until we come to *The Battle of the Five Armies*. Andy Serkis, who on *Hobbits* acted as director on the 'second unit' (leading an auxiliary crew delegated to film separate footage to Jackson's work with the primary film crew), noticed how the plots and characterizations increasingly drew on the seriousness of *Rings*: 'It starts off light, but gets darker' – rather like C.S. Lewis's observation that *The Hobbit* begins like a tale for children but ends like a Norse saga.[21] Jackson tried to give each film a different atmosphere: the first is a road movie, the second delves into the politics of Laketown and the confrontation with Smaug, the third analyzes war, from negotiation into conflict. Jackson thought of the third movie as a 'psychological thriller with action scenes interspersed in the middle of it. It has got a very tight narrative structure.'[22] Killing Smaug creates a power vacuum, a refugee crisis, and leads to a war – problems that Jackson was fascinated to unravel. He was also keen to have the various themes of the enmity between Elves and Dwarves, the fragility of political alliances, Thorin's madness, Thranduil's isolationism, and the various family relationships and conflicts (centred around fathers such as Thranduil and Azog) continue and be reflected throughout the battle.[23] And the battle scenes themselves were shot to be grimly real. The vast, set-piece confrontation gave a chance to move on from the balletic swooping camera dives of the Battle of the Pelennor Fields in *Rings* and try to recreate the chaotic reality of a combat cameraman

(COMCAM) in the midst of the action – to 'get down and dirty'.[24] For Martin Freeman, it is the film in which 'Bilbo truly sees the horror of the war'.[25] Perhaps unsurprisingly, the on-set conversations during filming referenced Hitler, George W. Bush, Kofi Annan, Colonel Kurtz, Saddam Hussein, and the United Nations, and Cate Blanchett recalled Boyens describing part of the story in a way that 'I felt she had just watched Al Jazeera'.[26] This is the sense of doom that hangs over *The Battle of the Five Armies*: the knowledge that, despite intermittent victories, the world is entering a long decline; what comes afterwards is *The Lord of the Rings* and an end to enchantment.

Tolkien had tried to rewrite *The Hobbit*, repositioning it as a prequel to *The Lord of the Rings*; he was not able to do so – but Jackson accomplished this with apparent ease. However, Tolkien had written *The Hobbit* without thinking of a sequel, oblivious that *The Lord of the Rings* would be published nearly twenty years later and would require two revisions to *The Hobbit* – which remained an undeveloped and somewhat untidy intro-duction to Middle-Earth. Peter Jackson, on the other hand, had already filmed *Rings* a decade earlier and so his *Hobbits* could fundamentally and legitimately be a prequel – that was his start-ing point. And that allowed so many nuances to be included: from the split identity of Gollum and Sméagol to the power of the as-yet uncorrupted White Council to be fully exploited as the allied opposition against the lone enemy Sauron. For any or all the faults of *Hobbits*, Peter Jackson did make it a part of the narrative arc of *The Lord of the Rings* in a way that Tolkien himself never quite managed.

Casting the film also enabled Jackson to extend the *Rings* franchise by having several actors reprise their roles, which was slickly accomplished despite the passing of a decade. Most notable of these is Andy Serkis, who brought his fully realized Sméagol/Gollum character to the first *Hobbits* film, making the riddle-game even more subtle and sinister than it was in the revised book: Sméagol wants to play, but is in conflict with Gollum, evoking his erratic and pitiable relationships with Frodo and Sam in *Rings*. Remarkably, this was also the first scene to be shot – on account of it requiring only two actors.[27] There were also many new actors. The alliance between Smaug and the Necromancer is implicitly underlined by having Benedict Cumberbatch voice the former and appear as the latter in mocap, CGI, and ADR.

When it came to the technical aspects of filming and editing, Jackson massively increased his use of CGI. *Rings* had inspired James Cameron to make *Avatar* (2009). Cameron had had a script for the film since 1994 but did not think that the technology yet existed to make it – that was until he saw Jackson's *The Two Towers* and began working with Wētā.[28] In turn, *Hobbits* benefited from the post-*Avatar* development of digital landscapes, cityscapes, and scenery, and so did not need the 'bigiatures' – the detailed large-scale models of *Rings*; in the event, the higher frame rate used in filming meant that the models were not in any case detailed enough for scenes.[29] But New Zealand remained the setting for location shooting to anchor the scenes in a physical reality (and, less edifyingly, because of legislation passed during filming to remove union rights for New Zealand workers in the film industry).[30] Once again, there was a multi-media blending: super-seamless and hyper-sophisticated compared with Ralph Bakshi, but essentially on the same spectrum of mashing up the real with the unreal.

The *Hobbits* movies subsequently make prominent use of the 'digital creature' (Gollum, Azog) and of the 'digital multitude' (armies), not to mention the 'digital world'.[31] The increasing use of green screen (actors performing against a green background to allow digital details and even figures to be added later) meant that actors were acting effectively in a void with no personal

onscreen interaction. The confrontation between Thranduil and
Thorin in the Halls of the Elvenking, for example, was filmed as
two separate confrontations in which each actor had to perform
staring at a green 'tennis ball' – this allowed them to maintain
eye contact despite the difference in height between an Elf (6'
2") and a Dwarf (4' 6").[32] But even seasoned players found this
trying. Ian McKellen openly admitted his difficulties. Early in
the shoot, in order to create the scene of Gandalf (5' 9") with the
thirteen Dwarves, two different sets were needed:

> they were all in one and I was alone in a different, green-
> screen one. All I had for company were 13 photographs of
> the Dwarves ... Pretending you're with 13 other people
> when you're on your own, it stretches your technical ability
> to the absolute limits. And I cried. I cried. Then I said out
> loud, 'This is not why I became an actor.' Unfortunately
> the microphone was on and the whole studio heard.[33]

While this process may undoubtedly add to the mood of
uncertainty, like all special effects it may come at the expense of
characterization. There was already an element of this in Ralph
Bakshi's film, putting spectacle before character, and the Jackson
Rings and especially *Hobbits* have a tendency to dazzle the audience with visual spectacle while the characters risk becoming
incidental and superficial. But as Professor of Film and Media
Kristen Whissel argues, while CGI effects may disrupt the
narrative of a film by drawing attention to their technological
brilliance, it is nevertheless possible to examine 'their narrative
function, their relationship to the development of character
and story, their peculiar mode of signification, and the kinds of
spectatorship they make possible or even demand'.[34] In other
words, CGI is, at heart, just another, albeit powerful, tool for
the film-maker, and has become as familiar and ubiquitous as

make-up and costumes. In any case, film critic Ian Nathan, who interviewed Jackson on set, saw that for all the CGI special effects that will be 'brought to bear on The Hobbit trilogy, Jackson is still dangling actors on piano wires and constructing sets enshrouded in their own wintry weather patterns'.[35]

The same attention to physical detail seen in *Rings* is also evident in *Hobbits*. Smaug was originally a winged Dragon with four legs, but was remodelled as a wyvern (with two legs and two wings) to make his movements more articulate, his wings becoming as expressive as hands.[36] The biggest problem was having thirteen Dwarves. This does not really matter in the book – they move as a unit, several are barely described, and Bilbo remains peripheral to their group. Onscreen, however, they each needed a clear identity and a degree of the audience's sympathies. 'I imagined 13 guys with long hair and beards,' remembered Jackson, 'and I thought, "How are we ever going to know which dwarf is which?"'[37] Hence the writers and Wētā created 'iconic silhouettes' for each one – different styles, costumes, gear, and beards – which even went down to the level of uniquely distinctive underwear. With the visual impact of the Dwarves in mind, Richard Armitage (Thorin Oakenshield) stood at 6' 2", but as Graham McTavish (Dwalin) was even taller, Armitage was provided with lifts in his shoes 'because they wanted me to be bigger than him!'[38] As with *Rings*, many character inflections were developed on the spot. Luke Evans, who played Bard, had a noticeable Welsh accent, which became a linguistic signature of Dale society – effectively a Welsh diaspora – and the Dale people who have settled in Laketown accordingly speak with a Welsh lilt.[39]

Jackson's reworking of *The Hobbit* amounts, then, not simply to making it visually consistent with *Rings*, but, most obviously in special effects, to magnifying them through CGI far beyond the visual spectacle of the earlier three films. These are movies that luxuriate in preposterously excessive spectacle – despite the book itself being far more modest and domestic than the self-consciously epic *Lord of the Rings*. Yes, there is a Dragon, some large Spiders (though nothing like Shelob), Goblins, and three foolish Trolls, but Smaug's chilling assault on Laketown is a deliberate anticlimax in the book, and even the Battle of the Five Armies is not presented as a dazzling climax as Bilbo is merely a bystander who is knocked unconscious before it is decided. Tolkien is not valorizing brute heroism, but the subtleties of survival. Yet for Jackson, the battle, from the loosing of the first salvo of arrows to the final rout of the Orcs, dominates the eponymous final film – and actually begins with a ferocious clash between the Elves of Mirkwood and the Dwarves of the Iron Hills before Azog arrives with his forces. Viggo Mortensen (Aragorn) commented in 2014 (before the release of the final *Hobbits* film) that while *The Fellowship of the Ring* film has an 'organic' quality making it 'grittier', the special effects snow-balled in *Two Towers* and *The Return of the King* films, and so 'with *The Hobbit*, one and two, it's like that to the power of 10'.[40] The ironically titled *Desolation of Smaug* depicts a vast Dwarven kingdom inside the Lonely Mountain that literally dwarfs the Moria of *Rings* depicted a dozen years earlier – but then Moria had already been overtaken as a subterranean kingdom in *An Unexpected Journey* (2012), when Thorin and Company find themselves in the caves of the Great Goblin beneath the Misty Mountains. Above and below ground in *Hobbits* there are immense vistas – spatial dimensions are vertiginously extended and exaggerated, almost to non-Euclidean levels. Armies consist of vast numbers and, most overwhelmingly, Smaug's hoard is of such fabulous wealth that it is effectively infinite: the gold is so profuse that it overwhelms every other manufactured material on the screen – stonework, iron, and timber. Tolkien's own illustration of Smaug's stolen wealth was a not inconsiderable heap, but no bigger than the mound of a small motte-and-bailey castle; in *Hobbits*, however, Smaug – the size of an airliner – is smothered in gold, literally lives in gold: the scale is oceanic.

The dominant use of CGI in *Hobbits* was also part of a wider strategy. Jackson wanted to try something different from the material authenticity of *Rings* and so made the daring decision to film in 3D and in 48fps (frames per second) – twice the industry standard frame rate. He was again pushing the boundaries of cinema convention in a Middle-Earth production. The aim was to make the experience more real – to dissolve the distinction between cinema and actuality by shifting from 2D moving images on a flat screen to a super-crisp 3D experience that appears to be happening in the space between the viewer and the screen. As Jackson himself described it,

> shooting at 48 fps gives you much more of an illusion of real life. The reduced motion blur on each frame increases sharpness and gives the movie the look of having been shot in 65mm or IMAX. One of the biggest advantages is the fact that your eye is seeing twice the number of images each second, giving the movie a wonderful immersive quality. It makes the 3D experience much more gentle and hugely reduces eyestrain. Much of what makes 3D viewing uncomfortable for some people is the fact that each eye is processing a lot of strobing, blur and flicker. This all but disappears in HFR [high frame rate] 3D.[41]

Many reviewers, however, were not convinced. *LA Times* film critic Kenneth Turan complained that, 'Though Jackson and other zealots for high frame rate would have you believe that the new system is more immersive, the truth is just the opposite.' For him, 'audiences looking for a rich, textured, cinematic experience will be put off and disconcerted by an image that looks more like an advanced version of high definition television than a traditional movie'.[42] Other critics compared the look of films to reality TV shows, high-definition footage of sports matches, and video games. Jackson was uncowed: 'HFR 3D is "different" – it won't feel like the movies you're used to seeing, in much the same way as the first CDs didn't sound like vinyl records … I think it's critical that filmmakers employ current technology to increase the immersive, spectacular experience that cinema should provide. It's an exciting time to be going to the movies.'[43]

The hyper-realist photographic stock of *Hobbits* presents everything in total clarity, a seamless *mise-en-scène*, meaning that the films do lack the dreamlike fluidity and slipperiness of traditional cinema. It can indeed be immersive, disorientating, and strange, and the cinema experience of *Hobbits* was itself an unexpected journey: the films do possess an unnerving reality. Jackson had stopped using 'swoopy' camera pans such as plummeting from the summit of Isengard to the ground, in part because it had become too popular in films such as the *Harry Potter* series (2001–11).[44] Instead, he began to add post-production scenes by himself using a handheld camera on a mo-cap stage and feeding his movements into the digital Wētā environments: 'Rather than any kind of filmmakery style, it's going to feel like you are a CNN cameraman in the middle of *The Battle of the Five Armies*.'[45] Jackson was the ultra-auteur, the camera his only actor.

From these hours and hours of footage, the films were again created in the editing suite. The number of takes was phenomenal: Jackson shot eight or nine takes for every scene, but second-unit director Andy Serkis provided thirty or forty.[46] In particular, Serkis recalled that Bilbo and the Dwarves running to escape the Wargs was 'the Helm's Deep of *The Hobbit*', with hundreds of shots from every angle.[47] There was also subsequent postpartum pick-up filming for fine tuning, extra shots, bridge scenes, and even whole new sequences – much as Tolkien drafted and redrafted his own characters, episodes, and plots. Perhaps unsurprisingly, the first film was allegedly finished only eight days before it was premièred.

But the première was, in effect, only the end of the beginning of *Hobbits*. Ian Nathan stated in *Empire* magazine that with *Hobbits*, Jackson was actively editing with expanded box-set DVD editions in mind, 'deliberately leaving things out of the theatrical cuts that people don't need to worry about for that particular film, and yet knowing they will see the light in his more elaborate, detailed versions – the ones fans take as canon' – such as Girion (from whom Bard is descended) failing to kill Smaug with black arrows, or Thranduil's desire for white gems inspiring the animosity of the Dwarves.[48] In addition, both *Rings* and *Hobbits* have contributed to video gaming in content, development, and marketing. As suggested, inconsequential remarks in Tolkien's text of *The Hobbit* were, in the hands of Jackson, Walsh, and Boyens, developed into epic sequences in the films – an example being Tolkien's single, undeveloped reference to were-worms in the book in a passing comment made by Bilbo. In *The Battle of the Five Armies*, these creatures are spectacularly harnessed by the Orcish armies and herald their onslaught by erupting from the ground, propelling the Elves and Dwarves into a hurried pact against them. But they also play a part in the spin-off video games *The Hobbit* (2003) and (as 'Were-Wyrms') in *The Desolation of Mordor* (2018).

Gaming and merchandizing in general have grown into a vast and lucrative empire, covering thousands of products. At one end of this spectrum, cultural critic Brian Rosebury has described playing cards branded to the films, such as *Top Trumps: The Lord of the Rings*, and a 2002 *Lord of the Rings* Christmas advent calendar: this is simple 'relabelling' – taking pre-existing cultural products and associating them with the films through, for example, artwork. Such relabelling is nothing new: Laurence Sterne's quirky eighteenth-century novel *Tristram Shandy* (1759–67) inspired a craze of cash-in merchandise, from ladies' fans to soup. More sophisticated relabelling includes a special edition of the board game Trivial Pursuit based on *Rings*; marketed in 2004 it includes over 2,400 questions – 600 of which are on two interactive DVDs and feature the voice of Andy Serkis as Gollum.

The deeper impact of Middle-Earth on the gaming world can be seen in the inaugural fantasy RPG (role-playing game) *Dungeons & Dragons* (*D&D*; 1974, 1977), which typifies the cross-media Tolkienian phenomenon of drawing on literature, film, art, music, and other games, and which has peaked with online video games.[49] *D&D* also created a market for 25mm lead figures of heroes and monsters, exemplified by the meticulously crafted Ral Partha models of the 1970s, which in turn created the opportunity to wage large-scale pitched battles governed by the first *Lord of the Rings* rulebook, *Middle Earth War Games Rules*, published by SELWG in 1976.[50] Lead figures of the Company of the Ring (plus Gollum) were also directly modelled on the characters in Bakshi's film. Early table-top games include the bestselling Middle-Earth board games of *The War of the Ring*, *Gondor: The Siege of Minas Tirith*, and *Sauron* (being the War of the Last Alliance) produced by SPI (Simulations Publications, Inc.) in 1977. Traditional table-top war games and RPGs have also been branded under licence from New Line Cinema, such as Games Workshop's *Middle-earth™: Battle Strategy Game* that has nearly a dozen expansion packs, including *Scouring of the Shire™*, accompanied by their own beautifully designed figurines based on the characters in Jackson's films.[51]

Early video games include *The Hobbit* (1982) for BBC Micro, Commodore, and ZX Spectrum (the game included a copy of the book) and the Parker Brothers' *The Lord of the Rings: Journey to Rivendell* for the Atari 2600 console (intended for 1983, but not released).[52] *The Hobbit* video game was followed by disappointing attempts to gamify *The Lord of the Rings* as *Lord of the Rings: Game On* (1984) and *Shadows of Mordor* (1987) which were constrained by limitations in graphics and vocabulary, although *The Hobbit* was popular at the time. In contrast, far more sophisticated items are the much more recent Playstation 2 games – Vivendi's *The Fellowship of the Ring* (2002) and Electronic Arts' (EA) *The Two Towers* (also 2002) – which, despite being standard adventure video games, are visualized as versions of *Rings*. Moreover, in the case of *The Two Towers*, EA acquired the gaming rights from New Line and so were able to incorporate Peter Jackson's actual footage, props, CGI, and even the actors themselves into the games. In doing so, they revolutionized the adaptation of films into games – and also of games into films: sequences in *Hobbits* such as the White Council clashing with the Ringwraiths in Dol Guldur show how symbiotic the two media have become.[53] Meanwhile, the Saul Zaentz Company (doing business as Tolkien Enterprises), in conjunction with New Line Cinema, licensed EA to produce the strategy game *Battle for Middle-Earth* in 2004 (*Battle for Middle-Earth II* followed in 2006). Other licensed video games include the *Lord of the Rings Online* (*LOTRO*) MMO (massive multiplayer online game) developed by Turbine, Inc. (2007) and *Lego: The Lord of the Rings* released by Warner Bros. Interactive Entertainment (WBIE) (2013).[54] The commercialization of these gaming franchises has been unashamedly transparent: as Barry Atkins points out, the games' 'fidelity to Jackson's vision (and not Tolkien's) is contractually policed, as the initial screens of any of the video games make clear through their copyright notices that mark out the limits of ownership for EA when compared to that of New Line Cinema'.[55] Clearly, then, for these games it is Peter Jackson's movies that are the defining experience to be replayed, and not Tolkien's original book: they are a chance for players to triumph as film stars through a series of choreographed moves in Jackson's moving-image Middle-Earth, rather than immerse and lose and simply imagine themselves in Tolkien's text.

By 2005 there was a flood of merchandise being produced under licence from Middle-earth Enterprises (which had changed its name from Tolkien Enterprises in 2010), and the company now turned its attention to licensing merchandise based on the books. The thirty-three current licensees run from Ashland Fly – which makes fishing flies and notes that Déagol found the ring while fishing (but not that he was almost immediately strangled by Sméagol) – to Middle-Earth bottled water (from New Zealand), to the Orcrist guitar overdrive effects pedal, to bespoke wooden Hobbit holes.[56] There has also been a steady stream of souvenirs from authentic Wētā Workshop swords and cloaks to commemorative Bank of New Zealand coins, as well as T-shirts and hoodies, crockery and glassware, and a goblet modelled on Frodo's head. The One Ring, meanwhile, can be purchased on eBay for as little as £1.27.

◆ ◆ ◆

Critics have objected to Jackson's adaptations because his focus on 'battles, spectacle, and his own interpolated material, is at the expense of the core matters of characterization and theme and their careful construction through the tone, language, and pacing of bridging scenes'.[57] He was, however, faced with an impossible adaptation: cinema was never going to replicate a three-volume novel, so Jackson transposed Middle-Earth, recreating it; that may have created a 'manifestly different interpretation', but this was not only recognizably Middle-Earth, it was already directly familiar to readers (although they may not have realized it) through earlier retellings, and has since become just as familiar to those who have never opened the books.[58] With *Rings*, then,

Jackson established an innovative fantasy-film genre cinematic template distinct from Tolkien's literary text, but, I suggest, *Rings* had the comparable quality that Jackson was living in the story and discovering it as he made the films.[59] *Hobbits* had to conform to this template – and it did: the box-office success of *Hobbits* was on an equal footing with that of *Rings* – that alone is a compelling enough argument to have a three-film version. And the overall statistics for Peter Jackson's six Middle-Earth films speak for themselves: '706 days of principal photography, over 50,000 VFX [visual effects] shots, 18 Oscars and $5.8 billion in global box office'.[60] Middle-Earth has become the fourth largest entertainment franchise worldwide.[61]

Jackson may be thrilled to see his influence in films such as *Kingdom of Heaven* (2005), *Narnia* (2005, 2008, 2010), and especially in the swooping shots of *Harry Potter*, and while it is certain HBO's *Game of Thrones* (2011–19) would have been 'unthinkable without Jackson's trailblazing world-building and proof of concept that fantasy adaptations could transcend the D&D audience', his influence is far more profound.[62] Already in 2004 critic Courtney Booker was arguing that since the 1960s the mediaeval period in the popular imagination had been deeply coloured by Tolkien's Middle-Earth and its reworkings; after *Rings*, however, it will be Jacksonesque.[63] As literary critic Marek Oziewicz points out, Jackson's films now overshadow the books 'whether or not one is familiar with the novel', and will 'inevitably overshadow one's past and future encounters with the literary texts'.[64] It is certain that no future film of *The Hobbit* or *The Lord of the Rings* will escape the influence of *Rings* and *Hobbits*, and it is difficult to imagine any writing on Tolkien or Middle-Earth also being untouched – if only by deliberately refusing to acknowledge them. We therefore await the Amazon Prime Video series *The Rings of Power* with great interest...[65]

The Art of War

Is there too much fighting and warfare in the films of *Rings* and *Hobbits*? The movie battle scenes have been compared with computer games, having no compunction about mass killing – rather, they turn slaughter into a joke as Legolas and Gimli keep a lighthearted score of their kills. The films certainly draw out the prevalence of warfare in the books: *The Lord of the Rings* is a novel about a war, so frontline action is inevitable as well as the management of supplies, troop movements, and borders, and the defence of strategic positions, such as Faramir's hopeless attempt to retake Osgiliath; there is also much about the 'home front' in depicting the roles and responsibilities of non-combatants during wartime. All three services (land, sea, air) are deployed in the War of the Ring, and there are even subtle differences of equipment and tactics – the Orcs, for example, use longer arrows than the Elves, while Saruman's Orcs are identified by unusual battle-gear and the unfamiliar insignia of the white hand; Tolkien pays close attention to emblems, crests, and heraldry – as does Jackson.[66] The armies of Mordor have few Horsemen but a variety of weapons of mass destruction, including Trolls and the *mûmakil* (grown to disproportionate size in *Rings*), and so rely on a strategy of force of numbers rather than the outflanking manoeuvres and surprise tactics that characterize the allies of the west, which was also often the case in the Second World War itself; it also appears that all of the swords in Tolkien's Middle-Earth appear to be one-handed, but the Elves at the Battle of the Last Alliance in *Rings* and at the Battle of the Five Armies in *Hobbits* brandish two-handed swords – Wētā Workshop drawing on the whole panoply of different blades and fighting styles for visual effect. The terms of engagement, meanwhile, although appearing to abide by the principles of 'just war', are in fact often in contravention of these justifications for military action, creating unsettling ambiguity. Excessive force is common; war crimes are committed.[67]

What constitutes a 'just war'? It is an ancient concept and emerges from shared cultural assumptions about the ethics of warfare. St Thomas Aquinas, writing in the thirteenth century, outlined the justifications for war in his work *Summa Theologica* (1265–73), offering defensible moral conditions for going to war: just war (*justum bellum*), the justice of war (*jus ad bellum*), just conduct (*jus in bello*), and subsequent accountability (*jus post bellum*) – principles to be taken in conjunction.[68] Arguably the most defensible is having just cause in self-defence or responding to unprovoked aggression: hence in 1939 Britain declared war on Nazi Germany in response to the invasion of Poland, believing that after years of German expansion and rearmament it was now threatened by invasion. In this case, war could also be seen as the last resort, as Prime Minister Neville Chamberlain had already attempted appeasement with the Munich Treaty of 1938. War was declared by a proper authority (the accountable national government) with the intention of assisting an ally (rather than simply being in the national interest to seize territory), and with reasonable chances of success – although arguably Britain's resistance to the Axis powers did not have favourable prospects, and certainly Germany did not think Britain would resist. Finally, there were identifiable goals, proportional to the means – liberating subjugated countries and peoples, and, in Europe, overcoming the tyranny of Fascism and Nazism. In the course of the war, other issues had to be decided, such as identifying legitimate targets, and defining what actually constituted proportionate force; the legality of assassination, exceptional rendition, and torture; establishing how prisoners-of-war were to be treated and the responsibilities of the victors over the defeated; and the role of civilians – what (if any) discrimination would be made to prevent civilian casualties?

To defeat Germany (and in response to the London Blitz), civilian cities were in fact bombed – notably Dresden in 1945;

to defeat Japan, two atomic bombs were dropped. This was 'total war', as Prime Minister Winston Churchill declared to the House of Commons in August 1940: 'The whole of the warring nations are engaged, not only soldiers, but the entire population, men, women and children. The fronts are everywhere.'[69] In contrast to the strong calls for the appeasement of Nazi Germany in 1938 and 1939 (reflected, perhaps, in *The Lord of the Rings* in the chapter 'The Council of Elrond'), there was horror when the Nazi concentration camps were revealed, and in retrospect total war appeared justified. Meanwhile, the Nuremberg Trials following the hostilities convicted Nazi war criminals, ten of whom were hanged, while another committed suicide shortly before execution; many others were subsequently tried and hanged, including the public execution of female SS guards of the Stutthof concentration camp in Poland, and the summary shooting of Mussolini, his partner, and entourage – after which the bodies were publicly abused and mutilated.

Tolkien's experience of the First and Second World Wars has since led the leading critic Tom Shippey to develop his thinking and argue that Tolkien, with C.S. Lewis, George Orwell, William Golding, and Kurt Vonnegut, can be considered a group of 'traumatized authors': authors who have first-hand experience of some of the most horrific excesses of the twentieth century. He argues that *The Lord of the Rings*, Lewis's *That Hideous Strength* (1945), Orwell's *Animal Farm* (1945) and *Nineteen Eighty-Four* (1949), Golding's *Lord of the Flies* (1954), and T.H. White's *The Once and Future King* (1958) are 'all books insistently marked by war'.[70] Although there seems to be little evidence elsewhere that Tolkien was traumatized by his experiences, Shippey's point does draw the insistent theme of war in *The Lord of the Rings* into sharp relief.[71] From his schooldays to the first publication of *The Fellowship of the Ring*, Tolkien lived through two world wars, the rise of Fascism, Nazism, and Stalinism, and, in Shippey's words, 'the routine bombardment of civilian populations, the use of famine as a political measure, the revival of judicial torture, the "liquidation" of whole classes of political opponents, extermination camps, deliberate genocide and the continuing development of "weapons of mass destruction" from chlorine gas to the hydrogen bomb.'[72] One could add to this the industrialization of war and killing, and the obsession with mass surveillance and internal security. Traditional literary responses were simply inadequate in responding to this new world; the only way of addressing this horror was, Shippey argues, obliquely, which is why 'The dominant literary mode of the twentieth century has been the fantastic'.[73] Fantasy writing also offers potential consolation, and Thomas W. Smith has suggested that fantasy writers 'as different as Tolkien, Ursula LeGuin, William Golding, George Orwell, Aldous Huxley, J.K. Rowling, C.S. Lewis, Kurt Vonnegut, or Philip Pullman understand their work as a kind of recovery from disillusionment and disenchantment'.[74]

But rather than classify Tolkien as a 'traumatized author' or some sort of Romantic Modernist, we should let the books and the films address these points. Who declares the War of the Ring? Middle-Earth slides into open conflict after years of aggression from Mordor, and certainly Gondor and Rohan are justified in defending their lands and peoples. Is open war the last resort? There are attempts by Saruman to approach Sauron, but this results in his corruption and betrayal of the White Council. Does the war against Sauron have a reasonable chance of success? No, and the Battle of the Black Gate is a completely lost cause: as Gandalf concedes, 'We must walk open-eyed into [Sauron's] trap'.[75] There is a clearly identifiable goal – to annihilate Sauron – effectively accomplished by assassination (destroying the One Ring). This reveals, as I have already suggested, that waging the war is a sideshow – which seriously questions its proportionality. Sauron is, however, a legitimate target, and following the war prisoners are generally set free.

Also to be taken into account is the extreme aggression of Sauron and Saruman. Rohan villages are sacked by Isengard Orcs, Théoden's horror – 'they are burning as they come, rick, cot, and tree' – being reminiscent of Cardinal Mercier, Primate of Belgium, who in 1920 had condemned the German war crimes at Louvain, denouncing their 'burning of our towns . . . and massacre of civilians'.[76] Helm's Deep likewise is attacked when it is full of civilians (a questionable decision by Théoden to shelter them there), the city of Minas Tirith is besieged and the heads of Gondorian soldiers are catapulted over the walls by Mordor Orcs to destroy morale, while in The Shire, the peaceable Hobbits are viciously suppressed by Sharkey's ruffians.[77] There is an attempt at negotiation with the Mouth of Sauron, whose punitive terms include detailed territorial plans that he will oversee from Isengard, creating a 'Greater Mordor' with a focus on the east and the south, and the depopulation of the remaining northern and western lands.[78] It should be remembered that against the treaty presented by the Mouth, Aragorn too is attempting to rebuild an empire by uniting northern and southern kingdoms: this is a political game of territorial gain, power, and dominion in which one imperial project is countered by asserting another. Attempting to intimidate the western envoys, the Mouth then claims to have tortured Frodo, presenting Frodo's *mithril* coat and other items as evidence that he has been captured.[79] In the book, the encounter with the Mouth of Sauron is a despairing vision of the future; in *Rings*, however, Jackson must make the confrontation much more dramatic, which he does by expressing Aragorn's despair in an act of pure fury: decapitating the Mouth. Aragorn's brutal retaliation may be cinematically effective in expressing the desperation of his plight, but it is also a *de facto* war crime.[80]

There are other negotiations too: principally with Saruman

among the ruins of Isengard, which is virtually a kangaroo court as Saruman has already been defeated and imprisoned, and Gandalf can act as judge, jury, and gaoler. Parleys also form a key plot device in *The Hobbit*. Bilbo speaks with Smaug, drawing attention to his linguistic dexterity and eloquence, duelling with riddling language, and providing a gloss on his adventures that underlines the status of his story as a story.[81] Parleys also take place between Bard and Thorin, emphasizing that the opposing parties are in an absolute impasse, and then, covertly, between Bilbo and Bard and the Elvenking – Bilbo negotiating not on behalf of the Dwarves but delivering the Arkenstone as the ultimate bargaining chip to break the deadlock.[82] These debates add doubt to the validity of going into battle, highlighting that it is not a straightforward decision but follows the result of diplomatic negotiations bedevilled with uncertainties and impediments, and fraught with risk; neither side is wholly innocent.

If the War of the Ring can be considered a just war, there are nevertheless important caveats. First, the allies of the West use the Rangers of Ithilien as masked and camouflaged resistance fighters to ambush troops on the move, which could equally be considered terrorism – as suggested by Kirill Yeskov's novel *The Last Ringbearer* (1999), a rewrite of *The Return of the King* from the point of view of the Orcs.[83] Frodo is interrogated by Faramir and, in *Rings*, is frog-marched to Ithilien; the Rangers also threaten to shoot Gollum out of hand in both book and film.[84] Gollum has already been tortured by Sauron (the opening scene of the BBC radio series), but Gandalf tortures him too to extract information: he admits that he 'had to be harsh', that he put 'the fear of fire on him', and so 'wrung the true story out of him'.[85] It is an extraordinary confession that few readers take notice of – but Gollum is a non-combatant, not only a civilian but a stateless person and weirdly 'timeless' too, being out of his own time; he has been stripped of his identity and his rights; he also has severe psychiatric disorders. Thranduil tortures and then summarily executes an Orc in *Hobbits*, while in *Rings*, as mentioned, Aragorn beheading the Mouth of Sauron during the actual armistice talks is a moment of sheer lawless, Tarantino-inspired cinema. And then there is the cold-blooded slaying of Orcs, who are never offered any mercy but rather become mere points in Gimli and Legolas's killing game.[86] The Rohirrim too are utterly ruthless, chanting deathsongs as they ride into battle.[87]

This attitude towards the Orcs needs an explanation: Orcs are considered irredeemable, and there is a genocidal aim to destroy them without mercy.[88] It seems impossible, then, that they are 'Fallen' or corrupted Elves: they are purely a manifestation of evil, devoid of personality or rights, and to be eradicated – like a virus. Saruman is a scientist creating a new generation of organic fighting machines – not dissimilar to the Nexus series of replicants engineered by the Tyrrel Corporation in the film *Blade Runner* (1982), and also possibly akin to Victor Frankenstein in Mary Shelley's novel of 1818. Azog's prosthetic arm in *Hobbits* suggests that the Orcs can evolve into cyborgs, and the development of 'fully autonomous weapons' ('killer robots') suggests a more contemporary way of perceiving Orcs as programmable killing machines. Sauron is strongly associated with war machines in *The Lost Road*, and, according to Treebeard, Saruman has a mind of 'metal and machines' – there is a whole subterranean industry at Isengard, which perhaps evokes H.G. Wells's Morlocks in *The Time Machine* (1895), and secret forges and mythological metallurgy in the creation of weaponry is in any case associated with the Fall.[89] Orcs are, then, bioengineered, enfleshed weapons, programmed to obey and to kill. In this way, they are a principle of evil, perhaps indeed built from bits of Elves, but not fully sentient. Having said that, the Hobbits Merry and Pippin, and then Frodo and Sam do gain insights into Orc society – hearing them speak, argue, and fight with each other, revealing that they are ruled by oppression and fear, and would rebel against their masters, if they could. But it is only the Hobbits who learn this – or think they do.

For Tolkien, Orcs are evil, but in ways that expose the contradictions of evil and how to combat it. Tolkien himself never resolved the problem of evil, or even established the origins of the Orcs – which would surely have influenced the ways in which they are treated in the books. In Tolkien's thinking, they are best understood as symbolic of sin – something that can affect anyone yet should be resisted and mercilessly fought against. In *Rings* and *Hobbits* they are celebrated for their visual grotesqueness, but the cinema has in any case a fascination with the dark side, with criminal society, and with the visualization of ultraviolence that contributes directly to the presentation of Azog in particular – but ultimately Orcs are equivalent to zombies: monsters that can be casually exterminated because they are not a recognizable life-form. As for Gimli and Legolas's inhuman killing sprees, being a Dwarf and an Elf they are not quite humane as they are not actually Human – they are different species, even if their slaughtering is a form of self-fashioning based on bold brags in the mead hall of Heorot in *Beowulf*. But the Orcs are not a separate species, still less a race: they represent what is evil in free people; they are not eradicated so much as absolved.

Massacring Orcs is not, however, heroic, and Gimli and Legolas and Tauriel are simply conducting the business of battle. The nature of heroism has changed radically in the past century as a result of the industrialization and mechanization of warfare, and is changing today with the advent of 'killer robots'. Tolkien's heroes negotiate between being traditional chivalric knights and contemporary defenders of justice, in which heroic values can only be acknowledged as being heroic if they can be translated into real situations: heroism is valueless as an abstract notion

– its worth is wholly practical. So Tolkien's heroism is, again, resolutely pragmatic: it is a manifesto or a template by which one can live one's life. Less so, perhaps, in the films, which have a clear Hollywood agenda of cinegenic actors making personal sacrifices and performing heroic deeds. Perhaps more effective and viable is the depiction of heroism in audio adaptations. Radio, relying on words and sound, frees the heroic from the prolixity of prose and from the insistence of visual aesthetics to create a more 'theatrical' space for the expression of direct Human values. Robert Stephens, in the BBC radio adaptation, created a compelling Aragorn that was broadcast into households across the globe – quite different from Viggo Mortensen's majestic figure that graced ten thousand silver screens: Mortensen's Aragorn was seen to lead, to fight, to excel, but the triumphs of Stephens's Aragorn were staged in the imagination of the listener, and so shimmer with an auratic energy.

Much of Tolkien's academic work related to heroism: *Beowulf* and *The Battle of Maldon* are both concerned with the social values and consequences of heroism, which are severely questioned in Tolkien's drama *The Homecoming of Beorhtnoth Beorhthelm's Son*. We hear the warriors confronting doom with defiance, boasting being part of the psychology of battle and the bravery and loyalty of 'Northern Courage'. This is strongly evident in the Roman historian Tacitus' work *Germania*, describing the values of the Northern barbarian tribes:

> When it comes to battle, it is a disgrace for a chief to be surpassed in bravery by his retinue, likewise for the retinue not to equal the bravery of their chief. And indeed it means lifelong infamy and shame to leave a battle alive when one's chief has fallen. To defend and protect him and to give him the credit for one's own deeds of valour are the most solemn obligations of their oath of allegiance.

The chiefs fight for victory, their followers for their chief.[90]

For Tolkien, *The Battle of Maldon* exemplifies this loyalty: Byrhtnoth is chivalrous but wrong – being the ealdorman, or ruling lord, he cannot be disobeyed, yet he is too foolish to be heroic; Tolkien compares the Maldon tactics with the charge of the Light Brigade, but the implicit parallel is with the British generals of the Great War ordering troops to go 'over the top'.[91] As he knew only too well, 'we may remember that the poet of *Beowulf* saw clearly: the wages of heroism is death'.[92] *Maldon* therefore articulates the Anglo-Saxon expression of heroic will: 'the clearest statement of the doctrine of uttermost endurance in the service of indomitable will', and in words spoken by a subordinate.[93] Interestingly, Tolkien also complicates the ethos of the poem, Leofsunu fearing reproach if he returns from the battle alive. This is similar to *Sir Gawain and the Green Knight* – Gawain being on a quest that can only end in his death – and even paralleled too in the resurrection of Christ as told in the Gospels, with which Tolkien audaciously ends his essay 'On Fairy-Stories' as being the most affirmative story of escape from death. 'Northern Courage', then, is heroism in the face of certain death: 'Disaster is foreboded', in *Beowulf*, 'Defeat is the theme.'[94] This certainty is what gives poetry to the hand-to-hand warfare in *Maldon*, an elegiac halo to the arenas of battle in the novel, and a choreographic beauty to the scenes of carnage in the films. And death does come – to Thorin, Fili, and Kili; to Gandalf, Boromir, and Théoden – and, moreover, in *Rings* to the Lothlórien lieutenant Haldir; while other characters are wounded beyond healing. And the dead are lamented in verse, song, and story from *Maldon* to Middle-Earth.

Until Tolkien's essay was published, *The Battle of Maldon* had been seen as a celebration of incipient chivalry, but it is really a critique of 'Northern Courage' – a *'severe'* critique, according to

Tolkien.[95] Nevertheless, 'Northern Courage' obviously resonates with *The Lord of the Rings*: the hopeless mission that will end in the ruin of all things. The whole anti-quest is doomed to fail, from Frodo offering to take the Ring to Mordor, to Aragorn leading the Host of the West into their final battle. Interestingly, Jackson's films tend to celebrate 'Northern Courage' more than the book does, balancing the compelling cinema of charismatic leadership against the quieter and more individual heroism of Frodo and Sam, neither of whom is a leader. The Hobbits' courage is not 'Northern Courage' in the conventional sense, then, but is a recasting of the credo in terms of individual will, resolution, and determination. The trenches of the Great War were no place for 'Northern Courage' either, except in the most personal and subjective ways; neither were the theatres of the Second World War. The reality of technological warfare destroyed a theory of heroism that had, in fact, been pointedly criticized for over a thousand years – even while it continued to inspire literature and national myths.

In contrast, the Hobbits have quite different forms of engagement and heroism – what amounts to a Baden-Powell 'boy scout' model of pragmatic ingenuity, inspired by the practical and expedient skills of different peoples of the British Empire and Commonwealth. This is continuous with the early scenes of the Hobbits when we hear about Frodo scrumping mushrooms from Maggot's fields: they are like the 'Outlaws' of Richmal Crompton's *Just William* stories of the 1930s – there's an unruliness, a freedom, a recklessness, a lack of moral certitude that looks back to Bilbo's tricksy thefts, lies, and deceptions, but which in *The Lord of the Rings* is transformed into pragmatism, tenacity, and resourcefulness. These proclivities are remodelled again as the Hobbits approach the frontline. Pippin pledges allegiance to Denethor and, in parallel, Merry becomes Théoden's esquire – except this is not quite in parallel as Gondor and Rohan are two different military cultures fighting different wars and, initially, different enemies.[96] Rohan is overrun, Helm's Deep is besieged, and there is immediate conscription; Minas Tirith is already on a war footing, food is rationed, the day is timetabled around the armed forces, there is a blackout enforced. Pippin and Merry offering their swords thus reflect the issues of joining up that complicated the wartime recruitment tactics, particularly during the Great War. Both enlist voluntarily, but for Merry it is a sudden sentimental decision, whereas Pippin is intimated by Denethor and does so out of a sense of duty (or guilt) to the Steward as reparation for Boromir's death and for his own survival. Both act on the spur of the moment, driven by impulsive emotions rather than reason – what Treebeard would consider rather too hasty – but it is also a desire to belong to a martial community, to join with like-minded comrades.

So against the disasters of war, Tolkien offers friendship and fellowship – one of his abiding themes and *the* principal concern of his greatest writing, clubs and collaborations being central to Tolkien throughout his life. Friendship and loyalty also have wider associations of hospitality and familiarity that are of course also expressed throughout Tolkien's work, as well as in later reworkings: they remain powerfully domestic bulwarks to the threats of apocalyptic evil. If anything, this camaraderie is emphasized in later adaptations due to the cinematic logic of having multiple leads – one thinks of Hollywood classics such as *The Magnificent Seven* (1960) or *The Great Escape* (1963) – as well as exploring complex buddy triangles such as Frodo–Gollum–Sam. Heroism, for Tolkien, lies not in an individual's will but in collective endeavour – in co-operation and collaboration, from slaying the Lord of the Nazgûl to, most ironically, destroying the Ring.

Unforgettably, it is Éowyn who delivers the deathblow to the Witch-King of Angmar, Lord of the Nazgûl – a scene almost perfectly realized in *Rings*.[97] There are, notoriously, few women in Tolkien's books – although perhaps more than are usually realized. In *The Silmarillion*, for example, Nienna redeems the discord of Melkor in the 'Ainulindalë'; Melian of Doriath is the most powerful figure in the kingdom, protecting Gondolin with a magical Girdle (and also mother of Lúthien, who bewitches Morgoth with her singing); Tuor follows the advice of his wife Idril in escaping Gondolin; Haleth was the female chieftain of the Haladrin and led them through Nan Dungortheb; there are several women in 'The Children of Húrin' (Morwen, Niënor, Finduilas); and royal succession in Númenor was by first-born, regardless of gender. Moreover, in *The Lord of the Rings*, Sméagol's society was matriarchal, Gilraen was the mother of Aragorn and placed him in Rivendell, and there are often overlooked characters such as Lobelia, Rosie, Goldberry, and Ioreth. But they are clearly outnumbered by male characters.

One reason for this is that *The Lord of the Rings* is war writing, and in Britain women did not go into battle during the First and Second World Wars, although they were required by the government to work and in the 1940s served as nurses, air-raid wardens, agricultural labourers (the 'land army'), plumbers, factory workers, ship builders, mechanics, engineers, drivers (including ambulances, fire engines, and tanks), and pilots delivering fighters and bombers; in all, some 100,000 women served in uniform. Tolkien reflects this in characters such as Ioreth, who works in the House of Healing in Minas Tirith. But in Éowyn he shows that women can be warriors – and highly effective warriors at that.

Éowyn knows she is trapped, and that her prospects are limited. Like Galadriel, Éowyn fulfils the traditional role as cup-bearer to the royal court, a position carrying particular authority in Germanic and Norse society: Éowyn is cup-bearer for Théoden and later Aragorn, and again at the coronation

of Éomer, effectively anointing the new king. But this is not
enough and she rebels against this symbolic domesticity, arguing with Aragorn that 'All your words are but to say: you are a
woman, and your part is in the house', and that once 'the men
have died in battle . . . you have leave to be burned in the house,
for the men will need it no more'. She asserts her noble blood,
of the House of Eorl, but also her warrior skills: 'I can ride and
wield blade, and I do not fear either pain or death.' Aragorn
then asks what she does fear; she answers, 'A cage.'[98] As Virginia Woolf wrote in *A Room of One's Own* (1929), 'I thought
how unpleasant it is to be *locked out*; and I thought how it is
worse perhaps to be locked in'.[99] Éowyn disguises herself by
(Shakespearean) crossdressing, a disguise that covers her other
offences, such as disobeying her king (and adoptive father) and
rejecting her duty as defender of people, and she is of course
seeking death (as Merry notices). But for Gandalf, her 'spirit
and courage' are 'at least the match' of Éomer's, but while he had
'horses, and deeds of arms, and the free fields', she was forced to
wait on Théoden as he fell into senility.[100] She more than proves
herself on the field and realizes her personal destiny: Éowyn's
gender is weaponized, much as sexual acts are weaponized in
Game of Thrones.[101] In this, Tolkien draws on the Anglo-Saxon
poem 'Judith' in the Nowell Codex – the same manuscript that
contains the sole copy of *Beowulf*. 'Judith' retells the Biblical tale
of Judith and Holofernes – in short, Judith is a wise and powerful woman whose people are threatened by Assyrians led by
Holofernes, so she decapitates him as he lies in a drunken stupor
in his bedroom. It was a popular subject for Anglo-Saxon poets
as it shows a woman taking up arms, and was written during
the incessant Viking raids that were plundering England; it is
these qualities that Tolkien recasts in a modern setting. Éowyn,
then, demonstrates that as a woman she is uniquely fitted for a
role on the battlefield and as an agent of providence – which is

why she knowingly releases her hair before putting the undead wraith to death. Further, she *laughs* in the face of her enemy – an utterly uncanny moment: it is eucatastrophic laughter – a foretold fate and a pivotal moment that vanquishes supernatural evil. Éowyn's act is a repudiation of the old values of 'Northern Courage' because, like Judith, she fights and wins: she does not fail – it takes a woman to do so.

Healed by Aragorn and recuperating, like so many other characters Éowyn then consciously has to sacrifice her proven power and find a new role. She meets Faramir and can surpass the limitations of her shield-maiden role as a healer and eventual ruler, which, as Tolkien mentioned in a letter, accounts for the speed of her affections for Faramir: they are in a war they are sure they will still lose, they are 'under the expectation of imminent death'.[102] Éowyn struggles, then, between public duty and personal fulfilment – and she has also been sexually objectified by Wormtongue for years – but having confirmed her rank among the foremost warriors of Rohan she transcends the doomed doctrine of 'Northern Courage' and, in doing so, is a foreshadow of final victory.

The Nature of War

Tolkien is a tree-hugger – everyone knows that. He lingers over the flora of his natural descriptions, he condemns the destruction of habitats – especially when caused by industrialization – and he is renowned for his love of, yes, trees. He had favourite trees in Oxford, he writes about sentient and animate trees, his trees oppose an industrialist oppressor, his trees are sagacious and charitable. Tolkien is a nature writer, even though his nature writing is not quite of our world: he writes of herbs, blossoming flowers, the passing seasons, and has a kinship with animals, many of which speak, or at least think, in his books – the Hobbits are gardeners and the Elvenking is crowned for the seasons.[103] The farmers outside Minas Tirith still keep crop fields and orchards beyond the city, and in *Rings* Faramir leads his hopeless force of 200 Gondor knights through the city streets on his way to try to reclaim Osgiliath as women throw flowers of good fortune before them. Sam, barely tempted by the Ring, is briefly deluded to imagine replanting Mordor, restoring barrenness to a 'garden of flowers and trees'.[104] Such is the detail of plant life that a 400-page book of the *Flora of Middle-Earth* has been published, detailing over 140 plants described in Tolkien's work, from those familiar today such as hart's-tongue and saxifrage, to the powerful drug kingsfoil and the otherworldly mallorn-tree.[105] There is throughout Tolkien's writing a strong sense that Humans occupy just a part of Middle-Earth, sharing it with many other species.

But Tolkien's trees in particular, and his environmental vision more generally, have been simplified through popular accounts of his concerns, as well as through a simplistic rendering of the Ents in *Rings*. While the revival of the White Tree of Gondor later becomes symbolic of the revival of the fortunes of that country, the more baleful aspects of woodland are an important reminder that nature, in Tolkien, can viciously strike back. This is more prevalent and more troubling in the books, but is featured in the films as well. Early in *The Fellowship* the opinionated Hobbit personage Daddy Twofoot is muttering about the Old Forest at the borders of The Shire – 'That's a dark bad place' – and the Hobbit Fredegar Bolger describes it as 'a nightmare'; nevertheless, Frodo, Merry, Pippin, and Sam decide to pass through it anyway in order to lose the Black Riders (an episode usually cut from later adaptations).[106] The Hobbits of Buckland have been in an uneasy truce with this magical wood for generations, a truce that eventually broke down into open confrontation when the Forest tried to break into Buckland through a protective hedge and invade The Shire. The Hobbits, being a pre-industrial farming community, therefore have to manage the land and control woodlands – which in this case necessitated burning parts of the Forest to keep it within its borders, and in doing so creating a large, unwooded clearing inside, where the felled trees had been burnt.

When Frodo and the Hobbits venture within the Forest, they find it 'dark and damp'; the word 'dark' being reiterated: 'the dark trees', the 'dark' River Withywindle, the 'dark opening' in the trunk of a willow tree, and there are 'queer gnarled and knobbly faces that gloomed dark against the twilight' – foreshadowing the experiences of Merry and Pippin in Fangorn.[107] It is no surprise, then, that they begin to feel 'that all this country was unreal, and that they were stumbling through an ominous dream that led to no awakening'.[108] The Forest then retaliates against the trespassing Hobbits first by leading them astray – the trees seeming to guide them deeper and deeper into the dark woods so they become completely disorientated – then by befuddling them by congealing the Forest atmosphere so that they become unbearably languorous, and finally by attempting to imprison them in a great tree: Old Man Willow. Within three days of leaving Frodo's home the Hobbits are lost, with no guide, and two of them are trapped and held captive in the knotty entrails of timber: their mission already foundering. Frodo and Sam want to cut down the Willow-Man and do start to set fire to him, but Merry and Pippin pegged within beg them to stop as the tree starts to crush them.

In the event they are rescued by the strange figure of Tom Bombadil (of whom more later). Following Tom to his home, reality dissolves – the dreamlike forest becomes a place of multiplying shadows, branches and trunks of trees hanging across their path, wreathed in mist rising from the river and fog from the earth.[109] When they finally reach the House of Tom Bombadil, his wife Goldberry observes, 'you are still afraid, perhaps,

of mist and tree-shadows and deep water, and untame things',
and Tom explains that Old Man Willow is an especially mali-
cious tree.[110] The Old Forest is not picturesque, this countryside
is not sentimentalized as a natural space – it is wild, dangerous,
and hostile.

The Hobbits' next encounter with sentient wood is the Ent
Treebeard, who despite his apparent wisdom is oblivious of
Hobbitry, decides they are starveling Orcs and so considers
stamping on them, and eventually goes on the rampage heed-
less of friend or foe when he sees that Saruman's Orcs have been
chopping down his forest of Fangorn to provide fuel for military forges and foundries. It is worth remembering that in early
drafts the Giant Treebeard was an evil character who imprisoned
Gandalf and later deceived Frodo, and that he does have a somewhat ambivalent morality. He commands the ominous wood of
the Huorns that appears before Helm's Deep and which liquid-
ates the retreating Orcs, revealing a much more sinister side
to living trees: truly a dark ecology. In Tolkien's book, Gandalf
leads the way through this woodland, which, like the Old Forest, is dark and vaporous, the stifling atmosphere within burning
with wrath; even Legolas is unsettled. Once calm, Treebeard's
opinions too prove wayward and, indeed, hasty: charged with
guarding Saruman, he nevertheless lets him go, thus initiating
Saruman's devastation of The Shire in the guise of Sharkey,
and the felling of many more trees. For all his sturdiness, tre-
mendous physical strength, and deliberation, Treebeard is also
ill-informed, erratic, and impulsive.

Treebeard and the Ents' whirlwind unleashed against Isengard, inspired as it is by Saruman's deforestation of Fangorn, is
both chaotic and devastating, but how different are Saruman's
aggressive tree-clearances to the Brandybuck Hobbits cutting
and burning the Old Forest? Likewise, while Gimli feels that
the Huorns have a 'hatred of all that go on two legs', Legolas

claims that their hate is restricted to Orcs – yet the Huorns do
to the Orcs exactly what the Willow-Man tries to do to the
Hobbits (perhaps he too thinks that they are odd little Orcs). In
the words of scholar Verlyn Flieger, Tolkien's attitude towards
trees is 'complicated, contradictory'.[111] She identifies 'two unrec-
oncilable attitudes' in *The Lord of the Rings*: that wild nature
cannot coexist with cultivated nature, and that wild nature will
eventually be tamed – and so be no longer wild. Lothlórien,
for instance, is, unlike Fangorn, cultivated, whereas Mirkwood,
'where the trees strive one against another and their branches
rot and wither', has been neglected and abandoned.[112] The lost
Entwives, who were gardeners, are also part of this problem,
and there is a basic contradiction in that the Ents are untamed
whereas the Entwives were tamers, creating not only an eternal
tension between them, but what will also lead to their extinction.
There is a hopeless tragedy here: the Ents are a forlorn hope,
the last of their kind, fighting not for themselves or their children (there are no 'Entings'), but for the Earth, Middle-Earth,
itself. But in that they will fail: there will be no 'rewilding' of
Middle-Earth. In his polemic *Defending Middle-Earth* (2004),
Patrick Curry calls for 'woodsmanship' to conserve and sus-
tain nature – a shepherding of the trees rather than either
exploiting woodlands, or just allowing them to grow without
interference.[113] In more pejorative language, this is management: interventionist ecological policies driven by politics and
economics are now unavoidable – and were too in Tolkien's time
after centuries of national forestry to provide the raw materials
for ships and housing and commodities. Tolkien said himself
that 'nobody in ancient England thought anything about oaks,
trees, I mean they'd devastated the whole of the south-eastern
country for smelting, for building ships and so on; no, it's not
a new thing'.[114] There is, in other words, no place for untamed
Ents, no place for the truly wild in a country such as Britain.

Tolkien's environmentalism is anything but straightforward: it is a battleground, and the fighting continues.

Some of these subtleties do remain in *Rings* and *Hobbits*. While the cinematic Treebeard (voiced by John Rhys-Davies, who also played the part of Gimli) is gentle and compassionate (and certainly not over-hasty), it is clear that he can be roused to high passions and has a devastating temper. The Ents destroy Isengard almost carelessly. Meanwhile, Peter Jackson's vision of Mirkwood in *An Unexpected Journey* is a phantasmic forest that twists reality into a maze of outlandish and branching tree trunks, all bent upon bewilderment. This is hardly the stuff of a benevolent arboretum: it is a dendrophobic nightmare. But most intriguingly, Jackson includes a version of Old Man Willow in the extended edition of his *Two Towers* film. Merry and Pippin awake in Fangorn, but Treebeard has already gone about his business and they are left alone – or so they think. As they drink water from the River Entwash, they are seized by a tree that closes its roots around their ankles and buries them within – until Treebeard returns, admonishes the tree, and warns the Hobbits that the forest is waking up: 'It isn't safe.' He goes on to tell them that the trees 'have grown wild and dangerous. Anger festers in their hearts. Black are their hearts. Strong is their hate. They will harm you if they can.'[115] His words are reminiscent of Tom Bombadil's warning about the trees of the Old Forest, filled with malice and 'a hatred of things that go free upon the earth', and of Willow-Man, whose 'heart was rotten, but his strength was green'.[116] The passage is remarkable for the visceral loathing felt by trees for living things at liberty, for their brutal violence and viciousness, and for the insidious and corrupting influence of Old Man Willow.

Ents are consequently weaponized nature – whether by stealth (Huorns) or in direct attack (Ents) – and the depths of woods and forests are not, for Tolkien, necessarily placid places.

They are inimical environments of organic leaf and magical timber, they create their own (sometimes ruthless) laws and values
of thoughts 'dark and strange', they exist outside the comprehension of the peoples of Middle-Earth: that is what Tolkien
means by the primitive neologism 'tree-ish'.[117] And in these
ways, Tolkien was strikingly ahead of the thinking of his time
and very much chimes with contemporary ecological thought
on the rights of trees, woodland, and forestry: we need to coexist
with them and understand that they are very different beings
from other living things. The Ents may be passing, but these
are still places where we should tread warily, where the very
ground is treacherous and the flora devious; where wood has
latent powers, can awaken, and wage war. That is part of their
dark enchantment.

Tom Bombadil knows all about the trees, but he is a hugely
problematic figure – the most problematic in all of Tolkien's
Middle-Earth. Of all the contradictions in characters, all the
ambiguities and incongruities, there is none bigger than Bombadil: 'a very odd character', as Tolkien described him.[118] From
the outset Tom is a mystery – a figure who pre-dates Tolkien's
writing of *The Lord of the Rings*, he is literally outside Middle-
Earth, while in Tolkien's notes he is 'the Aborigine of this land'
and is therefore 'Eldest', having seen the first raindrop and the
first acorn.[119] A deity of sorts, he exists in his own Puckish
world.[120] He is almost a Tolkien figure, a mischievous and contradictory authorial presence, contemplating and enjoying the
world around him, and cheering it with frivolous songs.

Tom narrates the Old Forest, focusing on Old Man Willow
and the malevolence of trees. He is completely immune to the
One Ring – it not only has no effect on him, but he can also
see through its veil of invisibility when Frodo briefly slips it on.
He rescues the Hobbits twice and provides generous hospitality; he eases their nightmares; he arms them – Merry's weapon

proving decisive in helping to annihilate the Witch-King. Sam, too, recalls Tom while in Shelob's Lair as he lays his hand on his sword from the Barrow, and one of Frodo's last memories before he leaves Middle-Earth is of Bombadil.[121] Tolkien wrote to Nevill Coghill, the mediaevalist scholar and translator of Chaucer, that Tom would not be explained. He wanted to leave him as a deliberate loose end that did not fit the tale of the One Ring, suggesting that, to paraphrase Shakespeare, there are more things in Middle-Earth than are dreamt of in your stories and histories, lore and legendaria.[122] He will not, should not be explained. In the words of Goldberry, to whom he is happily married, it is simple: 'He is'.[123]

The most recognizable aspect of Tom Bombadil – his singing – is nonetheless worth investigating further. Tom sings the land in nonsense songs that cast a spell.[124] The Hobbits have already been singing while walking or washing, but Tom's songs are incantations of protection against evil, freeing them from Old Man Willow and dispelling the Barrow-Wight, and so they deepen the import of verse and song, alerting the reader to its significance. And there is a great deal of singing subsequently: Frodo sings disastrously at The Prancing Pony, and Aragorn is introduced with a verse; Sam sings of Gil-Galad, and Aragorn of Tinúviel; Gimli sings of the Dwarrowdelf, and Legolas of Nimrodel. At Lothlórien, Frodo and Sam compose a song on Gandalf. In Rohan there are no books but many songs, Théoden declaring that even their defeat 'will be glorious in song', and that the last ride out of the Hornburg will 'make such an end as will be worth a song'.[125] Treebeard sings; even Gollum sings when he reaches the Dead Marshes. Sam takes the Ring because he fears that there will be no more songs; at almost the same time, Pippin is singing to Denthor. The Rohirrim sing battle songs on the Pelennor Fields, and celebrate their dead in song; and Sam sings to locate Frodo in the Tower of Cirith Ungol. Finally, a

Gondor minstrel celebrates Frodo and Sam, and Éowyn and Faramir in song.

These are just a few of the extraordinary number of songs and verses in *The Lord of the Rings*: characters negotiate their way through time and space, through history and landscapes, by song. In Lothlórien, Sam feels as if he is '*inside* a song', finally bringing melody into harmony with place, and the Riders of Rohan cross the mountains to Gondor on a road made 'in years beyond the reach of song' – so song and time are related too, songs being a form of measurement, or a reckoning.[126] On one hand this connective tissue of song is a way of creating multiple layers of culture, and very few literary characters (outside of musical works such as John Gay's *The Beggar's Opera*, 1728) sing so much, save in children's literature (notably, *Winnie-the-Pooh*) and in Shakespeare. At best, characters bring their own refrains to impose identities on territory – and none more than Tom Bombadil. As the Hobbits leave The Shire and encounter two fearsome enemies, Tom's singing allows them to confound these dangers. So he arms them with song – rhymes as ready as their swords – uniting them with the manifold singing of the Free Peoples of Middle-Earth that is an echo of the divine music of the Ainur, Tolkien's symphonic creation myth.[127]

Woods and forests apart, the landscapes of Middle-Earth more generally are also part of the struggle: the jagged rockscapes of the Emyn Muil over which Frodo and Sam clamber and climb, before reaching the treacherous bogs of the Dead Marshes, then the toxic landscape beyond, redolent of the blasted panoramas of the Great War and the industrial wastelands around Birmingham and the Black Country as depicted in the social realist paintings of Edwin Butler Bayliss (1874–1950): sodden grey and black factoryscapes of smoking eyesores – if not seen by Tolkien, he was at least familiar with the grim subjects from his childhood.[128] The Hobbits become ghosts in an ashy landscape, spectres of a wartorn Gothic past: the land is 'diseased beyond all healing' and Sam is sickened by this septic terrain. Part of the uncanniness of the Black Riders too is that they appear to be an emanation of what should be the familiar countryside of The Shire itself; in contrast, the Lothlórien cloaks given to the Company allow them to merge into the landscape.[129] Geography is felt and experienced: as Brian Rosebury suggests, Tolkien not only describes a landscape but charts its emotional effect on characters.[130]

Weather too is coerced into action by enemy forces: the weather on the Barrow-Downs is unpredictable and the Hobbits are lost in the fog, hostile meteorology is summoned by Saruman over the peak of Caradhras and again at the Hornburg when the Orcs attack in thunder and rain (part of the stunning *mise-en-scène* of the battle in *Rings*), and Sauron casts darkness over Gondor to shield the armies of Mordor. These disordered conditions cannot last, however, and changes in the wind from the sea disperse the shades of Mordor and a rainbow rises over Isengard after it has been flooded. Rain can also be purifying, and Frodo passes through rain to arrive in Valinor, being reminded of the rain he dreamt of while at the House of Tom Bombadil.[131] There is hope.

◆   ◆   ◆

One might expect that, having given an account of how deeply conflict soaks through diverse aspects of Tolkien's work, I will now move to considering the state of England in the 1940s and conclude this chapter on nationhood and national identity. After all, readers seem never to tire of presenting Tolkien's Englishness, commenting on Hobbiton being a Warwickshire village at the time of Queen Victoria's Diamond Jubilee (1897), 'The Scouring of The Shire' being an account of the post-war destruction of the English countryside (even though, for what

it is worth, Tolkien explicitly denied this), or even Tom Bombadil being a *genius loci* of the countryside of central England.[132]
But, looking towards my final chapter, I will instead start to
show how Tolkien today is not caught in nostalgia for an earlier,
parochial England, but is now very much for the twenty-first
century.

The first point to make is that Peter Jackson's films have come
to define particular features of Middle-Earth – in particular The
Shire. Hobbiton is no longer a middle-England village at the
time of Victoria's Jubilee, but a location on Alexander Farm in
the Waikato region of New Zealand (a variety of tours are, of
course, available).[133] This is global Middle-Earth. The battles
that form the spectacular set-pieces of three of Jackson's films
affect the entirety of *Rings* and *Hobbits*. Because cinema is a
visual medium, and because Jackson's huge team were scrupu-
lously attentive to every aspect of staging, there is a constant
texture of warfare throughout, with swords, Orcs, and danger
of every sort barely off the screen – the only scenes that really
escape the omnipresent sense of conflict are the Shire and Grey
Havens scenes that book-end *Rings*. Jackson succeeds in weap-
onizing not only trees and song, landscapes and weather, but his
whole medium – in editing, intercutting, and tracking shots,
as well as props, CGI, and mo-cap. His comments on filming
the Battle of the Five Armies, in which he effectively saw himself as a COMCAM, represent the zenith of this ambition and
more than anything else define that final movie as one of the
most battle-hardened fantasy experiences to date. Like *Rings*,
the final *Hobbits* film raised the barrier for fantasy action movies
through its almost persistent quality of being in a state-of-
emergency from the very opening scene in which the commercial hub of Laketown finds itself at the frontline: the target
of Smaug's aerial offensive, facing imminent destruction, its
citizens become homeless refugees. The fact that the movie can

begin with Smaug being shot from the skies and crashing into the blazing city indicates that there is far worse to come. This is cinema as a war machine in which an army of technicians cry 'havoc' and let slip the dogs of war, unleashing hell. The spin-off battle video games followed suit, and many of the weapons, including WMD Smaug, are available as replicas. Even the poster showed Bilbo threatening the viewer with his sword Sting – which in the book never left its scabbard during the conflict.

Although such thrills and spills are standard for action movies, *Rings* (and also *Hobbits*) works particularly well through the mixing of styles and genres I have discussed, the innovative technology, and the equivocal moralities. This ends up in pandemonium, a wonderfully imaginative and creative mayhem, a unique cinema experience. The books, one may think, do not reflect this exhilarating intensity – certainly the children's *Hobbit* does not – but re-read the singing of the Rohirrim at the Battle of the Pelennor Fields, which is conducted in great, stirring symphonic/mythic/Biblical prose, or the moment of the destruction of the One Ring, where Tolkien's language detonates like a volcano – the very crack of doom.[134] Literature is not film, but the reason that the movies resonated with readers was because they captured the memory of certain scenes, if recast, rescripted, restaged. In the words of Todd McCarthy of the *Hollywood Reporter*, 'After six films, 13 years and 1031 minutes of accumulated running time (far more if you count the extended versions), Peter Jackson has concluded his massively remunerative genuflection at the altar of J.R.R. Tolkien with a film that may be the most purely entertaining of any in the collection'.[135] For many, then, Jackson did succeed in encapsulating the lucid, ludic 'core' of Tolkien's original.[136]

SEVEN

Conclusion: Weird Things

Unrest and uncertainty are our lot.
Johann Wolfgang von Goethe,
letter to Sophie von La Roche (1774)

In the BBC Radio 4 religious programme *Beyond Belief*, first broadcast on 30 September 2013, the historian of Paganism Professor Ronald Hutton discussed the problem of forgiveness in Tolkien's Middle-Earth writings. Gollum, he argued, was the single case in which forgiveness proves an effective strategy in *The Lord of the Rings*. Both Sauron and Saruman are forgiven – Sauron by Elves and Humans at the beginning of the Second Age after the final defeat of Morgoth, and Saruman by Tree-beard and then the Hobbits after the War of the Ring – but in both cases this forgiveness brings about further catastrophe: in the first case in the forging of the Rings of Power, and in the second in the industrialization of The Shire. Nevertheless, forgiveness – at least the idea of forgiveness – does run deep in the novel: even the Orcs, who appear to be utterly demonized and never offered any quarter (see Chapter Six), are, during the Siege of Gondor, actually spoken of with sympathy by Gandalf – 'I pity even his slaves' – although that amounts to very little in practice. Even more surprisingly, Tolkien himself grappled with the problem of evil and the Orcs in a long letter written in 1954, suggesting that to describe Orcs as 'irredeemably bad' would be 'going too far' – but the letter, which shows Tolkien thinking aloud through these issues, was never sent as he thought he was taking himself too seriously (and, more to the point, was perhaps not necessarily accurate).[1] The questions of forgiveness and redemption were not resolved.

Hutton adds, moreover, that the only two characters who express a faith in the afterlife are Aragorn and Théoden – the latter going to join his 'fathers'.[2] This may mean that he is going to be with them in spirit in an afterlife, or simply lie with them in an earth barrow among standing stones: Hutton's opinion is that this is 'never made clear and I think that is deliberate'. In *The Hobbit*, Thorin Oakenshield is more explicit – he is going to 'the halls of waiting to sit beside my fathers, until the world is renewed', and the otherworldly and immortal Elves have of course the Undying Lands of Valinor.[3] But for Humans and Hobbits, any afterlife is at best uncertain, at worst simply nonexistent. In the wider context of Middle-Earth, in addition to only the vaguest hints of an afterlife there is also no institutionalized religion, priesthood, sacred ritual, or prayer (except in two enigmatic cases); there are no intercessionary saints, or everyday references to god or the gods; there is no consistent moral code, and the nature of evil cannot be understood (see Chapter Three, and elsewhere). *The Lord of the Rings*, then, appears to be a decidedly secular work. Yet Tolkien himself felt that his novel was 'fundamentally religious and Catholic', although direct religious references had been deliberately cut because the 'religious element' is 'absorbed into the story and the symbolism', presumably in instances such as the repeated temptation of the One Ring – although these revisions are not noticeably evident in early drafts.[4]

But the elimination of the Church and explicit spirituality from the narrative has two far-reaching consequences, especially for readers today. The first is summarized by Hutton:

> I think the truly significant thing is that neo-Pagans, who weren't around when Tolkien was writing his masterpiece, can read it and enjoy it with the same full-bloodedness as devout Christians – and that's the mark of a great story-teller: ... if ... one can *only* understand the true 'message', the hidden message of *The Lord of the Rings*, if you are a devout Christian, I think that both diminishes Tolkien as a storyteller, and is inappropriate to a multi-faith, multi-ethnic, multicultural society. It also doesn't come to terms with the success of *The Lord of the Rings* among a vast areligious and other-religious readership.[5]

So what is this true 'message' of the book? The answer lies in the 'Akallabêth' – which Tolkien only added to the legendarium after the 'Quenta Silmarillion' had already been through many versions, but which several times distracted him from completing *The Lord of the Rings*. The 'Akallabêth' was Tolkien's version of the myth of the deluged island of Atlantis or Lyonesse, and Tolkien was not alone in being drawn to the story. In his poem 'Fragments' (1920), for example, the poet (and later Poet Laureate) John Masefield imagines that although 'green and greedy seas' have deluged Atlantis, its gold still glitters from the depths:

> The Atlanteans have not died,
> Immortal things still give us dream.[6]

For Tolkien, this is Númenor, which likewise lives on through immortal things. Númenor is the bringer of dreams: relics and artefacts, monuments and architecture, bloodlines and rootstock, myth and legend – and versions of the history of Númenor appear not only in additions to 'The Silmarillion', but also in *The Lost Road*, *The Notion Club Papers*, independent works such as 'The Drowning of Anadûnê' and 'The Death of Saint Brendan', and throughout *The Lord of the Rings*, which is saturated in references to Númenor (or Westernesse – a term taken by Tolkien from the thirteenth-century mediaeval romance *King Horn*). The Númenóreans, or Sea-Kings, were highly admired as Elf-Friends, innovators of arts and crafts, pioneers of trade and agriculture, and guardians of scholarship and learning. Their impact was felt across Middle-Earth: they introduced crops and grapevines and founded the kingdom of Gondor; they raised, for example, Weathertop (Amon Sûl), the Seat of Seeing (Amon Hen), the colossal figures of the Argonath on the River Anduin, and the impervious tower of Orthanc at Isengard; and they guarded the *palantíri*. Their august lineage, meanwhile, endured through Denethor, Boromir, Faramir, and Aragorn. But the 'Akallabêth' is the story of their downfall – a story of greed and pride and corruption that annihilated the greatest Human civilization on Middle-Earth. The destruction of the island of Númenor is a counterpoint to the bloody and destructive history of the Silmarils of the First Age, dominates the history of the Second Age, and insistently haunts the Third Age through 'Isildur's Bane': the One Ring.

Their doom was bound to the endless strife of the First Age, at the end of which Melkor – known as Morgoth, the 'Dark Foe' – was thrust through the Door of Night into the Timeless Void and out of the comprehension of Middle-Earth. But the evil he had planted remained and took root, nurtured by the mightiest of his lieutenants: Sauron. Sauron had appeared to repent following the expulsion of Morgoth: he worked with the Elves and offered his aid to the Númenóreans. Yet Sauron's arrival in Númenor was a calculated stratagem. In contrast to the immortal Elves, Humans had been introduced to Middle-Earth with the 'gift' of death – they leave the world, and go 'whither the Elves know not': death defines the Human condition.[7] So at its founding, Númenor had a mountain that was sacred to Eru Ilúvatar, the godhead, and at the foot of this, the Pillar of Heaven, lay the tombs of their kings, placing death and memorialization at the heart of Númenórean identity.[8]

Sauron swiftly corrupted the people of Númenor by feeding their lust for immortal life. Three Númenórean kings became bound to him as Ringwraiths, and their last monarch, Ar-Pharazôn, who had seized the throne of the Sea-Kings, was converted to worship Melkor and instructed to build a huge domed temple around an altar of fire on which not only animals but even Humans were sacrificed – in other words, the single instance of organized religion in Middle-Earth is this diabolical cult. Sauron filled the island with temples and tombs, fortresses and mechanized 'engines', and inspired the Númenóreans to become imperialist capitalists and slavers.[9] Moreover, the island of Númenor was in sight of Valinor, the Undying Lands, although its people were forbidden ever to set foot there. Sauron convinced the Númenóreans to sail on to Valinor in the vain hope that they would become deathless and assume the immortality granted to the Elves when they landed on its shores, but at the moment the fleets of Ar-Pharazôn committed this unpardonable trespass, a giant tidal wave destroyed Númenor and buried the ships and their crews and warriors for eternity in catachthonic vaults.[10] A handful of rebels managed to escape the inundation – Elendil, his son Isildur, and their followers; Sauron also survived, although following the disaster he was never again able to take a pleasing Human form.

The 'Akallabêth' is a text dominated by mortal power and progress, the fear of death, and loss and memory. Moreover, just as Sauron and Saruman are tainted by technology, the industrialization of Númenor is not depicted as progress but as the triumph of totalitarian evil, and ultimately as calamitous. Indeed, in the unfinished novel *The Lost Road*, this Númenórean modernity is summarized by Christopher Tolkien as 'the withdrawal of the besotted and aging king from the public view, the unexplained disappearance of people unpopular with the "government", informers, prisons, torture, secrecy, fear of the night; propaganda in the form of the "rewriting of history"... [and] the multiplication of weapons of war' – including metal ships that travel without sails, fortifications, and missiles.[11] Although *The Lost Road* remained fragmentary and was not published for decades, the panoply of state terrorism he described – threat, incarceration, and ideologically revised history – was as horrifyingly present to Tolkien as it was to George Orwell. Orwell's response was to imagine this modern tyranny as a near-future allegorical dystopia; Tolkien's response was to travel back in time, conceiving Fascism as a primaeval and apocalyptic evil that resonates through and distorts Human history.

The story of Númenor is, then, a meditation on death, and how humanity tries to transcend death through technological progress, political ideology, and aggressive imperialism. This is why Númenor became increasingly important to Tolkien – he had lived through two world wars yet was drawing to the end of a long life. Reflecting on *The Lord of the Rings* in 1956, Tolkien had claimed that the book was about '*Power*'; however, in a letter written two and a half years later, he now considered power a 'relatively unimportant' theme; rather it is 'mainly concerned with Death, and Immortality; and the "escapes": serial longevity, and hoarding memory'.[12] Moreover, in an interview recorded just five years before he died, Tolkien declared that 'Stories, frankly always our human stories, frankly always are about one thing: death. The inevitability of death', before immediately (and unexpectedly) quoting the final words of Simone de Beauvoir's book *Une mort très douce* (1964) on the death of her mother: 'There is no such thing as a natural death: nothing that happens to a man is ever natural, since his presence calls the world into question. All men must die: but for every man his death is an accident and, even if he knows it and consents to it, an unjustifiable violation.'[13] Tolkien then addressed the interviewer directly: 'Well you may agree with those words or not, but those [words: i.e. de Beauvoir's words] are the key-spring of *The Lord of the Rings*.'[14]

To Fail Better

Much as death pervades Middle-Earth, Tolkien's life and writings breathe failure – the doom of 'Northern Courage' – if laced with strange, unexpected, even eucatastrophic success. He failed to finish many works: most obviously *The Silmarillion*, a rewrite of *The Hobbit* (which led to him disowning the book), and a sequel to *The Lord of the Rings* ('The New Shadow', which he barely started). His other creative works – *Farmer Giles of Ham*, *The Adventures of Tom Bombadil* (1961), and *Smith of Wootton Major* (1967) – may have been respectable successes (going through eleven, nine, and seven impressions, respectively, until the mid-1970s), but the vast majority of his fiction was published posthumously on the back of *The Lord of the Rings*, which exhausted well over forty impressions in different formats in the same period in the UK alone.[15] That book – like *The Hobbit*, for which it was originally a straightforward sequel – was of course a resounding success, although the publishers had little faith in it; nor indeed did Tolkien have much faith in them, attempting at one stage to abandon Allen & Unwin for Collins. Neither did Tolkien manage to retain control of his own posterity, being compelled to sell many of his drafts of *The Hobbit* and *The Lord of the Rings* (in a pile of paper seven feet high) – and then the film rights – for comparatively trifling sums (see Chapter Five).

He also failed to finish (or abandoned) a host of academic projects – including most significantly, perhaps, the Clarendon edition of Chaucer's poetry and prose – and he never consolidated his research and insights in Anglo-Saxon and Middle English philology and literature into a single career-defining book. Instead, Tolkien's immense learning was scattered through teaching notes and lectures, short articles and book reviews, and the extraordinarily generous assistance he gave to partner academics in the field. Much of his knowledge, such as his single-word studies, was also recondite in the extreme – fascinating to the specialist, but baffling to more general readers. A handful of longer pieces aside, Tolkien was almost a miniaturist in his academic work, from his early days as a lexicographer for the *Oxford English Dictionary* to his later editorial projects, and so it is ironic that he wrote one of the longest and most successful novels of the twentieth century. And yet essays such as his note on the word *ofermod* in *The Battle of Maldon* remain in print after some seventy years as a coda to his drama *The Homecoming of Beorhtnoth Beorhthelm's Son*, so in one important sense he did bring Anglo-Saxon philology to a global audience.

Nevertheless, Tolkien's professional career was frustrating and his academic reputation has been contested – and still raises hackles – and is inevitably now coloured by his literary reputation.[16] Members of the University of Oxford English Faculty were still rankling at Tolkien's influence on the undergraduate syllabus in the 1980s, and perhaps do so even now. His literary reputation is equally controversial, particularly among the chattering classes: his works are regularly dismissed *unread* by supposedly professional critics, and only very seldom taught in UK universities or schools – the present author having been one of the very few guardians of the flame for many years; in contrast, *Harry Potter* seems to be compulsory, at least at primary school level.[17] On the other hand, this disdain can perhaps be countered by pointing out that it is a massive failure of imagination by critics and academics themselves not to recognize the attraction that these books – and now the films – possess, and to acknowledge the tastes of the reading and film-going public accordingly.

In any case, Tolkien was aware of his perceived shortcomings and writes failure into his narratives. His characters keep failing: Aragorn and Gandalf (both repeatedly), Boromir and Denethor, Saruman and Treebeard. Frodo fails in his quest, Thorin dies in his, Bilbo has already failed. The Dwarves of Moria fail – twice – and the Dwarves of the Lonely Mountain seem about to precipitate a war between the Free Peoples of Middle-Earth in the most titanic failure of goodwill. Galadriel is in exile, the Elves are doomed, and Middle-Earth itself is failing, losing its enchantment, destined to become our own material world, the colours of wonder drained away. Peter Jackson's *Rings* also carry this sense of failure and doom: in *The Fellowship of the Ring*, Aragorn is first seen to fail when he is caught off-guard by Arwen in his search for the herb kingsfoil, and this functions as a capsule of Aragorn's greater failings throughout the three films where eventually a scene is added in which Elrond has to ride to Aragorn with the reforged sword Andúril to warn him that Arwen is dying and persuade him to 'Put aside the Ranger – become what you were born to be': to accept his fate as King of the Reunited Kingdom.[18] Aragorn is not, then, represented as the all-conquering hero-to-be-king, but as a fallible being who has failed in the past and risks failing again.

Likewise, despite *The Silmarillion* being completed by Christopher Tolkien with the assistance of Guy Gavriel Kay, the subsequent publications *Unfinished Tales*, the multi-volume

History of Middle-earth, and single-volume editions of the three 'Great Tales' have exposed the published *Silmarillion* as a broken text that fundamentally simplifies the gestation and development of key narratives, as well as underplaying and even distorting the role of characters such as Galadriel.[19] And yet only a dedicated Tolkien aficionado would now spend the required time making sense of the manifold and entangled versions of these multiple texts, which include such gambits as making the 'Dark Lord' Sauron a cat, portraying the siege of Gondolin as an armoured tank assault, and imagining the descent of Númenor into totalitarianism as an allegory of Nazism. Christopher Tolkien has since written that the published *Silmarillion* of 1977 was 'an error' because there was no 'framework' for the editorial decisions he was forced to make about the impossibly complex and contradictory texts he was faced with: texts that, as I have described, were written and rewritten, revised and amended, reshaped and reworked over more than half a century; but at the time, what else could Christopher Tolkien do?[20] It was a labour of love and brought the First Age – or at least a version of it – to the reading public, and so made possible the later, voluminous *History of Middle-earth* and the separate publication of the 'Great Tales'. Moreover, despite its failure to convey the legendarium in all its eldritch splendour, the 1977 *Silmarillion* does include some blazingly intense passages, such as the fall of the Elven King Fingolfin, who, like Elendil challenging Sauron at the gates of Mordor, calls forth Morgoth from the depths of his fortress, Angband, to face him in single combat – in which, of course, he can only fail. Or the exquisitely fearful tale of Beren and Lúthien that weaves the fell English folklore of vampires and werewolves into the kaleidoscopic tapestry of Middle-Earth, and can be retrospectively seen to have shaped the doomed, mortal relationship of Aragron and Arwen. But although *The Silmarillion* may be an acquired taste, it is anything but a clarification, and in fact satisfyingly complicates many aspects of Tolkien's vision.[21]

The Silmarillion is also a reminder that Tolkien predominantly writes about non-Human species – the Elves – and that when he does write about the Human Númenóreans, it is to describe their ruinous failings. Careful readers will have noticed that, especially in the last chapter, I describe the different peoples of Middle-Earth as different *species* rather than as different *races* – an issue that has bedevilled Middle-Earth studies. Dimitra Fimi has examined Tolkien's attitudes to race, noting that for much of Tolkien's career 'race was still a valid scientific term', and that it was only in essays written around 1959–60, after the publication of *The Lord of the Rings*, that he addressed racist terms used between Elves. She concludes that Tolkien's terminology for the different peoples of Middle-Earth derived from 'philology and linguistics, anthropology and folklore', as well as from spiritual influences and Romantic notions of primitivism: 'it is not a consistent world': indeed, it is not.[22] Patrick Curry, meanwhile, argues that 'the races in Middle-earth are most striking in their variety and autonomy', which seems to him 'an assertion of the wonder of multicultural difference' as well as 'bioregionalism'; he also places emphasis on the friendship between Gimli and Legolas (representative of two peoples estranged for thousands of years after warring over a Silmaril), and the marriage between Aragorn and Arwen, which he describes as 'interracial'.[23]

These relationships should not, however, be racially defined, but understood as bonds between different, albeit intelligent, species. W.H. Auden recognized this distinction, writing that, 'In the Secondary World of Middle-earth, there exist, in addition to men, at least seven species capable of speech and therefore of moral choice – Elves, Dwarves, Hobbits, Wizards, Ents, Trolls, Orcs', and within these various species that populate Middle-Earth are different races. Among the Hobbits there are brown-skinned Harfoots, heavy-built Stoors, and light-skinned Fallohides; likewise among Elves (such as the golden-haired Vanyar, the usually dark-haired Noldor, and the woodland Silvan Elves), Humans (identifiable races include Gondorians, Drúedain, and Haradrim), Ents (likened to different species [*sic*] of trees – Quickbeam, for example, being Rowan), and Orcs (Uruks, Uruk-Hai, and Snagas); only the Dwarves appear to belong to a single race as they were independently created by Aulë (effectively a demi-god) rather than by Ilúvatar, who created Elves and Humans (as well as, presumably, Hobbits and Ents). So Middle-Earth is teeming with diversity in races and species, as well as in flora and fauna – indeed, diversity is one of its characteristics – but the only hybrid mixing of *species* (as opposed to *races*) appears to be between Elves and Humans (very rarely), and between Orcs and Humans (only rumoured); the mixed-race marriage between the Rohanic Éowyn and the Númenórean Faramir, for example, passes without comment.[24] The philosopher Thomas Nagel's celebrated thought experiment 'What Is It Like to Be a Bat?' (1974) considers such inter-species exchanges as vital reminders of what is unknown, unknowable, and incommunicable between different species, arguing that there may be 'humanly inaccessible facts', facts 'beyond the reach of human concepts . . . facts which *could* not ever be represented or comprehended by human beings'.[25]

But before taking the issues of speciesism further, consider the diversity of Tolkien's Middle-Earth, and its relationship to national identities. Peter Ackroyd defines Englishness through characteristics such as diversity, adaptation and assimilation, a sense of place, and heterogeneity.[26] So if, as suggested (and deferred) at the end of the last chapter, *The Lord of the Rings* is about Englishness – a 'mythology of their own' for the English, much as the legendarium is 'dedicated' to England – it is not through being a nationalist epic of monarchy, military triumphalism, and the Empire, but as a quiet appreciation of language, landscape, diversity, modern heroism, failure, doubt, and decline: a precarious love song to what, in another context, Tolkien described as 'this sunlit archipelago in the midst of the Great Seas'.[27] But Tolkien himself – and as ever – is a contrarian when it comes to nationhood, and during the Second World War he entertained provocative and problematic views on governance. On 29 November 1943, for instance, he wrote to Christopher on his attraction to anarchy – 'philosophically understood, meaning abolition of control', as opposed to 'whiskered men' throwing bombs – and yet at the same time to '"unconstitutional" Monarchy'. He even asserted that he would 'arrest anybody who uses the word State' and 'execute them if they remained obstinate!' That closing exclamation mark reveals, I hope, that this is tongue-in-cheek banter rather than a manifesto for what would amount to state [sic] terrorism. But Tolkien then admitted that he did indeed have sympathy for 'the growing habit of disgruntled men of dynamiting factories and power-stations' – in other words, he simultaneously and paradoxically asserted 'a preference for complete absence of government and for the complete centralization of power'.[28] But the most interesting comment in these letters, militant and exasperated by turns, is a passing remark on the national identity of England: for Tolkien, it is an 'inanimate realm' – a 'thing that has neither power, rights nor mind'.[29]

Reread that last line: Tolkien does not believe that the nation is an active presence, he does not accept that countries, as countries, have any self-determination and agency. The political scientist Benedict Anderson has argued that communities are imagined into existence by a variety of activities such as mapping and defining borders, building archives and museums, and honouring historical relics. Communal identity is also constructed through writing and culture, shared history and a continuity with the past, law and institutions, failure and defeat (again), and in folk memory and traditions.[30] All of these are present in Middle-Earth: cartography, for example (as described in Chapter Three), the Hobbits have their 'Mathom-house' for useless objects while Aragorn carries his broken sword – which in *Rings* is exhibited in Rivendell – and the dead tree of Minas Tirith is a vestige of Númenor that defines the nation-state of Gondor. But Tolkien himself was far more interested in linguistic definitions of identity rather than those based on genetic ancestry, stating in his paper on 'English and Welsh' that individuals act and express and articulate through a shared language, and so 'Language is the prime differentiator of people – not of "races", whatever that much-misused word may mean in the long-blended history of western Europe.'[31] He goes on to acknowledge that Britain was settled by 'racially ... mixed invaders' – a favourite theme of earlier English antiquarianism that embraced and celebrated hybridity – by which he of course means different languages.[32] For Tolkien, then, national identities are as diverse and conflicted as almost every other aspect of his writing.

In the English literary tradition more generally, national identity derives from eighteenth-century politics and is a dimension of the 'Gothic'.[33] Volumes could be written on Tolkien and the Gothic, on how to make sense of a world acknowledged as broken, imperfect, and inhospitable, and despite Tolkien's explicit dismissal of the genre of Gothic literature, *The Lord of the Rings* is steeped in Gothic motifs.[34] Middle-Earth is littered with ancient and ruined architecture. There are many subterranean tunnels and passages, from Moria to the Paths of the Dead. History is governed by a prophecy concerning fragments ('Seek for the sword that was broken') that in turn motivates the Council of Elrond to decide on the fate of the One Ring, while the Witch-King Lord of the Nazgûl is protected by a foretelling that he shall not be slain by any living man.[35] The dead walk in the shape of Ringwraiths, Barrow-Wights, and Oathbreakers. Furthermore, there is a strong influence from the Shakespearean tragedies *Hamlet*, *King Lear*, and *Macbeth*, which themselves influenced later Gothic literature. *The Lord of the Rings* is also suffused with obscurity – meteorological, topographical, architectural, material, textual, spiritual, and psychological. There is mist on the road to Bucklebury Ferry, fog on the Barrow-Downs, and the Great Darkness on the Pelennor Fields – as well as the terrible deluge that engulfs Númenor. Impassable places include Mirkwood and the Old Forest, Caradhras and (without Gollum) the Dead Marshes; and there are terrifying built environments – the Barrow-Downs, Moria, Orthanc, Minas Morgul, Barad-Dûr, Dol Guldur, and Angband. Material disguises range from the dark shrouds of the Black Riders to the Elven cloaks of Lothlórien, from Éowyn's disguise as Dernhelm to Frodo and Samwise dressing as Mordor Orcs. Textual obscurities are at the very heart of Tolkien's Middle-Earth in invented and often untranslated languages, found manuscripts such as Thorin's Map, prophetic songs and verses, inscriptions and engravings, unfinished books and forgotten poems. Spiritual mystery is implicit – and suggestively understated – in half-acknowledged prayers: Sam's invocation when faced with Shelob is spoken in a language he does not understand, while Faramir's contemplation of Númenor remains unexplained. As to psychological issues, there are prophetic dreams, visions, shifts in perception caused by the Ring, split identities, and derangement – and monsters too: Smaug, the Watcher in the Water, the Fell Beasts on which the Nazgûl ride, and Shelob.

Dreams in particular create alternative realities in Middle-Earth. The Hobbits dream almost constantly. At Buckland, Frodo dreams of a sea of trees, the sea, a white tower; in the Old Forest all four become drowsy and Sam dreams that he has been thrown into the River Withywindle by a tree. At the House of Tom Bombadil, Frodo has a vision of Gandalf on Orthanc, Pippin dreams of a willow tree, and Merry dreams of water. They are drowsy again on the Barrow-Downs where the distances are 'hazy and deceptive'; Frodo dreams and awakes in the Barrow; Merry dreams of the Barrow dead – memories of the Men of Carn Dûm become hauntingly present through the portals of standing stones.[36] Merry dreams again when he is overcome by the 'Black Breath' of the Riders at Bree, and Frodo dreams of a horn sounding and galloping riders; Frodo, again, dreams of dark wings passing.[37] The dreams continue at Rivendell, and in the Misty Mountains, and in Moria. Frodo's dreams then seem to coalesce in the Mirror of Galdriel: he sees a White Wizard, Bilbo (among his manuscripts, while rain beats against his window), the sea and ships, and the Eye. Lothlórien is like a dream. Sam wonders whether he is dreaming when he thinks he sees Gollum on the River Anduin. Frodo has hyper-real visions on Amon Hen, the Seat of Seeing – yet seeing as through a 'mist'.[38] Merry and Pippin's journey being marched by the Orcs is a 'dark and troubled dream', repeatedly falling into 'evil dreams'.[39] Merry describes the movement of the Huorns as dreamlike – 'I thought I was dreaming an Entish dream' – while Pippin has an almost Einsteinian dream of relativity when riding with Gandalf to Minas Tirith, as if 'he and Gandalf were still as stone, seated upon the statue of a running Horse, while the world rolled away beneath his feet'.[40] Frodo stares at the lights of the Dead Marshes as if in a dream, and while on watch hallucinates between sleeping and waking; even Gollum has 'secret dreams'.[41] Although their dreams in Ithilien are more peaceful, they quickly turn to nightmare. Shelob is revealed as 'horrible beyond the horror of an evil dream', and Merry leaves the battlefield of the Pelennor Fields in a trance: 'a meaningless journey in a hateful dream'.[42] When Frodo hears Sam singing in the Tower of Cirith Ungol he of course thinks he is dreaming; later, in Mordor he dreams of fire, and is rescued from Mount Doom 'in a dream'.[43] Sam thinks that he has been dreaming until he sees Frodo's hand missing the third finger, and later, back in The Shire, declares it all 'seems like a dream' – as does Merry.[44] Not so for Frodo: for him, returning feels 'more like falling asleep'.[45]

When listed in this way, the sheer number of dreams the Hobbits dream – or believe they dream – is remarkable. The dreams create a continuous sense of unreality, of insecurity – especially concerning Frodo, who becomes indistinct, even spectral. These dreams are wholly individual and unshared experiences, emphasizing the isolation of characters – again, particularly Frodo. Humans dream too: Aragorn dreams of Horses, Faramir's prophetic dream sends Boromir to Rivendell and he repeatedly dreams of Númenor being engulfed, and Éowyn hears dark voices in dreams. For the people of Minas Tirith, the coming of the king is like a communal reverie – to be cherished, if also to be doubted – but for the Host of the West, the march to the Black Gate is a 'hideous dream' and Mordor is a ghastly delirium. Collective nightmares such as this challenge the fabric of reality, while also suggesting the impossibility of representing what is real.[46]

Much of the plot of *The Lord of the Rings* turns on characters remembering and forgetting, which devolves the action to personal experience – in the words of the philosopher Mary Warnock, memory is 'essentially emotional in character ... Since it can be called knowledge, its object is what is true. But the truths are of the heart not of the head.'[47] In other words, memory is a combination of fact and fiction, something that Tolkien recognized in having dreams seep into experience, and in the insistent uncertainties and hesitations of characters. Storytelling can be a powerful structuring device of memory: a poetic pattern that works alongside – or against – objectively true facts in order to anchor and stabilize identity, but it is also elusive and constructed and unprovable, and, except in the mind, no longer exists. As Johanna Lindbladh describes the process, 'memory cannot be isolated to a fixed point in the past, but has to be considered both as a fragment of an actual perception in the past, and as the result of a narrative process ... a process which is intimately connected with the individual's attempt to create meaning in his or her life'.[48]

This is perhaps one reason Frodo cannot tell his story properly and why it falls to Sam to finish the book. Literary description cannot recover the old Frodo, cannot rediscover his sense of self or reconstruct his identity. He cannot write himself back into his old existence in The Shire, and it is what he writes, not what he experiences, that becomes the story. This is another reason why Frodo has to be removed from Middle-Earth to Valinor: he must find a wholly different – even alien – world, in which his true narrative makes sense and the chaos of his being can be resolved, and that is the Elvish world of Faërie where magic remains even as it has disappeared from Middle-Earth. So we do not and cannot know what really happens to Frodo: after three volumes and half a million words, the story fails – the tale is a testament to its own inability to be told. Neither is Frodo's experience of trauma representative of a generation, as was the 'shell shock' (now redefined as PTSD) of First and Second World War veterans. His ordeal is almost entirely private, shared only with Sméagol (who by the end of the book has been entirely consumed in the fires that forged the Ring), and, to a lesser extent, the other three Ringbearers: Isildur (already dead), and Bilbo and Sam (both of whom also leave for Valinor). Frodo's is not a shared grief, but wholly singular, intensely isolating, and hence unutterable (profoundly so – from the depths): it is, as I have suggested, horrific, in the sense that Eugene Thacker writes of horror: not the fear of death but the 'dread of life'.[49] There is no catharsis here, no release from pity and terror – two words that run through the book like Wagnerian refrains, that together harmonize strangely in the unresolved Tristan chord.

Literature is, arguably, the most effective way to deal with traumatic experiences. The social psychologist Michael Billig cites philosopher Henri Bergson in arguing that 'the conventional categories of psychologists are unsuitable vehicles for describing the fleeting, fragmentary and deeply personal qualities of inner experience: the skills of novelists or poets are better equipped for such a task'.[50] As noted, Tolkien's story is filled with other storytellers, each of whom is trying to make sense of their own predicament. Frodo is a traumatized writer trying to rebuild his identity, Sam is a conscious myth-maker, Gollum's narrative theory is so frenziedly incoherent and solipsistic it takes Gandalf to translate it into an intelligible form; Saruman, in contrast, is a supremely artful phantasmagoric propagandist, while Treebeard is a limited nostalgist (see Chapter Three). What is called the 'poetics' of memory recognizes that 'individual and collective memory is enigmatic, fragmented, intimately connected to our senses and feelings' and therefore challenges 'traditional definitions of knowledge and truth'.[51]

Yet the tale that is told is of two Hobbits taking the Ring into Mordor alone, led for parts of the way by a mad Tom o' Bedlam figure: it is itself mad. If Frodo's anti-quest had failed, it would have appeared to subsequent chroniclers to have been completely inexplicable – a chaotic episode in history that no narrative could relate in a structured way, a black hole into which the past collapses. Yet it succeeds, against all odds and chance, despite all power and sense. As an attempt to overthrow an imperial totalitarian power, this mission defies meaning – and this is the reason for all the uncertainty, ambiguity, and hesitancy in *The Lord of the Rings* – they are devices of irresolution, doubt, and happenstance that oppose the oppressive logic of Mordor tyranny. And in the final reckoning, evil is, daringly, also recruited to complete the anti-quest: as the theologian Catherine Madsen points out, 'The scene at the Crack of Doom is one of immense moral ambiguity: good does not triumph over evil, but depends on evil to deliver it' – such is the power of pity.[52]

It is on such fragile and insecure pivots that Tolkien turns his tale. And so although Tolkien sees history as a long defeat rather than as a triumphal progress, Aragorn does indeed re-unite the kingdoms, the Hobbits do rebuild The Shire, and the exiled Elves do finally return to Valinor. Indeed, the passing of the Elves brings some sort of closure. It is arguably their presence in the wrong world for thousands of years that leads to one appalling disaster after another: they have allowed not only the disruptions of magic and Faërie into the material world of Middle-Earth, but also their blood-feuds, clan vendettas, racial warfare, and thirst for vengeance. With Elvish mystery and magic come far-reaching turmoil and a threat to the fabric of reality: in other words, until the Elves go there is always the danger that the Middle-Earth will be fractured and reshaped again – as it was first by the warring Elves at the end of the First Age, and secondly by the Human yearning for Elvish immortality towards the end of the Second Age. They have to go.

Stuff and Nonsense

There is a lot of stuff in Middle-Earth – exquisite gems, magic rings, fabled swords, and ancestral talismans – as well as the more general matter of clothes and armour, megaliths and monuments, food and drink. A supernatural aura suffuses many of these things: stones (standing stones, Seeing Stones, ruins), trees (waking, walking, warring), and paths (traces and memories of ancient footsteps, sentient and animate, seeming to plot). Some things are more mundane (rations, gear), others immense, international enterprises – such as the outbreak of total war and the mass mobilization of armed forces across Middle-Earth, activating communities in different ways. In the context of all this stuff and all these happenings, many of the peoples of Middle-Earth are materialistic and often covetous in the extreme – the Elves fight for centuries over the Silmarils; Dwarves are proverbially avaricious and bring ruin on themselves through mining too greedily or contracting Dragon sickness in the face of opulent golden hoards; and even Hobbits can be jealous and acquisitive, apt to pilfer from family (the Sackville-Bagginses) and friends (Bilbo and the Arkenstone). This attention to solid objects, goods and chattels, treasure and riches gives Middle-Earth a palpable grain of reality, as well as imaginative affluence. Peter Jackson's *Rings* productions are physically tangible too, with real props to give them the heft of reality, and there was an immediate market for replica artefacts from Wētā Workshop.

Much of this stuff is simply weird. The bedrock of Tolkien's Middle-Earth writing consists of a very English eeriness – what today is often described as 'folk horror'. There are haunted ruins, stone circles, the undead; strange truths hidden in riddles and nursery rhymes; superstitions, herblore, and witchcraft; ancient inscriptions, cryptic manuscripts, and secret writings; amoral nature spirits and sentient landscapes; occult rites, drugs, and altered states; cryptobotany and cryptozoology; deluged territories that cry out for recognition; temporal distortions; and, nearly everywhere, the 'Uncanny'. These elements are often radically developed, especially in cinematic adaptations, which can draw on a rich inheritance of earlier stage, film, and television to incorporate elements from *Hamlet* to *Doctor Who*. Tolkien's works and their legacy are, then, both familiar and unfamiliar – and this is also one of their key themes: the search for home. Indeed, the very chapter titles of *The Hobbit* contrast the homely ('A Short Rest', 'A Warm Welcome', 'On the Doorstep') with the unhomely ('An Unexpected Party', 'Queer Lodgings', 'Not at Home'), often ironically and in puns. Bilbo, Frodo, and Sam often think of home; Aragorn has yet to find his; and Thorin's Company have lost theirs.

Recent philosophy, in part inspired by Tolkien's literary contemporary H.P. Lovecraft (see Chapter Four), has focused on such 'weird realism' and how thinking in particular about objects can challenge or displace Human assumptions of the world by focusing on the perspective of things – such as a ring – and it is striking how Tolkien's work exemplifies such approaches. As the philosopher Graham Harman argues, 'It remains unclear just what objects are, but it is already clear that they far exceed the human-centered'.[53] So can reality be perceived from the perspective of objects rather than the perspective of Humans; can objects be at the centre of things? What are objects, and what can they teach us about species? Harman claims that '"Object" can refer to trees, atoms, and songs, and also to armies, banks, sports franchises, and fictional characters.'[54] The world therefore teems with stuff – loads of stuff everywhere, all the time – which persistently exposes the limitations of Human comprehension and perspectives. This school of thought, known as 'Object-Oriented Ontology' or 'Speculative Realism', whispers of a world that is delineated and governed by things that we, as Humans, cannot understand – or even define – any more than we can know what it is like to be a bat: what is it like, now, to be a hammer, or the University of Oxford English Faculty?[55] For the radical philosopher Eugene Thacker, these 'blind spots' are an abiding concern because, for him, the world remains 'superlatively beyond human comprehension'.[56] Yet for Tolkien, buoyed by his Tridentine Catholic convictions and a sublime faith in eucatastrophe, this sense of being beyond comprehension is not a cause of 'cosmic pessimism' and a demonstration of the futility of thought, but the source of wonder.[57]

The One Ring clearly has agency and its own, alien sentience; it can also grow and shrink. Harman describes plutonium as a 'strange artificial material' that possesses 'an additional reality ... that is in no way exhausted by the unions and associations in which it currently happens to be entangled', a reality that is 'yet to be determined'.[58] The Ring too has additional realities 'yet to be determined': when it is heated it remains cold but reveals a verse in a strange language; when it is worn it confers invisibility, enabling a character to be both there and not there; it emanates an aura of madness that is irresistible to some yet disregarded by others.[59] Moreover, what becomes the key episode of *The Hobbit* – the finding of the Ring – is told and retold in *The Lord of the Rings* (being written and, importantly, rewritten by Tolkien) because that scene too contains 'additional realities' and latent significance. Similarly, the *palantír* possesses a similarly almost radioactive power that tempts Pippin into stealing it from Gandalf, leads to the confusion not only of Denethor but also of Sauron, and which can be weaponized by Aragorn in confronting Sauron.[60] The definition of objects – things – can, furthermore, be extended to include concepts, experiences, and activities, such as hospitality, sleep, songs, the dark, species, and, indeed, words: words are more stuff.

Tolkien treats words as historical artefacts, relics of past cultures, remnants of the past. Words can have a physical presence in inscriptions, such as those over the Gate of Moria or the 'many runes' engraved on the sword Andúril.[61] With swords such as Andúril, Glamdring, and Orcrist, Tolkien draws on the runic swords in Anglo-Saxon poems such as 'Solomon and Saturn', in which the Devil cuts curses into weapons, and in the *Völsunga Saga*, where Sigurd receives a sword from Brynhild decorated with runes of victory.[62] Other swords of the period were described as being named, inscribed with serpentine patterns, treated as dynastic heirlooms, or being plundered from barrows or other hoards – much as are the principal weapons in Middle-Earth. Similarly, the writing in the Book of Mazarbul, the account of the attempted resettlement of Moria, is also a corporeal remain. It is written in different hands and a mix of runes and script that indicates the various different scribes who contributed to it – Ori's hand, for example, is identified by his characteristic style of Elvish lettering – and the book is marked with other legible signs too, such as bloodstains and burns. Moreover, the text also includes such subtleties as the archaic spellings of *'yestre day'* and *'novembre'*.[63]

Tolkien's use of archaisms is particularly revealing as it introduces to Middle-Earth what could be called 'linguistic strata' – layers of the history of the English language. Tom Shippey, for example, notes that the vocabulary and grammar used by Elrond give his speech a formal and antiquated air, but other characters are more fluid and move from one linguistic register or style to another, reflected in the narrative.[64] When Aragorn addresses the Oathbreakers and unfurls his standard, Tolkien's account becomes more Biblical with the exclamation 'behold!', an indication that Aragorn is growing in confidence and exercising his regal authority.[65] Tolkien uses the same word when Denethor reveals he is armed, and again when the Witch-King faces Gandalf and bares his nothingness, and again when the Fell Beast dives towards the Pelennor Fields.[66] Similarly, the word 'lo!' is used in the account of Théoden's charge into battle, again of the Fell Beast, and also of Aragorn's discovery of a scion of the White Tree of Gondor.[67] In all but the last instance, these words are Tolkien's in narration, which then merges with Aragorn's own way of speaking as another assurance of his reclaimed majesty.

Fey is a key word for eeriness in Middle-Earth. The *Oxford English Dictionary* defines it in a number of ways: obsolete meanings include 'fated to die' or 'accursed', but in the nineteenth

century it acquired a more potent sense: 'possessing or displaying magical, fairylike, or unearthly qualities'.[68] In *The Lord of
the Rings*, the word glides through these different meanings,
a strange brew of being in possession of unearthly powers yet
doomed to die. Éowyn speaks of the change in Aragorn when
he takes the Paths of the Dead – 'Fey I thought him, and like
one whom the Dead call'; likewise, Éomer laments that Aragorn
has fallen into a 'fey mood'.[69] Pippin describes Denethor on the
pyre as 'fey and dangerous'; Théoden sounds the charge and
in doing so bursts his banner-bearer's horn – 'Fey he seemed';
when Éomer believes he sees Éowyn lying dead slain 'A fey
mood took him' and he is consumed with lethal rage.[70] Most
strikingly, Frodo is seized by a 'fey mood' when he thinks he has
escaped Shelob's Lair and is recklessly running towards a band
of Orcs.[71] He bears magic (the Ring) but is ill-fated – again via
the Ring, but also more immediately he is about to be poisoned
by Shelob and left for dead by Sam. So *fey* encapsulates the
tension in Middle-Earth between the charm of Faërie and the
destruction it brings.[72]

Much as he does in *The Hobbit*, Tolkien also introduces deliberately unfamiliar words, often variations of obscure terms whose
meaning can only be guessed at by context – although even
then they remain partially hidden. These words are effectively
'occulted'– the etymology of *occult* being 'hidden, concealed, surrounded by shadows'.[73] Some are simple enough: Tolkien may
have coined various of the compound words he uses, such as
herb-master and *oathkeeper*, and these are representative of his
style of writing that repeatedly compounds different elements.[74]
Other words, however, are far more challenging. What is a *hythe*,
a word used three times in the chapter 'Farewell to Lórien'?[75]
What does *thrawn* mean, or *freshet*, or *gangrel*?[76] These are
archaic or dialect or half-invented terms.[77] Tolkien redefines
the word *weapontake* from the original *wapentake* (derived from

Old Norse and meaning a subdivison of a shire) and literalizes it to mean the taking up of weapons.[78] In particular, there is a little constellation of words beginning *dwimmer-*: Saruman is 'dwimmer-crafty', 'Dwimordene' is the Rohanic name for Loth-lórien, and Éowyn scorns the Witch-King of Angmar with the curse, 'Begone, foul dwimmerlaik, lord of carrion'.[79] These words are not in the *OED* in these forms. The lexicographers Peter Gilliver, Jeremy Marshall, and Edmund Weiner point out that the latter is a variant of *demerlayk* (linked to *dweomercræft*) and means 'magic, practice of occult art, jugglery', but that Tolkien's spelling is unique. It is impossible to divine this precise meaning from the context, and one is only left with the vague impression that words beginning *dwimmer-* relate to some baleful and despised sorcery.[80] As these lexicographers point out, Tolkien was not the only writer who harvested the *OED* for words – possibly Thomas Hardy and E.R. Eddison did so, and certainly James Joyce and Tolkien's friends W.H. Auden and C.S. Lewis – but Tolkien, as ever, takes the practice further by reworking and redefining the words at climactic moments.[81] When Théoden falls and Éowyn faces the Lord of the Nazgûl, Tolkien's prose becomes giddying, as if unveiling a vast prophecy – there is a sense of years being swept away in face of confrontation between the Witch-King, under the delusion that he is protected from harm, and his nemesis Éowyn, and so she reaches beyond the English language and the understanding of the reader to name the unnameable Nazgûl and expose his terminal weakness.[82]

These words, then, are tiny caskets of meanings made up of antique shards from ancient speech, revealing the diverse and varied elements that come together in a language. Tolkien had his own invented languages too, of which there are many untranslated words and lines in the novel (see Chapter Three). Frodo listens to untranslated song in Lothlórien, and, attacking Shelob, Sam cries out in Elvish, 'a language which he did not know'; he then discovers that the Ring actually enables its wearer to understand foreign languages.[83] Orcish is not only untranslated but there is so much variation between the contrasting dialects of different tribes or races that they cannot understand one another and resort to the Common Speech.[84] Peter Jackson's films reflect this sense of linguistic dislocation and confusion by introducing untranslated passages of Elvish that were specially composed by linguist David Salo simply in order to appeal to 'the minority of viewers who know something about the languages'; Salo also wrote Elvish lyrics for the soundtrack.[85]

When it came to inventing names, however, rather than use his invented languages as a direct source, Tolkien would typically make up a name out of nothing and only then try to analyze what it might mean, deciphering it through his assorted vocabularies of the different Elvish and other Middle-Earth languages, theorizing how it could have come into existence and what further nuances it might contain. One of the footnotes to *The Return of the King*, for example, glosses the name 'Sharkey' as 'probably Orkish [*sic*] in origin: *sharkû*, "old man"', Saruman himself comments on the usage of the word in Isengard, and there is a further note in Appendix F.[86] Tolkien, like his character Michael Ramer in *The Notion Club Papers*, seems 'to hear fragments of language and names that are not of this country' – and not of this world.[87]

This attention to objects and words, at least potentially, destabilizes the Human-centred perception with new ways of seeing; this perspective is most apparent in Tolkien's repeated emphasis on non-Human species and is key to understanding Middle-Earth today. In the 'Quenta Silmarillion', the majority of the plot concerns the rebel Elves and their ferocious honour-shame loyalties. Humans feature in the 'Great Tales' ('Beren and Lúthien', 'The Children of Húrin', and 'The Fall of Gondolin'), but elsewhere they are incidental to much of the plot and action. In *The Hobbit*, Humans do not appear at all until the final third of the book, and even then, with the exception of the opaque character Bard, play a minor role. In *The Lord of the Rings*, while Humans are certainly present, the central character Aragorn is descended from Númenóreans and therefore of a mightier stamp than everyday folk, living to the grand old age of 210. Other Human characters are often sidelined and are generally unreliable – even untrustworthy – such as Barliman Butterbur and Boromir (also of Númenórean descent). In the second and third volumes Humans are primarily defined by their strategic military role in leading (or failing to lead) the armies of Rohan, Gondor, and other nations, and although the story ends at the beginning of the Fourth Age, which will apparently be the age of Humans, it holds little interest. Tolkien's Middle-Earth, then, is fundamentally not centred on Humans. What of Hobbits, though – can a case be made to suggest that they can stand in for Humans? Although they are furry-footed, hole-dwelling, and, again, long-lived, in the Prologue to *The Lord of the Rings* Tolkien wrote that Hobbits 'are relatives of ours' and later suggested that they are essentially Human.[88] Hobbits are certainly *humane* (the original, now obsolete, meaning of the word being 'civil, courteous, or obliging towards others'), but Tolkien does repeatedly stress their physical differences (from height to stamina); their cultural differences (there is little high culture at all in The Shire, and popular culture is focused on food, gardening, singing and dancing, and oral storytelling); and their social and political differences (no internecine conflict, technological progress, or colonial or commercial aspirations). They are also, of course, superseded by Humans and have, according to Tolkien, all-but disappeared from the world today.

In addition to the ever-present characterization of non-Human species, Tolkien also draws the reader into non-Human perspectives, into new sensitivities and insights. Gimli provides several moments of 'Dwarrowcentric' thinking in his love of rocks, caves, and the subterranean. Tolkien describes the Glittering Caves, but then invites the reader to perceive them with both Dwarvish and Elvish eyes – Dwarrowcentric and Alvocentric perceptions, respectively – the latter having no language for the husbandry and cultivation of stone.[89] Gimli's rock-solid sense of selfhood and being is then shattered in the remarkable passage when he enters the Paths of the Dead and the reader enters his mind: he becomes 'lithophobic', terrified of stones. The Dwarf should literally be in his element under the mountain, but his mind splinters 'and at once a blindness came upon him, even upon Gimli Glóin's son who had walked unafraid in many deep places of the world'.[90] This is Dwarrowcentric dread, a horror experienced by a Dwarvish – a non-Human – consciousness, that leaves Gimli 'crawling like a beast' before he escapes 'in some other world'.[91] Similarly, Treebeard gives an Entish account of Middle-Earth – essentially the view from the trees, where time and space function differently, where identity (the individual Ent) and the community (the forest) coexist – a sensibility that cries out for trees to be given rights.[92] As the 'geologian' (or Christian environmentalist philosopher) Thomas Berry puts it in *The Great Work*, 'every being has rights to be recognized and revered. Trees have tree rights, insects have insect rights, rivers have river rights, mountains have mountain rights.'[93]

Tolkien therefore helped to normalize non-anthropocentric (Human-centred) narratives, which had already been developing in works from Anna Sewell's *Black Beauty* (1877) to George Orwell's *Animal Farm*, and even in Franz Kafka's *Metamorphosis* (1915, translated 1933). *The Lord of the Rings*, however, is quite different: it is neither a children's book nor a political allegory nor a grotesque Expressionist novella, yet the text abounds in non-anthropocentric capacities of an arresting range and complexity, and through all the labyrinthine intricacies of his legendarium Tolkien musters 'Otherness' on every page. These alternative viewpoints do not simply cover the various species of Elves, Dwarves, Hobbits, and so forth, but include a pensive Fox and a soar of giant Eagles, yammering Spiders and evil things 'in spider-form', trees and running water, and objects such as the One Ring and the *palantíri*.[94] Most explicitly, Aragorn describes the Black Riders as living in a different world of sensory experience: 'They themselves do not see the world of light as we do, but our shapes cast shadows in their minds, which only the noon sun destroys'; however, 'in the dark they perceive many signs and forms that are hidden from us' and 'at all times they smell the blood of living things' and also feel their presence: 'Senses, too, there are other than sight or smell', and their Horses can see for them.[95]

When we read Tolkien, then, we should never forget that we are persistently being presented with non-Human perspectives, and this is in part where the popularity of the books lies (although few perhaps recognize it): in the ludic, the playfulness, and the permission to become Other.[96] For critics such as Patrick Curry, Middle-Earth becomes a 're-enchantment' of the world of Modernity: recovering values of community, the natural world, and the spiritual – 'that dimension of life which cannot be quantified, controlled or exploited', but which is nevertheless imperilled.[97] He suggests that *The Lord of the Rings* 'imaginatively re-connects its unprejudiced readers with a world that is still enchanted, that is, a world in which nature – including, but also greatly exceeding, humanity – is still mysterious, intelligent, inexhaustible, ensouled'.[98] This is a sentient world in which humanity and Human perspectives are only a part, and which also looks forward to focusing on the non-Human. In this, he takes inspiration from the philosopher Zygmunt Bauman, who argues that this post-modernity 'can be seen as restoring to the world what modernity, presumptuously, had taken away;

as a *re-enchantment* of artifice that has been dismantled; the modern conceit of meaning – the world that modernity tried hard to *disenchant*.[99] Such 'enchantment' is key to understanding Tolkien's fascination with fairy stories, and in combining multiple non-Human and object-centred viewpoints, his work can offer a refreshingly positive perspective on current crises.[100] In a comparable way, in his environmental study *The Song of the Earth* Jonathan Bate maintains that 'we cannot do without thought-experiments and language-experiments which imagine a return to nature, a reintegration of the human and the Other. The dream of deep ecology will never be realized upon the earth, but our survival as a species may be dependent on our capacity to dream it in the work of our imagination.'[101] Ultimately, this flexible thinking can offer a far more positive way of delineating the Human and engage with the urgent challenges that currently confront us.

This is why I return to the ambiguity I have been tracing through this book. The historian Michael Saler comments that *The Lord of the Rings*, 'while a lavish fantasy . . . is also rigorously rational' – but it is this I wish to challenge.[102] *The Lord of the Rings* may give the *impression* of being a rational fantasy, but it is in fact a contained chaos – which is why it is so beguiling, if only often implicitly so. C.S. Lewis was closer to the mark when he reviewed *The Lord of the Rings* as being at 'the cool middle point between illusion and disillusionment' – but even this is too lucid an assessment.[103] In a letter, Tolkien responded to people who asked him what *The Lord of the Rings* was all about: 'It is not "about" anything but itself.'[104] Counter-intuitively, then, Tolkien's theory of 'subcreation', in which a writer should strive to create a Secondary World, entailed *not* the crafting of a continuously coherent imagined world, but the creation of domains as messy, inconsistent, unsure, changeable, and bewildering as the real world – or worlds; as Coleridge said of Shakespeare,

Tolkien is *'myriad-minded'*.[105] Truth, experience, the creative imagination, and values in a Fallen world are fractured, fragmentary, and elusive.

Some critics have noticed this, if occasionally reluctantly. Verlyn Flieger suggests that Tolkien's tone is 'multi-valent', and that

> *The Lord of the Rings* subverts (we might even say deconstructs) itself by looking like a medieval, or pseudo-medieval, or imitatively medieval fantasy epic/romance/fairy tale, while in specific places in the narrative sounding like . . . a surprisingly contemporary twentieth-century novel . . . And here Tolkien is not only not medieval, he is emphatically modern, or – dare I say it? – post-modern.[106]

No, not postmodern – Tolkien's Tridentine Catholic faith saw to that, finding a way of presenting a relativistic and non-Human-centred world that was rooted in the hope of eucatastrophe in the face of inevitable failure. Robert Eaglestone too sees an interplay of different discourses in different speeches, and treats this as evidence of trauma – not being able to make sense of the characters' predicaments: 'it is precisely the "traumatized" mixture of these different discourses, from the level of vocabulary, style and syntax, and up to the level of plot and character, that gives the book not only its literary strength but also opens it to polyvalent ideological interpretations which have, in part, ensured its popularity' – although this assessment runs the risk of treating Middle-Earth as a symptom of psychological disturbance.[107] More constructively, the mediaevalist Michael Drout has identified the need to investigate the function of authorship and the author in *The Lord of the Rings* by allowing the text to speak for itself rather than be anchored to Tolkien's own commentaries in his letters and in subsequently published material, tempting as this may be.[108]

But perhaps the most considered and influential recent reading of Middle-Earth (both books and films) comes in the philosopher and literary critic Timothy Morton's polemic *Ecology Without Nature*, which touches on several of the points I have been considering. For Morton, The Shire 'depicts the world bubble as an organic village', and so Tolkien depicts the 'victory of the suburbanite, the "little person," embedded in a tamed yet natural-seeming environment . . . the wider world of global politics is blissfully unavailable to them'. As such, 'Tolkien's work embodies a key nationalist fantasy, a sense of "world" as real, tangible yet indeterminate'. Keying Tolkien into his critique of early-nineteenth-century Romantic definitions of environmentalism, Morton claims that, 'If ever there was evidence of the persistence of Romanticism, this is it.'

Morton then goes on to connect Tolkien's creation with the German philosopher Martin Heidegger's environmental philosophy, and the 'deep ontological sense in which things are "around" – they may come in handy, but whether they do or not, we have a care for them'. This sense of superfluous detail that allows for plausible chance and providence accurately captures the capaciousness of Middle-Earth. However, surprisingly, Morton then narrows Tolkien's breadth: 'wherever we go in this world, however strange or threatening our journey, it will always be familiar, insofar as it has all been planned in advance, mapped out, accounted for . . . just a gigantic version of the ready-made commodity'.[109] The past six chapters of this book have tried to counter this prevailing – if untenable – idea: that Middle-Earth is a holistic and uniform conception. It is anything but. And surely the book (if not the films) expose the failure of The Shire: The Shire itself is living in a 'feigned' history, a story that the Hobbit community tells about itself, yet which has only the barest reality.[110] 'The Scouring of The Shire' episode coerces the Hobbits of The Shire into a painful and alarming international history, fulfilling the Elf Gildor's prediction that the Hobbits cannot fence out the world forever, decentring them from their homeland: 'it is not your own Shire ... Others dwelt here before hobbits were; and others will dwell here again when hobbits are no more.'[111] Frodo feels only too keenly that his homecoming is like falling asleep – at least until the Hobbits encounter Sharkey's ruffians – but Jackson's *Rings* cuts 'The Scouring of The Shire' so that the return to The Shire is instead like *waking* from a dream, as Sam, for example, feels. Jackson's Shire has not changed – it is impervious to the outside world, and Hobbiton is completely oblivious of the War of the Ring. This means that the characters on their respective 'journeys' have ultimately changed little and at the end the film seeks a closure its audience cannot understand – the voyage to Valinor. The final scenes are therefore a sidestep into an opaque mystery, where the audience cry because the three remaining Hobbits cry, and because the epic cinematic experience is over.

Adam Roberts, one of the most intelligent and insightful commentators on Tolkien's work, has also responded to Morton's argument, noticing that 'something is missing from this analysis', which is 'precisely the unexpected thing (the unexpected party) that Morton claims the novel erases'. This, for Roberts, is the figure of Tom Bombadil: 'He does not represent, but literally embodies, the irreducibility of "nature" as something other than the "human" world' because

> one of the things that is so wonderful about Tom Bombadil is precisely the way he doesn't fit the well-tooled story model, the 'road' that the film-makers trod. It is precisely his gnarly peculiarity, his oddity, his naffness (blue coat, yellow boots! Endless fol-de-rol singing!). His non-identity. He represents ... a sort of narrative hesitation – that's why Jackson and his screenwriters ditched him for their film version.[112]

Morton presents Tolkien as a seamless and consistent writer when patently he is not, and Bombadil is the quintessential figure of disruption. What is thrilling about Tolkien's writing is the precariousness of it all – something that was very difficult to translate into Peter Jackson's films. In any case, neither does Tolkien include Romantic egotism or individualism except as pejoratively – his characters are much more collaborative and cooperative.

But Tolkien's writing does possess an important quality associated with Romantic poetry, something that John Keats recognized in Shakespeare. He called it '*Negative Capability*', when one is 'capable of being in uncertainties, Mysteries, doubts, without any irritable reaching after fact and reason'.[113] This for me, in the closing pages of this book, perfectly sums up Tolkien's achievement – his capacity for the undecided, the unsure, and the unknowable. Similarly, Jackson's films are a multi-valent 'stereophony of echoes, citations, references', and if they do, to a degree, iron out 'negative capability' to unify Middle-Earth into a coherent vision, the gaps do remain. Furthermore, the experience of reading the book *after* having seen the films is likely to be disorientating, alien, and even 'uncanny'. And this is one reason for writing this book – to make those inconsistencies sing, and to tease out the fault lines in later versions . . .[114]

A House of Healing

Images of contagion and contamination, pollution and poison seep through Tolkien's texts in the depravity of Morgoth and Sauron, the venomous blandishments of Saruman, and the conflicts aroused by the One Ring. Mordor is like a sump of these cognates, and more: it is tainted, dirty, septic, noxious, and fouled – a sick and diseased land – and its infections spread through Middle-Earth through infestations of Orcs. This imagery may well have been influenced by Tolkien's experience of the Spanish 'Flu pandemic (1918–20) as he does describe deliberate pestilences sent from Angband in the First Age, and the 'Great Plague' sent from Mordor in the Second Age, the latter being biological warfare waged by Sauron that depopulated parts of Middle-Earth. Although viral spread was a staple image of pandemic for the period surrounding the Great War (as described at the time by Sabine Baring-Gould, and later by John Carey), it is also mixed with Tolkien's more personal experience of gas attacks on the frontline as well as the industrial effluence and smog of early twentieth-century Birmingham.[115]

Early theories of the spread of epidemics and pandemics included the theory that the words uttered by an infected person would, literally, communicate the disease to another – much as Saruman's mellifluous voice spreads his deceits and duplicity. Folkloric fears of the 'Evil Eye' also became part of medical practice. The fourteenth-century medical historian Gabriele de' Mussis, who chronicled the Black Death, believed that 'one infected man could carry the poison to others, and infect people and places . . . *by look alone*' – hence, doctors would blindfold their patients so as not to be seen and fall victim themselves.[116] This adds a sinister aspect to the Eye of Sauron – it is not merely a way of placing Middle-Earth under incessant surveillance, shadowing its peoples, it not only represents the objectification of individuals on a massive scale: it is also a vector of discord and malice, able to spread disease.

In addition, I have emphasized that much of *The Lord of the Rings* was written during the Second World War – a time of rationing, blackouts, severe restrictions on travel and personal liberties, if not lockdown and quarantine. Here, and in Tolkien's other writings, there are cities under siege, curfews (including one imposed on The Shire), mass surveillance, and the ever-present threat of incarceration, from the ruins of Moria to the bowers of Lothlórien, the depths of Helm's Deep to the charnel horror of Shelob's Lair, the deathly Tower of Cirith Ungol even to the Lockholes in The Shire, converted from storage tunnels into prison cells. Saruman is imprisoned in Orthanc and, we later learn, Thráin in the dungeons of Dol Guldur. In the First Age, Morgoth's fortress of Angband (literally, the 'iron prison') is in part a prison complex of dungeons and torture chambers, surrounded by vast walls and the cliffs of Thangorodrim from which one prisoner, Maedhros, is suspended, and to which another, Húrin, is bound. Following the breaking of the world at the end of the First Age, the Second Age saw the fall of Númenor and the everlasting imprisonment of Ar-Pharazôn 'The Golden' and his host in the Caves of the Forgotten. Meanwhile, there are several incarcerations and self-incarcerations in *The Hobbit*: in the Trollshaws, in Goblin Town, in the webs of the Mirkwood Spiders, in the dungeons of the Halls of the Elvenking, in barrels, and in the Lonely Mountain. We are now only too familiar with being locked up, our freedoms restricted. Such internments are also featured, if, like the books, *avant la lettre*, in the imagery of Jackson's *Rings* and *Hobbits*, which contrast the hyper-dynamic battle panoramas with claustrophobic scenes between a limited number of characters, such as the four Hobbits cowering under the roots of a tree in *The Fellowship of the Ring*, Azog caught beneath the ice, Frodo cocooned in Shelob's webs, and the centre-piece of *The Hobbit*, 'Riddles in the Dark'. Tolkien himself said in his 1968 interview with the BBC, 'Well, it is meant to be escapist, because I use escapism in its proper sense, as a man getting out of prison.'[117]

Frodo's alienation at the end of *The Lord of the Rings* amounts to a perpetual quarantine from his people; moreover, his long-term trauma, which regularly manifests itself in physical symptoms of illness, parallels the spectrum of lingering post-viral fatigue conditions today, including those variously known as 'post-Covid syndrome', 'chronic Covid-19', and 'Long Covid'.[118] Many of the issues raised in this concluding chapter – and in this book more generally – suggest, then, how Tolkien's Middle-Earth might help us think through the pandemic to life in a post-Covid world: living with failure, loneliness, loss, alienation, anxiety, fear, grief, and the inescapability of death; the values of pity and forgiveness, the consolations and anguish of memory; most overwhelmingly, the ongoing struggle to deal with radical uncertainty.[119] Human society has succumbed to an invisible non-Human agency that has shut down borders and industry, incarcerated communities, destroyed international travel, and ignited conspiracy theories. Medical science has been conscripted as an agent of state control, exposing the raw politics of modern health care through what are 'acceptable' death tolls. Repeated lockdowns have reimagined city centres as eerie, phantasmagoric, and above all empty spaces – ruins in all but name. Movement restrictions, even at local levels, even to visit the dead and dying, have confined individuals within their homes and their thoughts, isolated and divided families, and triggered claustrophia, agoraphobia, and virophobia. How do we write the story of the pandemic – how do we even remember it? Can we take control of the stories told of infection and of the viral folklore to create a master narrative, or are we faced with a billion personal and irreconcilable histories? Those with job security, no children, and living in the countryside usually had a much 'better' pandemic than those interned in urban apartments, home-schooling children, and in fear of losing their livelihoods.

Ultimately in Middle-Earth, as I have argued, the question is: who controls the story of the Ring? Like Morgoth, Sauron tries to command the master narrative, but it is severed from his hand and falls into oblivion, before the thread is confusedly taken up by Gollum, Bilbo, Frodo, and Sam (and briefly, too, by

Déagol and Isildur) – each of whom creates their own story, each of which involves an ever-widening and problematic circle of friends and enemies, and each of which is riven with ambiguities and ironies. Both Jackson's *Rings* and *Hobbits* and also the later edition of the BBC radio adaptation make a point of dramatizing the writing of the script and the self-dramatization of the characters, underlining the fiction. So if there are too many tales here, then that is the point: to learn to live with stories that clash and collide, characters with non-Human consciousness, objects that brim with significance, and words that confound meaning precisely because they feed the imagination. Uncertainty, contradiction, and failure are more revitalizing and compelling in the arts than are dogmatism, inflexibility, and vainglory.

Rereading the texts and rewatching the films after Covid inevitably and, perhaps, indelibly changes their meaning: whatever the creators may have intended, they now become meditations on the nature of freedom, reminders of individual autonomy, advocates of alternative understandings, and philosophies of communal support. As such, they will last in our collective, multi-media culture for at least another generation. The Amazon Prime Video TV *The Rings of Power* series is one of the first major post-Covid (or rather, late-Covid) productions; whether or not it will embrace this challenge will be fascinating to discover. Despite some ridiculous outpouring online of uninformed opinion based on only the slimmest of evidence, we should learn to treat adaptations of Tolkien in the same way that we would the production of, say, a Shakespeare play or a Dracula movie: all of these adaptations – like Tolkien's own rewritings – are simply versions.

According to John Howe, concept artist on *The Rings of Power*, the series brings new experiences such as sea-faring Elves as well as black Hobbits, while offering 'self-sacrifice and situations in which we are smaller than [the threats] we face'.[120]

But in fact, it offers far, far more. According to *Empire* magazine, '*The Lord of the Rings: The Rings of Power* stakes a good claim to being the biggest, most anticipated TV show of all time.'[121] It has been suggested that the rights and production costs have been $250 million and $462 million ('minus a large tax rebate'), respectively.[122] All five TV seasons are already mapped out and effectively comprise a fifty-hour movie. The show's online trailer broke records (as had that for Jackson's *Fellowship of the Ring*) with 257 million views. Writers J.D. Payne and Patrick McKay have claimed that, with the series, they wanted to distance themselves from *Rings* and *Hobbits* – and instead focus on the Second Age of Middle-Earth to explore 'how Sauron rose, how the mythical island of Númenor fell – and the forging of 19 rings that would ultimately shape Middle-earth's destiny'.[123] In this they are taking inspiration from Tolkien's long and wistful letter to Milton Waldman, in which he imagined that he would 'draw some of the great tales in fullness, and leave many only placed in the scheme, and sketched' and so 'leave scope for other minds and hands, wielding paint and music and drama' – or film, or television . . .[124]

Key characters are the younger Galadriel (played by Morfydd Clark), a fresh-faced Elrond (Robert Aramayo), and Gil-Galad (Benjamin Walker – Gil-Galad has only a second or two of screen-time in Jackson's *Rings*). However, it is the casting of British comedian Lenny Henry as the Harfoot Hobbit, Sadoc Burrows, that has created the most striking image for the series. The nomadic Harfoots are (rightly) darker-skinned Hobbits who combine the fond affection of Jackson's portrayal with a far wider sense of Hobbit diversity and identity which, two decades on from *Rings*, seems entirely appropriate to the twenty-first century. For Lenny Henry himself, 'Finally, in this show, kids are going to see people of colour taking up space in the centre of a fantasy series.'[125]

There are some interesting departures from *Rings* and *Hobbits*, such as the action being much more one-on-one than 10,000-on-10,000, but on the other hand, the attention to detail of Moria in its heyday is plumb within Jackson's fully realized Middle-Earth: 'How could they build a society beneath the earth?' asks producer Ron Ames. 'How would you grow their food? How would you exchange air? How would you channel water and where would light trickle in?'[126] Interestingly, director J.A. Bayona, responsible for the first two episodes, also seems to have returned to the physical sets of *Rings* rather than the green screens of *Hobbits* (despite the prevalence of CGI), while also denying being overly influenced by the sex and violence of HBO's *Game of Thrones* series. Indeed, Bayona's contention is nothing less than his declaration that '*The Rings of Power* is not television ... It's a new form we're creating here.'[127] It may well be so. And if it really does bomb – which seems to me to be highly unlikely – it will nevertheless renew interest in the earlier movie versions, and also, of course, in Tolkien's book.

•   ◆   •

Tolkien's crisscrossing, interlaced, and knotted strands of history, folklore, and his legendarium are not only subtle and fluid, but frequently clamorous and confusing, insistently and often aggressively disorientating the reader. This should at least encourage vigilant reading. The best radio and film adaptations also achieve this inner turmoil, this necessary inconsistency, if in different ways. But can this high drama of creativity provide any comfort as we sink further into the 'Anthropocene', the mess we have created of catastrophic Human intervention in the environment that has precipitated climate change and accelerated and globalized the Covid-19 pandemic? Middle-Earth is a mysterious and perilous realm, often inimical to sentient life, and with secrets deeper than the Dwarves delved in

Moria. The Old Forest is a telling example of antagonistic ecology – aggressive to the point that the Hobbits burnt down many of its trees, and still bearing unfathomable arboreal grudges. It is not a sentimentalized arcadia for pastoral ecologists: it is a hallucinatory, weird, and lethal landscape – like Harman's thought experiment with plutonium, the Old Forest has an 'additional reality' to that perceived by the Hobbits, an 'occulted world' that while making 'its presence known to us . . . in doing so reveals the unknown'.[128] And what is revealed is not some 'inner truth', but 'the "hiddenness" of the world' – at its worst, 'a blank, anonymous world that is indifferent to human knowledge, much less to our all-too-human wants and desires'.[129]

There is, however, a more positive possibility. If we accept that the world is not centred on Human wants and desires, we can still act as shepherds to its environment, and carers for the health and wellbeing of living things, and bequeath this to future generations through our cultural imagination: through literature and the moving image. For many, the lasting memory of lockdown and pandemic will be the unfamiliar, even eerie, contours that daily life took on: everyday objects and activities became unhomely and uncanny, giving a sobering appreciation of what had been lost, from birthday parties to shows and festivals, but in consequence encouraging us to value them more, through memory, and through hope. In other words, like the Old Forest, our 'uncanny' world can still be navigated through 'song'. The creative imagination, challenged by the most real of threats, remains our best – and perhaps ultimately our only – way through the woods, through current obscurity, and *The Lord of the Rings* both exemplifies and advocates such inspired artistry. We should never return to sleepwalking through our lives, but question and celebrate the everyday to live in an enhanced – if fearful – state of creative and imaginative awareness, and yearn, as Tolkien himself plaintively put it, for a 'kinder world'.[130]

So, to return to the Ring in books and films. Be inventive: read and reread favourite passages, skip bits: to quote the French critic Roland Barthes, 'it is the very rhythm of what is read and what is not read that creates the pleasure of the great narratives: has anyone ever read Proust, Balzac, *War and Peace*, word for word? (Proust's good fortune: from one reading to the next, we never skip the same passages.)'![131] The same could be said of *The Lord of the Rings* – few readers read every line of Elvish, or even every poem – despite Tolkien's poetry being probably the most widely published of the twentieth century. Make the text different every time – much as Tolkien himself wrote it, and Sir Peter Jackson edited it.[132] The texts, because of their radical ambivalence, will in any case be experienced differently every time, stimulating different responses. They have 'infinite variety', and can enable us, in the words of William Blake,

> To see a World in a Grain of Sand
> And a Heaven in a Wild Flower
> Hold Infinity in the palm of your hand
> And Eternity in an hour.[133]

But after so much doubt and unease, whatever their dreams and desires, this book should end with a smile. The 'Ring Verse', part of which is inscribed on the One Ring and which is heralded with such dread, was composed while J.R.R. Tolkien lay in the bath in his house at 20 Northmoor Road, Oxford: a true 'Eureka' moment: 'I still remember kicking the sponge out of the bath when I got to the last line, thinking, "That will do it all right," and jumped out.'[134]

Afterword: Power

O'er my thoughts
There hung a darkness, call it solitude.
William Wordsworth,
The Prelude (1850)

Episode one of the first season of *The Rings of Power* (*Power*) was streamed on Amazon Prime Video on 2 September 2022 in the teeth of a social media storm. A handful of stills, a few suggestive minutes of trailers, and a concatenation of interviews and rumour created an atmosphere equal parts hopeful expectation and committed cynical rejection. The eight weekly episodes were certainly ambitious, audacious, and often arresting; opinion was divided, but the critical reception eventually proved overwhelmingly positive.[1]

Visually, the episodes are spectacular: Valinor is presented as a set-piece lit by the two radiant trees Telperion and Laurelin; Khazad-Dûm is seen in all its extravagant glory and industry at the height of its dominion – and in striking contrast to the cyclopean ruin of Moria it has become in *Rings*; Númenor is a glittering island civilization garlanded with stupendous memorials to past triumphs – a land apart. Many of these sets are physically built environments enhanced with abundant material detail and enriched with CGI to intensify real-earth locations to magnificent Middle-Earth proportions. This extraordinary richness is evident, for example, in the Elvish kingdom of Lindon in which every leaf was hand-painted, or in the unique calligraphy developed for the Adûnaic inscriptions and graffiti glimpsed in Númenor. Further, intangible elements added to the realism – such as seafood being grilled during shooting for the harbour scenes to create the aromas of a coastal port – and the actors spent weeks developing their characters and relationships and honing their skills of fighting, riding, and swimming, as well as learning how to survive being hurled against walls.

This emphasis on realism extends to the 4K (Ultra-High Definition) cinematography, which unflinchingly shows every detail of characters' faces in unforgiving close-up. As with the innovative use of HFR film stock for *Hobbits*, this is a fantasy world that breaks with the dreamy cinematic convention of 24fps to bring a startling level of palpable, corporeal reality to Middle-Earth – and furthermore the lighting of scenes is often dazzlingly luminous, bringing even greater clarity in clear contrast to the shadowy, often ethereal atmospheres of Peter Jackson's *Rings*. As if reflecting on this new lucidity, Galadriel (Morfydd Clark) observes early in the first episode, 'we thought our light would never dim'; it will take millennia for this divine light to darken into the sombre hues of the Third Age.[2]

Power is effectively an adaptation of a non-existent work – or rather a vast expansion and reworking of two skeleton texts outlining Númenórean history and the chronology of the Second Age that appear in Appendices A and B of *The Lord of the Rings*, accompanied by a few scattered comments elsewhere, such as on the history of Khazad-Dûm. This material – barely a dozen pages – is in any case radically reworked, most noticeably in timelines. The key events of the Second Age are telescoped so that the rise of Sauron, the arrival of the Istari, the founding of Mordor, the forging of the Rings, the fall of Númenor, and the Battle of the Last Alliance all occur within a few years of each other, rather than across centuries. Added to this are major events from the Third Age, such as the discovery of *mithril*, the appearance of the Balrog of Moria, and the migrations of the Periannath (being the Harfoots, a nomadic race of Hobbits). And much new and pivotal material is added: the trials of Galadriel and new character Halbrand (Charlie Vickers); the plight and politics of the Southlanders in escaping or joining with the Orcs; the tensions between the Elves and the Southlanders, the Dwarves, and the Númenóreans; and the challenges faced by the itinerant Harfoots and the troubles brought on them by The Stranger (Daniel Weyman).

Despite radically reshaping the meagre and fragmentary sources there are nevertheless details that anchor *Power* in Tolkien's work. The very first episode is titled 'A Shadow of the Past', alluding to chapter two of *The Lord of the Rings* – 'The Shadow of the Past'. The sacred Harfoot book of migrations may remind viewers of the many physical texts that are preserved in Middle-Earth, notably the Book of Mazarbul in Moria, while the lettering of the Harfoot codex also bears distinct similarities to Tolkien's Goblin alphabet derived from Finno-Uggric pictographs in his *Father Christmas Letters* – much like the itinerant Humans bearing antlers who briefly and inexplicably appear in the first episode. The Númenórean Queen Regent Míriel (Cynthia Addai-Robinson) dreams of 'The Great Wave' that engulfs her island, a foreshadowing of doom – a recurrent dream of Tolkien himself that he bequeathed to Faramir as a race memory of the downfall of his ancestors, Faramir being peculiarly receptive to visions from beyond the wall of sleep. Adar's name means 'father' not only in Elvish, but is a word Tolkien had borrowed from the Gothic: it begins The Lord's Prayer, 'Atta unsar tu in himinam'.[3] The Harfoot leader Sadoc Burrows (Lenny Henry) sends The Stranger to the forest of Greenwood the Great, which in the Prologue to *The Lord of the Rings* is revealed to be the original name for Mirkwood and an ancient dwelling place of the Periannath before they crossed the Misty Mountains and moved west.[4] Most perturbingly, Galadriel's character in *Power* is predicated on a statement she makes in book about Sauron, 'I perceive the Dark Lord and know his mind' – from this came the idea that she had once had a close personal relationship with him; it is, then, with eerie deliberation that Halbrand's first words to Galadriel – 'the tides of fate are flowing' – are repeated by Galadriel to Frodo after he has offered her the Ring.[5]

There are also verbal echoes in lines delivered by the characters of *Power*. The atmosphere of the Harfoot feast and Sadoc's speech beginning 'Most agreeable, honorable Harfoots' is reminiscent of Bilbo's birthday party and his opening words '*My dear People*'.[6] Also among the Harfoots, Poppy Proudfellow (Megan Richards) sings the walking song 'This Wandering Day', which contains the line, 'That not all who wonder or wander are lost' – manifestly alluding to Gandalf's verse in his letter introducing Strider to the Hobbits: '*Not all those who wander are lost*'.[7] Celebrimbor (Charles Edwards) comments that Dwarves sculpt the rock of the mountains, echoing Gimli's rocklore in *The Two Towers* that the Caverns of Helm's Deep are 'glades of flowering stone'.[8] Most strikingly, when the Three Hunters (Aragorn, Gimli, Legolas) are pursuing the Uruk-Hai and their captives Merry and Pippin, Aragorn finds the brooch from Pippin's Elven cloak left as a clue, remarking 'Not idly do the leaves of Lórien fall.'[9] In *Power*, it is Nimloth the Fair, the White Tree of Númenor, that literally sheds its leaves in a sinister omen of impending disaster. Queen Míriel comments that 'the faithful believe that when the petals of White Tree fall 'tis no idle thing, but the very tears of the Valar themselves' – prefiguring the language of Aragorn centuries later and weaving the White Tree of Gondor, a seedling of Nimloth, into the image.[10] Perhaps the most knowing acknowledgement of Tolkien, however, is the opening title sequence of each episode, which portrays Tolkien's musical creation myth described in the 'Ainulindalë', the Music of the Ainur. This is accomplished by cymatics, a technique that visualizes noise: a metal 'Chladni' plate is strewn with sand and vibrated with sounds, thereby causing the particles to form patterns.

Power therefore hints at Tolkien's work through subtle use of language and imagery, creating almost subliminal frames of reference. Yet it is the films, primarily Jackson's *Rings* and *Hobbits*, that bear the closest kinship to *Power*. The first few minutes of Jackson's *Fellowship* (like Bakshi's adaptation) outlines the plot of *Power*, focusing on Galadriel and the Rings, the Battle of the Last Alliance, and the monstrous figure of Sauron – who appears at the climax of the battle wearing a distinctive helmet modelled on a horse's skull and surmounted by six spikes to represent the 'cruel pinnacles and iron crown of the topmost tower of Barad-dûr'.[11] This six-horned helmet is depicted several times in *Power*, either directly as Sauron's armoured headgear, or indirectly as a shadow or reflection, and the skull masks of the Orcs mirror this huge horse-skull helm. Another Jackson innovation is that the Elves at the Battle of the Last Alliance fight with two-handed swords, which are favoured by Galadriel's élite commando unit in *Power* – and even the Elf Gil-Galad (Benjamin Walker), who only appears for a few seconds in the film but is a major character in *Power*, looks strikingly similar.[12] The title lettering for the opening episode of *Power* evokes the patina of the golden script of *Rings* and *Hobbits* before becoming more polished in later episodes, and there are similar panning shots over stylized hand-drawn maps based on Christopher Tolkien's cartography for the book. Immediately noticeable too is the musical score: Howard Shore is credited with the main title, but this is lavishly extended by composer Bear McCreary into a series of recognizable leitmotifs for different characters, peoples, and locations, making it continuous with Shore's approach yet thematically wholly distinct. McCreary deliberately selected styles and instrumentation to contrast the soundtrack of *Power* with that of *Rings*, as the series depicts the realms and civilizations of an earlier, lost age – hence, the music of Númenor mixes Near and Middle-Eastern instruments with Arthurian warhorns.[13]

Later scenes often quote explicitly from Jackson's films. The magical duel between The Stranger and the Mystic The Dweller (Bridie Sisson) recalls that of Gandalf and Saruman, and possesses the same gritty physicality as Jackson's scene. The flowers cast before the Númenórean warriors as they march to their ships repeats a tradition introduced by Jackson in which the citizens of Gondor cast flowers before Faramir's doomed horsemen as they leave Minas Tirith – the ritual has no direct source in Tolkien's work. The hurtling charge of the Númenórean horse warriors, meanwhile – led by Galadriel in a furious bloodlust – is a breathtaking sequence that restages the iconic ride of the Rohirrim in Jackson's *Two Towers*. However, this time there is no snatching of victory from certain defeat: in the grim world of *Power* the Númenóreans arrive just too late and the literal fall-out from their clash with Adar's forces is catastrophic rather than eucatastrophic, devastating their expeditionary force and blinding their queen. Characters also echo those in *Rings*. Halbrand's (apparent) reluctance to accept his destiny as King of the Southlanders clearly recalls Aragorn's doubts in claiming the throne of Gondor – which is a major turning point in Jackson's third film.[14] In *Power*, it is Galadriel who – ironically – exhorts Halbrand to accept his destiny and lead his people. Moreover, Charlie Vickers, who plays the renegade Halbrand, shares the same mix of rugged charisma and collected vulnerability of Viggo Mortensen, and, again like Mortensen, applied himself to the physical demands of his role, training daily with Morfydd Clark for the raft and underwater scenes, for instance, that took two months to film.

More generally, the Balrog of Khazad-Dûm is directly inspired by Jackson's awe-inspiring demon, and the Orcs too are indebted to *Rings* and *Hobbits*, and although their skin is generally paler they have the same hideous variety in their bodily disfigurements and arms and armour. The Dwarves of Khazad-Dûm are straightaway recognizable from *Hobbits* – not only in their prosthetic noses, magnificent and idiosyncratic beards, robust sense of humour and expression, cantankerous belligerence, and formidable physical prowess, but also in their Scottish accents and moments of comic relief – all features exemplified by Billy Connolly's portrayal of Dain in Jackson's *Five Armies*. But the Dwarves of *Power* are also extensively developed beyond Jackson as a thriving established civilization, rather than as the remnants of a dispossessed people. Disa (Sophia Nomvete), wife of Prince Durin (Owain Arthur), is the first female Dwarf in Middle-Earth to appear onscreen, and is lightly bearded with sideburns and gentle facial fuzz. She is, moreover, a 'resonator' – able to sing to stone in a spiritual form of dowsing or geological echolocation that can both detect seams of precious metals as well as freeing miners lost under rockfalls.[15] More minor physical details such as the Harfoot's feet, which are large, bony, and sparsely-haired are also based on Jackson's Hobbits as inspired by Bakshi's animation, rather than being thickly-furred as described by Tolkien. Tolkien specifically defined the Harfoots as a racial strain of brown-skinned Hobbits – small, beardless, nimble, and favouring 'highlands and hillsides'; however, casting in *Power* is race-blind so Sir Lenny Henry (Sadoc Burrows) and Markella Kavenagh (Nori Brandyfoot) are both Harfoots.[16] Despite some reactionary social media postings, this is a non-issue today, and the racial identity of the Harfoots – like the Scoto-Dwarves – is instead based in language, society, customs, and culture, consistent with Tolkien's own definitions of race.[17] Linguistically, the Harfoots speak with an Irish lilt and Sadoc even uses the Anglo-Irish dialect word *eejit* or 'idiot', while Poppy's song 'This Wandering Day' has a strong flavour of Irish folksong.[18] Furthermore, the cultural legacy of the Harfoots to Third-Age Hobbits is revealed through the prevalent imagery of circles in their society – the wheels of their wagons and the annual cycle of their migration, circular symbols that are eventually translated into the round doors and windows of the Hobbit holes of The Shire.

Alongside these visual references, there are several direct and indirect verbal quotations in *Power* from the book and the films. Jackson's *Fellowship* memorably opens with Galadriel murmuring that, 'The world is changed: I feel it in the water, I feel it in the earth, I smell it in the air'. The lines are taken from the end of the book – they are almost word-for-word Treebeard's final farewell to Galadriel and Celeborn as they leave Isengard – whereas her later line 'History became legend . . . legend became myth' is, in contrast, adapted from Gandalf's account of the One Ring at the fireside of Bag End in only the second chapter of the book: 'And there in the dark pools amid the Gladden Fields . . . the Ring passed out of knowledge and legend'.[19] Although *Power* opens in hope and light, it rapidly descends into centuries of conflict and war and revenge – again narrated by Galadriel; and in the bitter passage of time and the fruitless pursuit of Sauron 'year gave way to year' – calling to mind the desolate pessimism that begins *Rings*.[20]

More positive is Nori Brandyfoot's fascination with The Stranger – 'I was supposed to find him' – which suggests other forces are stirring:

> He could have landed anywhere and he landed here. I know it sounds strange, but somehow I just know it's important. It's like there's a reason this happened, like I was supposed to find him: me.[21]

This too is a half-quote, adapted from Gandalf pondering how the Ring came to Hobbiton. Again by the fireside in Bag End, in the novel Gandalf says to Frodo,

> Bilbo was *meant* to find the Ring, and *not* by its maker. In which case you also were *meant* to have it. And that may be an encouraging thought.[22]

In Jackson's hands, however, Gandalf utters these words in consolation to Frodo under more dramatic and hazardous conditions: journeying in the dark through Moria. In all three cases, then, there is a sense of providence or fate or doom alighting upon the Hobbit characters. Moreover, in Jackson's scene, Gandalf, having made his gnomic observation, then decides which of three tunnels to take through the Mines:

> Ah! It's that way ... the air doesn't smell so foul down here. If in doubt, Meriadoc, always follow your nose! (laughs)[23]

Tolkien's Gandalf lacks this levity: 'I do not like the feel of the middle way; and I do not like the smell of the left-hand way: there is foul air down there ... I shall take the right-hand passage.'[24] Jackson's pithy scene has replaced Tolkien's more prolix

Gandalf in the popular mind, and the same lines provide the watershed moment at the end of the final episode of the first season of *Power*. The Stranger is unsure which direction to take, but he resolves the dilemma with a smile:

> There's a sweet smell on the air this way. When in doubt, Elanor Brandyfoot, always follow your nose.[25]

The Stranger therefore anticipates the language that Gandalf has already used on the big screen – even to the extent of using Nori's full name – in a scene extensively reworked by Jackson and chronologically occurring thousands of years in the future.

Yet despite their evident reverence for Tolkien and Jackson, showrunners Patrick McKay and J.D. Payne are determined to make their own mark on Middle-Earth. Although they inhabit paradise, from the outset the Elves are violent and unruly – they do not have the gracious serenity, wisdom, and gravitas of Third-Age Elves, but, in the words of Morfydd Clark, are 'messy'.[26] Many wear their hair close-cropped in military style, but even as warriors these Elves are fallible and mutinous, bickering with each other and questioning orders. There is dissension throughout Elf society, which is not only chauvinistic in excluding the mixed-species Half-Elf Elrond (Robert Aramayo) from assemblies, but is also cynically hypocritical in nevertheless exploiting him as a political pawn and a spy. There are tensions between the Human Southlanders and the Elvish watch garrisoned near their settlements – the Elves are considered supercilious colonialists patronizing the Southlanders, and the Southlanders routinely insult the Elves as 'knife-ears' and 'pointies'.[27] Neither are the Dwarves Elf-friends. Although Prince Durin has a brotherly love for Elrond, trust between Elves and Dwarves is at best precarious and constantly under threat, particularly once *mithril* and its miraculous properties are discovered. Dwarvish society too is riven with politics, notably in the clashes between the pig-headed King Durin, who is markedly intolerant and dismissive of the Elves, and his recalcitrant son and heir – whose wife Disa has ambitions to take over the kingdom. Winding through these plots are tangled mixed-species relationships which seem based on mutual misunderstanding – Galadriel and Halbrand, Bronwyn and Arondir (despite the warning that hybrid relationships between Elves and Humans are not only extremely rare, but also doomed), the bromance of Elrond and Durin, and Nori and The Stranger (who in the opening episodes is virtually mute).[28] As Charlie Vickers says of Halbrand's relationship with Galadriel and of Elves generally, 'I'm sure they see things differently to Humans, and they feel things differently' – this is a world of diverse and disparate and disconnected peoples.[29]

Galadriel is the key character in the first season of *Power*, although she does not figure directly in the Dwarf or Harfoot plots. McKay and Payne's Galadriel is very different from previous incarnations – neither the unearthly seer of Tolkien's Lothlórien, nor the dark queen 'terrible as the Dawn' of Jackson's *Fellowship*, nor the video avatar battling in Dol Guldur of Jackson's *Five Armies*, but thousands of years younger and with evergreen wounds of family grief and personal failure.[30] She is commander of the northern armies and warrior of the wastelands, but war-weary, her plate armour flecked with rust and her chainmail disintegrating after centuries of military campaigning. Her four brothers have been slain in the wars (and, curiously, she also claims that her husband Celeborn is dead), her élite force deserts her, and her mission to seek and destroy Sauron is aborted by Gil-Galad. Yet if her company do not respect her leadership, neither does she respect the decisions of her own king.

Galadriel is, then, an enticing but deeply flawed character:

a decisive leader and a dazzling fighter, an outsider and a loner whose closest friend is the Half-Elf Elrond. Her swordplay blends lightning dexterity with balletic agility and she handles her warhorse with acrobatic verve.[31] As such, Galadriel most resembles the character Tauriel in *Hobbits*, described by the actor Evangeline Lilly as 'a killing machine'.[32] Galadriel's skills in combat also give her not only a towering sense of entitlement but also at times a staggering arrogance – for example in her high-handed dealings with Queen Míriel – as well as almost messianic delusions, declaring at one point to Halbrand that,

> Ours was no chance meeting. Not fate, nor destiny, nor any of the words men use to speak of the forces they lack the conviction to name. Ours was the work of something greater ... Together we will redeem both our bloodlines.[33]

While Galadriel's ambiguous identity as a rebel and an exile haunts *The Lord of the Rings* and Tolkien's subsequent attempts to revise 'The Silmarillion', these same ambiguities – and her disastrous misjudgements – dominate *Power* in a way that binds it to Tolkien's shifting conception of Middle-Earth. When she portentously announces to Halbrand that 'Sometimes to find the light we must first touch the darkness', she is simply repeating the words of her dead brother Finrod with little grasp of their meaning.[34] Hence Halbrand's response is dismissive, contemptuous – 'What do you know of darkness?' – and he is, of course, horribly right: the stunning revelation that Halbrand is Sauron crushes Galadriel and casts doubt on all of her convictions, as well as overturning everything that Halbrand himself has said and done.[35]

Halbrand is not alone in exposing Galadriel's severe shortcomings. She is driven not only by a murderous passion to destroy Sauron, but also – chillingly – by a genocidal compulsion

to exterminate the entire Orc species. Her attitude that Orcs
are degenerate inferiors that deserve only extinction exemplifies the problems Tolkien faced when trying to define evil in
Middle-Earth, and also the moral issues that Jackson signals
in *Rings*. During her interrogation of Adar (Joseph Mawle),
for example, she ponders 'perhaps we should bring our prisoners into the sunlight'.[36] In other words, she proposes to torture
the Orcs by burning them alive under the sun – comparable
to Gandalf later torturing Gollum, and Thranduil executing his
Orc captive. Adar is shaken by this lawless threat, arguing that
Orcs are 'creations of the One, Master of the Secret Fire – the
same as you; as worthy of the breath of life, and just as worthy
of a home'.[37] *Power* thus presents the Orcs more sympatheti-
cally than earlier adaptations: they are literally battle-scarred,
their broken armour repaired with bones, but they are loyal to
their 'father' Adar. He safeguards his 'children' in the first attack
on the Southlanders by sending the Southlander defectors to
fight their own kind, and the consequent transformation of
the Southlands into shadowlands then provides the Orcs with
a homeland where volcanic smog will protect them from the
searing daylight. But Galadriel's response is that of the Angel
of Death:

> No. Your kind was a mistake. Made in mockery. And even
> if it takes me all of this age I vow to eradicate every last
> one of you. *You* shall be kept alive, so that one day – before
> I drive my dagger into your poisoned heart – I will whisper
> in your pikèd ear that all your offspring are dead and the
> scourge of your kind ends with you.

Adar responds with scathing dignity, 'I see that I am not the
only Elf alive that has been transformed by darkness . . .'.[38]
  Showrunner J.D. Payne has said of *Power* that,

The spirit of Tolkien is about disparate peoples who don't trust one another and look different from one another finding common ground in friendship and accomplishing big things ... That's the spirit we've tried to inculcate into every single comma and period in the show.[39]

While it is difficult to see these values reflected in Galadriel's homicidal cruelty, her failings are characteristic of the ambiguities of Middle-Earth so evident throughout *The Lord of the Rings* and its adaptations.

But despite the continuities with the works of Tolkien and Jackson, *Power* is inevitably a contemporary production reflecting the values of a new generation. It is certainly the case that there are multiple non-Human perspectives presented (Elves, Dwarves, Harfoots, Orcs, and a glimpse of Ents), different races (Southlanders and Númenóreans), children of every species (except Orcs, who are all Adar's children), and five strong, rebellious, and very different female characters – Galadriel, Bronwyn, Nori, Disa, and Míriel – none of whom are sexualized or objectified. Consequently, *Power* can be seen to be developing the diversity of Middle-Earth adaptations, and it was of course being written and filmed in the context of Black Lives Matter, which rapidly gained momentum in 2020, and the Me Too movement, which went viral when the offences of Harvey Weinstein, one-time producer of *Rings*, were made public.

The most significant world event of 2020 and the following years was the Covid-19 pandemic, and *Power* can perhaps be seen as a parable on the threat of contagion and the restrictions of lockdown – not least as the first season was filmed in New Zealand, ranked as the second safest country in the world during the pandemic.[40] Are the Orcs infiltrating the Southlands through underground tunnels and the Elves fading as the leaves of Lindon turn black representations of infection and contamination, with *mithril* as a wonder-drug vaccine? Perhaps – but more suggestive is the emphasis on isolation: Galadriel spurning the gift of her king and the divine grace of her people by plunging into the depths of the Sundering Seas and becoming a maverick lone wolf warrior in Middle-Earth; the Elves abandoning their watch over the Southlands; the Dwarves locked away in Khazad-Dûm and refusing aid to the Elves; the Númenóreans in splendid isolation on their island having cut all contact with Human and Elvish society on Middle-Earth and even having removed their king from power for his Elvish sympathies; and the close-knit Harfoot community passing through the countryside under camouflage, avoiding Humans, and overwhelmingly suspicious of The Stranger.

Isolation was an everyday consequence of pandemic restrictions, but isolationism also became a new political dogma throughout the West via Donald Trump's 'America First' policy (which soon became 'America Alone'), UK Brexit and renewed calls for Scottish independence, and the evaporation of European leadership caused by Angela Merkel stepping down as Chancellor of Germany, destabilizing the European Union and further weakening the West, which was already compromised by a chaotic US Republican administration.[41] Additionally, there are the increasingly dire perils of climate change: in 2019 alone 80,000 fires were lit in the Amazon rain forest, risking deforestation that would 'release billions of tons carbon into the atmosphere'.[42] Extreme weather has spiralled in recent years, despite a succession of international treaties and conferences including the Kyoto Protocol (effective from 2005), the Paris Accords (2015), and COP26 (2021).

In *Power*, isolationist peoples are inexorably drawn into international politics, and although the various plots focus on exile and loss and failure (Galadriel and The Stranger, Khazad-Dûm and Númenor, the Southlanders and the Rings of Power, respectively), the series does also offer a post-Covid sense of conciliation, consolation, and community – quite different from, for example, *Game of Thrones*, which in its amorality and brutality is unquestionably a pre-Covid fantasy. Similarly, the show is intensely aware of environmental crises, from the Harfoots finding blighted fruit in The Grove, to the calamitous climate change in the Southlands – the result of an ancient plot to trigger a volcanic eruption, release vast quantities of dust into the atmosphere to block out sunlight, and thus create a shadowland. In the face of such hopelessness, *Power* is essentially a protracted commentary on a moment in *The Lord of the Rings* in which Tolkien was musing to himself about the hardships of his own time, and which Peter Jackson dramatized into Frodo's decision to go to Mordor alone:

> 'I wish it need not have happened in my time,' said Frodo.
> 'So do I,' said Gandalf, 'and so do all who live to see such times. But that is not for them to decide. All we have to decide is what to do with the time that is given us.'[43]

The Rings of Power has been forged in the shadows of global crises, and reminds us that while we may hope that these things should not have happened in our lifetime, that is not for us to decide. But we can decide what we can do with the time we have – and for all the ruinous errors we may make, what makes this series part of Middle-Earth is its characteristically Tolkienian conviction that although failure may not be defeat, it is still, perhaps, nevertheless inevitable.

Notes

Abbreviations

Adventures of Tom Bombadil: J.R.R. Tolkien, *The Adventures of Tom Bombadil*, ed. Christina Scull and Wayne Hammond (London: HarperCollins, 2014).

Beowulf: J.R.R. Tolkien, *Beowulf: A Translation and Commentary, Together with Sellic Spell*, ed. Christopher Tolkien (London: HarperCollins, 2014).

Book of Lost Tales, i.: J.R.R. Tolkien, *The Book of Lost Tales I*, ed. Christopher Tolkien (London: HarperCollins, 1983).

Book of Lost Tales, ii.: J.R.R. Tolkien, *The Book of Lost Tales II*, ed. Christopher Tolkien (London: HarperCollins, 1984).

Carpenter: Humphrey Carpenter, *J.R.R. Tolkien: A Biography* (London, Boston, and Sydney: George Allen & Unwin, 1977).

Children of Húrin: J.R.R. Tolkien, *The Children of Húrin*, ed. Christopher Tolkien (London: HarperCollins, 2007).

Chron.: Christina Scull and Wayne Hammond, *The J.R.R. Tolkien Companion and Guide: Chronology* volume, revised and expanded edition in 3 vols (London: HarperCollins, 2017), and online addenda (https://www. hammondandscull.com/addenda.html).

Cilli, *Tolkien's Library*: Oronzo Cilli, *Tolkien's Library: An Annotated Checklist* (Edinburgh: Luna Press, 2019).

Fall of Arthur: J.R.R. Tolkien, *The Fall of Arthur*, ed. Christopher Tolkien (London: HarperCollins, 2013).

Farmer Giles: J.R.R. Tolkien, *Farmer Giles of Ham / The Adventures of Tom Bombadil* (London, Boston, and Sydney: Unwin Paperbacks, 1979).

Garth, *Great War*: John Garth, *Tolkien and the Great War: The Threshold of Middle-Earth* (London: HarperCollins, 2004).

Gilliver, et al., *Ring of Words*: Peter Gilliver, Jeremy Marshall, and Edmund Weiner, *The Ring of Words: Tolkien and the Oxford English Dictionary* (Oxford: Oxford University Press, 2006).

Green: *Green's Dictionary of Slang*, online edition.

Guide: Christina Scull and Wayne Hammond, *The J.R.R. Tolkien Companion and Guide: Guide* (in 2 vols, i. & ii.), revised and expanded edition in 3 vols (London: HarperCollins, 2017), and online addenda (https://www.hammondandscull.com/addenda.html).

Hobbit: J.R.R. Tolkien, *The Annotated Hobbit*, ed. Douglas A. Anderson (New York: Houghton Mifflin, 2002).

Letters: *The Letters of J.R.R. Tolkien*, ed. Humphrey Carpenter, with Christopher Tolkien (London, Boston, and Sydney: George Allen & Unwin, 1981).

Lost Road: J.R.R. Tolkien, *The Lost Road and Other Writings*, ed. Christopher Tolkien (London: HarperCollins, 1987).

LotR: J.R.R. Tolkien, *The Lord of the Rings*, 3 vols, 3rd edn (London, Boston, and Sydney: Unwin Paperbacks, 1979).

Monsters and Critics: J.R.R. Tolkien, *The Monsters and the Critics and Other Essays*, ed. Christopher Tolkien (London: HarperCollins, 2006).

Morgoth's Ring: J.R.R. Tolkien, *Morgoth's Ring: The Later Silmarillion Part One, The Legends of Aman*, ed. Christopher Tolkien (London: HarperCollins, 1993).

ODNB: *Oxford Dictionary of National Biography*, online edition.

OED: *Oxford English Dictionary*, online edition.

On Fairy-Stories: J.R.R. Tolkien, *Tolkien On Fairy-Stories: Expanded Edition, with Commentary and Notes*, ed. Verlyn Flieger and Douglas A. Anderson (London: HarperCollins, 2008).

Oxford Shakespeare: William Shakespeare, *The Oxford Shakespeare: The Complete Works*, gen. eds Stanley Wells and Gary Taylor (Oxford: Clarendon Press, 1988).

Peoples of Middle-earth: J.R.R. Tolkien, *The Peoples of Middle-earth*, ed. Christopher Tolkien (London: HarperCollins, 1996).

Rateliff: John Rateliff, *The History of The Hobbit: Part One, Mr. Baggins* and *Part Two, Return to Bag-End* (London: HarperCollins, 2007); 2 vols designated i. & ii.

Return of the Shadow: J.R.R. Tolkien, *The Return of the Shadow: The History of The Lord of the Rings, Part One*, ed. Christopher Tolkien (London: HarperCollins, 1988).

Road Goes Ever On: J.R.R. Tolkien and Donald Swann, *The Road Goes Ever On: A Song Cycle* (London: George Allen and Unwin Ltd, 1968).

Roberts, *Riddles of the Hobbit*: Adam Roberts, *Riddles of the Hobbit* (Basingstoke: Palgrave Macmillan, 2013).

Rosebury, *Tolkien: A Cultural Phenomenon*: Brian Rosebury, *Tolkien: A Cultural Phenomenon* (Basingstoke: Palgrave Macmillan, 2003).

Sauron Defeated: J.R.R. Tolkien, *Sauron Defeated: The History of The Lord of the Rings, Part Four*, ed. Christopher Tolkien (London: HarperCollins, 1992) [includes *The Notion Club Papers*].

Shaping of Middle-earth: J.R.R. Tolkien, *The Shaping of Middle-earth: The Quenta, The Ambarkanta and the Annals*, ed. Christopher Tolkien (London: HarperCollins, 1986).

Shippey, *Author of the Century*: Tom Shippey, *Tolkien: Author of the Century* (London: HarperCollins, 2000).

Shippey, *Road to Middle-earth*: Tom Shippey, *The Road to Middle-earth*, rev. edn (London: HarperCollins, 2005).

Silmarillion: J.R.R. Tolkien, *The Silmarillion*, ed. Christopher Tolkien (London, Boston, and Sydney: George Allen & Unwin, 1977; Unwin Paperbacks, 1979).

Songs for the Philologists: J.R.R. Tolkien, E.V. Gordon, and others, *Songs for the Philologists*, ed. and rev. Ronald Kyrmse (privately printed: n.p., 2007).

Treason of Isengard: J.R.R. Tolkien, *The Treason of Isengard: The History of The Lord of the Rings, Part Two*, ed. Christopher Tolkien (London: HarperCollins, 1989).

Unfinished Tales: J.R.R. Tolkien, *Unfinished Tales of Númenor and Middle-earth*, ed. Christopher Tolkien (London: HarperCollins, 1998).

War of the Jewels: J.R.R. Tolkien, *The War of the Jewels: The Later Silmarillion, Part Two – The Legend of Beleriand*, ed. Christopher Tolkien (London: HarperCollins, 1990).

War of the Ring: J.R.R. Tolkien, *The War of the Ring: The History of The Lord of the Rings, Part Three*, ed. Christopher Tolkien (London: HarperCollins, 1990).

Acknowledgements

1 Principally, 'The English Literary Tradition: Shakespeare to the Gothic', in Stuart Lee (ed.), *A Companion to J.R.R. Tolkien* (Oxford: Blackwell, 2014), 286–302; ' "The Ghostly Language of the Ancient Earth": Tolkien and Romantic Lithology', in Julian Eilmann and Will Sherwood (eds), *The Romantic Spirit in the Works of J.R.R. Tolkien* (Zurich: Walking Tree, 2023), 99–124; 'Nazgûl Taller Than Night: Tolkien and Speculative Realism', in Will Sherwood (ed.), *Twenty-first Century Receptions of Tolkien: Proceedings of the Tolkien Society Winter Seminar 2021* (Edinburgh: Luna Press, 2022), 38–57; 'Tolkien and the Gothic', in Lynn Forest-Hill (ed.), *The Return of the Ring: Proceedings of the Tolkien Society Conference 2012*, 2 vols (Edinburgh: Luna Publishing, 2016), ii. 25–34; 'Tolkien y la literatura gótica', in Martin Simonson and José R. Montejano (eds), *J.R.R. Tolkien y la Tierra Media: Once Ensayos*

sobre el Mayor Mito Literario del Siglo XX (Aces de Candamo: Jonathan Alwais, 2021), 269–310; *The Vampire. A New History* (New Haven and London: Yale University Press, 2018); and 'Viral Vampires', *Critical Quarterly* 62.4 (2020), 7–14; however, all of these readings could be developed further along their own lines.

2   See Jennifer Brooker, 'Language Re-Imagined in Middle Earth and Hundred-Acre Wood: Jokes, Rhymes, & Riddles in Works of J.R.R. Tolkien and A.A Milne' (2020); Chris Walsh, 'Gildor, Frodo and Bilbo: A Tolkien Puzzle', unpublished papers; and Jessica Yates, correspondence: my sincere thanks to all three for their insights.

Notes on the Text

1   See the Conclusion; the term 'Roma' is endorsed by the European Network Against Racism: see https://www.enar-eu.org/Frequently-asked-questions-1167

2   *LotR*, iii. 513; see p. 101 for a fuller discussion.

3   See Billy Bragg, *The Progressive Patriot: A Search for Belonging* (London: Bantam Press, 2006), 55: 'The hyphen in Anglo-Saxon is symbolic of our ancient multicultural traditions'; other writers such as Jeremy Paxman, *The English: A Portrait of a People* (Harmondsworth: Penguin, 1999) make a similar point; see also https://aeon.co/essays/why-we-should-keep-the-term-anglo-saxon-in-archaeology

4   *Sauron Defeated*, 157.

Foreword

1   Terry Pratchett, 'Cult Classic', in Karen Haber (ed.), *Meditations on Middle-Earth* (London, etc.: Earthlight, 2003), 75–83, at 78.

2   Book sales are difficult to assess due to the pirated paperback published in America by Ace, but it seems reasonable to put sales of both *The Lord of the Rings* and *The Hobbit* in excess of 100 million copies each. The first radio adaptation was proposed in August 1955 by Terence Tiller (see *Chron.*, 499ff.; and below, Chapter Five).

3   See BBC *Sounds* archive; also jockey Richard Dunwoody, swimmer Duncan Goodhew, and many others, while Will Carling would take *The Hobbit*.

4   For 'radical typology', see Laurence Coupe, *Mythology*, 2nd edn (London and New York: Routledge, 2009), 169–75.

5   https://www.deviantart.com/search?q=hobbit

6   John Heminges and Henry Condell, 'To the Great Variety of Readers', in 'Commendatory Poems and Prefaces', *Oxford Shakespeare*, xliii–xlix, at xlv.

One: Myriad Middle-Earths

1   *Beowulf: An Edition with Relevant Shorter Texts*, ed. Bruce Mitchell and
    Fred C. Robinson, rev. edn (Malden, MA, etc.: Blackwell Publishing,
    1998), 45.

2   The letter 'þ' is *thorn*, pronounced as 'th'; the letter 'ð' is *eth* or *edh*, also
    pronounced as 'th'.

3   *Beowulf and the Finnesburg Fragment*, trans. John R. Clark Hall, preface
    by J.R.R. Tolkien, ed. and intr. C.L. Wrenn (London, Boston, and
    Sydney: George Allen & Unwin, 1950), 20.

4   Some of these are mentioned by Garth, *Great War*, 19; for Arcastar
    Mondósaresse, see http://www.tolkienbooks.net/php/details.
    php?reference=72920

5   Richard Plotz, 'The Society', *Tolkien Journal*, 1.2 (1965), [1] (reprinted
    by the Mythopoeic Society: see https://dc.swosu.edu/tolkien_journal/
    vol1/iss2/1).

6   Carpenter, 26.

7   *Letters*, 218–19.

8   A Middle English word referring to both learning and magic (*OED*).

9   In his biography, Carpenter suggests that the profusion of names derives
    from Tolkien's various invented languages – but then admits that 'in
    practice he was often more arbitrary' (102).

10 See Robert Foster, *The Complete Guide to Middle-Earth* (London,
    Boston, and Sydney: Unwin Paperbacks, 1978).

11 *LotR*, ii. 80: his name is like the Λόγος of ancient Greek philosophy
    and early Christian theology – in the beginning was the Word, which
    brings the Creation into being and continues to unfold through time as
    Human history.

12 Tolkien's sober biographer, Humphrey Carpenter, admits that, early in
    his life, Tolkien was two people (39).

13 These biographical details are indebted to Carpenter, and to Scull and
    Hammond's *Chronology*; page references are given only in the case of
    direct quotation. Characteristically, Tolkien disparaged biographical
    criticism as 'an entirely vain and false approach to [an author's] works'
    (*Letters*, 414).

14 I generally refer to Tolkien as Ronald until he begins his studies at King
    Edward's School, where he would have been addressed as Tolkien (see
    Chron., 1).

15 Tolkien later claimed that the spider was a tarantula; as Rateliff
    points out, it was a 'wind scorpion', *solifugae* (Rateliff, i. 333). On early
    memories, Tolkien admitted in an interview with Denys Gueroult
    that what he vividly remembered as his childhood home was in fact 'a
    beautifully worked out pastiche' of his father's house in Bloemfontein
    and his grandmother's in Birmingham (Brian Sibley (ed.), *J.R.R.*

Tolkien: An Audio Portrait [documentaries 1964–98] (BBC Worldwide Ltd, 2001), CD 1, track 4).

16 The letter is reproduced in Catherine McIlwaine, *Tolkien: Maker of Middle-earth* (Oxford: Bodleian Library, 2018), 122–3.

17 According to Carpenter, 'the best story he had ever read' (30).

18 'The Story of Sigurd', in Andrew Lang (ed.), *The Red Fairy Book* (London: Longmans, Green, and Co., 1890), 357–67, at 366.

19 Sadly, Barry's building was demolished in the 1930s.

20 Carpenter, 35.

21 For Fr Francis's generosity, see Carpenter, 40.

22 Tolkien, 'English and Welsh', in *The Monsters and the Critics*, 162–97, at 192; the allusion is to John Keats's sonnet that describes his first reading of George Chapman's translations of the *Odyssey* and the *Iliad*.

23 Tolkien read a paper on Thompson to the Exeter College Essay Club on 4 March 1914 (*Chron.*, 58); Carpenter, 47–8.

24 *OED* defines the rare word *apolaustic* as 'concerned with or wholly devoted to seeking enjoyment; self-indulgent', and notes that it was used as a synonym for 'aesthetic' (see Gilliver, et al., *Ring of Words*, 39 n.7); Tolkien presumably took the word from the opening of Aristotle's *Nicomachean Ethics* (1. 5. 1–2) (see https://laudatortemporisacti. blogspot.com/2008/10/).

25 Quoted by *Chron.*, 59 (1 June 1914).

26 These wartime details are again indebted to Carpenter's *Biography*, and Scull and Hammond's *Chronology*, as well as to Garth, *Great War*; page references are only given in the case of direct quotation.

27 His translation of Kullervo was published in 2010. The tale of Túrin Turambar appears in 'The Children of Húrin', since published in various versions, including a single volume edition in 2007.

28 27 November 1914 (*Chron.*, 64), and 20 October 1913 (*Chron.*, 53); Tolkien later noted that Earp roomed with the composer William Walton.

29 See Hugh Lloyd Jones, 'Eric Robertson Dodds', *ODNB*.

30 'Parcels for Prisoners', *The Graphic* (13 May 1916): quoted by https://www.blogs.hss.ed.ac.uk/selcie/2021/03/01/fairy-fever-in-the-aftermath-of-the-first-world-war/

31 Maggie Atkinson, 'Visions of "Blighty": Fairies, War and Fragile Spaces,' *Libri & Liberi* 6.1 (2017), 39–62, at 42.

32 See https://www.blogs.hss.ed.ac.uk/selcie/2021/03/01/fairy-fever-in-the-aftermath-of-the-first-world-war/

33 *OED*, Green, and *Letters*, 95: *OED* and Green both cite first uses of the word in the armed forces, Green pre-dating *OED* by some years.

34 Philip Norman, 'The Hobbit Man', *Sunday Times Magazine* (15 January 1967), 36: quoted in *Chron.*, 89.

35 The word *legendarium* was coined by Tolkien himself in about 1951,

modelled on the nineteenth-century theological use to describe the canon of saints' lives; *OED*, citing Tolkien, defines the word as 'A body or system of myths, legends, stories, etc., concerning or relating to a particular fictional world; a work containing this' (see *Letters*, 149).

36 See Gilliver, et al., *Ring of Words*, 6–30.

37 See *Chron.*, 118–19; and *Unfinished Tales*, 5.

38 Exeter College archives: quoted by *Chron.*, 119; and see *Letters*, 445–6n.

39 See Christopher Tolkien's remarks in *Book of Lost Tales*, ii. 322; Brian Bates has written a detailed account of the correspondences between Anglo-Saxon England and Tolkien's Middle-Earth in *The Real Middle-Earth: Magic and Mystery in the Dark Ages* (London, Basingstoke, and Oxford: Pan Books, 2003).

40 For an account of the 'Father Christmas letters', see Alison Milbank's thought-provoking book *Chesterton and Tolkien as Theologians: The Fantasy of the Real* (London and New York: T&T Clark, 2009), 149–56.

41 See Julius B. Cohen and Arthur G. Ruston, *Smoke: A Study of Town Air* (London: Edward Arnold, 1912), 46, 35, 60–68.

42 'Éadig Béo Þu!' ('good luck to you!') is reprinted in Shippey, *Road to Middle-earth*, 401–3; see Verlyn Flieger, *A Question of Time: J.R.R. Tolkien's Road to Faërie* (Kent, OH: Kent State University Press, 1997), 243. These songs were privately printed by students at University College London in 1935 or 1936 under the title *Songs for the Philologists*; Tolkien was not made aware of the existence of the publication until 1940, by which time nearly every copy had been lost in a fire.

43 John M. Bowers has provided a definitive account of this edition in *Tolkien's Lost Chaucer* (Oxford: Oxford University Press, 2019).

44 Carpenter, 118.

45 Tolkien spoke in a sort of headlong mumble routinely punctuated by unexpectedly emphatic words and waylaid by sudden reflective pauses: on his vocal delivery, see Clyde Kilby, *Tolkien and The Silmarillion* (Berkhamsted: Lion Publishing, 1977), 83n.; and examples of audio recordings in Sibley (ed.), *Tolkien: An Audio Portrait*. Yet Tolkien could also declaim verse and prose resoundingly: see the recordings in J.R.R. Tolkien, *Essential Tolkien* (Caedmon, n.d.); J.R.R. Tolkien, and Christopher Tolkien, *The Homecoming of Beorhtnoth*, read by J.R.R. Tolkien and Christopher Tolkien (Tolkien Centenary Conference recording, 1992); and J.R.R. Tolkien and Christopher Tolkien, *The Tolkien Audio Collection* (HarperCollins, 2002).

46 See Rateliff, i. xi–xv; also *Chron.*, 147.

47 There may have been a veiled allusion here to C.S. Lewis's involvement with a group of National Trust activists, one of whom went under

the alias 'Bill Stickers': see Anna Hutton-North, *Ferguson's Gang: The Maidens Behind the Masks* (Great Britain: Lulu Inc., 2013).

48   See a passing reference in Carpenter, 179.

49   See Kris Swank, 'The Child's Voyage and the *Immram* Tradition in Lewis, Tolkien, and Pullman', *Mythlore* 38.1 (2019), 75–98; 'The Death of Saint Brendan' is appended to *The Notion Club Papers* (*Sauron Defeated*, 296–9).

50   Tolkien alludes to *Through the Looking-Glass* in '*Beowulf*: The Monsters and the Critics' (*Monsters and Critics*, 5–48, at 9).

51   See, for example, the illustration 'The White Dragon pursues Roverandom & the Moondog', J.R.R. Tolkien, *Roverandom*, ed. Christina Scull and Wayne G. Hammond (London: HarperCollins, 2013), [89].

52   Surprisingly, *Roverandom* has been set to music by Walter Mertens, who scored it for a concert band in 2015.

53   See *Chron.*, 173, 187; Jo appears to have been sold at the beginning of the Second World War (see Carpenter, 12).

54   But none of these stories were published until well after Tolkien's death: see Chapter Five.

55   Tolkien described his conversion in the poem 'Mythopoeia' (*Tree and Leaf including the poem Mythopoeia*, 2nd edn (London, Sydney, and Wellington: Unwin Hyman Limited, 1988), 97–101), which mixes storytelling with religious belief and personal friendship.

56   See *Chron.*, 196; Gordon's letter is quoted in *Chron.*, 198.

57   The edition was later published by the Early English Text Society in 1961.

58   See *Chron.*, 175.

59   For a sense of the range here, see *Chron.*, 184.

60   The Oxford English School established a Faculty Board in 1926, which was shortly after Tolkien took up his professorship; however, the Faculty was familiarly referred to as the 'English School' for decades after: see Maria Sachiko Cecire, 'The Oxford School of Children's Fantasy Literature: Medieval Afterlives and the Production of Culture', DPhil thesis (University of Oxford, 2011); and Scarlett Baron, 'A Short History of the Oxford English Faculty' (https://www.academia.edu/2550098/A_Short_History_of_the_Oxford_English_Faculty).

61   The sitting room, or parlour, was a private room in which to receive guests.

62   *Chron.*, 183. The Eagle and Child pub was named after the Eagle sent by Zeus to bring him Ganymede; Eagles also appear in Anglo-Saxon poems such as 'The Seafarer' and *The Battle of Maldon* as beasts (i.e. predators) of battle. The word *inkling* is used in *The Notion Club Papers* (which is effectively a fictionalized account of their meetings) in the sense of something or somewhere: see *Sauron Defeated*, 173; by 1954

they had decamped from the Eagle and Child after the landlord opened his parlour to the public, and instead met at the Lamb and Flag on the opposite side of the road.

63 See Rateliff, i. xvi.

64 See Carpenter, 179–80; Rateliff, i. xvii–xviii.

65 Rateliff conclusively demonstrates that Tolkien did not give up on the story and resort to improvised versions of the last chapters for his children, but in fact worked on it steadily until publication – disproving Carpenter's account (see Rateliff, ii. 633–6; Carpenter, 179–80).

66 See Gilliver, et al., *Ring of Words*, 162–4; and Arne Zettersten, *J.R.R. Tolkien's Double Worlds and Creative Process: Language and Life* (Basingstoke: Palgrave Macmillan, 2011), 43–5.

67 The letter 'ȝ' is 'yogh', usually pronounced as 'y' or 'gh', although sometimes harder as 'ch' in Scottish 'loch'.

68 Glossary, ed. Thomas Ruddiman, in Virgil, *Æneis*, trans. Gawin Douglas (Edinburgh, 1710), [531].

69 C.T.C.S., 'Popular Superstitions of Clydesdale. No. II. – *Fairies*', in *Edinburgh Magazine & Literary Miscellany* (October 1818), 326–31, at 329, also 330 (anglicized).

70 E.R. Eddison, *The Worm Ouroboros* (London: Jonathan Cape, 1922), 205: 'At length when winter was gone in middle earth, and the spring far spent, back came that last little martlet.'

71 *Letters*, 258; see https://apilgriminnarnia.com/2014/04/09/worm/

72 *Harper's Magazine* (June 1947), 508–9, at 508; reprinted in *Nones* (London: Faber and Faber, 1952), 57–62, at 58. Auden became Professor of Poetry at Oxford in 1956.

73 'The Nativity', I, ii., ll. 103–4; the text is taken from *Cynewulf's Christ: An Eighth Century English Epic*, ed. and trans. Israel Gollancz (London: David Nutt, 1892), 10 – a text with which Tolkien would have been familiar, the translation is also from this edition (11) [note: this version lacks accents].

74 See, for example, R.K. Gordon (ed. and trans.), *Anglo-Saxon Poetry* (London, Melbourne, and Toronto: J.M. Dent and Sons, 1954), 135; and S.A.J. Bradley (ed. and trans.), *Anglo-Saxon Poetry* (London: J.M. Dent, 1995), 208.

75 See Carpenter, 79; *Book of Lost Tales*, ii. 267–77; *Shaping of Middle-earth*, 213–18; and Garth, *Great War*, 44–7.

76 Carpenter, 72, quoting *The Notion Club* (*Sauron Defeated*, 236).

77 Carpenter, 83; Roberts treats the Cynewulf lines as a riddle Tolkien then tried to answer (*Riddles of the Hobbit*, 33).

78 *Shaping of Middle-earth*, 236.

79 See the letter of 10 June 1955 to his American publisher the Houghton-Mifflin Co. (*Letters*, 220; and Rateliff, i. 17).

80 See William Gray, *Fantasy, Myth and the Measure of Truth: Tales*

of Pullman, Lewis, Tolkien, Macdonald and Hoffmann (Basingstoke: Palgrave Macmillan, 2009), 69–74.

81 *Lost Road*, 63–4.

82 *Lost Road*, 98.

83 Rudyard Kipling, *Puck of Pook's Hill* (London: Penguin, 1991), 11.

84 *Lost Road*, 91n, 92–4.

85 *Lost Road*, 91n., 23.

86 *Lost Road*, 44, 55n.

87 Roberts, *Riddles of the Hobbit*, 30; see Maria Artamonova, 'Writing for an Anglo-Saxon Audience in the Twentieth Century: J.R.R. Tolkien's Old English Chronicles', in David Clark and Nicholas Perkins (eds), *Anglo-Saxon Culture and the Modern Imagination* (Cambridge: D.S. Brewer, 2010), 71–88. Tolkien's translations *into* Anglo-Saxon include *Sellic Spell*; as Christopher Tolkien states, this is 'a demonstration of [his] father's fluency in the ancient tongue' (*Beowulf*, 407).

88 For Ælfwine see *Lost Road*, 98; and Shippey, *Author of the Century*, 279, 281; the best account of *The Notion Club Papers* is Gray, *Fantasy, Myth and the Measure of Truth*, 74–80; see also Verlyn Flieger, 'Tolkien's Experiment with Time: *The Lost Road*, "The Notion Club Papers" and J.W. Dunne', *Mythlore* 21.2 (1996), 39–44.

89 *Notion Club*, 231, 240 and 257–9, 252–3; typically for Tolkien the language has two versions: the 'A' language (Avallonian) and the 'B' language (Adûnaic); there is also the Old Solar language (*Sauron Defeated*, 200).

90 *Sauron Defeated*, 234, 250.

91 *Lost Road*, 39.

92 *Fall of Arthur*, 136–9, 148–63.

93 *Fall of Arthur*, 160–68.

Two: Uncertainty

1 Tolkien himself, however, pointed out that references to religion in Middle-Earth 'are frequently overlooked': the verse 'A Elbereth Gilthoniel' is a prayer, and Faramir and his Rangers pray to the West (*Road Goes Ever On*, 65).

2 *Release – Tolkien in Oxford*, dir. Leslie Megahey (BBC, 1968): https://www.bbc.co.uk/archive/release--jrr-tolkien/znd36v4 ; and *Archive on 4*, 'Tolkien: The Lost Recordings', BBC Radio 4 (6 August 2016): https://www.bbc.co.uk/programmes/b07mvd5z; see Stuart D. Lee, 'Tolkien in Oxford (BBC, 1968): A Reconstruction', *Tolkien Studies* 15 (2018), 115–76, at 151.

3 More specifically, the Ring can be said to provoke intemperate desire, and covetousness is expressed by both the Sackville-Bagginses and Saruman – especially in his role as Sharkey.

4 *Hobbit*, [9].
5 See Shippey, *Author of the Century*, 46; for an exhaustive discussion
   of the origins of the word 'Hobbit', see Gilliver, et al., *Ring of Words*,
   142–52.
6 *Letters*, 31; Gilliver, et al., *Ring of Words*, 190–91.
7 Adam Roberts, 'How Many Species of Hobbits?', http://
   europrogovision.blogspot.com/2011/12/how-many-species-of-hobbits.
   html (27 December 2011); see also Benjamin Eldon Stevens, 'Ancient
   Underworlds in *The Hobbit*', in Brett M. Rogers and Benjamin Eldon
   Stevens (eds), *Classical Traditions in Modern Fantasy* (Oxford: Oxford
   University Press, 2017), 121–44.
8 It could reasonably be argued that only Gandalf, Beorn, the Spiders, and
   the people of Laketown are not Hobbits – the Trolls live in a cave, and
   even Rivendell, as the name suggests, is in a deep and secret valley.
9 Roberts, *Riddles of the Hobbit*, 94–7.
10 For numbers, see Rateliff, i. 185 (summarizing Wayne G. Hammond,
   with Douglas A. Anderson, *J.R.R. Tolkien: A Descriptive Bibliography*
   (Winchester: St Paul's Bibliographies, 1993), 4–71.
11 Shippey, *Author of the Century*, 18.
12 See Paul Thomas, 'Some of Tolkien's Narrators', in Verlyn Flieger and
   Carl Hostetter (eds), *Tolkien's Legendarium: Essays on The History of Middle-
   earth* (Westport, CT, and London: Greenwood Press, 2000), 161–81 –
   Thomas describes the narrator as 'self-conscious' and 'intrusive' and lists
   his various interjections; some of these points about the narrator are also
   made by Rateliff (i. 55–8), although we also differ in significant respects.
13 *Hobbit*, 12–13.
14 Lewis Carroll, *Alice's Adventures in Wonderland* and *Through the Looking
   Glass and What Alice Found There: The Centenary Edition*, ed. Hugh
   Haughton (London: Penguin, 1998), 186.
15 See my book *The Making of Percy's Reliques* (Oxford: Clarendon Press,
   1999), 239–40.
16 Carroll, *Through the Looking Glass*, 187. These are examples of Tolkien's
   compound words in *The Hobbit*; see Gilliver, et al., *Ring of Words*, for a
   list of his neologisms and unconventional usages (89–224); *Hobbit*, 227.
17 *Hobbit*, 19.
18 A philological child doubtless familiar with Joseph Wright's *English
   Dialect Dictionary* (1898–1905); the last two do not yet have separate
   entries in *OED*. 'Wuther' is well known as a raging wind; Emily Brontë
   described it as a provincial term; see Gilliver, et al., *Ring of Words*,
   99–100. Perhaps predictably, Tolkien believed that children should read
   books beyond their assigned reading age (!).
19 See Gilliver et al., *Ring of Words*, 135–6.
20 *Hobbit*, 55; for Joni Mitchell, see https://jonimitchell.com/music/song.
   cfm?id=131

21 *Hobbit*, 236.

22 Carroll, *Through the Looking Glass*, 185.

23 See Cilli, *Tolkien's Library*, items 320 and 321, p. 41. Tolkien alludes to 'Jabberwocky', for example, in '*Beowulf*: The Monsters and the Critics' (see above), and he translated the poem 'The Walrus and the Carpenter' from *Through the Looking-Glass* into his Elvish language Qenya – from memory (see J.R.R. Tolkien, *The Qenya Alphabet*, ed. Arden R. Smith (Mountain View, CA: Parma Eldalamberon, 2012): *Parma Eldalamberon* 20 (2012)).

24 *Letters*, 22.

25 Rateliff notes that several Hobbits have Wodehousian names (i. 47, 60).

26 Jack Zipes, *Breaking the Magic Spell: Radical Theories of Folk and Fairy Tales* (Lexington, KY: University Press of Kentucky, 1979), 169.

27 *Letters*, 159.

28 J.R.R. Tolkien, *The Hobbit*, 2nd edn (London, Boston, and Sydney: George Allen & Unwin, 1951), [10].

29 Jorges Luis Borges, *Labyrinths: Selected Stories and Other Writings*, ed. Donald A. Yates and James E. Irby (London: Penguin Books, 1970), 27–43; it is no surprise that both Tolkien and Borges were darlings of the late sixties counterculture: see Chapter Five and Nicolas Roeg and Donald Cammell's 1970 film *Performance*.

30 *Hobbit*, [8]; Orcs are in fact mentioned only once in *The Hobbit* (*Hobbit*, 149).

31 John Lomax had recorded 'The Animals Marched in Two by Two' in 1934.

32 *Hobbit*, 125, 131.

33 *Hobbit*, 116; in contrast, see the final Dwarves' song (*Hobbit*, 274–5).

34 *Hobbit*, 25.

35 C.G. Jung, *Psychology of the Unconscious: A Study of the Transformations and Symbolisms of the Libido – A Contribution to the History of the Evolution of Thought*, trans. Beatrice M. Hinkle (New York: Moffat, Yard and Company, 1916), 349; see Cilli, *Tolkien's Library*, item 1152, p. 138. Although Tolkien later qualified this as mere longevity in Valinor, the clear implication in the novel is that the Ringbearers (and Gimli) share in the immortality of the Elves (*Letters*, 198–9).

36 *Hobbit*, 71, 392; Rateliff insists that this and comparable anachronisms are the voice of the narrator guiding a contemporary reader (i. 43, 318), but it is notable that the chaotic juxtapositions in early drafts of the story are not removed but rather revised to become more nuanced.

37 Interestingly, an early reader ('HABIT') wrote to the *Observer* that 'one of the book's charms appears to be its Spenserian harmonising of the brilliant threads of so many branches of epic, mythology, and Victorian fairy literature' (16 January 1938; quoted by Rateliff, ii. 855).

38 Roberts suggests that the runes form the first riddle of this book filled with riddles (*Riddles of the Hobbit*, 83).

39 Bowers, *Tolkien's Lost Chaucer*, 223; Tolkien interviewed by Denys Gueroult (see Sibley (ed.), *Tolkien: An Audio Portrait*, CD 1, track 4); also *Letters*, 235.

40 *Hobbit*, 47, who suggests that only the name Balin is Tolkien's own (see Rateliff, i. 23–4).

41 The superstition was first recorded in the *Athenian Mercury* (June 1695), quoted in John Aubrey's *Miscellanies* (1695): see John Aubrey, *Three Prose Works*, ed. John Buchanan-Brown (Fontwell: Centaur Press, 1972), 55.

42 *Hobbit*, 36.

43 William uses the word *lumme*, first recorded in Albert Chevalier's music-hall song 'A Coster's Courtship' (1888 – see Green). Tempting as it is to suggest that Tolkien's inspiration was George Bernard Shaw's *Pygmalion* (1913, 1914), Shaw's characters do not use words such as *lumme* or *blimey*, which were recent coinages, and, in any case, Tolkien was not impressed by Shaw (see Carpenter, 241).

44 Noted by Rateliff, i. 122–3.

45 *Hobbit*, 60, 63; Tolkien himself noted this point in his letter to the *Observer* (20 February 1938): *Letters*, 30–32; see Rateliff, ii. 855–65).

46 *Lost Road*, 53.

47 Tolkien ponders the Semitic qualities of the Dwarves in *Letters*, 229; see Renée Vink, '"Jewish" Dwarves: Tolkien and Anti-Semitic Stereotyping', *Tolkien Studies* 10 (2013), 123–45.

48 By 1971, it was clear that he had disowned 'Goblin Feet' (see *Hobbit*, 77n.).

49 Christina Rossetti, *Goblin Market and Other Poems*, 2nd edn (London and Cambridge: Macmillan and Co., 1865), 22.

50 It is perhaps worth remarking that there were Hobbit machines as well, such as forge-bellows, water-mill, and hand-loom (see *Hobbit*, 71–2; *LotR*, i. 17).

51 *Letters*, 229: see Rateliff, i. 79–80, 86–7; and 1965 BBC interview with Denys Gueroult (*Chron.*, 661, 789).

52 *OED* cites Tolkien as the source for the compound *riddle-game*: see Gilliver, et al., *Ring of Words*, 179–80.

53 Roberts, *Riddles of the Hobbit*, 56.

54 See Bradley (ed.), *Anglo-Saxon Poetry*, 368; and Roberts, *Riddles of the Hobbit*, 19.

55 Roberts, *Riddles of the Hobbit*, 55.

56 *Hobbit*, 84 – these words are common to all three editions.

57 Constance B. Hiett, 'The Text of *The Hobbit*: Putting Tolkien's Notes in Order', *English Studies in Canada* 7.2 (1981), 212–24, at 223 n.22.

58 Roberts, *Riddles of the Hobbit*, 4.

59 Shippey, *Author of the Century*, 24; Roberts thinks things are more

complicated than Shippey allows (see Roberts, *Riddles of the Hobbit*, 68).

60   See *Saga Heiðreks Konungs ins Vitra: The Saga of King Heidrek the Wise*, ed. and trans. Christopher Tolkien (London, etc.: Thomas Nelson and Sons, 1960), especially 36, 38–9; see Roberts, *Riddles of the Hobbit*, 47.

61   The fish riddle is reiterated in *LotR* in a slightly different version (ii. 282); the Sphinx riddle is adapted in several English nursery rhymes.

62   *Letters*, 31 (letter to the *Observer*), 123: see Roberts, *Riddles of the Hobbit*, 68–9; Roberts also forwards an elaborate argument that the answers to the riddle-game form an acrostic of *Alvissmæl* ('All-Wise's Saying') in the *Elder Edda* (*Riddles of the Hobbit*, 85–6); for further suggestions and possible sources, see Rateliff, i. 168–74.

63   Jorge Luis Borges, 'John Wilkins' Analytical Language', in *The Total Library: Non-Fiction 1922–1986*, ed. Eliot Weinberger; trans. Esther Allen, Suzanne Jill Levine, and Eliot Weinberger (London: Penguin Books, 2001), 229–32, at 231: it is wonderful that such a fiction appears in Borges's *Non-Fiction*, thereby casting doubt on categorizing his work as either non-fiction or fiction.

64   In the early drafts the Spiders were specifically female, but in the published version they are gender neutral (see Rateliff, i. 320).

65   *Hobbit*, 89.

66   *Saga Heiðreks Konungs*, 44. This is one of the 'known unknowns' of Norse mythology: Baldr (the name is variously spelt) was impervious to weapons except those made from mistletoe; when the tainted god Loki discovered this, he had Baldr's blind brother fire a mistletoe arrow at him during games in which the gods were amusing themselves with the invulnerability of Baldr. Baldr died and as he was placed on his funeral ship, Odin whispered something in his ear.

67   A similar point is made by Roberts, *Riddles of the Hobbit*, 92–3.

68   Perhaps William Brown, of Richmal Crompton's contemporaneous *Just William* stories, could give Bilbo a decent run for his money – if over many more tales.

69   Rateliff, i. 167.

70   The original chapter was first republished in 1985: see Marvin Kaye with Saralee Kaye (eds), *Masterpieces of Terror and the Supernatural: A Collection of Spinechillling Tales Old & New* (London: Little, Brown, 2002), 632–45, 652–3.

71   *Hobbit*, 110n., 141, 287; see Shippey, *Road to Middle-earth*, 46.

72   Gilliver, et al., *Ring of Words*, 206–7 (see *Letters*, 381n.; and Rateliff, i. 217 quoting a further letter).

73   'Ruddoc Hana' ('Who Killed Cock Robin?') was published in *Songs for the Philologists*, 8–9.

74   Quoted by Kim Hjardar and Vegard Vike, *Vikings at War*, trans. Frank Stewart (Oxford and Philadelphia: Casemate, 2016), 98–9.

75 Tolkien's source was an illustration in E.V. Gordon's *An Introduction to Old Norse* (Oxford: Clarendon Press, 1927), 28: Tolkien assisted Gordon on the publication (see Rateliff, i. 284, quoting William H. Green).

76 See Jacqueline Simpson and Steve Roud, *A Dictionary of English Folklore* (Oxford: Oxford University Press, 2000), 20.

77 For a survey of 'The Dolittle Theme', see Rateliff, i. 266–8.

78 For Tolkien's own ambivalent attitude towards Spiders, see *Guide*, ii. 1252–5.

79 Lord Dunsany, 'The Fortress Unvanquishable, Save for Sacnoth', in *The Sword of Welleran and Other Stories* (London: George Allen & Sons, 1908), 169–210, at 190.

80 Dunsany, 'The Lord of Cities', in *Sword of Welleran*, 213–28. Dunsany also wrote of Hlo-hlo, a Spider idol that guards a gigantic diamond, which appears to animate and pursue Thangobrind the Jeweller to a mysterious end, despite the jeweller inflicting grievous wounds on the demi-god. Again, this creature is humanoid – in spite of 'his shocking limbs and that demoniac body, his face was serene', and he holds the gemstone in his lap. This may seem to be an antecedent for the giant Spiders of Mirkwood, but a dismissive critique of the story written by Tolkien in 1963 indicates that he was unaware of the tale before then (Lord Dunsany, 'The Distressing Tale of Thangobrind the Jeweller', in *The Book of Wonder* (Boston: John W. Luce & Company, 1912), 11–19, at 13: see Cilli, *Tolkien's Library*, item 541, p. 68; and *Chron.*, 655). Conan the Barbarian battles with a Spider the size of a pig in Robert E. Howard's story 'The Tower of the Elephant' (1933), but there is no evidence that Tolkien knew the story. Clark Ashton Smith, one of the horror writer H.P. Lovecraft's circle, also wrote a short story called 'The Seven Geases' about Atlach-Nacha, a giant Spider with a humanoid face; this was published in 1934, but Tolkien was not aware of it. Jennifer Brooker has more plausibly suggested Jeremias Gotthelf's short story *Die Schwarze Spinne* (1842) as a possible source (personal communication); Tolkien was also perhaps influenced by the second-century satire *A True Story* by Lucian of Samosata.

81 Arthur Rackham (illus.), *Mother Goose: The Old Nursery Rhymes* (London: William Heinemann, n.d. [1913]), [41]. The third book of Enid Blyton's Magic Faraway Tree series, which is based on the Norse myth of Yggdrasil, includes Miss Muffet's giant Spider taking several of the central characters prisoner by wrapping them in a web cocoon (*The Folk of the Faraway Tree*, 1946). Blyton may well have been influenced by *The Hobbit*; likewise, Edgar Rice Burroughs, whose novella 'John Carter and the Giant of Mars' (in Book Eleven of the *John Carter of Mars* series, 1941), contains a passing reference to a great Martian Spider, and 'A Wild Ride' (1942) also has a large Spider-like monster. In correspondence, Jessica Yates generously reminded me of the M.R.

James story 'The Ash-Tree' (*Ghost-Stories of an Antiquary* (London: Edward Arnold, 1912), 81–112), which surely must also have been on Tolkien's mind.

82   Gilliver, et al., *Ring of Words*, 165.

83   Gandalf's advice and Beorn's advice: *Hobbit*, 150, 144.

84   'Sir Orfeo', ll. 281–4 (122); Tolkien translated the poem in 1943 or 1944.

85   See the Wilton Diptych of the late fourteenth century. The possible link with Herne the Hunter seems to have developed much later.

86   *Hobbit*, 179.

87   *Hobbit*, 300–301; Rateliff, ii. 720–22.

88   Robert Browning, 'The Pied Piper of Hamelin; A Child's Story', in *Selected Poems*, ed. Daniel Karlin (London: Penguin, 2004), 30–38; for Tolkien's archaeological sources, see Rateliff, i. 448–50.

89   See Rateliff, i. 453.

90   *Hobbit*, 210.

91   *Hobbit*, 227–8; Gilliver, et al., *Ring of Words*, 193–5.

92   *Hobbit*, 228.

93   Zipes, *Breaking the Magic Spell*, 171.

94   *Hobbit*, 227, 235.

95   Shippey, *Author of the Century*, 38–9; Rateliff, ii. 523–4; Job 41:9–34.

96   *Hobbit*, 230.

97   Shippey, *Author of the Century*, 45.

98   These instruments disappeared, as Tolkien himself noted (Rateliff, i. 63).

99   Despite the ink spilt suggesting that the Arkenstone is a recovered Silmaril, there are too many objections to this being the case (see Rateliff, ii. 603–9).

100 *Hobbit*, 317, 278.

101 For Shippey, the death of Smaug 'seems more like the First World War … than any legendary battle from the Dark Ages' (*Author of the Century*, 40).

102 The contract, in the Tengwar alphabet, is discussed by Rateliff, i. 105–7, and reprinted as the frontispiece to his second volume.

103 *Hobbit*, 77, 249.

104 *Hobbit*, 284.

105 Noted by Mark Atherton, *There and Back Again: J.R.R. Tolkien and the Origins of the Hobbit* (London and New York: I.B. Tauris, 2012), 165.

106 *Hobbit*, 313; note that in *LotR* this poem is revised into the song 'The Road Goes Ever On and On' (i. 58).

107 *Hobbit*, 311, 314. Green defines *queer* as, primarily, 'an all-purpose negative' and cites George Henderson's *Keys to Crookdom*: 'Queer also is used to mean mentally deficient, strange' (New York and London: D. Appleton & Co, 1924).

108 Although he does 'reimburse' Thranduil with part of the share of his treasure.

109 See Atherton, *There and Back Again*, 67.
110 Aristotle, *Poetics*, ed. and trans. Stephen Halliwell, Loeb Classical Library 199 (Cambridge, MA: Harvard University Press, 1995), ch. XIII, 71.
111 *Hobbit*, 22, 24, 82, 86, 223; see too Debbie Sly, 'Weaving Nets of Gloom: "Darkness Profound" in Tolkien and Milton', in George Clark and Daniel Timmons (eds), *J.R.R. Tolkien and his Literary Resonances: Views of Middle-Earth* (Westport, CT: Greenwood Press, 2000), 109–19.
112 The comic cannibalism of the trolls is repeated in *The Lord of the Rings* in Sam's song, 'Troll sat alone on his Seat of Stone' (*LotR*, i. 276–7) – again, note the deliberate inconsistency of tone here.
113 *Hobbit*, 317.
114 *Hobbit*, 14.
115 Roberts, *Riddles of the Hobbit*, 13.

Three: The Ambiguity of Evil

1 *LotR*, i. 105.
2 *LotR*, i. 357.
3 *Letters*, 221.
4 C.S. Lewis, 'The Gods Return to Earth' (*Time and Tide* 35 (14 August 1954), 1082–3), reprinted in C.S. Lewis, *Image and Imagination: Essays and Reviews*, ed. Walter Hooper (Cambridge: Cambridge University Press, 2013), 109–10, at 99: see Carpenter, 222; the award took place at a dinner at the Criterion Restaurant in London on 10 September 1957 (*Chron.*, 539).
5 *Chron.*, 845–6.
6 For the dating of 'Leaf by Niggle' see *Guide*, i. 659.
7 Simon Armitage has translated *The Owl and the Nightingale* (London: Faber & Faber, 2021); Tolkien was familiar with Carlyle's Shandean novel from his teaching at Leeds (see Cilli, *Tolkien's Library*, item 318, p. 40).
8 *Sauron Defeated*, 167.
9 Quoted by Carpenter, 207.
10 Quoted from Rayner Unwin, *George Allen & Unwin: A Remembrancer* (London: Merlin Unwin, 1999), 99, in *Chron.*, 414, which relates these negotiations.
11 Letter of 15 November 1952, quoted in *Chron.*, 414.
12 B.L. Joseph, *Elizabethan Acting* (London: Oxford University Press, 1951), [v].
13 *Chron.*, 425.
14 *Letters*, 221.
15 Walter Hooper recalls this in a charming memoir, 'The Inklings', in

Roger White, Judith Wolfe, and Brendan N. Wolfe (eds), *C.S. Lewis & His Circle: Essays and Memoirs from the Oxford C.S. Lewis Society* (Oxford: Oxford University Press, 2015), 197–213, at 211.

16 *Letters*, 183.

17 *Letters*, 183.

18 *Letters*, 247.

19 *The Homecoming* was also repeated on 17 June 1955 (*Chron.*, 482).

20 Letter of 29 January 1955, quoted by *Chron.*, 472; see https://www.theguardian.com/film/2022/mar/12/hoard-of-the-rings-lost-scripts-for-bbc-tolkien-drama-discovered

21 *Chron.*, 484–5, sadly, not all of this material could be included in the appendices and so did not reach the public until 1980, when it was published in *Unfinished Tales*.

22 *Chron.*, 488, see also 491.

23 'The Homecoming of Beorhtnoth Beorhthelm's Son', in J.R.R. Tolkien, *Tree and Leaf / Smith of Wootton Major / The Homecoming of Beorhtnoth* (London, Boston, and Sydney: Unwin Paperbacks, 1979), 149–75, at 152; typically, Tolkien translated these lines in a slightly different way in the drama script.

24 Interestingly, in the definitive unabridged audiobook version brilliantly performed by Brian Inglis, this Prologue appears at the end of the *Fellowship* recording.

25 As Dimitra Fimi points out, the Elves invented the runic alphabet, which was adopted and adapted by the Dwarves and others; moreover, these Elvish runes differ from the Anglo-Saxon runes of *The Hobbit* (*Tolkien, Race and Cultural History: From Fairies to Hobbits* (Basingstoke: Palgrave Macmillan, 2008), 189–92).

26 See Bowers, *Tolkien's Lost Chaucer*, 241.

27 *LotR*, iii. 525. This gambit is discussed by Margaret Hiley, ' "Bizarre or dream like": J.R.R. Tolkien on *Finnegans Wake*', in Martha C. Carpentier (ed.), *Joycean Legacies* (Basingstoke: Palgrave Macmillan, 2015), 112–26.

28 The first lines of The Lord's Prayer in Gothic, from D. Gary Miller, *The Oxford Gothic Grammar* (Oxford: Oxford University Press, 2019), 476.

29 See Hazel K. Bell, 'Fiction Published with Indexes in Chronological Order of Publication', *The Indexer* 25.3 (April 2007), 1–9: of seventy-three works (including later scholarly editions) to 2006, Bell lists only eleven indexed books of fiction published before 1954 with indices prepared or sanctioned by the author (including two each by D'Israeli and Carroll, although she overlooks Samuel Richardson's indices); she discusses the sequence of *LotR* indices on p. 4, and thereafter cites eleven of Tolkien's posthumous publications.

30 *LotR*, i. 12.

31 *LotR* (1954), i. 7.

32 *LotR*, i. 19.

33 *Letters*, 220.

34 Carpenter, 12.

35 T.A. Shippey, review of *Vølve: Scandinavian Views on Science Fiction*, ed. Cay Dollerup, in *Review of English Studies* 31.124 (1980), 500.

36 See Tom Shippey, 'Tolkien as a Post-War Writer', *Mythlore* 21.2 (1996), 84–93(https://dc.swosu.edu/cgi/viewcontent.cgi?article=2133&context =mythlore) and *Road to Middle-earth*; see above, pp. 271–2.

37 *LotR*, i. 9.

38 Shippey, *Author of the Century*, 165–8.

39 *LotR*, i. 12.

40 Letter to Rayner Unwin (12 May 1955), quoted in *Chron.*, 478; for the number of times Tolkien uses allegory with consistency rather than vagueness see Shippey, *Author of the Century*, 161–8.

41 *Letters*, 246.

42 J.R.R. Tolkien, *Sir Gawain and the Green Knight/Pearl/Sir Orfeo*, ed. Christopher Tolkien (London: HarperCollins, 2006), 7 [describing *Pearl*].

43 For the relationship of *Animal Farm* to *The Lord of the Rings*, see Shippey, *Author of the Century*, 115–16; and Shippey, *Road to Middle-earth*, 375.

44 Tolkien, *Sir Gawain and the Green Knight*, 7.

45 The three laws are '(1) a robot may not injure a human being or, through inaction, allow a human being to come to harm; (2) a robot must obey the orders given it by human beings except where such orders would conflict with the First Law; (3) a robot must protect its own existence as long as such protection does not conflict with the First or Second Law' (quoted by https://www.britannica.com/topic/ Three-Laws-of-Robotics).

46 *LotR*, i. 12.

47 Malcolm Joel Barnett, 'Review: The Politics of Middle-Earth', *Polity* 1.3 (1969), 383–7, at 383.

48 See Anna Smol, '"Oh ... Oh ... *Frodo!*" Readings of Male Intimacy in *The Lord of the Rings*', *Modern Fiction Studies* 50.4 (2004), 949–79.

49 J.R.R. Tolkien, *A Secret Vice: Tolkien on Invented Languages*, ed. Dimitra Fimi and Andrew Higgins (London: HarperCollins, 2016), 91–3, 110; Cilli, *Tolkien's Library*, items 1149 and 1150, p. 138; see *Guide*, ii. 1055.

50 Hiley, 'Tolkien on *Finnegans Wake*', in Carpentier (ed.), *Joycean Legacies*, 118; Brian Rosebury also comments on Tolkien's links with his contemporaries (*Tolkien: A Cultural Phenomenon*, 147–54), but rejects the idea that he is a Modernist as his works lack irony (154), which somewhat underplays Tolkien's occasional ironic tone.

51 Stuart Lee's otherwise essential collection *A Companion to J.R.R. Tolkien* has only passing references (if any) to these writers: see, for example,

Anna Vaninskaya, 'Modernity: Tolkien and his Contemporaries', in Lee (ed.), *A Companion to J.R.R. Tolkien*, 350–66, at 364; nevertheless, see Shippey, *Author of the Century*, 310–18.

52	The ballad of 'Thomas the Rhymer' is quoted by Tolkien in *On Fairy-Stories*, 28–9.

53	Tolkien used the inscribed pottery of the 'Sherd of Amenartas' from H. Rider Haggard's *She* (1887) – another novel he admired – as inspiration for the Book of Mazarbul (*Peoples of Middle-earth*, 320).

54	*LotR*, i. 469.

55	*LotR*, i. 304.

56	*LotR*, iii. 452.

57	See *On Fairy-Stories*, 129.

58	Telepathy, often overlooked, is how Gandalf and the Elves returning to Lothlórien and Rivendell communicate (*LotR*, iii. 319–20).

59	*LotR*, i. 405–6.

60	*LotR*, ii. 431.

61	Twice: first in *LotR*, i. 408; then ii. 217 (in the construction 'tom-fool').

62	The key sourcebook here is Stuart Lee and Elizabeth Solopova, *The Keys of Middle-Earth: Discovering Medieval Literature through the Fiction of J.R.R. Tolkien*, 2nd edn (Basingstoke: Palgrave Macmillan, 2015).

63	It is no surprise that Alan Lee, the Oscar-winning artist and designer of Peter Jackson's films, lives on Dartmoor.

64	For Rohan, see Shippey, *Author of the Century*, 91–3. Once Tolkien had completely finished the novel he went on holiday to Italy – or 'Gondor' as he preferred to call it; further indication that Gondor has an Italian aspect is on the map he annotated for Pauline Baynes (see https://www.tolkiensociety.org/2015/11/tolkiens-annotated-map-of-middle-earth-transcribed/).

65	Sibley (ed.), *Tolkien: An Audio Portrait*, CD 1, track 18.

66	See Cilli, *Tolkien's Library*, item 279, p. 36; see also items 276–8; item 2200, p. 274; item 2271, p. 284; and items 835 and 1612, pp. 103, 196. Tolkien made notes on the invented languages of Swift's *Gulliver's Travels* (see Tolkien, *A Secret Vice*, xli, 85–6).

67	See Shippey, *Author of the Century*, 102.

68	Charlotte Plimmer and Denis Plimmer, 'The Man Who Understands Hobbits', *Daily Telegraph Magazine* (22 March 1968), 31–5, at 32.

69	Sally Bushell, *Reading and Mapping Fiction: Spatialising the Literary Text* (Cambridge: Cambridge University Press, 2020), 199–236, at 220 (also https://www.bl.uk/20th-century-literature/articles/jrr-tolkien-as-mapmaker-in-the-hobbit).

70	*Farthing* literally means 'quarters', now obsolete except when referring to pre-decimal coinage.

71	*LotR*, ii. 64.

72	Shippey, *Author of the Century*, 112; see Benedict Anderson, *Imagined*

Communities: Reflections on the Origin and Spread of Nationalism, rev. edn (London and New York: Verso, 2006).

73 See Cilli, *Tolkien's Library*, item 1193, p. 143.

74 See *Hobbit*, 12; there are, of course, many reworkings of Merlin in the Arthurian cycles.

75 *LotR*, ii. 38.

76 *LotR*, ii. 39, 201.

77 See *Treason of Isengard*, 247, 262–3, and *LotR*, i. 462.

78 *LotR*, i. 120.

79 Roger Sale, *Modern Heroism: Essays on D.H. Lawrence, William Empson, & J.R.R. Tolkien* (Berkeley and Los Angeles: University of California Press, 1975), 212.

80 *LotR*, i. Foreword, 12; and *Letters*, 239.

81 *LotR*, i. 12.

82 *LotR*, i. 33.

83 *LotR*, i. 326.

84 *LotR*, i. 64; and Shakespeare, *Othello*, I. iii. 159.

85 *Hobbit*, 87.

86 'Monsters and Critics', 27.

87 See, for instance, Shippey's discussion of interlaced narratives (*Author of the Century*, 102–11).

88 Sam's song (*LotR*, i. 276–7) is based on Tolkien's 'Pēro & Pōdex' (reprinted in Rateliff, i. 101–2), which was written during his time at Leeds and published in *Songs for the Philologists* as 'The Root of the Boot'(19–20); it was only introduced into the novel with some doubts (see *Treason of Isengard*, 59).

89 *LotR*, i. 272.

90 *LotR*, i. 347.

91 *LotR*, i. 89 (Tolkien's capitalization).

92 *LotR*, ii. 275.

93 *LotR*, iii. 203.

94 Kathryn F. Crabbe comments that this pairing – or rather doubling – of Frodo with Sauron shows that the 'ultimate defeat' is 'not simply to lose the battle with evil, but to become incorporated into it' (*J.R.R. Tolkien* (New York: Frederick Ungar Publishing Co., 1981), 87).

95 *LotR*, iii. 275; note too that Beowulf wrenched off Grendel's arm, thus inflicting on him a mortal wound.

96 See *Hobbit*, 317.

97 *LotR*, i. 291.

98 *LotR*, i. 328.

99 *LotR*, i. 475.

100 *LotR*, ii. 209.

101 *LotR*, ii. 249.

102 *LotR*, ii. 361.

103 *LotR*, ii. 192; *LotR*, i. 474 (Tolkien's capitalization).

104 *LotR*, i. 351.

105 *LotR*, ii. 106, 108.

106 *LotR*, iii. 225.

107 *LotR*, iii. 248.

108 *LotR*, iii. 254.

109 *LotR*, iii. 102.

110 *OED*.

111 Shakespeare, *Macbeth*, IV. iii. 133.

112 In Tolkien's essay 'Nomenclature of *The Lord of the Rings*', he notes Shakespeare's use in *Macbeth* as referring to a peal of thunder on the Last Day, but states that his use is of a 'fissure', and that his source was a story by Algernon Blackwood (Tolkien, 'Guide to the Names in *The Lord of the Rings*: Nomenclature of *The Lord of the Rings*', in Jared Lobdell (ed.), *A Tolkien Compass: Fascinating Studies and Interpretations of J.R.R. Tolkien's Most Popular Epic Fantasies* (New York: Ballantine Books, 1975), 168–216, at 194; see *Guide*, ii. 1055).

113 For 'eucatastrophe' see *On Fairy-Stories*, 66–76; Shippey rightly sees Gollum's fall not as luck or chance but as the consequence of a series of decisions (*Author of the Century*, 143–7).

114 *LotR*, iii. 271.

115 Peter J. Schakel, *The Way into Narnia: A Reader's Guide* (Grand Rapids, MI and Cambridge: William B. Eerdmans Publishing Company, 2005), 30.

116 Shippey, *Author of the Century*, 133–8.

117 John Marenbon, 'Anicius Manlius Severinus Boethius', *The Stanford Encyclopedia of Philosophy* (Winter 2021 Edition), ed. Edward N. Zalta (https://plato.stanford.edu/archives/win2021/entries/boethius/).

118 Boethius, *The Consolation of Philosophy*, trans. and ed. Peter Walsh (Oxford: Oxford University Press, 2008), 82 (III. xii); see also *The Consolation of Philosophy*, trans. and ed. Victor Watts, rev. edn (London: Penguin Books, 1999) – Watts translates this as 'God rules the universe by the helm of goodness, that all things obey willingly' and, moreover 'evil is nothing' (82).

119 Boethius, *Consolation of Philosophy*, ed. Watts, 117 (V. i); the definition derives from Aristotle's definition of causality (Boethius, *Consolation of Philosophy*, ed. Walsh, 158n.).

120 Marenbon, 'Boethius'.

121 See Boethius, *Consolation of Philosophy*, ed. Watts, 116–17 (V. i).

122 Saint Augustine, 'Christian Instruction', trans. John J. Gavigan, OSA, in *The Fathers of the Church: Saint Augustine* (Washington, DC: The Catholic University Press of America, 2002), 30 (ch. 4).

123 On the remission of Galadriel, see *Release – Tolkien in Oxford*; *Archive on 4*, 'Tolkien: The Lost Recordings'; and Lee, 'Tolkien in Oxford (BBC, 1968)', 153.

124 Discussed by Shippey, *Author of the Century*, 130–31, and *passim*.
125 Boethius, *Consolation of Philosophy*, ed. Watts, 81 (III. xii).
126 Boethius, *Consolation of Philosophy*, ed. Watts, 30 (II. iv); Walsh's translation is very similar (Boethius, *Consolation of Philosophy*, ed. Walsh, 26); see Kathleen E. Dubs, 'Providence, Fate, and Chance: Boethian Philosophy in *The Lord of the Rings*', *Twentieth Century Literature* 27.1 (Spring, 1981), 34–42.
127 *LotR*, ii. 119.
128 *LotR*, ii. 143.
129 *LotR*, ii. 251.
130 Boethius, *Consolation of Philosophy*, ed. Walsh, 65 (III. xi); translated in the same way in Boethius, *Consolation of Philosophy*, ed. Watts, 77.
131 See Shippey, *Author of the Century*, 130ff.
132 *LotR*, i. 350.
133 *LotR*, iii. 227.
134 *LotR*, i. 425; interestingly this usage, 'To produce or generate as spawn or in large numbers; also, in contemptuous use, to give birth to' (*OED*), was first used by Shakespeare (*Measure for Measure*, III. i. 372).
135 *LotR*, ii. 107.
136 *Hobbit*, 51.
137 Sauron and Fëanor (who created the Tengwar alphabet) appear to be the only inventors of language in Middle-Earth.
138 *OED*.
139 *Unfinished Tales*, 348; *Return of the Shadow*, 118.
140 *LotR*, i. 377.
141 *LotR*, i. 377.
142 *LotR*, ii. 436.
143 Shippey, *Author of the Century*, 208–9; *LotR*, iii. 277; later, 25 March is also the birthdate of Sam and Rosie's first child (*LotR*, iii. 372); see my book *The Seasons: A Celebration of the English Year* (London: Atlantic, 2014), 103–4, 51.
144 W.H. Auden, 'At the End of the Quest, Victory', *New York Times* (22 January 1956), https://archive.nytimes.com/www.nytimes.com/books/01/02/11/specials/tolkien-return.html.
145 See Shippey, *Author of the Century*, 147.
146 *LotR*, iii. 364; Tolkien, contrarily, thought Frodo less 'Christ-like' as he was simply continuing the story: see Sibley (ed.), *Tolkien: An Audio Portrait*, CD 1, track 18.

Four: The Hesitancy of Good

1 Hugo Dyson of the Inklings, in contrast, was belligerently dismissive of the work-in-progress.
2 C.S. Lewis, *The Collected Letters of C.S. Lewis*, ed. Walter Hooper

(London: HarperCollins, 2006), iii. 287 (letter dated 15 May 1959).

3   See Andrew Lazo, who cites an unpublished letter by Lewis on his
    active role ('A Kind of Mid-Wife: J.R.R. Tolkien and C.S. Lewis –
    sharing influence', in Jane Chance (ed.), *Tolkien the Medievalist* (London
    and New York: Routledge, 2002), 36–49, at 40).

4   Walter Hooper, 'Preface', in C.S. Lewis, *On Stories, and Other Essays on
    Literature*, ed. Walter Hooper (Orlando, etc.: Harvest, 1982), ix–xxi,
    at x; see also Lazo, 'A Kind of Mid-Wife'.

5   *Return of the Shadow*, 13–15.

6   *Return of the Shadow*, 41.

7   *Return of the Shadow*, 42.

8   *Return of the Shadow*, 115–16.

9   *Letters*, 34; *Return of the Shadow*, 42–4, 48.

10 *Return of the Shadow*, 54.

11 *Return of the Shadow*, 75.

12 *Return of the Shadow*, 80.

13 *Return of the Shadow*, 80.

14 *Letters*, 40.

15 *Return of the Shadow*, 118.

16 *Return of the Shadow*, 154, 158.

17 *Return of the Shadow*, 221.

18 *Return of the Shadow*, 227.

19 *Return of the Shadow*, 233.

20 *Return of the Shadow*, 250–72.

21 *Return of the Shadow*, 269.

22 *Return of the Shadow*, 310–14; see *LotR*, i. 17ff.

23 *LotR*, i. 24–5 (see *Letters*, 231).

24 *Return of the Shadow*, 343.

25 *Return of the Shadow*, 355.

26 Shippey, *Author of the Century*, 52.

27 T.A. Shippey, 'The Curious Case of Denethor and the Palantír, Once
    More', *Mallorn* 57 (2016), 6–9, at 6.

28 *Return of the Shadow*, 381: another allusion to *The Tragedy of King Lear*,
    in Edgar's rhyme 'Child Roland to the dark tower came, / His word was
    still "Fie, fo, and fum; / I smell the blood of a British man"' (III. iv. 170);
    see also Robert Browning's poem 'Childe Roland to the Dark Tower
    Came' (*Selected Poems*, ed. Karlin, 93–9), in which the Dark Tower, the
    goal of a mysterious quest, stands on a desolate and rotting landscape
    through which a river runs, appearing to flow over the faces of the dead.

29 *Return of the Shadow*, 382–4; see also 397.

30 For more on the Company see *Treason of Isengard*, 114–15, and my
    essay 'The Decline and Fall of the Company of the Ring'.

31 *Adventures of Tom Bombadil*, 99–103; *LotR*, i. 306–9; *Treason of Isengard*,
    85; *War of the Ring*, x; and James Hogg, *The Jacobite Relics of Scotland;*

being The Songs, Airs, and Legends, of the Adherents to the House of Stuart (Edinburgh: William Blackwood, 1819), 218–19; see also Peter and Iona Opie (eds), *The Oxford Dictionary of Nursery Rhymes* (Oxford: Clarendon Press, 1952), 354.

32 The monarch's ability to cure the disease scrofula, the 'king's evil', by 'royal touch' was practised until 1714; the deposed Catholic king James II continued the tradition in exile, but it was dismissed as superstition by the Protestant William III (see Shakespeare, *Macbeth*, IV. iii. 147–60).

33 For more on the mood of the Company see my essay 'A Comparison of Fellowship and Company in *The Lord of the Rings*'.

34 *Return of the Shadow*, 442.

35 *Return of the Shadow*, 467.

36 *Return of the Shadow*, 462; see also *Treason of Isengard*, 116.

37 *Return of the Shadow*, 461; Christopher Tolkien's argument is based on paper stock (see *Treason of Isengard*, 67).

38 *Treason of Isengard*, 1.

39 Graham Harman, *Weird Realism: Lovecraft and Philosophy* (Winchester and Washington, DC: Zero Books, 2011), 3.

40 Harman, *Weird Realism*, 3.

41 Harman, *Weird Realism*, 9.

42 Harman, *Weird Realism*, 54.

43 Harman, *Weird Realism*, 9.

44 Tolkien refers to James's *Ghost-Stories of an Antiquary* in his notes on fairy stories (*On Fairy-Stories*, 261; and see Cilli, *Tolkien's Library*, items 1092 and 1093, p. 132). For a penetrating analysis of James's style here, see Henry Bartholomew, 'Theory in the Shadows: Speculative Realism and the Gothic, 1890–1920' (University of Exeter PhD thesis, 2021), 55.

45 M.R. James, 'Canon Alberic's Scrap-Book', *Ghost-Stories of an Antiquary*, 3–28, at 18–19. For a penetrating analysis of James's style here, see Henry Bartholomew, 'Theory in the Shadows: Speculative Realism and the Gothic, 1890-1920' (University of Exeter PhD thesis, 2021), 55.

46 Harman, *Weird Realism*, 234–5.

47 *Treason of Isengard*, 197.

48 *LotR*, i. 428–9. Gandalf's original words appear three times in the Ralph Bakshi film, but Peter Jackson uses them just once in *The Fellowship of the Ring* before Gandalf almost immediately revises his statement to 'You shall not pass' (Fran Walsh, Philippa Boyens, and Peter Jackson, *The Lord of the Rings: The Fellowship of the Ring*, screenplay typescript (New Line Cinema, 2001), 130–31).

49 *LotR*, i. 428–9.

50 *Treason of Isengard*, 209.

51 *Treason of Isengard*, 211.

52   *Treason of Isengard*, 212.
53   *Treason of Isengard*, 277.
54   *LotR*, i. 489.
55   *Unfinished Tales*, 296; *Peoples of Middle-earth*, 337.
56   Dwarves are almost completely absent, except in the appendices –
     although there are plenty of dead Dwarves, and they are the prevailing
     species in *The Hobbit*.
57   *LotR*, i. 473.
58   *LotR*, i. 450.
59   *LotR*, ii. 351.
60   *LotR*, ii. 177; see Lynn Forest-Hill, 'Underground Man', *Times
     Literary Supplement* (14 January 2011), 14–15, at 14; see too ensuing
     correspondence, *TLS* (21 January 2011), 4; and *TLS* (28 January
     2011), 4.
61   *LotR*, ii. 12–13, 27.
62   *Letters*, 211n.–12n. (comments repeated in *Letters*, 231).
63   The Anglo-Saxon phrase appears in *Beowulf*, 'The Ruin, 'The Wanderer',
     and elsewhere: see P.J. Frankis, 'The Thematic Significance of *enta
     geweorc* and Related Imagery in *The Wanderer*', *Anglo-Saxon England*
     2 (1973), 253–69; see Gilliver, et al., *Ring of Words*, 119–21; see also
     Verlyn Flieger, 'The Green Knight, the Green Man, and Treebeard', in
     Green Suns and Faërie: Essays on J.R.R. Tolkien (Kent, OH: Kent State
     University Press, 2012), 211–22.
64   *Letters*, 212n.; he added a further comment on gendered differences
     towards wild things and gardening being his inspiration from 'life'.
65   Mark 8:23–4; see Roberts, *Riddles of the Hobbit*, 28.
66   Algernon Blackwood, 'The Man Whom the Trees Loved', in *Pan's Garden:
     A Volume of Nature Stories* (London: Macmillan and Co., 1912), 3–99, at
     31, 9 (Blackwood's capitalization); *LotR*, ii. 83. Cilli, *Tolkien's Library*, lists
     several Blackwood titles which Tolkien knew (items 152–7, p. 21).
67   *Treason of Isengard*, 411.
68   *LotR*, ii. 79; perhaps Tolkien's hesitancy in introducing Hobbits into
     Middle-Earth is reflected in the fact that Treebeard and the Ents have
     never heard of Hobbits.
69   *LotR*, ii. 88, 93ff.
70   *LotR*, i. 69.
71   *LotR*, ii. 125.
72   *LotR*, i. 433.
73   *LotR*, iii. 311, 314.
74   Gimli and Legolas also have a rather odd conversation on city planning:
     LotR, iii. 176.
75   *LotR*, ii. 116.
76   *LotR*, ii. 124, 110.
77   *Treason of Isengard*, 428 – see Christopher Tolkien's interesting

speculations on the same page that it was an 'emanation' of Gandalf.

78   *Treason of Isengard*, 426; *LotR*, ii. 120.

79   *Treason of Isengard*, 442, 449; *Beowulf*, 21; the relevant lines are ll.
     237–57, see *Beowulf: An Edition with Relevant Shorter Texts*, ed.
     Mitchell and Robinson, 56.

80   *LotR*, ii. 141.

81   *Treason of Isengard*, 448.

82   *War of the Ring*, 54.

83   *War of the Ring*, 78.

84   *War of the Ring*, 66 – retained in the published version (*LotR*, ii. 240).

85   *LotR*, iii. 313.

86   *Treason of Isengard*, 340; see also *War of the Ring*, 184ff.

87   *Letters*, 70.

88   *War of the Ring*, 105, also 113–15.

89   *Letters*, 77.

90   *LotR*, ii. 335.

91   Erich Maria Remarque, *All Quiet on the Western Front*, trans.
     A.W. Wheen (London: Pan Books, n.d.), 147.

92   *LotR*, iii. 31.

93   *Letters*, 81.

94   *War of the Ring*, 190.

95   Defined by Christopher Booker as The Quest, Overcoming the
     Monster, Rebirth, Voyage and Return, Rags to Riches, Tragedy, and
     Comedy: see *The Seven Basic Plots: Why We Tell Stories* (London and
     New York: Continuum, 2004), especially 316–21.

96   Reproduced in McIlwaine, *Tolkien: Maker of Middle-earth*, 392–3.

97   *War of the Ring*, 357.

98   See Shippey, *Author of the Century*, 102–11. Shakespeare is the only
     source for Elves knitting up one's hair overnight; it is a verb that
     deserves to be revived (*Tragedy of King Lear*, II. ii. 173).

99   Shakespeare does very occasionally deploy a narrative voice addressing
     the audience as, for example, the allegorical figure of Rumour in *2.
     Henry IV*, or the Chorus in *The Winter's Tale*.

100 Shakespeare, *Tragedy of King Lear*, IV. v. 145.

101 *LotR*, i. 455 (Tolkien's emphasis), ii. 403.

102 *War of the Ring*, 337.

103 Daphne Castell, 'The Realms of Tolkien' [interview], *New Worlds SF* 50,
     no. 168 (1966), 143–54, at 151: see *LotR*, iii. 121.

104 Shakespeare, *Hamlet*, I. i. 138–45.

105 John Brand, *Observations on Popular Antiquities: including the Whole of
     Mr. Bourne's Antiquitates Vulgares, with Addenda to Every Chapter of that
     Work* (Newcastle-upon-Tyne, 1777), 54.

106 Brand, *Observations on Popular Antiquities*, 64.

107 Shakespeare, *Macbeth*, V. x. 12–16.

108 *War of the Ring*, 385.
109 *War of the Ring*, 401.
110 *Sauron Defeated*, 18; *Letters*, 103–4.
111 Popularized by Thomas Percy in 'An Essay on the Ancient English Minstrels', in *Reliques of Ancient English Poetry*, 3rd edn (London, 1774), i. pp. xix–lxxviii, at xxix.
112 *LotR*, iii. 246, 253.
113 *Sauron Defeated*, 4.
114 *Sauron Defeated*, 5; see also 6.
115 *Sauron Defeated*, 5.
116 *Sauron Defeated*, 38 – although, strangely, Christopher Tolkien does not think that this change is significant; the italics are presumably Christopher Tolkien's editorial intervention, although this is not made clear.
117 Shippey rather splits hairs over whether Frodo has free choice to claim the Ring or not at the Crack of Doom (*Author of the Century*, 140), but the words of the final version – 'I *will* not do this deed' (my italics) – and his statement of possession are clear: this is an act of will, an assertion of self. Tolkien conceded Frodo's failure in an interview, stating that 'Frodo actually failed' (see Sibley (ed.), *Tolkien: An Audio Portrait*, CD 1, track 18).
118 *Sauron Defeated*, 53.
119 See the 1st edn of *LotR* (1955), iii. 260–63, compared with the 2nd edn (1966), iii. 260–63.
120 *Sauron Defeated*, 89.
121 *LotR*, iii. 360.
122 As for the volume titles, Tolkien never resolved them to his complete satisfaction – in particular, *The Two Towers* remained ambiguous: were the two towers Orthanc and Cirith Ungol, or Orthanc and Minas Morgul (see *Letters*, 170–71, 173, and 444n.)? His illustration of 1954, later used for the book cover, seems to show Minas Morgul and Orthanc (see *Guide*, i. 545; and Roberts, *Riddles of the Hobbit*, 131).
123 *LotR*, iii. 334.
124 *LotR*, iii. 338, 341.
125 *LotR*, iii. 360.
126 *LotR*, iii. 362.
127 *LotR*, iii. 365.
128 Eugene Thacker, *In the Dust of This Planet [Horror of Philosophy, vol. 1]* (Winchester and Washington, DC: Zero Books, 2011), 98.
129 *LotR*, ii. 403.
130 *LotR*, iii. 377.
131 *LotR*, iii. 378; from 2002 the text was revised, adding a comma after 'Well'.
132 *Letters*, 231. *OED* defines a *metafiction* as 'Fiction in which the author

self-consciously alludes to the artificiality or literariness of a work', and
then quotes a review of Austin Wright's novel *Tony and Susan* (1993)
that, quite unexpectedly, captures something of the metafictionality of
LotR: 'a metafiction that ingeniously comments on the experience of
reading it, but which, as fiction, retains a feverish psychic grip' (*Observer*
(18 September 1994), Review section, 19/1).

133 Foreword, *LotR* (1954), i. 7.
134 See Shippey, *Author of the Century*, 68; Bowers notes that Chaucer was
also partial to including unexplained references in his work (*Tolkien's
Lost Chaucer*, 238).
135 See *Farmer Giles*, 13, 38.
136 *LotR*, i. 251–2.
137 Roberts mentioned some of these (*Riddles of the Hobbit*, 127–9).
138 *LotR*, iii. 275; see Shippey, *Author of the Century*, 153.
139 *LotR*, i. 491, 457.
140 *LotR*, i. 230; see, for example, Shakespeare's *Merchant of Venice* (II. vii. 65).
141 *LotR*, ii. 38.
142 Shakespeare, *Tragedy of King Lear*, I. iv. 212–13.
143 *Letters*, 88.
144 *LotR*, iii. 141, 296ff.
145 *LotR*, i. 121.
146 *LotR*, ii. 299.
147 *LotR*, ii. 299.
148 *LotR*, ii. 281.
149 *LotR*, ii. 280.
150 Shakespeare, *Tragedy of King* Lear, IV. vi. 39–40; *LotR*, iii. 258.
151 *LotR*, ii. 428.
152 See, for example, *LotR*, iii. 52, 72, 172.
153 *LotR*, ii. 123.
154 *LotR*, iii. 160.
155 *LotR*, iii. 57–8, 102.
156 Tom Shippey: first discussed in *Author of the Century*, 172; then in an
appendix on 'Peter Jackson's Film Versions' in *Road to Middle-Earth*,
409–29, at 425; then in 'Curious Case of Denethor and the Palantír,
Once More', 8.
157 First appears *LotR*, ii. 235, then chapter ii. 241ff.
158 *LotR*, iii. 65.
159 *LotR*, i. 464.
160 *LotR*, ii. 19; see above, p. 65.
161 *LotR*, ii. 310.
162 *LotR*, ii. 363.
163 *LotR*, i. 343, ii. 34, ii. 41.
164 *LotR*, ii. 36.
165 *LotR*, ii. 217.

166 *LotR*, ii. 227, 233.

167 *LotR*, ii. 232.

168 *LotR*, ii. 260.

169 *LotR*, ii. 440.

170 *LotR*, i. 489, iii. 268.

171 *LotR*, iii. 267.

172 *LotR*, iii. 100, 102, 113, 202.

173 *Monsters and Critics*, 31.

174 *LotR*, iii. 207–10.

175 Shippey suggests that the Ring is 'addictive' (*Road to Middle-earth*, 126), although this does not explain its effect on, say, Boromir or Sam (see Roberts, *Riddles of the Hobbit*, 117–18).

176 Roberts, *Riddles of the Hobbit*, 133.

177 *LotR*, ii. 119 (see Roberts, *Riddles of the Hobbit*, 132).

178 See Roberts, *Riddles of the Hobbit*, 133.

179 *LotR*, iii. 137.

180 *LotR*, iii. 115, 152; very few of Tolkien's characters deliberately commit suicide, although many fight against insuperable, suicidal odds; Túrin, the doomed hero of the First Age, is a rare exception.

181 Timothy Morton, *Ecology Without Nature: Rethinking Environmental Aesthetics* (Cambridge, MA: Harvard University Press, 2007), 98.

182 Verlyn Flieger describes this as 'an image of post-modern indeterminacy' (Verlyn Flieger, 'A Post-Modern Medievalist', in *Green Suns and Faërie*, 251–61, at 259; see also Flieger, 'A Distant Mirror: Tolkien and Jackson in the Looking-Glass', in *Green Suns and Faërie*, 292–303, at 300–302).

183 *Letters*, 220; see also 284.

184 *Letters*, 239: see Michael Piret, 'W.H. Auden and Inklings', in White, Wolfe, and Wolfe, *C.S. Lewis & His Circle*, 122–34, at 129–31.

185 *Letters*, 213.

186 See Robert Eaglestone, 'Introduction', in Robert Eaglestone (ed.), *Reading The Lord of the Rings* (London and New York: Continuum, 2005), 1–11, at 4–7, which draws on Paul Fussell's *The Great War and Modern Memory* (Oxford: Oxford University Press, 1975), *Killing in Verse and Prose* (London: Bellew Publishing, 1988), and *Wartime* (Oxford: Oxford University Press, 1989); see too, of course, Garth, *Great War*.

187 *Le Monde*, 6 September 1973; reprinted in *Tolkien Studies* 5 (2008), 186–8, at 186.

188 Roberts, *Riddles of the Hobbit*, 147.

189 See Shippey, *Author of the Century*, 219–20.

190 See Roberts, *Riddles of the Hobbit*, 157.

191 Clyde Kilby spent the summer of 1966 acting as Tolkien's secretary in an attempt to bring 'The Silmarillion' into order (see Kilby, *Tolkien and The Silmarillion*).

192 See *Letters*, 301–2.
193 *Letters*, 333; the letter is reproduced in McIlwaine, *Tolkien: Maker of Middle-earth*, 98–9.
194 A.N. Wilson, *Iris Murdoch as I Knew Her* (London: Arrow Books, 2004), 224; Wilson also makes various comments about Christopher Tolkien, noting that he was 'one of the best lecturers in the English faculty' (252).
195 *Release – Tolkien in Oxford*; see *Archive on 4*, 'Tolkien: The Lost Recordings'; and Lee, 'Tolkien in Oxford (BBC, 1968)'.
196 Quoted by Lee, 'Tolkien in Oxford (1968)', 120–21.
197 *Letters*, 389–90.

Five: Lucid Moments

1 Linda Hutcheon, *A Theory of Adaptation* (New York and London: Routledge, 2006), 8 [I am indebted to Prof. Debra Ramsay for this reference].
2 Hutcheon, *Theory of Adaptation*, 8; a palimpsest is an overwritten manuscript, 'a thing likened to such a writing surface, esp. in having been reused or altered while still retaining traces of its earlier form; a multilayered record' (*OED*).
3 For all games see https://www.youtube.com/watch?v=8dxdWikk-iA
4 *Guide*, i. 547–8; Tolkien's recording was issued as a complimentary cassette tape for the 1992 Tolkien Centenary Conference and is a very scarce item.
5 See https://genome.ch.bbc.co.uk/00695fd2a8ef46158c8b64b0e6319a1b
6 *Chron.*, 500–508, 523–4.; see Lee, 'Tolkien in Oxford (BBC, 1968)', 117–18; and https://www.theguardian.com/film/2022/mar/12/hoard-of-the-rings-lost-scripts-for-bbc-tolkien-drama-discovered
7 See *Letters*, 228.
8 See *Chron.*, 506.
9 *Letters*, 13, 198.
10 *Letters*, 261; see *Chron.*, 539.
11 See *Letters*, 270–77; and Janet Brennan Croft, 'Three Rings for Hollywood: Scripts for *The Lord of the Rings* by Zimmerman, Boorman, and Beagle', in *Fantasy Fiction Into Film*, ed. Leslie Stratyner and James R. Keller (Jefferson, NC: McFarland and Co., 2007), 7–20.
12 *Letters*, 270.
13 *Letters*, 274.
14 Denis O'Dell, with Bob Neaverson, *At the Apple's Core: The Beatles from the Inside* (London: Peter Owen, 2002), 201n., 103; O'Dell's full account is at 89–105 – even the exacting Tolkien scholars Hammond and Scull seem to have been spellbound by Beatles mythology (*Guide*, i. 23).
15 O'Dell, *At the Apple's Core*, 104. According to McCartney this idea was spiked by Tolkien himself, who was still at that stage holding the rights,

but this seems improbable (see 'Beatles Plan for Rings Film', CNN.com (28 March 2002): http://edition.cnn.com/2002/SHOWBIZ/Movies /03/28/rings.beatles/index.html).

16 See *Guide*, i. 1–8; 75¢ is equivalent to about $6.80 today.

17 Richard Plotz, 'The Silmarillion', *Tolkien Journal*, 1.2 (1965), 2 (reprinted by the Mythopoeic Society: see https://dc.swosu.edu/ tolkien_journal/vol1/iss2/1): this short article adds material to the letter to Plotz partially published in *Letters*, 359–62.

18 C.N. Manlove, *Modern Fantasy* (Cambridge: Cambridge University Press, 1975), 157; Manlove goes on to analyse Tolkien's work, 158–206.

19 David Bowie allegedly later auditioned for the Peter Jackson movies to play either Gandalf or Elrond (see Ben Child, 'David Bowie "Did Audition" for Lord of the Rings', *Guardian* (29 January 2016): https:// www.theguardian.com/film/2016/jan/29/david-bowie-auditioned- lord-of-the-rings-dominic-monaghan).

20 The word is Tolkien's coinage: see Gilliver, et al., *Ring of Words*, 216–18, 226.

21 For the 1960s Tolkien craze see Lin Carter, *Tolkien: A Look Behind The Lord of the Rings* (New York: Ballantine, 1969), 1–6.

22 Reviewed by David Hurwitz, https://www.classicstoday.com/review/ review-9704/

23 The deal for *The Hobbit* was more complicated: see above, pp. 245–8.

24 John Harlow and Rachel Dobson, '*Lord of the Rings* Is Worth £3bn but Tolkien Sold the Film Rights to Ward Off the Taxman', *Sunday Times* (15 December 2002): 16 (https://www.thetimes.co.uk/article/focus- tolkien-sold-film-rights-to-lord-of-the-rings-to-avoid-taxman- ttwv6qh3rlv). The sum in sterling was £104,602. The contract documents became public during the lawsuit made by the Tolkien Trust and HarperCollins, which by 1990 was the publisher of Tolkien's work, against New Line Cinema in 2008; it appears that the publisher George Allen & Unwin sold the rights for *The Hobbit* and *The Two Towers*, while the Sassoon Trustee and Executor Corporation (an overseas investment company) sold the rights for *The Fellowship of the Ring* and *The Return of the King*. The case was designated 'Christopher Reuel Tolkien v. New Line Cinema Corp., BC385294' (see Kristin Thompson, 'Tolkien Trust and HarperCollins suing New Line Cinema', *The Frodo Franchise: Lord of the Rings and Modern Hollywood*, 11 February 2008: http://www. kristinthompson.net/blog/2008/02/11/tolkien-trust-and-harpercollins- suing-new-line-cinema/). News that the case had been settled out of court broke on 8 September 2009 (see Kristin Thompson, 'Tolkien Trust Lawsuit's Settlement Official; Christopher Tolkien Comments', *The Frodo Franchise: Lord of the Rings and Modern Hollywood*, 8 September 2009: http://www.kristinthompson.net/blog/2009/09/08/tolkien- trust-lawsuits-settlement-official-christopher-tolkien-comments/). *The*

Hollywood Reporter carried the headline 'Tolkien Settlement: More than $100 Million', 8 September 2009: https://www.hollywoodreporter.com/business/business-news/tolkien-settlement-100-million-63321/

25 Text from *TheOneRing.net* ('greendragon' [Kristin Thompson], 'Tolkien Rights and the Amazon Television Deal – Some Insight' (15 November 2017): https://www.theonering.net/torwp/2017/11/15/104416-tolkien-rights-and-the-amazon-television-deal-some-insight/); also quoted, with minor changes, by Kristin Thompson, 'The Tolkien Trust Lawsuit: Developments since May', *The Frodo Franchise: Lord of the Rings and Modern Hollywood* (21 August 2008): http://www.kristinthompson.net/blog/2008/08/21/the-tolkien-trust-lawsuit-developments-since-may/; see also Douglas C. Kane, 'Clearing Up Misconceptions regarding the Tolkien v. New Line Lawsuit', *TheOneRing.net* (14 June 2008): http://www.theonering.net/torwp/2008/06/14/29016-clearing-up-misconceptions-regarding-the-tolkien-vs-new-line-lawsuit/#more-29016

26 The dramatist Peter Shaffer, author of the acclaimed play *The Royal Hunt of the Sun* (1964), may also have been considered.

27 John Boorman, *The Emerald Forest Diary* (New York: Farrar Straus Giroux, 1985), 20.

28 Boorman, *Emerald Forest Diary*, 20; pages were also glued to pieces of black card and annotated.

29 Boorman notes that Tolkien 'wrote asking me how I intended to make the film'; Boorman responded that it would be 'live action and he was much relieved', explaining that he had a 'dread that it would be an animation film and was comforted by my reply' (Boorman, *Emerald Forest Diary*, 21).

30 Boorman, *Emerald Forest Diary*, 21.

31 John Boorman and Rospo Pallenberg, *The Lord of the Rings*, screenplay typescript (n.d., n.p.), 34; there are some caustic summaries at https://greenjeans1978.livejournal.com/10857.html , apparently taken from postings by 'Ichjua' on http://forums.theonering.com/viewtopic.php?t=51271&postdays=0&postorder=asc&start=60

32 Quoted by James Fenwick, 'John Boorman's *The Lord of the Rings*: A Case Study of an Unmade Film', *Historical Journal of Film, Radio and Television* 42.2 (2022), 261–85, at 268.

33 Quoted by Fenwick, 'John Boorman's *The Lord of the Rings*', 269.

34 Christopher Lee was adamant he would be in the film, even auditioning for the role of Saruman – something he 'hadn't done for years and years and years!' (Brian Sibley, *The Lord of the Rings: Official Movie Guide* (London: HarperCollins, 2001), [33], see also 51.)

35 See Fenwick, 'John Boorman's *The Lord of the Rings*', 262.

36 See my book, *The Gothic: A Very Short Introduction* (Oxford: Oxford University Press, 2012), 133.

37   Boorman, *Emerald Forest Diary*, 20.
38   Dan Yakir, 'The Sorcerer: John Boorman interviewed by Dan Yakir',
     Film Comment, May–June 1981, Vol. 17, No. 3, special issue: 'Eccentric
     Cinema' (May–June 1981) 49–53, at 49.
39   Notably in *Zardoz* (1974), *Exorcist II: The Heretic* (1977), and *Excalibur*
     (1981): see Brian Hoyle, *The Cinema of John Boorman* (Lanham, MD,
     Toronto, and Plymouth: Scarecrow Press, 2012), 92–3, 124.
40   Boorman and Pallenberg, 30.
41   Boorman and Pallenberg, 30.
42   Boorman and Pallenberg, 43.
43   Boorman and Pallenberg, 46.
44   Boorman and Pallenberg, 47.
45   Boorman and Pallenberg, 52.
46   Boorman and Pallenberg, 64.
47   Boorman and Pallenberg, 69.
48   Boorman and Pallenberg, 76.
49   Boorman and Pallenberg, 106.
50   Boorman and Pallenberg, 116.
51   Boorman and Pallenberg, 117.
52   Boorman and Pallenberg, 126.
53   Boorman and Pallenberg, 137.
54   Boorman and Pallenberg, 138.
55   It is worth recalling that Tolkien had considered the possibility that
     Aragorn could marry Éowyn, before Arwen began to emerge as a
     counterpart to the Elf-maiden Lúthien.
56   Also known as 'The Lady and the Blacksmith' and by various similar
     titles.
57   Boorman and Pallenberg, 162.
58   Boorman and Pallenberg, 172.
59   Boorman and Pallenberg, 174.
60   Boorman and Pallenberg, 176.
61   Boorman and Pallenberg, 176.
62   Boorman and Pallenberg, 143.
63   Quoted by Fenwick, 'John Boorman's *The Lord of the Rings*', 268;
     Boorman, *Emerald Forest Diary*, 23.
64   See https://www.zaentz.com/middle-earth-enterprises.html; and
     Kristin Thompson, *The Frodo Franchise: The Lord of the Rings and Modern
     Hollywood* (Berkeley, Los Angeles, and London: University of California
     Press, 2007), 19, 23.
65   It has been suggested that Bakshi is satirizing the American Dream in a
     medium usually reserved for children: see James Craig Holte, 'Ethnicity
     and the Popular Imagination: Ralph Bakshi and the American Dream',
     Multi-Ethnic Literature of the United States 8.4 (1981), 105–13. Crumb
     was not, in fact, happy with the final result and promptly killed off Fritz.

66 Remarkably, *Pink Flamingos* was made by New Line Cinema, whose investment made Peter Jackson's *Rings* possible.

67 Term quoted by Holte, 'Ethnicity and the Popular Imagination', 110.

68 See https://filmschoolrejects.com/ralph-bakshi-lord-of-the-rings/

69 Bakshi seems to be the sole source for this information: see David Weiner, 'How the Battle for "Lord of the Rings" Nearly Broke a Director', *The Hollywood Reporter* (10 November 2018: https://www.hollywoodreporter. com/movies/movie-news/lord-rings-almost-starred-mick-jagger-1160023/). In 1976, Led Zeppelin had released both the album *Presence* and the film and accompanying live soundtrack *The Song Remains the Same*, and spent four months of 1977 touring the US before the remaining dates were cancelled after singer Robert Plant's five-year-old son Karac died; whether they would have had the time or the inclination to record *The Lord of the Rings* is an open question – they certainly did not need the money at this stage in their career. As for Jagger, Bakshi claims that his call came too late: this would presumably have been mid-1978 when the band had just released *Some Girls* and were touring the US to promote the album. Nevertheless, Bakshi later shot the video to the Stones' single 'Harlem Shuffle' on 7 February 1986, characteristically mixing live-action and animation (see Bob Mackin(?), *Rolling Stones – The Chronology: April 28, 1963 – March 24, 1986*, typescript, (n.p., 1986), 19).

70 See https://archive.nytimes.com/www.nytimes.com/books/01/02/11/ specials/tolkien-hobbittv2.html; Stephen Zito 'Bakshi Among the Hobbits', *American Film* 10 (September 1978), 58–63, at 62 (quoted by Christine Cornea, '2-D Performance and the Re-Animated Actor in Science Fiction Cinema', in Christine Cornea (ed.), *Genre and Performance: Film and Television* (Manchester: Manchester University Press, 2010), 148–65, at 159).

71 See https://archive.nytimes.com/www.nytimes.com/books/01/02/11/ specials/tolkien-hobbittv2.html

72 Tasha Robinson, 'Back with Bakshi' [interview with Ralph Bakshi], *The Onion A.V. Club* (2000): excerpt available at https://www.theonering. com/news/books/back-with-bakshi-the-onion-a-v-club/

73 There is some discussion of this unlikely meeting at http://newboards. theonering.net/forum/gforum/perl/gforum.cgi?post=893842;sb=post_ latest_reply;so=ASC;forum_view=forum_view_expandable;guest= 239893165

74 Robinson, 'Back with Bakshi'.

75 Regarding Brooks, see Shippey, *Author of the Century*, 319–20.

76 Michael Moorcock, 'Epic Pooh', reprinted in Harold Bloom (ed.), *J.R.R. Tolkien's The Lord of the Rings*, Bloom's Modern Critical Interpretations, new edition (New York: Bloom's Literary Criticism, 2008), 3–18, at 7; Moorcock unfortunately confuses Sauron with Saruman, which does not help his argument.

77 Moorcock, 'Epic Pooh', 8.
78 *Archive on 4*, 'Tolkien: The Lost Recordings'; see also Lee, 'Tolkien in Oxford (BBC, 1968)', 150. This is a bone of contention: for Tolkien's despair at 'the Machines' of modern life see *Letters*, 111, but also, more complexly, 145–6, where the 'Machine' is equated with 'Magic'; see Christopher Tolkien's comments in *A Film Portrait of J.R.R. Tolkien*, dir. Derek Baily (Landseer, 1996); see also some interesting comments by Alan Jacobs in 'Fall, Mortality, and the Machine: Tolkien and Technology', *The Atlantic* (27 July 2012): https://www.theatlantic.com/technology/archive/2012/07/fall-mortality-and-the-machine-tolkien-and-technology/260412/
79 It was not until Hawkwind's *Chronicle of the Black Sword* (1985) that Moorcock's work received the rock accolade of a concept album; for other 'Rock and Metal Inspired by Michael Moorcock's Multiverse', see https://rideintoglory.com/chronicle-of-the-black-sword-rock-and-metal-inspired-by-michael-moorcocks-multiverse/
80 Robinson, 'Back with Bakshi'.
81 Additionally, the Hawkwind sample is edited to end rather than begin with Frodo's cackle.
82 Bakshi's troubles in making the movie are summarized in his candid, if possibly overstated, interview with Weiner, 'How the Battle for "Lord of the Rings" Nearly Broke a Director'.
83 See https://www.imdb.com/title/tt0077869/awards/?ref_=tt_awd. This did not really compete with Zaentz's success as a producer with the two films that book-ended *The Lord of the Rings*: *One Flew Over the Cuckoo's Nest* (1975), which won five Academy Awards, and *Amadeus* (1984), with eight Academy Awards.
84 *LotR*, i. 18.
85 I have only anecdotal evidence for this: over a decade of teaching the films alongside the books to intelligent and well-informed undergraduates.
86 This was also the first scene shot by Jackson: see *Return to Middle Earth: Empire Classics* 3 (2018), 50–51 (originally published January and February 2004).
87 Brian Rosebury notes some of these allusions (see *Tolkien: A Cultural Phenomenon*, 208).
88 Andrew M. Butler, *Solar Flares: Science Fiction in the 1970s* (Liverpool: Liverpool University Press, 2012), 70.
89 Interestingly, the actor Anthony Daniels voiced C3PO in *Star Wars* and both Legolas and Déagol in *The Lord of the Rings*.
90 See Ned Raggett, 'The Trouble With Ralph Bakshi's *The Lord Of The Rings* & Other Tolkien Misadventures', *The Quietus*, 19 November 2018: https://thequietus.com/articles/25681-ralph-bakshi-the-lord-of-the-rings-animation-review-anniversary
91 See Alexander Sergeant, 'High Fantasy Disney: Recontextualising

The Black Cauldron', in Amy M. Davis (ed.), *Discussing Disney*
(Bloomington, IN: John Libbey Publishing, 2019), 53–70, at 64.

92 See Sergeant, 'High Fantasy Disney', 53.

93 See 'greendragon' [Thompson], 'Tolkien Rights and the Amazon
Television Deal'.

94 Raggett, 'The Trouble With Ralph Bakshi's *The Lord Of The Rings*'.

95 'Brian Sibley, Writer, BBC's *The Lord of the Rings* (1981)', interview
with Brian Sibley by 'The Nerd of the Rings': https://open.spotify.com/
episode/3y5fBGrKQ6jZsiDavz61kx

96 Comments taken from Sibley (ed.), *Tolkien: An Audio Portrait*.

97 Sibley's comment (and much of this information) is taken from his
essay 'The Making of the Rings' in the booklet that accompanies *The
Lord of the Rings*, BBC Radio Collection CD box (BBC Worldwide,
1995), 12, and the interview 'Brian Sibley, Writer, BBC's *The Lord of the
Rings* (1981)'. According to Sibley, the BBC's first choice for composer
was apparently William Walton – just possible, although he was in the
twilight of his career.

98 'Brian Sibley, Writer, BBC's *The Lord of the Rings* (1981)'.

99 Surprisingly, the critic Brian Rosebury, who has written on the
BBC series, considers it an 'honourable' failure (*Tolkien: A Cultural
Phenomenon*, 206); I, and many others, must disagree.

100 See 'Brian Sibley, Writer, BBC's *The Lord of the Rings* (1981)'.

101 'Brian Sibley, Writer, BBC's *The Lord of the Rings* (1981)'.

102 See 'The Taming of Smeagol [*sic*]', *Return to Middle Earth*, 35–7.

103 'Brian Sibley, Writer, BBC's *The Lord of the Rings* (1981)'.

104 'Brian Sibley, Writer, BBC's *The Lord of the Rings* (1981)'.

105 Thompson, *The Frodo Franchise*, 21–2.

106 Sibley, *Lord of the Rings: Official Movie Guide*, 11.

107 *Return to Middle Earth*, 12 (originally published July 2001); the
Middle-earth Enterprises website (Saul Zaentz Company) claims that
Jackson saw Bakshi's film on its release in New Zealand (https://www.
middleearth.com/history.html).

108 *Return to Middle Earth*, 7 (originally published January 2015).

109 Quoted by Thompson, *The Frodo Franchise*, 25.

110 *Return to Middle Earth*, 9 (originally published January 2015); Kristin
Thompson describes Weinstein's deal as 'draconian', and quotes him as
allowing only three weeks for Jackson and Walsh to find an alternative
(*The Frodo Franchise*, 27).

111 *Return to Middle Earth*, 9 (originally published January 2015).

112 See Thompson, *The Frodo Franchise*, 32–3.

113 See https://www.middleearth.com/timeline.html. New Line was not
only sued by the Tolkien Trust, but also twice by Saul Zaentz, and even
by Peter Jackson himself; the company became a division of Warner
Bros. in 2008 – coincidentally just days after the first lawsuit against

them was filed (see Rachel Abramowitz, 'A Ring of Mire', *Los Angeles Times* (2 July 2008): https://www.latimes.com/archives/la-xpm-2008-jul-02-et-brief2-story.html).

114 Raggett, 'The Trouble With Ralph Bakshi's *The Lord Of The Rings*'. The scene that Jackson admits to is Odo Proudfoot's oversized feet on the table at Bilbo's party: see the director's and writers' commentary to *The Fellowship of the Ring: Special Extended DVD Edition* (New Line Cinema, 2002).

115 Matt Skuta has edited a split-screen video comparing the two versions: https://www.youtube.com/watch?v=4t7KSarpfFM

116 *Return to Middle Earth*, 14 (originally published July 2001).

117 For the complexity of the chapter 'The Council of Elrond', see Shippey, *Author of the Century*, 77–82.

118 Sibley, *Lord of the Rings: Official Movie Guide*, 59.

119 *LotR*, i. 78, 84, 89.

120 *LotR*, iii: 170.

121 *Return to Middle Earth*, 79 (originally published December 2012).

122 Rosebury, *Tolkien: A Cultural Phenomenon*, 214.

123 See Rosebury, *Tolkien: A Cultural Phenomenon*, 219.

124 [Anon.], 'Greatest Battles', *Empire* magazine (September 2014), 60–63, at 63; Paul Bradshaw, 'The 10 Greatest Middle-Earth Moments', *Total Film* magazine (December 2014), 78–9, at 79; and *Return to Middle Earth*, 33 (originally published January 2003).

125 See Tyler Daswick, '15 Years Later, No One's Matched "LOTR"'s Battle at Helm's Deep', *Relevant Magazine* (18 December 2017): https://relevantmagazine.com/culture/movies/15-years-later-no-ones-matched-lotrs-battle-at-helms-deep/

126 Roberts, *Riddles of the Hobbit*, 131.

127 Rosebury, *Tolkien: A Cultural Phenomenon*, 216–17.

128 Sibley, *Lord of the Rings: Official Movie Guide*, 15.

129 Ian Nathan (ed.), *The Lord of the Rings: A Celebration*, supplement to *Empire* magazine (n.d.), 32; Fran Walsh, Philippa Boyens, and Peter Jackson, *The Lord of the Rings: The Return of the King* screenplay typescript (New Line Cinema, 2003), 130.

130 Quoted by Ben Child, 'Bored of the Rings? No more Tolkien, says Peter Jackson – but Ian McKellen suspects otherwise', *Guardian* (3 December 2014): https://www.theguardian.com/film/2014/dec/03/bored-of-the-rings-no-more-tolkien-says-peter-jackson-but-ian-mckellen-suspects-otherwise

131 *Return to Middle Earth*, 14 (originally published July 2001).

132 Sibley, *Lord of the Rings: Official Movie Guide*, 11.

133 Flieger, 'A Distant Mirror', at 298.

134 *Return to Middle Earth*, 45 (originally published January 2004).

135 These are mainly deleted scenes available on YouTube rather than in the 'Director's Cut' extended editions (although, admittedly, some may be

apocryphal); the best compilation is currently 'Unreleased Lord of the Rings': https://www.youtube.com/watch?v=4CxqTBTAeBQ

136 Brian Sibley, *Lord of the Rings: Official Movie Guide*, 95.

137 For Viggo Mortensen's snapped front tooth, see *The Lord of the Rings: The Return of the King, Special Extended DVD Edition*, dir. Peter Jackson (2004).

138 Brian Sibley, *Lord of the Rings*, 83.

139 See Thompson, *The Frodo Franchise*, 93–4; altogether there were over 500 bows and 10,000 arrows made (Brian Sibley, *The Lord of the Rings™: The Making of the Movie Trilogy* (London: HarperCollins, 2002), 104).

140 See Sibley, *Lord of the Rings™*, 82–3.

141 He went on to say that the fight with the cave troll at Balin's tomb was his 'Harryhausen scene': 'I wanted that monster fight to contain all the gags and moments I enjoyed seeing in Ray's films' (https://www.tate.org.uk/art/tate-etc/peter-jackson-on-ray-harryhausen).

142 Sibley, *Lord of the Rings™*, 123.

143 Mark Langer, 'The End of Animation History' (paper presented to the Ottawa Student Animation Festival: Teacher's Symposium, Ottawa, Canada, 19 October 2001): quoted by Bob Rehak, *More Than Meets the Eye: Special Effects and the Fantastic Transmedia Franchise* (New York: NYU Press, 2018), 136.

144 Rehak, *More Than Meets the Eye*, 130, and see 132–3; Andy Serkis has since recorded his own unabridged version of *The Lord of the Rings* in his inimitable, chicory style (2021).

145 See Sean Cubitt and Barry King, 'Dossier: Acting, On-Set Practices, Software, and Synthespians', in Harriet Margolis, Sean Cubitt, Barry King, and Thierry Jutel (eds), *Studying the Event Film: The Lord of the Rings* (Manchester: Manchester University Press, 2012), 111–25, at 124.

146 Rehak, *More Than Meets the Eye*, 113. It is extraordinary that Andy Serkis did not receive an Oscar for the part.

147 *LotR*, ii. 404.

148 Rehak, *More Than Meets the Eye*, 111–12.

149 The lines occur in Tolkien's verse and are in the script in both English and Elvish (Walsh, Boyens, and Jackson, *The Fellowship of the Ring* screenplay, 70).

150 *Popbitch* (8 October 2021); Weinstein seems to be the grotesque Orc leader at the Pelennor Fields who is eventually killed.

151 See https://www.youtube.com/watch?v=o_8ZLMMfFIk; and Carpenter, 138.

152 See Lisa Hopkins, *Screening the Gothic* (Austin: University of Texas Press, 2005), 146.

153 *LotR*, ii. 119.

154 See *Return to Middle Earth*, 124–5.

155 *Return to Middle Earth*, 46 (originally published January 2004).

156 *Return to Middle Earth*, 16 (originally published July 2001); and Sibley, *Lord of the Rings: Official Movie Guide*, 84.

157 Sibley, *Lord of the Rings*, 16; see Cubitt and King, 'Dossier: Acting, On-Set Practices, Software, and Synthespians', in Margolis, et al. (eds), *Studying the Event Film*, 121–2.

158 See, for example, Cubitt and King, 'Dossier: Acting, On-Set Practices, Software, and Synthespians', in Margolis, et al. (eds), *Studying the Event Film*, 117.

159 Richard Jordan, 'Battlefield Middle-Earth', *Total Film* magazine (December 2014), 62–9, at 68.

160 Sibley, *Lord of the Rings™*, 143; see also Sibley, *Lord of the Rings: Official Movie Guide*, 36.

161 See Judith Bernanke, 'Howard Shore's Ring Cycle: The Film Score and Operatic Strategy', in Margolis, et al. (eds), *Studying the Event Film*, 176–84.

162 Harold Bloom (ed.), *Modern Critical Views: J.R.R. Tolkien* (Philadelphia: Chelsea House Publishers, 2000), 2.

163 *Return to Middle Earth*, 53; see Craig Hight, 'One (Special Extended Edition) Disc to Rule Them All', in Margolis, et al. (eds), *Studying the Event Film*, 32–9. Interestingly, Jackson has claimed that the original theatrical releases are the 'definitive versions': 'I regard the extended cuts as being a novelty for the fans that really want to see the extra material' (quoted by Sean Cubitt and Barry King, 'Dossier: Materials for a Study of the *Lord of the Rings* Trilogy and its Audiences', in Margolis, et al. (eds), *Studying the Event Film*, 27–31, at 30).

164 Danny Butt, 'Creative Industries in Hobbit Economies: Wealth Creation, Intellectual Property Regimes, and Transnational Productions', in Margolis, et al. (eds), *Studying the Event Film*, 84–92, at 87; Ryan Reynolds, Henry Bial, and Kimon Keramidas, 'Tourist Encounters', in Margolis, et al. (eds), *Studying the Event Film*, 239–48; and Thompson, *The Frodo Franchise*, 283. For more technical statistics, see Sean Cubitt and Barry King, 'Dossier: Production and Post-Production', in Margolis, et al. (eds), *Studying the Event Film*, 135–68.

165 Sibley, *Lord of the Rings: Official Movie Guide*, 16.

Six: Just War

1 Reported in *Huffington Post* (11 January 2021): https://www.huffpost.com/entry/gene-deitch-the-hobbit_n_1198864. Deitch's original blogposts appear to have been removed following his death in 2020, but accounts can still be found online.

2 See https://www.awn.com/genedeitch/chapter-twentythree-hobbitalized

3   See https://www.youtube.com/watch?v=UBnVL1Y2src
4   No correspondence from Tolkien has come to light concerning this
    production, leading Hammond and Scull to conclude that Tolkien had
    nothing to do with it (*Chron.*, 863).
5   See https://archive.nytimes.com/www.nytimes.com/books/01/02/11/
    specials/tolkien-hobbittv2.html
6   Further possible similarities are suggested by Matt Skuta at https://
    www.youtube.com/watch?v=goOjPcncrzg
7   *Return to Middle Earth*, 72 (originally published December 2012).
8   See 'Hobbit History' timeline in Paul Bradshaw, Jamie Graham,
    and Jonathan Crocker, 'There and Back Again', *Total Film* magazine
    (December 2014), 72–7, at 79; and Jordan, 'Battlefield Middle-Earth', 64.
9   Jordan, 'Battlefield Middle-Earth', 64 (square brackets given in
    original).
10 *Hobbit*, 130.
11 Matthew Leyland, 'The Hobbit: An Unexpected Journey', *Total Film*
    magazine (February 2012), 70–74, at 74.
12 Ian Nathan, 'Into the Woods', *Empire* magazine (August 2013), 62–71,
    at 68.
13 Nathan, 'Into the Woods', 68; and *LotR*, i. 9.
14 Nathan, 'Into the Woods', 71.
15 Nathan, 'Into the Woods', 71.
16 *Return to Middle Earth*, 102 (originally published January 2015).
17 Nathan, 'Into the Woods', 70 (second ellipsis in original).
18 Nathan, 'Into the Woods', 66.
19 Jordan, 'Battlefield Middle-Earth', 64.
20 *Return to Middle Earth*, 86 (originally published December 2013).
21 *Return to Middle Earth*, 68 (originally published September 2012).
22 Ian Nathan, 'Winter is Coming', *Empire* magazine (September 2014),
    80–7, at 83; he also comments that, 'Uniquely in the Middle-earth
    canon, The Battle of the Five Armies isn't a road movie' (83).
23 Jordan, 'Battlefield Middle-Earth', 66.
24 *Return to Middle Earth*, 101 (originally published January 2015).
25 *Return to Middle Earth*, 100 (originally published January 2015).
26 *Return to Middle Earth*, 102–5, 104 (originally published January 2015);
    elsewhere in the films, the Great Goblin (played with aplomb by Barry
    Humphries) was apparently partly based on Kim Jong-il of North
    Korea, (*Return to Middle Earth*, 75 (originally published December
    2012)).
27 See https://www.dailyhindnews.com/the-hobbit-what-was-the-first-
    scene-shot-in-the-entire-trilogy-cinema-news/
28 James Clarke, *The Cinema of James Cameron: Bodies in Heroic Motion*
    (New York and Chichester: Wallflower Press (Columbia University
    Press), 2014), 133.

29   *Return to Middle Earth*, 75 (originally published December 2012); for
     the models used in the *Rings* films see, for example, Sibley, *Lord of the
     Rings™*, 57–67.

30   Employment Relations (Film Production) Amendment Act (2010): see
     New Zealand Journal of Employment Relations 36.3 (2011): special issue
     'The "Hobbit Law": Exploring Non-standard Employment'.

31   See Kristen Whissel, *Spectacular Digital Effects: CGI and Contemporary
     Cinema* (Durham, NC: Duke University Press, 2014).

32   Brian Sibley, *The Hobbit: The Battle of the Five Armies* (London:
     HarperCollins, 2014), [53]; heights taken from 'Character Comparative
     Heights' table drafted for *Rings*, reproduced in Sibley, *Lord of the Rings:
     Official Movie Guide*, [75].

33   *Return to Middle Earth*, 72 (originally published December 2012), 74.

34   Whissel, *Spectacular Digital Effects*, 7.

35   Nathan, 'Into the Woods', 66.

36   See John Howe's comments in Daniel Falconer, *Smaug: Unleashing the
     Dragon* (London: HarperCollins, 2014), [28].

37   Leyland, 'The Hobbit', 73.

38   Matthew Leyland, 'Step by Step: Essentials for an Unexpected Journey',
     Total Film magazine (February 2012), 73.

39   See Jordan, 'Battlefield Middle-Earth', 65.

40   Tim Robey, 'Viggo Mortensen Interview: Peter Jackson Sacrificed
     Subtlety for CGI', *The Telegraph* (14 May 2014): https://www.telegraph.
     co.uk/culture/film/10826867/Viggo-Mortensen-interview-Peter-
     Jackson-sacrificed-subtlety-for-CGI.html

41   Peter Jackson, 'Q&A on HFR 3D', Facebook website (posted 19
     November 2012) [I am indebted to Prof. Debra Ramsay for this
     reference].

42   Kenneth Turan, '"The Hobbit: An Unexpected Journey" lacks a Certain
     Ring', *Los Angeles Times* (12 December 2012): https://www.latimes.com/
     entertainment/la-xpm-2012-dec-12-la-et-mn-hobbit-review-
     20121213-story.html [I am indebted to Prof. Debra Ramsay for this
     reference].

43   Jackson, 'Q&A on HFR 3D'.

44   Nathan, 'Winter is Coming', 84.

45   *Return to Middle Earth*, 97 (originally published September 2014).

46   Nathan, 'Winter is Coming', 84.

47   *Return to Middle Earth*, 69 (originally published September 2012).

48   Ian Nathan, 'An Extended Journey', *Empire* magazine (August 2013),
     71.

49   Sergeant, 'High Fantasy Disney', 58.

50   SELWG being the South East London Wargames Group.

51   Rosebury, *Tolkien: A Cultural Phenomenon*, 194–5.

52   The prototype is available at https://atariage.com/features/lotr/. Other

games are included (with links) on the website https://screenrant.com/
lord-of-the-rings-cancelled-projects-fans-hoping-for/
53 For a detailed account, see Thompson, *The Frodo Franchise*, 224–53.
54 Details from https://www.middleearth.com/timeline.html
55 Barry Atkins, 'Games', in Eaglestone (ed.), *Reading The Lord of the Rings*, 151–62.
56 See https://www.middleearth.com/current-licensees.html
57 Janet Brennan Croft, 'Mithril Coats and Tin Ears: "Anticipation" and "Flattening" in Peter Jackson's *The Lord of the Rings* Trilogy', in Janet Brennan Croft (ed.), *Tolkien on Film: Essays on Peter Jackson's The Lord of the Rings* (Altadena, CA: Mythopoeic Press, 2004), 63–80, at 71.
58 Hutcheon, *A Theory of Adaptation*, 8.
59 See Marek Oziewicz, 'Peter Jackson's *The Hobbit*: A Beautiful Disaster', *Journal of the Fantastic in the Arts* 27.2 (96) (2016), 248–69, at 255.
60 *Return to Middle Earth*, 109.
61 See https://www.middleearth.com/history.html
62 See Bradshaw, et al., 'There and Back Again', 75–6; and *Return to Middle Earth*, 109.
63 Courtney M. Booker, 'Byte-Sized Middle Ages: Tolkien, Film, and the Digital Imagination', *Comitatus* 35 (2004), 145–74, at 173.
64 Oziewicz, 'Peter Jackson's *The Hobbit*', 249.
65 See 'greendragon' [Thompson], 'Tolkien Rights and the Amazon Television Deal'
66 *LotR*, ii. 14.
67 Tolkien's most distressing catalogue of war crimes occurs in *The Children of Húrin*, which includes torture, sexual violence, mutilation, the murder of women, and the desecration of the dead.
68 The title is difficult to translate, broadly meaning a synthesis of the highest theological thinking.
69 House of Commons debate 20 August 1940, in *Hansard*, vol. 364, col. 1160 (https://api.parliament.uk/historic-hansard/commons/1940/aug/20/war-situation).
70 Shippey, 'Tolkien as a Post-War Writer', 84.
71 See Eaglestone, 'Introduction', in Eaglestone (ed.), *Reading The Lord of the Rings*, 3.
72 Shippey, *Road to Middle-earth*, 324–5.
73 Shippey, *Author of the Century*, vii.
74 Thomas W. Smith, 'Tolkien's Catholic Imagination: Mediation and Tradition', *Religion and Literature*, vol. 38.2 (2006), 73–100: 81.
75 *LotR*, iii. 187.
76 *LotR*, ii. 165; see 'Louvain: The Unpardonable Crime', *The Times* (9 April 1920), quoted by Forest-Hill, 'Underground Man', 15.
77 *LotR*, iii. 112.

78 *LotR*, iii. 200.
79 *LotR*, iii. 199.
80 See entry on 'Perfidy' by Vera Rusinova, *Max Planck Encyclopedias of International Law* (2011), at *Oxford Public International Law* (Oxford: Oxford University Press, 2021: http://opil.ouplaw.com).
81 Jonathan D. Evans, 'Semiotics and Traditional Lore: The Medieval Dragon Tradition', *Journal of Folklore Research* 22.2/3 (1985), 85–112, at 107.
82 *Hobbit*, 278, 288.
83 See https://ymarkov.livejournal.com/270570.html
84 *LotR*, ii. 337.
85 *LotR*, i. 85.
86 *LotR*, ii. 172.
87 *LotR*, iii. 133.
88 Even the published *Silmarillion* is equivocal on this point: it is only '*held true* by the wise of Eressëa' [my emphasis] that Elves captured by Melkor 'by slow arts of cruelty were corrupted and enslaved' thus breeding the Orcs, 'the vilest deed of Melkor' (*Silmarillion*, 58); for Orcs and evil, see a useful summary by David Tneh, 'Orcs and Tolkien's Treatment of Evil', *Mallorn* 52 (2011), 37–43. The abiding problem of the origin of Orcs (or Goblins) is summarized by Rateliff, i. 137–43; in a long but unsent letter to a Catholic theologian written in September 1954, Tolkien tried to make sense of the Orcs; they clearly made imaginative sense to him, even if their nature and origins were obscure – and, like many things in Middle-Earth, would probably remain so (see *Letters*, 187–96, at 195; and *Morgoth's Ring*, 408–24).
89 *Lost Road*, 48; and *LotR*, ii. 90, 198; on the Fall, see Shippey, *Author of the Century*, 240–41.
90 Tacitus, *Agricola and Germany*, ed. and trans. Anthony R. Birley (Oxford: Oxford University Press, 1999), 44–5: see sections 7 and 14 of *Germania*; see also interesting comments by Richard Z. Gallant in 'The Noldorization of the Edain: The Roman-Germani Paradigm for the Noldor and Edain in Tolkien's Migration Era', in Hamish Williams (ed.), *Tolkien and the Classical World* (Jena: Walking Tree, 2021), 305–27.
91 'The Homecoming', 171, 173.
92 *Monsters and Critics*, 26.
93 'The Homecoming', 169.
94 *Monsters and Critics*, 30.
95 'The Homecoming', 172 (Tolkien's emphasis); however, critics such as Shippey and Drout disagree that the poet is critical: see Michael D.C. Drout, 'J.R.R. Tolkien's Medieval Scholarship and its Significance', *Tolkien Studies* 4 (2007), 113–76, at 143.
96 See Shippey, *Author of the Century*, 98–102.

97 This is also staged reasonably well in the animation of *The Return of the King*.
98 *LotR*, iii. 63.
99 Virginia Woolf, *A Room of One's Own* (London: Hogarth Press, 1931), 37.
100 *LotR*, iii. 169.
101 George R.R. Martin has acknowledged his debt to Tolkien – 'we are all still walking in Bilbo's footsteps': see Karen Haber, 'Introduction', in Haber (ed.), *Meditations on Middle-Earth*, 1–5, at 5; see too Poul Anderson's 'Awakening the Elves' in the same volume (21–32, at 21).
102 Leslie A. Donovan, 'The Valkyrie Reflex in J.R.R. Tolkien's *The Lord of the Rings*: Galadriel, Shelob, Éowyn, and Arwen', in Chance (ed.), *Tolkien the Medievalist*, 106–32, at 126; and *Letters*, 324.
103 *Hobbit*, 183.
104 *LotR*, iii. 210.
105 See Walter S. Judd and Graham A. Judd, *Flora of Middle-Earth: Plants of J.R.R. Tolkien's Legendarium* (Oxford: Oxford University Press, 2017); see too Dinah Hazell's shorter work *The Plants of Middle-Earth: Botany and Sub-Creation* (Kent, OH: Kent State University Press, 2006).
106 *LotR*, i. 41; i. 150.
107 *LotR*, i. 153, 157, 160, 163, 168.
108 *LotR*, i. 168.
109 *LotR*, i. 167.
110 *LotR*, i. 170–71.
111 Verlyn Flieger, 'Taking the Part of Trees: Eco-Conflict in Middle-Earth', in Clark and Timmons (eds), *Tolkien and His Literary Resonances*, 147–58, at 147.
112 *LotR*, i. 456; see Shippey, *Author of the Century*, 206. Mirkwood was the primaeval Germanic forest mentioned by William Morris in *The House of the Wolfings* (1889).
113 Patrick Curry, *Defending Middle-Earth – Tolkien: Myth and Modernity*, 2nd edn (Boston and New York: Houghton Mifflin, 2004), 48–86, 156.
114 *Release – Tolkien in Oxford*; *Archive on 4*, 'Tolkien: The Lost Recordings'; and see also Lee, 'Tolkien in Oxford (BBC, 1968)', 161.
115 Fran Walsh, Philippa Boyens, Stephen Sinclair, and Peter Jackson, *The Lord of the Rings: The Two Towers* screenplay typescript (New Line Cinema, 2002), 78.
116 *LotR*, i. 179.
117 *LotR*, i. 179; ii. 75.
118 Sibley (ed.), *Tolkien: An Audio Portrait*, CD 1, track 18.
119 *Return of the Shadow*, 121; and *LotR*, i. 180.
120 See Kipling, *Puck of Pook's Hill*, 11.
121 See Kerry Brooks, 'Tom Bombadil and the Journey for Middle-Earth', *Mallorn* 55 (2014), 11–13.
122 The letter (21 August 1954) is quoted at https://wayneandchristina.

wordpress.com/2014/12/30/tom-bombadil-addenda-corrigenda/ ; see also *Adventures of Tom Bombadil*, 7–26.

123 *LotR*, i. 172.
124 *LotR*, i. 165, 194.
125 *LotR*, ii. 151, 177.
126 *LotR*, i. 455; iii. 75.
127 The 'Ainulindalë: The Music of the Ainur' was published in *Silmarillion*, 15–24.
128 Bayliss's paintings are remarkable protests against industrialization: see https://www.wolverhamptonart.org.uk/ebb/
129 *LotR*, i. 129, 481.
130 Rosebury, *Tolkien: A Cultural Phenomenon*, 84.
131 It rains too when Bilbo returns to Bag End: rainfall is transitional.
132 *LotR*, i. 12–13; and Shippey, *Author of the Century*, 63.
133 See https://www.hobbitontours.com/
134 *LotR*, iii. 133, 269.
135 Todd McCarthy, ' "The Hobbit: The Battle of the Five Armies": The Final Visit to Middle-Earth is the Most Purely Entertaining', in *The Hollywood Reporter* (1 December 2014): see https://www.hollywoodreporter.com/movies/movie-reviews/hobbit-battle-five-armies-film-752865/
136 *Letters*, 270.

Conclusion: Weird Things

1 *LotR*, iii. 100; *Letters*, 195 (see Chapter Six, note 88, above).
2 *LotR*, iii. 138.
3 *Hobbit*, 300–301.
4 *Letters*, 172.
5 See https://www.bbc.co.uk/sounds/play/b03bqchj
6 John Masefield, 'Fragments', in *The Poems and Plays of John Masefield*, 2 vols (New York: Macmillan, 1920), i. 104–7, at 107.
7 *Silmarillion*, 47, 48.
8 *Silmarillion*, 313–14.
9 *Silmarillion*, 330.
10 *Silmarillion*, 317.
11 *Lost Road*, 77.
12 *Letters*, 246, 284; Tolkien's comment on power is quoted in Chapter Three.
13 Simone de Beauvoir, *A Very Easy Death* [*Une mort très douce*], trans. Patrick O'Brian (Harmondsworth: Penguin, 1969), 92; Tolkien had a newspaper clipping of the lines in his pocket, from which he read.
14 *Release – Tolkien in Oxford*; *Archive on 4*, 'Tolkien: The Lost Recordings'; and see Lee, 'Tolkien in Oxford (BBC, 1968)', 156.
15 See www.tolkienbooks.net/

16 See, for example, Drout, 'Tolkien's Medieval Scholarship', 113–76.

17 See Shippey, *Author of the Century*, xx–xxiv. Disappointingly, in April
    2002 the usually magnanimous BBC Radio 4 literary quiz *The Write
    Stuff* devoted a programme to Tolkien in which the panellists – with
    the notable exception of Nigel Williams – mixed condescension with
    indifference (see https://www.bbc.co.uk/programmes/m0001923).

18 Walsh, Boyens, and Jackson, *Return of the King*, screenplay, 69; Elrond
    also persuades Aragorn to take the Dimholt Road to raise an army of
    the undead, loyal to the King of Gondor.

19 See Douglas Charles Kane, *Arda Reconstructed: The Creation of the
    Published Silmarillion* (Bethlehem, PA: Lehigh University Press, 2009).

20 *Lost Tales*, i. 5, also 6.

21 Even those who professedly admire *The Lord of the Rings* can be
    dismissive of *The Silmarillion*: see Niall Ferguson interviewed on
    Great Lives: J.R.R. Tolkien, Creator of The Hobbit, BBC Radio 4 (10
    December 2021: https://www.bbc.co.uk/programmes/m00127zh); for
    more trenchant criticism, see the character Linda Snell's objections in
    the long-running British radio soap opera, *The Archers* (29 March 2018:
    https://www.bbc.co.uk/programmes/p062gfrw).

22 Fimi, *Tolkien, Race and Cultural History*, 159; Tolkien's essay 'Quendi
    and Eldar' is reprinted in *War of the Jewels* (see especially 373).

23 Curry, *Defending Middle-Earth*, 33.

24 Not that Tolkien, however, felt that the matter was ever adequately
    resolved, writing to his favoured illustrator Pauline Baynes as late as
    1970, he stated that Hobbits were part of the Human race and that
    Gollum himself is therefore essentially Human – or at least could be
    defined as such fifteen years after the publication of *The Lord of the
    Rings* (see unpublished letter quoted by Rateliff, i. 186–7). Tolkien
    noted earlier mixed-race unions between the Dúnedain and other
    Human races (including the Rohirrim) in Appendix A, on 'Gondor and
    the Heirs of Anárion'.

25 Thomas Nagel, 'What Is It Like To Be a Bat?', *Mortal Questions*
    (Cambridge: Cambridge University Press, 1979), 165–80, at 171.

26 See Peter Ackroyd, *Albion: The Origins of the English Imagination*
    (London: Chatto and Windus, 2002).

27 *Letters*, 231, 144; *Sauron Defeated*, 204.

28 Paul Romney, '"Great Chords": Politics and Romance in Tolstoy's *War
    and Peace*', *University of Toronto Quarterly* 80.1 (2011), 49–77: 74; see
    Chester N. Scoville, 'Pastoralia and Perfectibility in William Morris and
    J.R.R. Tolkien', in Jane Chance and Alfred K. Siewers (eds), *Tolkien's
    Modern Middle Ages* (London: Palgrave Macmillan, 2005), 93–103, at 95.

29 *Letters*, 63–4: see also 65, 73, 107, 115, 215, 246.

30 See Anderson, *Imagined Communities*.

31 'English and Welsh', *Monsters and Critics*, 166.

32 'English and Welsh', *Monsters and Critics*, 171.
33 See Groom, *The Gothic*, 54–64.
34 Of course, for Tolkien the Gothic meant something very different: see my essays 'Tolkien and the Gothic' and 'Tolkien y la literatura gótica'.
35 *LotR*, i. 322.
36 *LotR*, i. 187.
37 *LotR*, i. 235.
38 *LotR*, i. 519–20.
39 *LotR*, ii. 52, 57.
40 *LotR*, ii. 211, 258.
41 *LotR*, ii. 319.
42 *LotR*, ii. 420, iii. 158.
43 *LotR*, iii. 276.
44 *LotR*, iii. 374.
45 *LotR*, iii. 335, see also 370.
46 *LotR*, iii. 175.
47 Mary Warnock, *Memory* (London: Faber & Faber, 1987), 90.
48 Johanna Lindbladh, 'Introduction', in Johanna Lindbladh (ed.), *The Poetics of Memory in Post-Totalitarian Narration* (Lund: Centre for European Studies, 2008), 5–13, at 6.
49 Thacker, *In the Dust of This Planet*, 98.
50 Michael Billig, 'A Psychoanalytic Discursive Psychology: From Consciousness to Unconsciousness', *Discourse Studies* (2006), 8.1, 17–24, at 18.
51 Lindbladh, 'Introduction', in Lindbladh (ed.), *The Poetics of Memory*, 5.
52 Catherine Madsen, '"Light from an Invisible Lamp": Natural Religion in *The Lord of the Rings*, in Jane Chance (ed.), *Tolkien and the Invention of Myth: A Reader* (Lexington, KY: University Press of Kentucky, 2004), 35–47, at 41.
53 Graham Harman, *Towards Speculative Realism: Essays and Lectures* (Winchester and Washington, DC: Zero Books, 2010), 116.
54 Harman, *Towards Speculative Realism*, 147.
55 Harman, *Towards Speculative Realism*, 116.
56 Thacker, *In the Dust of This Planet*, 9, 126.
57 See Eugene Thacker, *Cosmic Pessimism* (Minneapolis, MN: Univocal Publishing, 2015).
58 Harman, *Towards Speculative Realism*, 103.
59 Robert Eaglestone also has interesting points to make about invisibility, relating it to narrative structure and the separation of some characters from their authenticating communities: see 'Invisibility', in Eaglestone (ed.), *Reading The Lord of the Rings*, 73–84.
60 First appears *LotR*, ii. 235, then ii. 241ff.
61 *LotR*, i. 361.
62 K.S. Whetter and R. Andrew McDonald, '"In the Hilt is Fame":

Resonances of Medieval Swords and Sword-Lore in J.R.R. Tolkien's *The Hobbit* and *The Lord of the Rings*', in *Mythlore* 25.1/2 (2006), 5–28.

63 *LotR*, i. 418–19.
64 See Shippey, *Author of the Century*, 70.
65 *LotR*, iii. 69.
66 *LotR*, iii. 106, 120, 135.
67 *LotR*, iii. 133, 135, 303.
68 Gilliver importantly notes that the words *fey* and *fay* are unrelated (*Ring of Words*, 131).
69 *LotR*, iii. 80.
70 *LotR*, iii. 118, 133, 140.
71 *LotR*, ii. 419.
72 Elsewhere, in *Children of Húrin*, for example, Brandir utters 'fey laughter' towards the climax of the tragedy (252) and Túrin, blind in the mist of Morgoth, is 'fey and witless' (255, see also 203, 204).
73 See Thacker, *In the Dust of This Planet*, 52–4.
74 Gilliver, et al., *Ring of Words*, 77.
75 *LotR*, i. 482, 485, 490: 'a small haven or landing place on a river' (*OED* Old English: *hithe*).
76 *Thrawn* (*LotR*, i. 510): 'twisted, crooked' (*OED*, Scottish and Irish English); *freshet* (*LotR*, i. 434, ii. 322): 'small stream of fresh water' (*OED*, Old French, archaic); *gangrel* (*LotR*, ii. 331, 366): 'lanky, loose-jointed' (*OED*, English regional northern, rare); Tolkien also uses *gangrels* (*LotR*, iii. 329) in the sense of wandering beggars or vagrants (*OED*, English regional northern, Scottish).
77 Of *gangrel*, the *OED* notes that in 'later usage probably influenced by Tolkien's use'.
78 *LotR*, iii. 82; see Gilliver, et al., *Ring of Words*, 209.
79 *LotR*, ii. 42, ii. 144–5, iii. 136.
80 Gilliver, et al., *Ring of Words*, 108–10.
81 Gilliver, et al., *Ring of Words*, 79ff.
82 The Lord of the Nazgûl is what Thacker, writing on Lovecraft, calls 'blasphemous life': '*Blasphemous life is the life that is living but that should not be living*' (Thacker, *In the Dust of This Planet*, 104).
83 *LotR*, ii. 425; for the Ring's powers of comprehension, see *LotR*, ii. 432.
84 *LotR*, ii. 53, 54.
85 See https://www.elvish.org/gwaith/movie_intro.htm
86 *LotR*, iii. 362n, 362, 520; see also 'Nomenclature of *The Lord of the Rings*', 186.
87 *Sauron Defeated*, 251.
88 *LotR*, i. 18, 17.
89 'Alvocentric': derived from the Middle English *alve*, meaning elf.
90 *LotR*, iii. 65.

91 *LotR*, iii. 67; for a longer discussion, see my essay '"The Ghostly Language of the Ancient Earth": Tolkien and Romantic Lithology'.

92 See Curry, *Defending Middle-Earth*, 48–86, 154–7; and Robert Macfarlane, 'Should This Tree Have the Same Rights as You?': https://www.theguardian.com/books/2019/nov/02/trees-have-rights-too-robert-macfarlane-on-the-new-laws-of-nature

93 Thomas Berry, *The Great Work: Our Way Back into the Future* (Bell Tower: New York, 1999), 5.

94 *LotR*, ii. 417.

95 *LotR*, i. 255.

96 This may also account for the deliberate assuming of names, costumes, and masks at conventions: it is healthy role-play.

97 Curry, *Defending Middle-Earth*, 153.

98 Curry, *Defending Middle-Earth*, 152.

99 Zygmunt Bauman, *Intimations of Postmodernity* (London and New York: Routledge, 1992), x; Curry, *Defending Middle-Earth*, 13.

100 *On Fairy-Stories*, 59–66, especially 63–4.

101 Jonathan Bate, *The Song of the Earth* (London: Picador: 2000), 37–8; see also Lawrence Buell, *The Future of Environmental Criticism: Environmental Crisis and Literary Imagination* (Malden, MA, Oxford, and Carlton, Vic.: Blackwell Publishing, 2005), 107.

102 Michael Saler, *As If: Modern Enchantment and the Literary History of Virtual Reality* (Oxford: Oxford University Press, 2012), 159; Saler does subsequently admit that Middle-Earth is 'riven with fissures' (188).

103 C.S. Lewis, 'Tolkien's *Lord of the Rings*', in *On Stories, and Other Essays*, ed. Hooper, 83–90, at 87 [this text is a combination of two reviews of the book: 'The Gods Return to Earth', in *Time and Tide* (14 August 1954), and 'The Dethronement of Power', also in *Time and Tide* (22 October 1955)].

104 *Letters*, 220; see also 284, where he makes the same point.

105 Samuel Taylor Coleridge, *Biographia Literaria*, ed. James Engell and W. Jackson Bate (Princeton: Princeton University Press, 1984), ii. 19.

106 Verlyn Flieger, 'A Post-Modern Medievalist', in *Green Suns and Faërie*, 256; see also Flieger, 'A Distant Mirror: Tolkien and Jackson in the Looking-Glass', 292–303, at 300–302.

107 Eaglestone, 'Introduction', in Eaglestone (ed.), *Reading The Lord of the Rings*, 9.

108 See Michael D.C. Drout, 'Towards a Better Tolkien Criticism', in Eaglestone (ed.), *Reading The Lord of the Rings*, 1–28.

109 Morton, *Ecology Without Nature*, 98.

110 *LotR*, i. 12.

111 *LotR*, i. 120.

112 Adam Roberts Project, 'Morton on Tolkien' (4 December 2011): http://europrogovision.blogspot.com/2011/12/morton-on-tolkien.html

113 John Keats, *The Letters of John Keats*, ed. Maurice Buxton Forman, 4th edn (London, New York, Toronto: Oxford University Press, 1952), 71.

114 Roland Barthes, *Image–Music–Text*, trans. Stephen Heath (London: Fontana Press, 1977), 160.

115 See Sabine Baring-Gould, 'The Dead Finger', in *A Book of Ghosts*, 2nd edn (London: Methuen, 1904), 274–95, at 295; and John Carey, *The Intellectuals and the Masses: Pride and Prejudice among the Literary Intelligentsia, 1880–1939* (London: Faber and Faber, 1992), 25–6.

116 Gabriele de' Mussis, in Rosemary Horrox (ed. and trans.), *The Black Death* (Manchester: Manchester University Press, 1994), 14–26, at 17 [my emphasis]; see Nick Groom, *The Vampire: A New History*, 15–18, and 'Viral Vampires', 9–10.

117 *Release – Tolkien in Oxford*; see *Archive on 4*, 'Tolkien: The Lost Recordings'; and Lee, 'Tolkien in Oxford (BBC, 1968)', 154.

118 [Editorial,] 'Long COVID: Let Patients Help Define Long-Lasting COVID Symptoms', *Nature* (7 October 2020): https://www.nature.com/articles/d41586-020-02796-2

119 See, for example, Michael G. Wheaton, Alena Prikhidko, and Gabrielle R. Messner, 'Is Fear of COVID-19 Contagious? The Effects of Emotion Contagion and Social Media Use on Anxiety in Response to the Coronavirus Pandemic', *Frontiers in Psychology* (January 2021), article 567379, 1–9 (https://www.frontiersin.org/articles/10.3389/fpsyg.2020.567379/full).

120 Al Horner, 'The New Age: The Rings Return Promises to be Epic – But this isn't your Dad's Middle-Earth . . .', *Empire* magazine (Summer 2022), 83.

121 Al Horner, 'The World Is Changed', *Empire* magazine (July 2022), 52–61, at 54.

122 Horner, 'The World Is Changed', 54 – although this is disputed in the same article (60).

123 Horner, 'The World Is Changed', 55.

124 *Letters*, 145.

125 Horner, 'The World Is Changed', 60.

126 Horner, 'The World Is Changed', 58, 60.

127 Horner, 'The World Is Changed', 58.

128 Thacker, *In the Dust of This Planet*, 52.

129 Thacker, *In the Dust of This Planet*, 54.

130 The phrase is used in *Children of Húrin*, 189.

131 Roland Barthes, *The Pleasure of the Text*, trans. Richard Miller (New York: Hill and Wang, 1975), 11.

132 This is what makes audiobooks such a distinct experience, because every word, sentence, and passage is given equal weight.

133 Shakespeare, *Antony and Cleopatra*, II. ii. 242; William Blake, 'Auguries

of Innocence', *Blake: The Complete Poems*, ed. W.H. Stevenson, 2nd edn (London and New York: Longman, 1989), 589 (ll. 1–4).

134 *Release – Tolkien in Oxford*; see *Archive on 4*, 'Tolkien: The Lost Recordings'; and Lee, 'Tolkien in Oxford (BBC, 1968)', 138.

Afterword: Power

I would like again to thank Jessica Yates and Chris Walsh, as well as Dan Carey, Jeremy de Chavez, Timothy Feather, Andrew Moody, Mark Phillips, Ricardo Pinto, Yongyu Benedict Quan, Glenn Timmermans, and Chengcheng Jo You for their help. In this Afterword, actors' names are given only for those characters who are mentioned more than once; references to *The Rings of Power* (*RoP*) are given only for direct quotations.

1 84% positive on Rotten Tomatoes (https://www.rottentomatoes.com/tv/the_lord_of_the_rings_the_rings_of_power).
2 *RoP*, episode 1, 0.04.20.
3 *LotR*, i. 347; Quenya *atar*, Sindarin *adar* (see https://www.elfdict.com/w/adar); see above, p. 101.
4 *LotR*, i. 19; *LotR*, iii. 454.
5 *LotR*, i. 473, 475; *RoP*, episode 1, 0.27.52.
6 *RoP*, episode 3, 0.43.20; *LotR*, i. 49; Jackson's film cuts the first three words and goes straight to the list of names.
7 *RoP*, episode 5, 0.5.30–0.7.10; *LotR*, i. 230; not included in *Rings*.
8 *RoP*, episode 2, 0.14.58; *LotR*, ii. 189.
9 *LotR*, ii. 25; Walsh, Boyens, Sinclair, and Jackson, *The Two Towers*, screenplay, 20.
10 *RoP*, episode 3, 0.18.44; Míriel's words are repeated in the next episode, rallying Númenor to aid the Southlanders (*RoP*, episode 4, 1.03.30).
11 *LotR*, iii. 264.
12 Mark Ferguson in *The Fellowship of the Ring* (2001); Benjamin Walker in *The Rings of Power* (2022).
13 https://bearmccreary.com/project/the-lord-of-the-rings-the-rings-of-power/
14 See above, p. 303.
15 *RoP*, episode 2, 0.37.25.
16 *LotR*, i. 20.
17 See above, p. 305.
18 *RoP*, episode 3, 0.42.15.
19 Walsh, Boyens, and Jackson, *Fellowship of the Ring*, screenplay, 5 [ellipsis in original]; *LotR*, iii. 314–15; *LotR*, i. 80.
20 *RoP*, episode 1, 0.7.50.
21 *RoP*, episode 2, 0.9.15.

22 *LotR*, i. 84; Gandalf later ponders on the 'strange chance, if chance it was' of Bilbo finding the Ring (*LotR*, i. 328).
23 Walsh, Boyens, and Jackson, *Fellowship of the Ring*, screenplay, 122.
24 *LotR*, i. 409.
25 *RoP*, episode 8, 1.00.30.
26 *The Official The Lord of the Rings: The Rings of Power Podcast* (Amazon Music), Ep. 1: 'A Shadow of the Past', 6.43.
27 *RoP*, episode 1, 0.38.45, 0.48.06.
28 *RoP*, episode 1, 0.42.30.
29 *Official Podcast*, Ep. 3: 'Adar', 18.00.
30 Walsh, Boyens, and Jackson, *Fellowship of the Ring*, screenplay, 146. Tolkien's Galadriel may be as equally fierce but is more measured than Jackson's: see *LotR*, i. 474.
31 Galadriel's moves are based on those of Ukrainian Cossacks (*Official Podcast*, Ep. 7: 'The Eye', 21.30).
32 See above p. 255.
33 *RoP*, episode 3, 0.56.42.
34 *RoP*, episode 5 0.48.40.
35 *RoP*, episode 5, 0.48.50.
36 *RoP*, episode 6, 0.48.20.
37 *RoP*, episode 6, 0.49.35.
38 *RoP*, episode 6, 0.50.00.
39 https://www.hollywoodreporter.com/tv/tv-features/the-rings-of-power-showrunners-interview-season-2-1235233124/
40 Bloomberg's Covid Resilience Ranking: https://www.bloomberg.com/graphics/covid-resilience-ranking/
41 https://www.theatlantic.com/international/archive/2020/10/donald-trump-foreign-policy-america-first/616872/
42 https://www.washingtonpost.com/climate-environment/top-scientists-warn-of-an-amazon-tipping-point/2019/12/20/9c9be954-233e-11ea-bed5-880264cc91a9_story.html
43 *LotR*, i. 78; Walsh, Boyens, and Jackson, *Fellowship of the Ring*, screenplay, 169; see above, p. 231.

Works Cited and Selected Reading

All Shakespearean quotations and allusions are referenced to *The Oxford Shakespeare: The Complete Works*, gen. eds Stanley Wells and Gary Taylor (Oxford: Clarendon Press, 1988). Biblical citations are from the King James Authorized Version (Oxford and New York: Oxford University Press, 1997). *ODNB* refers to *The Oxford Dictionary of National Biography*, and *OED* to *The Oxford English Dictionary* – both online editions; likewise, *Green's Dictionary of Slang* also refers to the online edition. To keep this bibliography readable, references in the endnotes to journalism, broadcasts, recorded music, and webpages are (with a few notable exceptions) not repeated here.

Works by Tolkien

J.R.R. Tolkien, *The Adventures of Tom Bombadil*, ed. Christina Scull and Wayne Hammond (London: HarperCollins, 2014).

———, *The Annotated Hobbit*, ed. Douglas A. Anderson (New York: Houghton Mifflin, 2002).

———, *Beowulf: A Translation and Commentary, Together with Sellic Spell*, ed. Christopher Tolkien (London: HarperCollins, 2014).

———, *Beren and Lúthien*, ed. Christopher Tolkien (London: HarperCollins, 2017).

———, *The Children of Húrin*, ed. Christopher Tolkien (London: HarperCollins, 2007).

———, *The Fall of Arthur*, ed. Christopher Tolkien (London: HarperCollins, 2013).

———, *The Fall of Gondolin*, ed. Christopher Tolkien (London: HarperCollins, 2018).

——, *Farmer Giles of Ham / The Adventures of Tom Bombadil* (London, Boston, and Sydney: Unwin Paperbacks, 1979).

——, *The Father Christmas Letters* (London, Boston, and Sydney: Unwin Paperbacks, 1978).

——, *Finn and Hengest: The Fragment and the Episode*, ed. Alan Bliss (London: HarperCollins, 2006).

——, *The History of Middle-earth*, ed. Christopher Tolkien (London: HarperCollins, 1983–96), 12 vols:

The Book of Lost Tales I, ed. Christopher Tolkien (London: HarperCollins, 1983).

The Book of Lost Tales II, ed. Christopher Tolkien (London: HarperCollins, 1984).

The Lays of Beleriand, ed. Christopher Tolkien (London: HarperCollins, 1985).

The Shaping of Middle-earth: The Quenta, The Ambarkanta and the Annals, ed. Christopher Tolkien (London: HarperCollins, 1986).

The Lost Road and Other Writings, ed. Christopher Tolkien (London: HarperCollins, 1987).

The Return of the Shadow: The History of The Lord of the Rings, Part One, ed. Christopher Tolkien (London: HarperCollins, 1988).

The Treason of Isengard: The History of The Lord of the Rings, Part Two, ed. Christopher Tolkien (London: HarperCollins, 1989).

The War of the Ring: The History of The Lord of the Rings, Part Three, ed. Christopher Tolkien (London: HarperCollins, 1990).

Sauron Defeated: The History of The Lord of the Rings, Part Four, ed. Christopher Tolkien (London: HarperCollins, 1992) [includes *The Notion Club Papers*].

Morgoth's Ring: The Later Silmarillion, Part One – The Legends of Aman, ed. Christopher Tolkien (London: HarperCollins, 1993).

The War of the Jewels: The Later Silmarillion, Part Two – The Legend of Beleriand, ed. Christopher Tolkien (London: HarperCollins, 1994).

The Peoples of Middle-earth, ed. Christopher Tolkien (London: HarperCollins, 1996).

——, *The History of Middle-earth*, 12 vols in 3 (London: HarperCollins, 2002).

——, *The Hobbit*, 2nd edn (London, Boston, and Sydney: George Allen & Unwin, 1951).

——, *The Hobbit*, 3rd edn (London, Boston, and Sydney: Unwin Paperbacks, 1979).

——, *The Hobbit*, new edn (London: HarperCollins, 2009).

——, *The Lay of Aotrou and Itroun, together with The Corrigan Poems*, ed. Verlyn Flieger (London: HarperCollins, 2016).

——, *The Legend of Sigurd and Gúdrun*, ed. Christopher Tolkien (London: HarperCollins, 2009).

——, *The Letters of J.R.R. Tolkien*, ed. Humphrey Carpenter, with Christopher Tolkien (London, Boston, and Sydney: George Allen & Unwin, 1981).

——, *The Lord of the Rings*, 3 vols, 1st edn (London, Boston, and Sydney: George Allen & Unwin, 1954–5).

——, *The Lord of the Rings*, 3 vols, 2nd edn (London, Boston, and Sydney: George Allen & Unwin, 1966).

——, *The Lord of the Rings*, 3 vols, 3rd edn (London, Boston, and Sydney: Unwin Paperbacks, 1979).

——, *The Lord of the Rings*, 3 vols, new edn (London: HarperCollins, 1999).

——, *The Lord of the Rings*, new edn (London: HarperCollins, 2014).

——, *The Monsters and the Critics and Other Essays*, ed. Christopher Tolkien (London: HarperCollins, 2006).

——, *Mr Bliss* (London, Boston, and Sydney: George Allen & Unwin, 1982).

——, *The Nature of Middle-earth: Later Writings on the Lands, Inhabitants, and Metaphysics of Middle-earth*, ed. Carl F. Hostetter (London and Dublin: London: HarperCollins, 2021).

——, 'The Nomenclature of *The Lord of the Rings*', in Jared Lobdell (ed.), *A Tolkien Compass: Fascinating Studies and Interpretations of J.R.R. Tolkien's Most Popular Epic Fantasies* (New York: Ballantine Books, 1975), 168–216.

——, 'Prefatory Remarks', in *Beowulf and the Finnesburg Fragment*, trans. John R. Clark Hall, preface by J.R.R. Tolkien, ed. and intr. C.L. Wrenn (London, Boston, and Sydney: George Allen & Unwin, 1950).

——, *Roverandom*, ed. Christina Scull and Wayne Hammond (London: HarperCollins, 2013).

——, *A Secret Vice: Tolkien on Invented Languages*, ed. Dimitra Fimi and Andrew Higgins (London: HarperCollins, 2016).

——, *The Silmarillion*, ed. Christopher Tolkien (London, Boston, and Sydney: George Allen & Unwin, 1977).

——, *The Silmarillion*, ed. Christopher Tolkien (London, Boston, and Sydney: Unwin Paperbacks, 1979).

——, *The Silmarillion*, ed. Christopher Tolkien, new edn (London: HarperCollins, 1992).

——, *Sir Gawain and the Green Knight / Pearl / Sir Orfeo*, ed. Christopher Tolkien (London: George Allen & Unwin, 1975).

——, *Smith of Wootton Major*, ed. Verlyn Flieger (London: HarperCollins, 2005).

——, *The Story of Kullervo*, ed. Verlyn Flieger (London: HarperCollins, 2015).

——, *Tales from the Perilous Realm: Farmer Giles of Ham / The Adventures of Tom Bombadil / Leaf by Niggle / Smith of Wootton Major* (London: HarperCollins, 2002).

——, *Tolkien On Fairy-Stories: Expanded Edition, with Commentary and Notes*, ed. Verlyn Flieger and Douglas A. Anderson (London: HarperCollins, 2008).

——, *Tree and Leaf* (London: HarperCollins, 2009).

——, *Tree and Leaf/Smith of Wootton Major/The Homecoming of Beorhtnoth* (London, Boston, and Sydney: Unwin Paperbacks, 1979).

——, *Tree and Leaf including the poem Mythopoeia*, 2nd edn (London, Sydney, and Wellington: Unwin Hyman Limited, 1988).

——, *Unfinished Tales of Númenor and Middle-earth*, ed. Christopher Tolkien (London: HarperCollins, 2001).

J.R.R. Tolkien and E.V. Gordon (eds), *Sir Gawain & the Green Knight* (Oxford: Clarendon Press, 1930).

J.R.R. Tolkien, E.V. Gordon, and others, *Songs for the Philologists*, ed. and rev. Ronald Kyrmse (privately printed: n.p., 2007).

J.R.R. Tolkien and Donald Swann, *The Road Goes Ever On: A Song Cycle* (London: George Allen and Unwin Ltd, 1968).

Art by Tolkien

Wayne G. Hammond and Christina Scull, *The Art of The Hobbit* (London: HarperCollins, 2011).

——, *The Art of The Lord of the Rings by J.R.R. Tolkien* (London: HarperCollins, 2015).

——, *J.R.R. Tolkien: Artist & Illustrator* (London: HarperCollins, 1995).

J.R.R. Tolkien, *Drawings by J.R.R. Tolkien*, Catalogue of an Exhibition at the Ashmolean Museum . . . and at The National Book League . . . (Oxford: Ashmolean Museum; London: The National Book League; and London, Boston, and Sydney: George Allen & Unwin, 1976).

——, *Pictures by J.R.R. Tolkien*, ed. Christopher Tolkien (London, Boston, and Sydney: George Allen & Unwin, 1979).

Selected Other Reading

Peter Ackroyd, *Albion: The Origins of the English Imagination* (London: Chatto and Windus, 2002).

Benedict Anderson, *Imagined Communities: Reflections on the Origin and Spread of Nationalism*, rev. edn (London and New York: Verso, 2006).

Poul Anderson, 'Awakening the Elves', in Karen Haber (ed.), *Meditations on Middle-Earth* (London, etc.: Earthlight, 2003), 21–32.

Maria Artamonova, 'Writing for an Anglo-Saxon Audience in the Twentieth Century: J.R.R. Tolkien's Old English Chronicles', in David Clark and Nicholas Perkins (eds), *Anglo-Saxon Culture and the Modern Imagination* (Cambridge: D.S. Brewer, 2010), 71–88.

Aristotle, *Poetics*, ed. and trans. Stephen Halliwell, Loeb Classical Library 199 (Cambridge, MA: Harvard University Press, 1995).

Simon Armitage (trans.), *The Owl and the Nightingale* (London: Faber & Faber, 2021).

Mark Atherton, *There and Back Again: J.R.R. Tolkien and the Origins of the Hobbit* (London and New York: I.B. Tauris, 2012).

Barry Atkins, 'Games', in Robert Eaglestone (ed.), *Reading The Lord of the Rings* (London and New York: Continuum, 2005), 151–62.

Maggie Atkinson, 'Visions of "Blighty": Fairies, War and Fragile Spaces', *Libri & Liberi* 6.1 (2017), 39–62.

John Aubrey, *Three Prose Works*, ed. John Buchanan-Brown (Fontwell: Centaur Press, 1972).

Henry Bartholomew, 'Theory in the Shadows: Speculative Realism and the Gothic, 1890–1920' (University of Exeter PhD thesis, 2021).

W.H. Auden, 'At the End of the Quest, Victory', *New York Times* (22 January 1956), https://archive.nytimes.com/www.nytimes.com/books/01/02/11/specials/tolkien-return.html

——, 'Good and Evil in *The Lord of the Rings*', *Critical Quarterly* 10 (1968), 138–42.

——, *Nones* (London: Faber and Faber, 1952).

——, 'Under Which Lyre: A Reactionary Tract for the Times', *Harper's Magazine* (June 1947), 508–9.

Saint Augustine, 'Christian Instruction', trans. John J. Gavigan, OSA, in *The Fathers of the Church: Saint Augustine* (Washington, D.C.: The Catholic University Press of America, 2002).

Francis Bacon, *The Advancement of Learning*, ed. G.W. Kitchin (London and Melbourne: J.M. Dent & Sons Ltd, 1973).

Tino Balio, *United Artists, Volume 2, 1951–1978: The Company That Changed the Industry* (Madison, WI: Wisconsin University Press, 2009).

Sabine Baring-Gould, 'The Dead Finger', in *A Book of Ghosts*, 2nd edn (London: Methuen, 1904), 274–95.

Malcolm Joel Barnett, 'Review: The Politics of Middle-Earth', *Polity* 1.3 (1969), 383–7.

Roland Barthes, *Image–Music–Text*, trans. Stephen Heath (London: Fontana Press, 1977).

——, *The Pleasure of the Text*, trans. Richard Miller (New York: Hill and Wang, 1975).

Jonathan Bate, *The Song of the Earth* (London: Picador: 2000).

Brian Bates, *The Real Middle-Earth: Magic and Mystery in the Dark Ages* (London, Basingstoke, and Oxford: Pan Books, 2003).

Zygmunt Bauman, *Intimations of Postmodernity* (London and New York: Routledge, 1992).

Hazel K. Bell, 'Fiction Published with Indexes in Chronological Order of Publication', *The Indexer* 25.3 (April 2007), 1–9.

Beowulf: An Edition with Relevant Shorter Texts, ed. Bruce Mitchell and Fred C. Robinson, rev. edn (Malden, MA, Oxford, and Chichester: Blackwell Publishing, 1998).

Judith Bernanke, 'Howard Shore's Ring Cycle: The Film Score and Operatic Strategy', in Harriet Margolis, Sean Cubitt, Barry King, and Thierry Jutel (eds), *Studying the Event Film: The Lord of the Rings* (Manchester: Manchester University Press, 2012), 176–84.

Thomas Berry, *The Great Work: Our Way Back into the Future* (Bell Tower: New York, 1999).

Michael Billig, 'A Psychoanalytic Discursive Psychology: From Consciousness to Unconsciousness', *Discourse Studies* 8.1 (2006), 17–24.

Algernon Blackwood, 'The Man Whom the Trees Loved', in *Pan's Garden: A Volume of Nature Stories* (London: Macmillan and Co., 1912), 3–99.

William Blake, *Blake: The Complete Poems*, ed. W.H. Stevenson, 2nd edn (London and New York: Longman, 1989).

Harold Bloom (ed.), *J.R.R. Tolkien's The Lord of the Rings*, Bloom's Modern Critical Interpretations, new edn (New York: Bloom's Literary Criticism, 2008).

—— (ed.), *Modern Critical Views: J.R.R. Tolkien* (Philadelphia: Chelsea House Publishers, 2000).

Boethius, *Consolation of Philosophy*, trans. and Joel C. Relihan (Indianopolis, IN: Hackett Publishing Company, Inc., 2001).

——, *The Consolation of Philosophy*, trans. and ed. Peter Walsh (Oxford: Oxford University Press, 2008).

——, *The Consolation of Philosophy*, trans. and ed. Victor Watts, rev. edn (London: Penguin Books, 1999).

Christopher Booker, *The Seven Basic Plots: Why We Tell Stories* (London and New York: Continuum, 2004).

Courtney M. Booker, 'Byte-Sized Middle Ages: Tolkien, Film, and the Digital Imagination', *Comitatus* 35 (2004), 145–74.

John Boorman, *The Emerald Forest Diary* (New York: Farrar Straus Giroux, 1985).

Jorge Luis Borges, 'John Wilkins' Analytical Language', in *The Total Library: Non-Fiction 1922–1986*, ed. Eliot Weinberger; trans. Esther Allen, Suzanne Jill Levine, and Eliot Weinberger (London: Penguin Books, 2001), 229–32.

——, 'Tlön, Uqbar, Orbis Tertius', in *Labyrinths: Selected Stories and Other Writings*, ed. Donald A. Yates and James E. Irby (London: Penguin Books, 1970), 27–43.

John M. Bowers, *Tolkien's Lost Chaucer* (Oxford: Oxford University Press, 2019).

S.A.J. Bradley (ed. and trans.), *Anglo-Saxon Poetry* (London: J.M. Dent, 1995).

Paul Bradshaw, 'The 10 Greatest Middle-Earth Moments', *Total Film* magazine (December 2014), 78–9.

Paul Bradshaw, Jamie Graham, and Jonathan Crocker, 'There and Back Again', *Total Film* magazine (December 2014), 72–7.

Billy Bragg, *The Progressive Patriot: A Search for Belonging* (London: Bantam Press, 2006).

John Brand, *Observations on Popular Antiquities: including the Whole of Mr. Bourne's Antiquitates Vulgares, with Addenda to Every Chapter of that Work* (Newcastle-upon-Tyne, 1777).

Jennifer Brooker, 'Language Re-Imagined in Middle Earth and Hundred-Acre Wood: Jokes, Rhymes, & Riddles in Works of J.R.R. Tolkien and A.A Milne', unpublished paper (2020).

Kerry Brooks, 'Tom Bombadil and the Journey for Middle-Earth', *Mallorn* 55 (2014), 11–13.

Robert Browning, *Selected Poems*, ed. Daniel Karlin (London: Penguin, 2004).

Lawrence Buell, *The Future of Environmental Criticism: Environmental Crisis and Literary Imagination* (Malden, MA, Oxford, and Carlton, Vic.: Blackwell Publishing, 2005).

Sally Bushell, *Reading and Mapping Fiction: Spatialising the Literary Text* (Cambridge: Cambridge University Press, 2020).

Andrew M. Butler, *Solar Flares: Science Fiction in the 1970s* (Liverpool: Liverpool University Press, 2012).

Danny Butt, 'Creative Industries in Hobbit Economies: Wealth Creation, Intellectual Property Regimes, and Transnational Productions', in Margolis, Cubitt, King, and Jutel (eds), *Studying the Event Film*, 84–92.

C.T.C.S., 'Popular Superstitions of Clydesdale. No. II. – *Fairies*', in *Edinburgh Magazine & Literary Miscellany; A New Series of The Scots Magazine* 3 (October 1818), 326–31.

John Carey, *The Intellectuals and the Masses: Pride and Prejudice among the Literary Intelligentsia, 1880–1939* (London: Faber and Faber, 1992).

Humphrey Carpenter, *J.R.R. Tolkien: A Biography* (London, Boston, and Sydney: Unwin Paperbacks, 1977).

——, *The Lord of the Rings: Souvenir Booklet Commemorating Twenty Five Years of its Publication* (n.p. [London, Boston, and Sydney]: George Allen & Unwin, 1980).

Lewis Carroll, *Alice's Adventures in Wonderland* and *Through the Looking Glass and What Alice Found There, The Centenary Edition*, ed. Hugh Haughton (London: Penguin Books, 1998).

Lin Carter, *Tolkien: A Look Behind The Lord of the Rings* (New York: Ballantine, 1969).

Daphne Castell, 'The Realms of Tolkien' [interview], *New Worlds SF* 50, no. 168 (1966), 143–54.

Maria Sachiko Cecire, 'The Oxford School of Children's Fantasy Literature: Medieval Afterlives and the Production of Culture', DPhil thesis (University of Oxford, 2011).

Jane Chance (ed.), *Tolkien the Medievalist* (London and New York: Routledge, 2002).

—— (ed.), *Tolkien and the Invention of Myth: A Reader* (Lexington, KY: Kentucky University Press, 2004).

Jane Chance and Alfred K. Siewers (eds), *Tolkien's Modern Middle Ages* (London: Palgrave Macmillan, 2005).

Oronzo Cilli, *Tolkien's Library: An Annotated Checklist* (Edinburgh: Luna Press, 2019).

George Clark and Daniel Timmons (eds), *J.R.R. Tolkien and His Literary Resonances: Views of Middle-Earth* (Westport, CT: Greenwood Press, 2000).

James Clarke, *The Cinema of James Cameron: Bodies in Heroic Motion* (New York and Chichester: Wallflower Press (Columbia University Press), 2014).

Julius B. Cohen and Arthur G. Ruston, *Smoke: A Study of Town Air* (London: Edward Arnold, 1912).

Samuel Taylor Coleridge, *Biographia Literaria*, ed. James Engell and W. Jackson Bate, 2 vols (Princeton: Princeton University Press, 1984).

Christine Cornea, '2-D Performance and the Re-Animated Actor in Science Fiction Cinema', in Christine Cornea (ed.), *Genre and Performance: Film and Television* (Manchester: Manchester University Press, 2010), 148–65.

Laurence Coupe, *Mythology*, 2nd edn (London and New York: Routledge, 2009).

Kathryn F. Crabbe, *J.R.R. Tolkien* (New York: Frederick Ungar Publishing Co., 1981).

Janet Brennan Croft, 'Mithril Coats and Tin Ears: "Anticipation" and "Flattening" in Peter Jackson's *The Lord of the Rings* Trilogy', in Janet Brennan Croft (ed.), *Tolkien on Film: Essays on Peter Jackson's The Lord of the Rings* (Altadena, CA: Mythopoeic Press, 2004), 63–80.

——, 'Three Rings for Hollywood: Scripts for *The Lord of the Rings* by Zimmerman, Boorman, and Beagle', in *Fantasy Fiction Into Film*, ed. Leslie Stratyner and James R. Keller (Jefferson, NC: McFarland and Co., 2007), 7–20.

Richmal Crompton, *Just William* (London: Newnes, 1922), et al.

Sean Cubitt and Barry King, 'Dossier: Acting, On-Set Practices, Software, and Synthespians', in Margolis, Cubitt, King, and Jutel (eds), *Studying the Event Film*, 111–25.

——, 'Dossier: Materials for a Study of the *Lord of the Rings* Trilogy and its Audiences', in Margolis, Cubitt, King, and Jutel (eds), *Studying the Event Film*, 27–31.

——, 'Dossier: Production and Post-Production', in Margolis, Cubitt, King, and Jutel (eds), *Studying the Event Film*, 135–68.

Patrick Curry, *Defending Middle-Earth – Tolkien: Myth and Modernity*, 2nd edn (Boston and New York: Houghton Mifflin, 2004).

Cynewulf's Christ: An Eighth Century English Epic, ed. and trans. Israel
    Gollancz (London: David Nutt, 1892).
S.R.T.O. d'Ardenne, *An Edition of Þe Liflade ant te Passiun of Seinte Iuliene*
    (Oxford, etc.: Early English Text Society, 1960).
Amy M. Davis (ed.), *Discussing Disney* (Bloomington, IN: John Libbey
    Publishing, 2019).
Simone de Beauvoir, *A Very Easy Death [Une mort très douce]*, trans. Patrick
    O'Brian (Harmondsworth: Penguin, 1966).
Gabriele de' Mussis, in Rosemary Horrox (ed. and trans.), *The Black Death*
    (Manchester: Manchester University Press, 1994), 14–26.
Leslie A. Donovan, 'The Valkyrie Reflex in J.R.R. Tolkien's *The Lord of the
    Rings*: Galadriel, Shelob, Éowyn, and Arwen', in Chance (ed.), *Tolkien the
    Medievalist*, 106–32.
Michael D.C. Drout, 'J.R.R. Tolkien's Medieval Scholarship and its
    Significance', *Tolkien Studies* 4 (2007), 113–76.
——, 'Towards a Better Tolkien Criticism', in Eaglestone (ed.), *Reading The
    Lord of the Rings*, 1–28.
Kathleen E. Dubs, 'Providence, Fate, and Chance: Boethian Philosophy in
    The Lord of the Rings', *Twentieth Century Literature* 27.1 (Spring, 1981),
    34–42.
Lord Dunsany, *The Book of Wonder* (Boston: John W. Luce & Company,
    1912).
——, *The Sword of Welleran and Other Stories* (London: George Allen &
    Sons, 1908).
Robert Eaglestone, 'Introduction', in Eaglestone (ed.), *Reading The Lord of the
    Rings*, 1–11.
——, 'Invisibility', in Eaglestone (ed.), *Reading The Lord of the Rings*, 73–84.
Robert Eaglestone (ed.), *Reading The Lord of the Rings* (London and New
    York: Continuum, 2005).
E.R. Eddison, *The Worm Ouroboros* (London: Jonathan Cape, 1922).
[Editorial,] 'Long COVID: Let Patients Help Define Long-Lasting
    COVID Symptoms', *Nature* (7 October 2020).
William Empson, *Seven Types of Ambiguity* (Harmondsworth: Penguin,
    1995).
Jonathan D. Evans, 'Semiotics and Traditional Lore: The Medieval Dragon
    Tradition', *Journal of Folklore Research* 22.2/3 (1985), 85–112.
Daniel Falconer, *Smaug: Unleashing the Dragon* (London: HarperCollins,
    2014).
James Fenwick, 'John Boorman's *The Lord of the Rings*: A Case Study of
    an Unmade Film', *Historical Journal of Film, Radio and Television* 42.2
    (2022), 261–85.
Dimitra Fimi, *Tolkien, Race, and Cultural History: From Fairies to Hobbits*
    (Basingstoke: Palgrave Macmillan, 2008).
Verlyn Flieger, 'A Distant Mirror: Tolkien and Jackson in the

Looking-Glass', in *Green Suns and Faërie: Essays on J.R.R. Tolkien* (Kent, OH: Kent State University Press, 2012), 292–303.

——, 'The Green Knight, the Green Man, and Treebeard' in *Green Suns and Faërie*, 211–22.

——, *Green Suns and Faërie: Essays on J.R.R. Tolkien* (Kent, OH: Kent State University Press, 2012).

——, 'A Post-Modern Medievalist' in *Green Suns and Faërie*, 251–61.

——, *A Question of Time: J.R.R. Tolkien's Road to 'Faerie'* (Kent, OH: Kent State University Press, 1997).

——, 'Taking the Part of Trees: Eco-Conflict in Middle-Earth', in Clark and Timmons (eds), *Tolkien and His Literary Resonances*, 147–58.

——, 'Tolkien's Experiment with Time: *The Lost Road*, "The Notion Club Papers" and J.W. Dunne', *Mythlore* 21.2 (1996), 39–44.

Verlyn Flieger and Carl Hostetter (eds), *Tolkien's Legendarium: Essays on The History of Middle-Earth* (Westport, CO, and London: Greenwood Press, 2000).

Lynn Forest-Hill (ed.), *The Return of the Ring: Proceedings of the Tolkien Society Conference 2012*, 2 vols (Edinburgh: Tolkien Society, 2016).

——, 'Underground Man', *Times Literary Supplement* (14 January 2011), 14–15.

Robert Foster, *The Complete Guide to Middle-Earth: From The Hobbit to The Silmarillion* (London, Boston, and Sydney: Unwin Paperbacks, 1978).

P.J. Frankis, 'The Thematic Significance of *enta geweorc* and Related Imagery in *The Wanderer*', *Anglo-Saxon England* 2 (1973), 253–69.

Paul Fussell, *The Great War and Modern Memory* (Oxford: Oxford University Press, 1975).

——, *Killing in Verse and Prose* (London: Bellew Publishing, 1988).

——, *Wartime* (Oxford: Oxford University Press, 1989).

Richard Z. Gallant, 'The Noldorization of the Edain: The Roman-Germani Paradigm for the Noldor and Edain in Tolkien's Migration Era', in Hamish Williams (ed.), *Tolkien and the Classical World* (Jena: Walking Tree, 2021), 305–27.

John Garth, *Tolkien and the Great War: The Threshold of Middle-Earth* (London: HarperCollins, 2004).

——, *The Worlds of J.R.R. Tolkien: The Places that Inspired Middle-Earth* (London: Frances Lincoln, 2020).

Peter Gilliver, Jeremy Marshall, and Edmund Weiner, *The Ring of Words: Tolkien and the Oxford English Dictionary* (Oxford: Oxford University Press, 2006).

E.V. Gordon, *An Introduction to Old Norse* (Oxford: Clarendon Press, 1927).

—— (ed.), *Pearl* (Oxford: Clarendon Press, 1953).

R.K. Gordon (ed. and trans.), *Anglo-Saxon Poetry* (London, Melbourne, and Toronto: J.M. Dent and Sons, 1954).

William Gray, *Fantasy, Myth and the Measure of Truth: Tales of Pullman,*

Lewis, Tolkien, Macdonald and Hoffmann (Basingstoke: Palgrave Macmillan, 2008).

Nick Groom, 'A Comparison of Fellowship and Company in *The Lord of the Rings*', unpublished paper.

——, 'The English Literary Tradition: Shakespeare to the Gothic', in Stuart Lee (ed.), *A Companion to J.R.R. Tolkien* (Oxford: Blackwell, 2014), 286–302.

——, '"The Ghostly Language of the Ancient Earth": Tolkien and Romantic Lithology', in Julian Eilmann and Will Sherwood (eds), *The Romantic Spirit in the Works of J.R R. Tolkien* (Zurich: Walking Tree, 2023), 99–124.

——, *The Gothic: A Very Short Introduction* (Oxford: Oxford University Press, 2012).

——, *The Making of Percy's Reliques* (Oxford: Clarendon Press, 1999).

——, 'Nazgûl Taller Than Night: Tolkien and Speculative Realism', in Will Sherwood (ed.), *Twenty-first Century Receptions of Tolkien: Proceedings of the Tolkien Society Winter Seminar 2021* (Edinburgh: Luna Press, 2022), 38–57.

——, *The Seasons: A Celebration of the English Year* (London: Atlantic, 2014).

——, 'Tolkien and the Gothic', in Forest-Hill (ed.), *The Return of the Ring: Proceedings of the Tolkien Society Conference 2012*, ii. 25–34.

——, 'Tolkien y la literatura gótica', in Martin Simonson and José R. Montejano (eds), *J.R.R. Tolkien y la Tierra Media: Once Ensayos sobre el Mayor Mito Literario del Siglo XX* (Aces de Candamo: Jonathan Alwars, 2021), 269–310.

——, *The Vampire: A New History* (New Haven and London: Yale University Press, 2020).

——, 'Viral Vampires', *Critical Quarterly* 62.4 (2020), 7–14.

Karen Haber, 'Introduction', in Haber (ed.), *Meditations on Middle-Earth*, 1–5.

Karen Haber (ed.), *Meditations on Middle-Earth* (London, etc.: Earthlight, 2003).

Wayne G. Hammond, with Douglas A. Anderson, *J.R.R. Tolkien: A Descriptive Bibliography* (Winchester: St Paul's Bibliographies, 1993).

John Harlow and Rachel Dobson, '*Lord of the Rings* Is Worth £3bn but Tolkien Sold the Film Rights to Ward Off the Taxman', *Sunday Times* (15 December 2002), 16.

Graham Harman, *Towards Speculative Realism: Essays and Lectures* (Winchester and Washington, DC: Zero Books, 2010).

——, *Weird Realism: Lovecraft and Philosophy* (Winchester and Washington, DC: Zero Books, 2011).

Dinah Hazell, *The Plants of Middle-Earth: Botany and Sub-Creation* (Kent, OH: Kent State University Press, 2006).

Constance B. Hiett, 'The Text of *The Hobbit*: Putting Tolkien's Notes in Order', *English Studies in Canada* 7.2 (1981), 212–24.

Craig Hight, 'One (Special Extended Edition) Disc to Rule Them All', in Margolis, Cubitt, King, and Jutel (eds), *Studying the Event Film*, 32–9.

Margaret Hiley, ' "Bizarre or dream like": J.R.R. Tolkien on *Finnegans Wake*', in Martha C. Carpentier (ed.), *Joycean Legacies* (Basingstoke: Palgrave Macmillan, 2015), 112–26.

Kim Hjardar and Vegard Vike, *Vikings at War*, trans. Frank Stewart (Oxford and Philadelphia: Casemate, 2016).

James Hogg, *The Jacobite Relics of Scotland; being The Songs, Airs, and Legends, of the Adherents to the House of Stuart* (Edinburgh: William Blackwood, 1819).

James Craig Holte, 'Ethnicity and the Popular Imagination: Ralph Bakshi and the American Dream', *Multi-Ethnic Literature of the United States* 8.4 (1981), 105–13.

Walter Hooper, 'The Inklings', in Roger White, Judith Wolfe, and Brendan N. Wolfe (eds), *C.S. Lewis & His Circle: Essays and Memoirs from the Oxford C.S. Lewis Society* (Oxford: Oxford University Press, 2015), 197–213.

——, 'Preface', in C.S. Lewis, *On Stories, and Other Essays on Literature*, ed. Walter Hooper (Orlando, etc.: Harvest, 1982), ix–xxi.

Lisa Hopkins, *Screening the Gothic* (Austin: University of Texas Press, 2005).

Al Horner, 'The New Age: The Rings Return Promises to be Epic – But this isn't your Dad's Middle-Earth . . .', *Empire* magazine (Summer 2022), 83.

Rosemary Horrox (ed. and trans.), *The Black Death* (Manchester: Manchester University Press, 1994).

Brian Hoyle, *The Cinema of John Boorman* (Lanham, MD, Toronto, and Plymouth: Scarecrow Press, 2012).

Laurence Hughes, 'There Were Giants in Those Days . . .': A Tolkien and C.S. Lewis Walking Tour of Oxford* (Oxford: Intelligent Walking Tours, 2015).

Linda Hutcheon, *A Theory of Adaptation* (New York and London: Routledge, 2006).

Anna Hutton-North, *Ferguson's Gang: The Maidens Behind the Masks* (Great Britain: Lulu Inc., 2013).

Montague Rhodes James, 'Canon Alberic's Scrap-Book', in *Ghost-Stories of an Antiquary* (London: Edward Arnold, 1912), 3–28.

Richard Jordan, 'Battlefield Middle-Earth', *Total Film* magazine (December 2014), 62–9.

B.L. Joseph, *Elizabethan Acting* (London: Oxford University Press, 1951).

Walter S. Judd and Graham A. Judd, *Flora of Middle-Earth: Plants of J.R.R. Tolkien's Legendarium* (Oxford: Oxford University Press, 2017).

C.G. Jung, *Psychology of the Unconscious: A Study of the Transformations and Symbolisms of the Libido – A Contribution to the History of the Evolution of Thought*, trans. Beatrice M. Hinkle (New York: Moffat, Yard and Company, 1916).

Douglas Charles Kane, *Arda Reconstructed: The Creation of the Published Silmarillion* (Bethlehem, PA: Lehigh University Press, 2009).

Marvin Kaye (ed.), with Saralee Kaye, *Masterpieces of Terror and the Supernatural: A Collection of Spinechilling Tales Old & New* (London: Little, Brown, 2002).

John Keats, *The Letters of John Keats*, ed. Maurice Buxton Forman, 4th edn (London, New York, Toronto: Oxford University Press, 1952).

Clyde Kilby, *Tolkien and The Silmarillion* (Berkhamsted: Lion Publishing, 1977).

Rudyard Kipling, *Puck of Pook's Hill* (London: Penguin, 1991).

Paul H. Kocher, *Master of Middle-Earth: The Achievement of J.R.R. Tolkien* (London: Thames and Hudson, 1972).

Andrew Lazo, 'A Kind of Mid-Wife: J.R.R. Tolkien and C.S. Lewis – Sharing Influence', in Chance (ed.), *Tolkien the Medievalist*, 36–49.

Alan Lee, *The Lord of the Rings Sketchbook* (London: HarperCollins, 2005).

Stuart D. Lee (ed.), *A Companion to J.R.R. Tolkien* (Malden, MA, Oxford, and Chichester: Wiley-Blackwell, 2014).

——, 'Tolkien in Oxford (BBC, 1968): A Reconstruction', *Tolkien Studies* 15 (2018), 115–76.

Stuart D. Lee and Elizabeth Solopova, *The Keys of Middle-Earth: Discovering Medieval Literature Through the Fiction of J.R.R. Tolkien*, 2nd edn (Basingstoke: Palgrave Macmillan, 2015).

C.S. Lewis, *The Collected Letters of C.S. Lewis*, ed. Walter Hooper, 3 vols (London: HarperCollins, 2000–2006).

——, *Image and Imagination: Essays and Reviews*, ed. Walter Hooper (Cambridge: Cambridge University Press, 2013).

——, 'Tolkien's *Lord of the Rings*', in *On Stories, and Other Essays*, ed. Hooper, 83–90 (adapted from C.S. Lewis, 'The Gods Return to Earth' (*Time and Tide* 35 (14 August 1954), 1082–3) and 'The Dethronement of Power' (*Time and Tide* (22 October 1955), 1373–4)).

Matthew Leyland, 'The Hobbit: An Unexpected Journey', *Total Film* magazine (February 2012), 70–74.

——, 'Step by Step: Essentials for an Unexpected Journey', *Total Film* magazine (February 2012), 73.

Johanna Lindbladh, 'Introduction', in Johanna Lindbladh (ed.), *The Poetics of Memory in Post-Totalitarian Narration* (Lund: Centre for European Studies, 2008), 5–13.

—— (ed.), *The Poetics of Memory in Post-Totalitarian Narration* (Lund: Centre for European Studies, 2008).

Elias Lönnrot (ed.), *The Kalevala, or The Land of Heroes* (Oxford: Oxford University Press, 1999).

Catherine McIlwaine, *Tolkien: Maker of Middle-earth* (Oxford: Bodleian Library, 2018).

——, *Tolkien Treasures* (Oxford: Bodleian Library, 2018).

Bob Mackin(?), *Rolling Stones – The Chronology: April 28, 1963 – March 24, 1986*, 1986, typescript, (n.p., 1986).

Catherine Madsen, '"Light from an Invisible Lamp": Natural Religion in *The Lord of the Rings*', in Chance (ed.), *Tolkien and the Invention of Myth: A Reader*, 35–47.

Eirikr Magnusson and William Morris (trans.), *Volsunga Saga: The Story of the Volsungs and Niblungs, with Certain Songs from the Elder Edda*, ed. H. Halliday Sparling (London: Walter Scott Publishing Co. Ltd, 1888).

C.N. Manlove, *Modern Fantasy* (Cambridge: Cambridge University Press, 1975).

John Marenbon, 'Anicius Manlius Severinus Boethius', *The Stanford Encyclopedia of Philosophy* (Winter 2021 Edition), ed. Edward N. Zalta (https://plato.stanford.edu/archives/win2021/entries/boethius/).

John Masefield, *The Poems and Plays of John Masefield*, 2 vols (New York: Macmillan, 1920).

Alison Milbank, *Chesterton and Tolkien as Theologians: The Fantasy of the Real* (London and New York: T&T Clark, 2009).

D. Gary Miller, *The Oxford Gothic Grammar* (Oxford: Oxford University Press, 2019).

John Milton, *Paradise Lost*, ed. Alastair Fowler (London and New York: Longman, 1971).

Michael Moorcock, 'Epic Pooh', reprinted in Bloom (ed.), *J.R.R. Tolkien's The Lord of the Rings*, 3–18.

Timothy Morton, *Ecology Without Nature: Rethinking Environmental Aesthetics* (Cambridge, MA: Harvard University Press, 2007).

Thomas Nagel, 'What Is It Like To Be a Bat?', *Mortal Questions* (Cambridge: Cambridge University Press, 1979), 165–80.

Ian Nathan, 'Into the Woods', *Empire* magazine (August 2013), 62–71.

——, 'Winter is Coming', *Empire* magazine (September 2014), 80–7.

—— (ed.), *The Lord of the Rings: A Celebration*, supplement to *Empire* magazine (n.d.).

New Zealand Journal of Employment Relations 36.3 (2011): special issue 'The "Hobbit Law": Exploring Non-standard Employment'.

Denis O'Dell, with Bob Neaverson, *At the Apple's Core: The Beatles from the Inside* (London: Peter Owen, 2002).

Peter and Iona Opie (eds), *The Oxford Dictionary of Nursery Rhymes* (Oxford: Clarendon Press, 1952).

Marek Oziewicz, 'Peter Jackson's *The Hobbit*: A Beautiful Disaster', *Journal of the Fantastic in the Arts* 27.2 (96) (2016), 248–69.

Thomas Percy, 'An Essay on the Ancient English Minstrels', in *Reliques of Ancient English Poetry*, 3rd edn, 3 vols (London, 1775), i. pp. xix–lxxviii.

Michael Piret, 'W.H. Auden and Inklings', in White, Wolfe, and Wolfe (eds), *C.S. Lewis & His Circle*, 122–34.

Charlotte Plimmer and Denis Plimmer, 'The Man Who Understands Hobbits', *Daily Telegraph Magazine* (22 March 1968), 31–5.

Richard Plotz, 'The Society', *Tolkien Journal*, 1.2 (1965), [1].

Arthur Rackham (illus.), *Mother Goose: The Old Nursery Rhymes* (London: William Heinemann, n.d. [1913]).

John Rateliff, *The History of The Hobbit: Part One, Mr. Baggins* and *Part Two, Return to Bag-End* (London: HarperCollins, 2007).

Bob Rehak, *More Than Meets the Eye: Special Effects and the Fantastic Transmedia Franchise* (New York: NYU Press, 2018).

Erich Maria Remarque, *All Quiet on the Western Front*, trans. A.W. Wheen (London: Pan Books, n.d. [1929]).

Return to Middle Earth: Empire Classics 3 (2018).

Patricia Reynolds and Glen GoodKnight (eds), *Proceedings of the J.R.R. Tolkien Centenary Conference, 1992* (Milton Keynes and Altadena, CA: Tolkien Society and Mythopoeic Press, 1995).

Ryan Reynolds, Henry Bial, and Kimon Keramidas, 'Tourist Encounters', in Margolis, Cubitt, King, and Jutel (eds), *Studying the Event Film*, 239–48.

Brian J. Robb and Paul Simpson, *Middle-earth Envisioned: The Hobbit and The Lord of the Rings: On Screen, On Stage, and Beyond* (New York: Race Point Publishing, 2013).

Adam Roberts, *Riddles of the Hobbit* (Basingstoke: Palgrave Macmillan, 2013).

Brett M. Rogers and Benjamin Eldon Stevens (eds), *Classical Traditions in Modern Fantasy* (Oxford: Oxford University Press, 2017).

Paul Romney, '"Great Chords": Politics and Romance in Tolstoy's *War and Peace*', *University of Toronto Quarterly* 80.1 (2011), 49–77.

Brian Rosebury, *Tolkien: A Cultural Phenomenon* (Basingstoke: Palgrave Macmillan, 2003).

Christina Rossetti, *Goblin Market and Other Poems*, 2nd edn (London and Cambridge: Macmillan and Co., 1865).

Vera Rusinova, 'Perfidy', *Max Planck Encyclopedias of International Law* (2011), at *Oxford Public International Law* (Oxford: Oxford University Press, 2021: http://opil.ouplaw.com).

Roger Sale, *Modern Heroism: Essays on D.H. Lawrence, William Empson, & J.R.R. Tolkien* (Berkeley and Los Angeles: University of California Press, 1975).

Michael Saler, *As If: Modern Enchantment and the Literary History of Virtual Reality* (Oxford: Oxford University Press, 2012).

M.B. Salu (ed.), *The Ancrene Riwle* (London: Burns & Oates, 1955).

Saga Heiðreks Konungs ins Vitra: The Saga of King Heidrek the Wise, ed. and trans. Christopher Tolkien (London, etc.: Thomas Nelson and Sons, 1960).

Peter J. Schakel, *The Way into Narnia: A Reader's Guide* (Grand Rapids, MI and Cambridge: William B. Eerdmans Publishing Company, 2005).

Chester N. Scoville, 'Pastoralia and Perfectibility in William Morris and J.R.R. Tolkien', in Chance and Siewers (eds), *Tolkien's Modern Middle Ages*, 93–103.

Christina Scull and Wayne Hammond, *The J.R.R. Tolkien Companion and Guide*, rev. edn, 3 vols (London: HarperCollins, 2006).

Jeanette Sears, *The Oxford of J.R.R. Tolkien and C.S. Lewis* (Oxford: Heritage Tours Publications, 2006).

Alexander Sergeant, 'High Fantasy Disney: Recontextualising *The Black Cauldron*', in Davis (ed.), *Discussing Disney*, 53–70.

Philip Shaw, *The Sublime* (London and New York: Routledge, 2006).

T.A. Shippey, 'The Curious Case of Denethor and the Palantír, Once More', *Mallorn* 57 (2016), 6–9.

——, review of *Vǫlve: Scandinavian Views on Science Fiction*, ed. Cay Dollerup, in *Review of English Studies* 31.124 (1980), 500.

Tom Shippey, *The Road to Middle-earth*, rev. edn (London: HarperCollins, 2005).

——, *Roots and Branches: Selected Papers on Tolkien* (Zollikofen: Walking Tree, 2007).

——, 'Tolkien as a Post-War Writer', *Mythlore* 21.2 (1996), 84–93.

——, *Tolkien: Author of the Century* (London: HarperCollins, 2000).

Brian Sibley, *The Hobbit: The Battle of the Five Armies* (London: HarperCollins, 2014).

——, *The Lord of the Rings™: The Making of the Movie Trilogy* (London: HarperCollins, 2002).

——, *The Lord of the Rings: Official Movie Guide* (London: HarperCollins, 2001).

Brian Sibley, illustrated by John Howe, *The Road Goes Ever On and On: The Map of Tolkien's Middle-Earth* (London: HarperCollins, 2009).

Jacqueline Simpson and Steve Roud, *A Dictionary of English Folklore* (Oxford: Oxford University Press, 2000).

Debbie Sly, 'Weaving Nets of Gloom: "Darkness Profound" in Tolkien and Milton', in Clark and Timmons (eds), *Tolkien and His Literary Resonances*, 109–19.

Thomas W. Smith, 'Tolkien's Catholic Imagination: Mediation and Tradition', *Religion and Literature* 38.2 (2006), 73–100.

Anna Smol, '"Oh . . . Oh . . . *Frodo!*" Readings of Male Intimacy in *The Lord of the Rings*', *Modern Fiction Studies* 50.4 (2004), 949–79.

Benjamin Eldon Stevens, 'Ancient Underworlds in *The Hobbit*', in Rogers and Stevens (eds), *Classical Traditions in Modern Fantasy*, 121–44.

'The Story of Sigurd', in Andrew Lang (ed.), *The Red Fairy Book* (London: Longmans, Green, and Co., 1890), 357–67.

Sandra Ballif Straubhaar, 'Myth, Late Roman History, and Multiculturalism in Tolkien's Middle-earth', in Chance (ed.), *Tolkien and the Invention of Myth: A Reader*, 101–17.

Kris Swank, 'The Child's Voyage and the *Immram* Tradition in Lewis, Tolkien, and Pullman', *Mythlore* 38.1 (2019), 75–98.

Tacitus, *Agricola and Germany*, ed. and trans. Anthony R. Birley (Oxford: Oxford University Press, 1999).

Eugene Thacker, *Cosmic Pessimism* (Minneapolis, MN: Univocal Publishing, 2015).

——, *In the Dust of This Planet [Horror of Philosophy, vol. 1]* (Winchester and Washington, DC: Zero Books, 2011).

Paul Thomas, 'Some of Tolkien's Narrators', in Flieger and Carl (eds), *Tolkien's Legendarium*, 161–81.

Kristin Thompson, *The Frodo Franchise: The Lord of the Rings and Modern Hollywood* (Berkeley: University of California Press, 2007).

David Tneh, 'Orcs and Tolkien's Treatment of Evil', *Mallorn* 52 (2011), 37–43.

'Turgon' [David E. Smith] (ed.), *The Tolkien Fan's Medieval Reader: Versions in Modern Prose* (Cold Spring Harbor, NY: Cold Spring Press Fantasy, 2004).

J.E.A. Tyler, *The Tolkien Companion*, ed. S.A. Tyler (London and Basingstoke: Macmillan London Ltd, 1976).

Rayner Unwin, *George Allen & Unwin: A Remembrancer* (London: Merlin Unwin, 1999).

Anna Vaninskaya, 'Modernity: Tolkien and His Contemporaries', in Lee (ed.), *A Companion to J.R.R. Tolkien*, 350–66.

Renée Vink, '"Jewish" Dwarves: Tolkien and Anti-Semitic Stereotyping', *Tolkien Studies* 10 (2013), 123–45.

Virgil, *Æneis*, trans. Gawin Douglas, ed. Thomas Ruddiman (Edinburgh, 1710).

Chris Walsh, 'Gildor, Frodo and Bilbo: A Tolkien Puzzle', unpublished paper.

Mary Warnock, *Memory* (London: Faber & Faber, 1987).

Sarah Wells (ed.), *The Ring Goes Ever On, Proceedings of the Tolkien 2005 Conference: 50 Years of The Lord of the Rings*, 2 vols (Coventry: Tolkien Society, 2008).

Michael G. Wheaton, Alena Prikhidko, and Gabrielle R. Messner, 'Is Fear of COVID-19 Contagious? The Effects of Emotion Contagion and Social Media Use on Anxiety in Response to the Coronavirus Pandemic', *Frontiers in Psychology* (January 2021), article 567379, 1–9.

K.S. Whetter and R. Andrew McDonald, '"In the Hilt is Fame": Resonances of Medieval Swords and Sword-Lore in J.R.R. Tolkien's *The Hobbit* and *The Lord of the Rings*', *Mythlore* 25.1/2 (2006), 5–28.

Kristen Whissel, *Spectacular Digital Effects: CGI and Contemporary Cinema* (Durham, NC: Duke University Press, 2014).

Elizabeth Whittingham, *The Evolution of Tolkien's Mythology: A Study of the History of Middle-earth* (Jefferson, NC: McFarland, 2007).

Toby Widdicombe, *J.R.R. Tolkien: A Guide for the Perplexed* (London: Bloomsbury, 2020).
Hamish Williams (ed.), *Tolkien and the Classical World* (Jena: Walking Tree, 2021).
A.N. Wilson, *Iris Murdoch as I Knew Her* (London: Hutchinson, 2003).
Virginia Woolf, *A Room of One's Own* (London: Hogarth Press, 1931).
Dan Yakir, 'The Sorcerer: John Boorman interviewed by Dan Yakir', *Film Comment*, special issue: 'Eccentric Cinema', 17.3 (May–June 1981), 49–53.
Arne Zettersten, *J.R.R. Tolkien's Double Worlds and Creative Process: Language and Life* (Basingstoke: Palgrave Macmillan, 2011).
Jack Zipes, *Breaking the Magic Spell: Radical Theories of Folk and Fairy Tales* (Lexington, KY: University Press of Kentucky, 1979).
Sue Zlosnik, 'Gothic Echoes', in Eaglestone (ed.), *Reading The Lord of the Rings*, 47–58.

Audio

Brian Sibley, 'Brian Sibley, Writer, BBC's *The Lord of the Rings* (1981)', interview by 'The Nerd of the Rings': https://open.spotify.com/episode/3y5fBGrKQ6jZsiDavz61kx
——, (ed.), *J.R.R. Tolkien: An Audio Portrait* [documentaries 1964–98] (BBC Worldwide Ltd, 2001).
The Spoken Word: British Writers (British Library, 2008).
J.R.R. Tolkien, *The Complete Lord of the Rings Trilogy & The Hobbit*, NPR drama, scripted by Bob Lewis and Bernard Mayes (HighBridge Company, 2003).
——, *Essential Tolkien* (Caedmon, n.d.).
——, *The Hobbit*, unabridged audiobook, read by Rob Inglis (HarperCollins, 2002).
——, *The Hobbit*, BBC drama, scripted by Michael Kilgariff (AudioGO Ltd, 2012).
——, *The Lord of the Rings*, BBC drama, scripted by Brian Sibley and Michael Bakewell (BBC Worldwide Ltd, 1995).
——, *The Lord of the Rings: Part One, The Fellowship of the Ring*, unabridged audiobook, read by Rob Inglis (Recorded Books, LLC, 1990; HarperCollins, 2002).
——, *The Lord of the Rings: Part Two, The Two Towers*, unabridged audiobook, read by Rob Inglis (Recorded Books, LLC, 1990; HarperCollins, 2002).
——, *The Lord of the Rings: Part Three, The Return of the King*, unabridged audiobook, read by Rob Inglis (Recorded Books, LLC, 1990; HarperCollins, 2002).
——, *The Lord of the Rings: The Collector's Edition Trilogy*, BBC drama, scripted by Brian Sibley and Michael Bakewell (BBC Audiobooks Ltd, 2003).

——, *The Silmarillion*, unabridged audiobook, read by Martin Shaw (HarperCollins, 2001).

J.R.R. Tolkien, and Christopher Tolkien, *The Homecoming of Beorhtnoth*, read by J.R.R. Tolkien and Christopher Tolkien (Tolkien Centenary Conference recording, 1992).

——, *The Tolkien Audio Collection* (HarperCollins, 2002).

There are many documentaries of Tolkien's life and works available online; the most significant are:

Archive on 4, 'Tolkien: The Lost Recordings', BBC Radio 4 (6 August 2016): https://www.bbc.co.uk/programmes/b07mvd5z

BBC interview with Denys Gueroult (recorded 1965, broadcast 1970): https://www.youtube.com/watch?v=bzDtmMXJ1B4

A Film Portrait of J.R.R. Tolkien, dir. Derek Baily (Landseer, 1996): https://www.youtube.com/watch?v=EwTWzA4dWRI

Release – Tolkien in Oxford, dir. Leslie Megahey (BBC, 1968): https://www.bbc.co.uk/archive/release--jrr-tolkien/znd36v4; an interview with Megahey on making the documentary is at https://podcasts.ox.ac.uk/tolkien-oxford-bbc-1968 (see also: https://fiddlersdog.blogspot.co.uk/2013/11/tolkien-in-oxford.html and more on the 1968 BBC interview is at tolkienlibrary.com/press/814-Tolkien-1968-BBC-Interview.php).

Films

Born of Hope, dir. Kate Madison ([independent:] 2009).

The Hobbit, dir. Gene Deitch (Rembrandt Films, 1966).

The Hobbit, dir. Arthur Rankin Jr and Jules Bass (Warner Bros. Home Video, 2001).

The Hobbit: An Unexpected Journey, Extended Edition, dir. Peter Jackson (Warner Bros. Entertainment Inc., 2013).

The Hobbit: The Desolation of Smaug, Extended Edition, dir. Peter Jackson (Warner Bros. Entertainment Inc., 2014).

The Hobbit: The Battle of the Five Armies, Extended Edition, dir. Peter Jackson (Warner Bros. Entertainment Inc., 2015).

The Hunt for Gollum, dir. Chris Bouchard ([independent:] 2009).

The Lord of the Rings, dir. Ralph Bakshi (Warner Bros. Entertainment Inc., 1978).

The Lord of the Rings: The Motion Picture Trilogy, dir. Peter Jackson (New Line Productions Inc., 2010).

The Lord of the Rings: The Fellowship of the Ring, Special Extended DVD Edition, dir. Peter Jackson (New Line Home Entertainment, 2002).

The Lord of the Rings: The Two Towers, Special Extended DVD Edition, dir. Peter Jackson (New Line Home Entertainment, 2003).

The Lord of the Rings: The Return of the King, Special Extended DVD Edition, dir. Peter Jackson (New Line Home Entertainment, 2004).

Performance, dir. Nic Roeg and Donald Cammell (Warner Bros. Entertainment Inc., 2007).

The Return of the King, dir. Arthur Rankin Jr and Jules Bass (Warner Bros. Home Video, 2001).

Film scripts

John Boorman and Rospo Pallenberg, *The Lord of the Rings*, screenplay typescript (n.d., n.p.).

Philippa Boyens, Guillermo del Toro, Peter Jackson, and Fran Walsh, *The Hobbit: An Unexpected Journey*, screenplay typescript (n.p., 2015) [screenplays of *The Hobbit: The Desolation of Smaug* and *The Hobbit: The Battle of the Five Armies* consulted online].

Fran Walsh, Philippa Boyens, and Peter Jackson, *The Lord of the Rings: The Fellowship of the Ring*, screenplay typescript (New Line Cinema, 2001).

Fran Walsh, Philippa Boyens, Stephen Sinclair, and Peter Jackson, *The Lord of the Rings: The Two Towers*, screenplay typescript (New Line Cinema, 2002).

Fran Walsh, Philippa Boyens, and Peter Jackson, *The Lord of the Rings: The Return of the King*, screenplay typescript (New Line Cinema, 2003).

Index